Challenges of the Developing World

Challenges of the Developing World

EIGHTH EDITION

Howard Handelman

Emeritus Professor, University of Wisconsin-Milwaukee

ROWMAN & LITTLEFIELD

Lanham • Boulder • New York • London

Executive Editor: Traci Crowell
Associate Editor: Molly White
Senior Marketing Manager: Karin Cholak
Marketing Manager: Deborah Hudson
Interior Designer: Rosanne Schloss
Cover Designer: Jen Huppert Design

Credits and acknowledgments for material borrowed from other sources, and reproduced with permission, appear on the appropriate page within the text.

Published by Rowman & Littlefield
A wholly owned subsidiary of The Rowman & Littlefield Publishing Group, Inc.
4501 Forbes Boulevard, Suite 200, Lanham, Maryland 20706
www.rowman.com

Unit A, Whitacre Mews, 26-34 Stannary Street, London SE11 4AB, United Kingdom

British Library Cataloguing in Publication Information Available

Library of Congress Cataloging-in-Publication Data
Names: Handelman, Howard, 1943–author.
Title: Challenges of the developing world / Howard Handelman.
Description: Eighth edition. | Lanham : Rowman & Littlefield, 2016. |
    Previously published by Pearson Education, Inc. under the title The challenge
    of third world development. | Includes index.
Identifiers: LCCN 2015043591 (print) | LCCN 2015044340 (ebook) |
    ISBN 9781442256873 (cloth : alk. paper) | ISBN 9781442256880 (pbk. : alk. paper) |
    ISBN 9781442256897 (electronic)
Subjects: LCSH: Developing countries—Economic conditions. | Developing
    countries—Economic policy. | Developing countries—Politics and government. |
    Economic development.
Classification: LCC HC59.7 .H299 2016 (print) | LCC HC59.7 (ebook) |
    DDC 338.9009172/4—dc23 LC record available at http://lccn.loc.gov/2015043591

Printed in the United States of America

To Maggie, Alice, Phoebe, and Kris

Brief Contents

Detailed Contents

Tables

★ ★ ★

Preface

FOR MANY WESTERNERS, the politics, economics, and cultures of the less developed countries (LDCs) seem remote until a major event bursts into the news and demands our attention, such as the Islamic State and the Syrian civil war. Other events have attracted our attention more gradually, including the emergence of China and now India as major economic powers.

The purpose of this book is to enhance our understanding of the political, economic, and cultural forces that lay behind these changes. With a combined population of over seven billion people, LDCs now account for nearly 90 percent of the world's total population, and this proportion will rise in the coming decades. *Challenges of the Developing World* examines and analyzes the politics of developing countries in Africa, Asia, Latin America, the Caribbean, and the Middle East in order to better understand major phenomena such as: civil war in the Middle East, the rise of Islamic militancy (Islamism), the ongoing struggle to attain and retain democracy in the LDCs, the growing economic might of India and East Asia, and the changing role of women in the politics of the developing world.

The list of LDCs includes desperately poor countries such as Nepal and Somalia and rapidly developing industrial powers such as China, Singapore, South Korea, and India. Some, like Jamaica and Costa Rica, are stable democracies; others, such as North Korea and Sudan, suffer under highly repressive dictatorships. All of them, however, share at least some of the aspects of political, economic, and social underdevelopment that this book evaluates.

NEW TO THIS EDITION

Since the publication of the last edition of this text, there have been a number of major developments that have merited new or extended discussion in this new edition.

- Corruption: This is a growing problem in the developing world and a mounting source of citizens' resentment that undermines the legitimacy of many governments. We explore the extent of such corruption and evaluate some attempts to reduce or contain it.
- The Millennium Development Goals and economic progress in the LDCs: During the last decade or more, the growth of the developing world's economies has lifted hundreds of millions out of severe poverty, mostly in China and India. We discuss what these developments were, the extent that they have been met, and the ways in which setting the development goal helped developing nations advance. Yet, such gains can be reversed by a global economic downturn such as the one that drove an additional 60 million people into extreme poverty in 2008–2009.
- The emergence of the Islamic State as the world's most powerful and brutal terrorist organization: We discuss the turmoil in Syria, Iraq, and Libya with a focus of the growing strength and militancy of Islamist groups.
- The persistence of ethnic conflict in Africa, Asia, and the Middle East: we examine some of the increased ethnic violence in the Arab World and parts of Africa.
- The continuing and growing role of women in the politics of the LDCs. We update and expand analysis of women in parliaments and congresses.

FEATURES

No text is capable of fully examining the individual political and socioeconomic systems of so many highly diverse countries. Instead, we will look for common issues, problems, and potential solutions.

We start in chapter 1 by exploring the nature of underdevelopment and then consider the leading theories attempting to explain underdevelopment and development. This edition presents new analysis on political corruption as both a result and a cause of underdevelopment. It also discusses the magnitude of migration (both within and outside of the LDCs) caused by war and economic deprivation.

Chapter 2 discusses what has been one of the most important political changes in world politics during the late twentieth and early twenty-first centuries—the wave of democratic transitions that has swept over the developing nations of Africa, Asia, Latin America, and the Middle East (as well as southern Europe and the former Soviet bloc of nations) in the past four decades. But, this edition also analyzes the failures of the so-called Arab Spring and the continued inability of most of the Arab World to democratize.

Chapters 3–5, respectively, on religion and politics, ethnic conflict, and women and development, analyze religious, ethnic, and gender issues that have often divided developing nations, but also provide identities that can be helpful in the processes of political and economic development. This edition evaluates the importance of militant Islamism in the Middle East and discusses the origins and rise of the Islamic State, especially in Syria and Iraq. Chapter 5, discussion on women and development, analyzes the socioeconomic status of women in the developing world and their growing role in the political system.

Chapter 6 discusses rural land concentration and poverty and their political consequences. It outlines the LDCs' explosive urban growth and analyzes both the problems and opportunities presented by this huge demographic change. It describes the many challenges the urban poor face regarding housing, employment, and crime and also their political activities. Next, chapter 7 on revolutionary change considers the definition of revolutions, how revolutions start, whether they succeed, and how they govern. We also examine the current and future prospects for revolution in the LDCs.

Chapter 8 on the military in politics updates data on the weight of military expenditures in national budgets and contains new coverage of the military's declining, but continuing, role. Finally, chapter 9, dealing with the political economies of developing countries, compares alternate paths to economic development and evaluates their relative effectiveness. It also analyzes the costs and benefits of globalization in the developing world.

As the preceding pages indicate, in many ways there is now greater cause for optimism about the LDCs: the continued spread of democracy (albeit with important setbacks); growing world concern over human rights; the military's declining political influence in many nations; ongoing economic growth in Asia and renewed vigor in Africa's previously lackluster economies; and impressive reductions in world poverty, especially in Asia.

At the same time, however, important problems persist or even worsen: ongoing internal and cross-national warfare continues to take too many lives in parts of Africa, Asia, and the Middle East; the wave of immigrants is flooding into Europe and to neighboring developing countries, especially those fleeing war-torn Syria and Afghanistan; many millions continue to die of preventable diseases, hunger, or even starvation, while many others lack adequate housing in urban centers or adequate farmland to feed their families in rural areas; corruption plagues both political and economic development in most countries, even in economic powerhouses like China and India; bureaucratic corruption is often matched by bureaucratic incompetence; and while women are beginning to play a greater role in the politics of the LDCs, gender gaps remain enormous in virtually all aspects of development and power, including horrors such as so-called female circumcisions and honor killings.

This text's discussion and analysis will hopefully shed further light on these important developments.

SUPPLEMENTS

Rowman & Littlefield is pleased to offer several resources to qualified adopters of *Challenges of the Developing World* and their students that will make teaching and learning from this book even more effective and enjoyable.

Test Bank. For each chapter in the text, test questions are provided in multiple choice, true-false questions, and essay formats. The test bank is available to adopters for download on the text's catalog page at http://rowman.com/ISBN/9781442256880.

Testing Software. This customizable test bank is available as either a Word file or in Respondus 4.0. Respondus 4.0 is a powerful tool for creating and managing exams that can be printed to paper or published directly to the most popular learning management systems. Exams can be created offline or moved from one LMS to another. **Respondus LE** is available for free and can be used to automate the process of creating print tests. **Respondus 3.5**, available for purchase or via a school site license, prepares tests to be uploaded to an LMS. Click here: http://www.respondus.com/products/testbank/search.php to submit your request.

Companion Website. Accompanying the text is an open-access Companion Website designed to engage students with the material and reinforce what they have learned in the classroom. For each chapter, flash cards and self-quizzes help students master the content and apply that knowledge to real-life situations. Students can access the Companion Website from their computer or mobile device; it can be found at http://textbooks.rowman.com/handelman8e.

eBook. The full-color eBook allows students to access this textbook anytime and anywhere they want. The eBook for *Challenges of the*

Developing World includes everything that is in the print edition in vibrant color, and features direct links to the Companion Website where students can access flash cards and self-quizzes to help test their understanding of the major concepts and terminology in each chapter. The eBook can be purchased at http://rowman.com/ISBN/9781442256880 or at any other eBook retailer.

ACKNOWLEDGMENTS

Because of the broad geographic and conceptual scope of any book on politics in LDCs, I am particularly indebted to others for their kind help and advice.

I would like to thank the many people at Rowman & Littlefield who have worked with me. I particularly appreciate Traci Crowell and Molly White for their guidance and support on this edition.

I appreciated and benefited from the comments of the many reviewers of the book: Reverend Michael J. Connolly, Gonzaga University; Joseph M. Dondelinger, Augustana College; Thomas F. Head, George Fox University; Edislav Manetovic, SUNY Old Westbury; David Penna, Gallaudet University; Holly Pottle, Texas Woman's University; Paul S. Rowe, Trinity Western University; Azamat Sakiev, University of North Georgia; Richard Stahler-Sholk, Eastern Michigan University; Kathleen Staudt, University of Texas at El Paso; and Timothy J. White, Xavier University.

I owe a particular debt to my wife, Dr. Kristin Ruggiero, for her insights and her careful proof reading and editing of the manuscript.

The quality of this book benefited enormously from their many insights, suggestions, and corrections. The usual caveat, of course, applies: Any remaining errors of fact or interpretation are my own responsibility.

Howard Handelman
Professor Emeritus
University of Wisconsin–Milwaukee

1

Understanding Underdevelopment

A rural village in the Indian state of Orissa. About two-thirds of India's population and almost half the population of all of the world's LDCs live in villages such as this, where standards of living and literacy rates are lower than in urban areas. *Robert Harding World Imagery/Alamy Stock Photo*

MOST AMERICANS FOCUS INFREQUENTLY on the **less developed countries** (LDCs) of Africa, Asia, the Middle East, the Caribbean, and Latin America. Media coverage of these countries is sporadic and tends to concentrate on tragedies or disturbances of various magnitudes—religious conflict and civil wars in the Middle East, a devastating earthquake in Haiti, ethnic conflict in Burma, and famine in North Korea. To almost any observer, the problems currently plaguing the developing world appear daunting. Warfare, internal violence, and massive human suffering beset the most troubled countries in these regions: insurgency and religious extremism in Syria, poverty in Bangladesh, ethnically based massacres in Burma (Myanmar)* and the Central African Republic, and political repression in Vietnam and Egypt. Of course, some of these problems exist in industrialized democracies as well, though in a milder form. For example, in recent times, both Northern Ireland and the Basque region of Spain have experienced ethnic violence and terrorism. Portions of Washington, DC have higher infant mortality rates than do Cuba and Singapore. Nevertheless, it is the scope and persistence of the developing world's political, economic, and social challenges that ultimately draw our attention.

Understanding the nature and causes of underdevelopment is a complex task complicated by theoretical debates between scholars and a profusion of terminology. Even the names given to the politically and economically less developed nations vary, with each having its own assumptions. In order to avoid repetitious usage, I interchangeably use the terms "less developed countries" (or LDCs), "developing world," "developing countries," "developing nations," and—occasionally—"Third World."†

DEVELOPING WORLD COMMONALITIES: THE NATURE OF UNDERDEVELOPMENT

Despite the substantial differences among them, developing countries still share a number of common characteristics. All of them suffer from at

---

*In 1989, the ruling military junta changed Burma's official name to Myanmar. However, human rights groups and some governments—including the United States and Britain—have not recognized that change. Burma also remains the name best known to people outside the country. Therefore, this book will call the country Burma.

†The term "Third World" was coined during the Cold War between the West and the Soviet, communist bloc. It related to the order in which the world's three major groups of nations experienced industrialization and other aspects of modernization. "First World" referred to the most developed countries in Europe, North America, Oceana, and Japan, which are generally capitalist and democratic. The "Second World"—now essentially defunct—consisted of later developing countries with communist economic and political systems. "Third World" countries are the less developed countries of Africa, Asia, Latin America and the Caribbean, and the Middle East. The term was found in much of the political science literature written during the Cold War and is still sometimes used in the mass media.

least some aspects of political, economic, or social underdevelopment. Although some of East Asia's newly industrializing countries (NICs)— for example, South Korea and Singapore—are no longer *economically* underdeveloped, they still share a vulnerability to global economic forces and continue to suffer from aspects of political underdevelopment. On the other hand, Costa Rica and Uruguay are relatively well developed politically and socially but manifest a number of the problems of economic underdevelopment. In short, while some developing countries are underdeveloped in all major aspects of modernization, others are far more advanced in some aspects of development than in others. As we shall see, economic, social, and political underdevelopments are closely related to each other, but they are not perfectly correlated. The basic disciplinary approach of this text is political science. However, it will also draw on theories and research from anthropology, economics, and sociology.

Economic Underdevelopment

Perhaps the most salient characteristic of most developing countries is poverty. At the national level, this is manifested by some combination of low per capita income, very unequal income distribution, poor **infrastructure** (including communications and transportation), limited use of modern technology, and low consumption of hydrocarbon and hydroelectric power. At the grassroots level, economic underdevelopment connotes widespread scarcity, substantial unemployment, substandard housing, poor health conditions, low literacy and educational levels, and inadequate nutrition.

While most developing countries are much poorer than nations in Western Europe and North America, there is also considerable variation among them and between world regions. Table 1.1 compares the per capita gross national income (GNI), human development, and life expectancy of the developing world's major regions with those of the United States. Purchasing power parity (PPP) means that, when two economies are compared, the exchange rate between their two currencies is adjusted so that the expenditure on a similar commodity (say, five pounds of rice) is the same in both currencies. As the first data column indicates, per capita income in the United States is more than three times higher than in the **Arab States** and more than sixteen times higher than **Sub-Saharan Africa**.* Of late, however, many developing nations—especially those in Asia and Sub-Saharan Africa—have been narrowing that gap by growing at a much faster economic rate than the United States and other developed countries.

---

*"Arab States" or "Arab World" refer to countries with primarily Arabic-speaking populations located in the Middle East and North Africa. "Sub-Saharan Africa" consists of those African nations that are located south of the Sahara Desert (i.e., south of the Arab countries of northern Africa).

Table 1.1   Income and Human Development

Region	Gross National Income (GNI) per Capita (PPP)[a]	Human Development Index (HDI)	Life Expectancy at Birth (years)	
			Male	Female
United States	52,308	0.914	76.5	81.3
Sub-Saharan Africa	3,152	0.502	55.6	58.0
East Asia	10,499	0.703	72.3	75.8
South Asia	5,195	0.588	65.7	68.9
Arab States	15,817	0.682	68.4	72.2
Latin America and the Caribbean	13,767	0.740	71.8	78.0

Source: United Nations Development Programme (UNDP), *Human Development Report.*

[a] PPP (purchasing power parity) means that these per capita incomes are adjusted to account for the purchasing power in each region.

The second data column in Table 1.1 shows the **Human Development Index (HDI)** of these regions. HDI is a composite statistic of life expectancy, education, and per capita income indicators. The highest possible HDI score a country may achieve is 1.000 and the lowest is .000 (though, in real life, no country is at either of these extremes).

Most development specialists consider the HDI to be a much better measure than per capita GNI of a nation's quality of life. For example, as the table shows, the Arab States have the highest per capita income of any developing region listed in the first data column. But their comparatively high GNI per capita ($15,817) is inflated by the huge oil income that the governments of many countries in the region earn (such as Saudi Arabia and Kuwait) and is not an accurate reflection of how well the average person lives. We can see this in the HDI scores, where the Arab States fall well behind East Asia and Latin America and the Caribbean.

The last data column demonstrates that both male and female life expectancy in the developing world lag well behind those in the United States (and in other developed countries). Only East Asia and Latin America and the Caribbean come close. Given the Arab States' high per capita income, it is instructive that it trails those two regions in both life expectancy and the HDI. In all three columns, South Asia (principally India and Pakistan) and especially Sub-Saharan Africa trail well behind.

Table 1.2 moves from the economic performance of developing world regions to an examination of individual countries in each of those areas: South Africa, Nigeria, and Mali (all in Sub-Saharan Africa); Iraq (an Arab State); Indonesia, Pakistan, and China (South and East Asia); Peru, Mexico, and Brazil (Latin America). The first data column in the

Table 1.2 Income and Income Inequality

Country	GDP ("Income") per Capita (PPP) ($)	Percentage of Population Living in Severe Poverty (earning <$2/day [PPP])	Share of Income Going to Poorest 20%	Share of Income Going to Richest 20%
South Africa	12,700	26.2	2.5	69.9
Nigeria	5,600	82.2	5.4	48.9
Mali	1,160	78.8	8.0	41.3
Iraq	14,670	21.2	8.8	38.5
Indonesia	10,250	43.3	7.6	43.7
Pakistan	5,100	50.7	9.6	39.5
China	13,130	18.6	4.7	47.1
Peru	11,510	8.0	4.2	50.1
Mexico	16,710	4.1	4.9	54.1
Brazil	15,900	6.8	3.4	57.2

Source: United Nations Development Programme (UNDP), *Human Development Report*; World Bank, *World Development Indicators.*

table, **GDP (gross domestic product)** per capita indicates the annual dollar value of goods and services produced per person.* The data illustrate the tremendous gap in living standards between most developed and less developed countries and the considerable variation within the developing world. On the one hand, the U.S. per capita GDP of approximately $55,000 (not in the table) is more than three times higher than the levels for Mexico or Brazil. On the other hand, the Mexican GDP per capita is about three times higher than Nigeria's and about fourteen times as high as Mali's.

While per capita income and product are useful indicators of a country's living standard, they do not give us a complete picture because they fail to take into account how equitably those quantities are distributed. For example, hypothetically, two nations may have the same per capita incomes, say $20,000 annually. However, in country "A," 40 percent of the population is poor, with annual incomes lower than $7,000, while the wealthiest 25 percent of the populace has an average income of $75,000. On the other hand, in country "B," with the same average income, earnings are far more evenly distributed, with almost everyone making between $15,000 and $25,000 annually. Thus, while the countries have the same *average* incomes, country A has far more poor people.

If we look at Table 1.2, we find that the countries with the lowest per capita GDPs tend to have the most severe poverty. So, for example,

---

*In popular usage, "per capita GDP" is often used interchangeably with "GNI per capita" or "per capita income."

Mali has a far lower average GDP than Mexico and a far greater percentage of its population living in severe poverty. But there are some clear exceptions to this pattern. Nigeria has a higher per capita GDP than Pakistan and far higher than Mali. Yet it has a larger share of its population in poverty than either. Similarly, while South Africa has a higher per capita GDP than Peru, it has more than three times as large a portion of its population living in poverty. The reason for anomalies such as these lies in how equally (or unequally) income is distributed in each country. Looking at the last data column reveals that the richest 20 percent of the Nigerian population ("the rich") earn almost half (48.9 percent) of their country's total income, while in South Africa the rich earn more than two-thirds (69.9 percent) of the national income. Correspondingly, the poorest portion of each population earns a very small percentage of national income (5.4 percent in Nigeria and a mere 2.4 percent in South Africa). In short, the extent of poverty in any country is a function of both its average income and how equally that income is distributed.

Social Underdevelopment

Poverty in the LDCs tends to correlate with poor social conditions such as high infant mortality and low literacy rates, which in turn reduces opportunities for human development in other areas. If LDCs are to modernize and develop economically, politically, and socially, they must extend and improve their educational systems and, thereby, raise the rate of literacy. An educated workforce contributes to higher labor productivity. Moreover, improved education also expands mass political participation and contributes to greater government accountability to the governed. Thus, not surprisingly, political scientists have found that countries with higher literacy rates are more likely to attain and maintain democratic governments.[1]

Table 1.3 presents data on several important indicators of social development and compares a number of LDCs with the United States. The first data column lists each country's HDI, which, as we saw earlier, is a composite measure of education, adult literacy, life expectancy, and per capita income. Alongside of the HDI scores, the numbers in parentheses show how each country's score ranks among almost two hundred nations in the world. Thus, for example, the United States' HDI of 0.914 ranks it fifth in the world (behind Norway, Australia, Switzerland, and the Netherlands).

Countries with greater average incomes, not surprisingly, tend to have higher HDIs, but that is not always true. The next column shows each country's world ranking on average income minus its rankings on HDI. Thus, for example, the United States has the fourteenth highest per capita income in the world (not shown in the table), but the fifth highest

Table 1.3   Human Development and Literacy

Country	HDI (rank)	Per Capita GNI Rank Minus HDI Rank	Percentage Adult Literacy (age 15+)
United States	0.914 (5)	+9	100
South Africa	0.658 (128)	−11	94
Nigeria	0.504 (152)	−4	60
Mali	0.407 (176)	+20	39
Iraq	0.612 (120)	−23	80
Indonesia	0.684 (108)	+16	94
Pakistan	0.537(146)	+10	58
China	0.719 (91)	+14	96
Peru	0.737 (82)	+33	94
Mexico	0.756 (71)	+17	95
Brazil	0.744 (79)	+15	93

Source: UNDP, *Human Development Report*; CIA, *The World Book Factbook*.

HDI. So, it is an "overachiever" in that its HDI ranking (fifth) is higher than we would have predicted based on its average income (fourteenth), giving it a score of (14 – 5 or +9). In this column, any country with a *positive* score has "overachieved" (i.e., its HDI rank is higher than we might have predicted based on its GNI rank) and, conversely, any country with a *negative* score has "underachieved."* The primary reason why a country overachieves is that its government has allocated an above average percentage of its spending toward improving health, sanitation, and education, while underachieving governments have spent a lower percentage of their revenue on improving these services.

Peru (+33) is the greatest overachiever in the table, followed by Mali and Mexico. So, Mali, though a desperately poor country, has a much higher than expected HDI score. Among all of the world's developing nations, the two highest overachievers are Cuba (+52)—which is known for its strong government educational and public health programs—and Grenada (+30).

On the other end of the spectrum, Iraq (–23) is the greatest underachiever in the table, an indication of how years of war and civil conflict have decimated the educational and health systems. Looking more broadly at all the LDCs, the greatest underachievers tend to be Middle Eastern countries deriving the major portion of their income from exporting oil. That income primarily benefits the government and the economic elite, while the country's educational and health facilities fail

---

*In this table, far more countries are "overachievers" than "under achievers." But if we had looked at the entire list of developing nations, the number of countries in each of these two groups would be about even.

Table 1.4   Quality of Life/Social Indicators

Country	Life Expectancy at Birth Male	Life Expectancy at Birth Female	Child Malnutrition: Percentage of Underweight Children < Age 5 (rank among 138 countries)[a]	Percentage of Children Enrolled in Primary School
South Africa	55	55	8.7 (72)	NA
Nigeria	52	54	31.0 (12)	64
Mali	53	57	27.9 (20)	64
Iraq	70	73	8.5 (94)	NA
Indonesia	70	75	19.9 (31)	92
Pakistan	65	69	31.6 (11)	72
China	73	77	3.4 (109)	NA
Peru	71	75	3.5 (103)	92
Mexico	73	78	2.8 (117)	96
Brazil	70	77	2.2 (121)	NA

Source: CIA, *The World Book Factbook*; The World Bank, *Databank*.

[a] *The World Factbook* rated 138 developed and developing countries for their rate of childhood malnutrition. The figures in parentheses express where each country ranked in terms of *the most* malnutrition.

to receive a commensurate share. These countries include Kuwait (–57), Oman (–50), Qatar (–36), and Saudi Arabia (–19). But the world's greatest underachiever is the tiny West African nation of Equatorial Guinea (the third-largest oil producer in Sub-Saharan Africa). While its oil wealth allows it to rank forty-fifth in the world in GNI per capita, it is an abysmal 136th on HDI, giving it a GNI – HDI score of –91. Much of its oil income falls into the hands of its brutal dictator, who has ruled the country since 1979 (making him one of the longest serving heads of state in the world), and is worth an estimated $600 million, while most of his subjects live in abject poverty.

The last column again shows how widely social conditions vary among LDCs, with Mali having an adult literacy rate of only 39 percent, while Brazil, Mexico, Peru, Indonesia, China, and South Africa all are 93–96 percent literate. In recent decades many developing nations have raised their literacy rates dramatically, with almost half of all LDCs currently exceeding 90 percent literacy and all but thirteen now over 50 literate.

Finally, Table 1.4 presents additional measures of the quality of people's lives: life expectancy, child malnutrition, and school enrollment. The first data column reveals how much lower life expectancy is in most African nations (as illustrated by Mali, Nigeria, and South Africa). While malnutrition, deadly diseases such as malaria, and, in some cases, civil violence account for much of that, a number of African countries have experienced sharp declines in life expectancy because of the HIV/AIDS pandemic. This was especially true of South Africa, which has the highest infection rate in the world. Overall life expectancy in that country (for females and males combined) had climbed to sixty-two years in the early 1990s and then began to fall because of AIDS to a low of fifty-two by 2007. That decline was accelerated by then president Thabo Mbeki (1999–2008), who denied that the disease was caused by a virus, refused foreign medical assistance, and failed to establish prevention or treatment programs. Experts at Harvard Medical School have estimated that 330,000 additional people died during Mbeki's administration as a result of his denial of scientific evidence.[2]

Since he left office, the new administration has adopted a very strong antiretroviral policy, reduced AIDS deaths dramatically and thereby increased life expectancy by more than four years, with similar improvements happening throughout Sub-Saharan Africa. The UN's World Health Organization (WHO) reports that "the increasing availability of antiretroviral therapy has reduced the spread of the epidemic, and the mortality due to AIDS has been decreasing since about 2005 [allowing African life expectancy at birth to increase from 50 years in 2000 to 58 years in 2013]."[3] Elsewhere in the developing world, life expectancy has increased steadily in recent decades, especially in East Asia and Latin America.

The next column presents the percent of children under five who are seriously underweight, a clear indicator of malnutrition. The numbers in parentheses following the percentage of malnourished children in each country show how the country ranks among 138 developed and developing nations. Thus, Pakistan, with nearly 32 percent of its children under age five suffering from malnutrition, ranks as the twelfth most malnourished of the 138 countries in the group. China and Brazil have both lowered child malnutrition impressively recently—China by introducing free-market practices that have raised the living standards of its huge rural population and Brazil through its Bolsa Familia, a highly successful government antipoverty program.

The last column presents the percentage of school-aged children enrolled in primary school. Here also there have been substantial improvements through most of the developing world, so that even in a very poor country, such as Mali, 64 percent of school-aged children are enrolled in school. Some of the most dramatic gains in the LDCs have been in education and literacy. At the same time, many Islamic countries, such as Pakistan, have lower school enrollments than their socioeconomic conditions would have us predict, because girls are less likely to attend school. But the high enrollment for Indonesia—the world's most populous Muslim country—demonstrated that this is not always true.

Political Underdevelopment

When Western political scientists first began to study LDCs systematically, they soon recognized that evaluating political systems in cultural and socioeconomic settings very different from their own was extremely challenging. While many modernization theorists believed that governments in the developing world should model themselves after Western industrialized democracies, they were also mindful of important differences between the regions that limited that possibility. For example, recognizing that most Western European countries did not fully democratize until they were well along the path to industrial development, scholars were often reluctant to criticize **authoritarian governments** in countries still at the early stages of economic development. A number of African social scientists added to the debate by arguing that their continent had extensive village- and tribal-based democracy that adequately substituted for competitive elections at the national level. Others feared that, in the ethnically divided countries of Africa and Asia, multiparty systems would inevitably develop along ethnic lines, further contributing to national disintegration.

Conscious of such land mines, many political scientists proposed political standards that they felt were free of ideological and cultural biases. Political development, they suggested, involves the creation of specialized and differentiated government institutions that effectively carry out necessary functions, such as collecting tax revenues, defending national borders, maintaining political stability, stimulating economic development, improving the quality of human life, and communicating with the citizenry. In addition, they argued, developed governments are responsive to a broad segment of society and respect the population's fundamental freedoms and civil rights. Presumably, any government satisfying these standards would enjoy a reasonable level of **legitimacy** (i.e., its own citizens would endorse its right to govern), which encourages individuals and groups to pursue their political objectives peacefully through established political institutions rather than through violent or other illegal channels. But, too many LDCs, Paul Collier notes, suffer from "bad governance"—a combination of corruption, catering to special interests and mismanagement.[4]

But while analysts agreed that governments should be responsive, representative, and nonrepressive, many of them also believed that a political system could be considered developed even if it was not democratic, at least as that term is defined in the West. Definitions of "full democracy" generally encompass the following basic components: fair and competitive elections in which opposition parties have a realistic chance of winning; universal or nearly universal adult suffrage; widespread opportunities for political participation; free and open mass media;

and government respect for human rights, including minority rights.[5] Many political scientists initially felt that it was unrealistic and perhaps culturally biased to expect that level of democracy to quickly flourish in developing countries. Similarly, others argued that many developing nations were not ready for democracy. Concerned about the high levels of violence and instability in those political systems, they claimed that the LDCs' first priority had to be political stability, even if that might initially require military rule or other forms of authoritarian government.[6]

More recently, however, troubled by extensive government repression in the developing world and the obvious failures of most authoritarian regimes, political scientists have begun to insist that democracy and some degree of socioeconomic equality must be understood as integral parts of political development.[7] The collapse of communist regimes in the Soviet Union and Eastern Europe, and more recently the overthrow of decades-old dictatorships in the Arab World exposed additional weaknesses in authoritarian systems. Beyond its obvious ethical attractions, democracy also has pragmatic appeal. For example, governments whose citizens hold them accountable through competitive elections are more likely to be more efficient and honest (although the disappointing records of democratic governments in countries such as Kenya and the Philippines demonstrate that there are no guarantees). Similarly, free and independent forms of mass media also help keep governments accountable. The disintegration of the Soviet bloc and the fall of many dictatorships throughout the developing world suggest that authoritarian regimes may be stable in the short run but are fragile in the long term. Thus, there is not necessarily a trade-off between democracy and political stability, as many had imagined. In fact, democracies are generally (but not always) immune to revolutionary insurrection and less susceptible to other forms of mass violence.

Only a restricted number of developing countries have fully met the standards of political development and democracy just listed—for example, the Bahamas, Uruguay, and Costa Rica. Others—such as Argentina, India, South Korea, and Taiwan—currently satisfy most of the criteria. Even a cursory review of the LDCs, however, reveals that most governments still fall short. At one extreme—in nations such as Somalia and Yemen—rebel groups or warlords have divided control over their country or rebels and corruption have so undermined the national governments that political scientists label them "failed states." Elsewhere in the developing world, many governments respond disproportionately to the demands of an affluent minority. Self-perpetuating and self-serving elites have ruled many Middle Eastern and North African nations, while some Sub-Saharan African governments serve the interests of dominant ethnic groups (ethnicities). Political corruption, bureaucratic inefficiency, and police repression are all endemic to much of the LDCs.

In the recent past, class-based revolutionary movements have erupted in various Asian and Latin American nations, and a number of African countries have been torn apart by ethnic civil wars (with some countries still suffering from such conflicts). Thus, until recently most LDCs were not democratic, stable, or legitimate. In the last decades of the twentieth century, however, democracy (and with it, government legitimacy) advanced in much of the developing world, most notably in Latin America and East Asia (see chapter 2).

Corruption: A Critical Obstacle to Political and Economic Development

Government corruption has been a problem in nearly every country in the world, developed and underdeveloped alike. But, it is particularly problematic in many developing nations, both because the scale has been so extensive and because its pervasiveness is more shocking in view of widespread poverty in their countries. Culprits vary widely: from high-ranking officials of Petrobras (the Brazilian state petroleum giant) who colluded with private contractors to steal millions of dollars in kickback schemes to Mexican traffic police shaking down innocent motorists for imagined traffic violations. Transparency International (TI), an independent organization that evaluates the level of corruption in nations worldwide—based on surveys of public opinion and on analysis by experts—issues an annual report ranking developed and developing countries according to their perceived level of corruption. In its latest (2015) ratings of 176 nations, TI ranked six developing countries—two in Asia (North Korea and Afghanistan), two in Sub-Saharan Africa (Somalia and South Sudan), one in North Africa (Sudan), and one in the Middle East (Iraq) as the world's worst offenders. Only one LDC (Singapore) was rated among the ten least corrupt nations.*

At the highest level of government, former Nigerian president Sani Abacha apparently siphoned off $1.1 billion from funds allocated to the country's armed forces, leaving the military ill-equipped to fight the powerful Boko Haram terrorists. At the local level, after the Indian parliament passed affirmative action legislation, setting aside seats at universities for lower-caste applicants, many of these seats were soon sold by corrupt school officials to more affluent students. The World Bank has estimated that up to 80 percent of Peru's logging exports are illegally harvested, much of it by loggers who bribe local officials to bypass laws protecting the rain forest. And in 2013, a respected Indian research

---

*Other developing countries among the twenty-five *least* corrupt were Barbados, the Bahamas, Hong Kong, Chile, Uruguay, and the United Arab Emirates. The United States was tied with Ireland, Barbados, and Hong Kong for seventeenth least corrupt.

institute reported that 30 percent of the winners in national and regional elections during the previous five years had faced subsequent criminal charges so far. Meanwhile, many of these convicted government officials can (and do) remain in office while they appeal their convictions, a process in India's incredibly slow court system that often takes ten to fifteen years to complete.

Government corruption has long been an impediment to economic growth, and a huge financial burden on millions of urban businessmen and village peasants, among others. It has also made people highly cynical about their political system and caused governments to lose legitimacy. But many people in the developing world grudgingly accept government corruption as an inescapable burden of life or, in some cases, refuse to believe that a beloved official could be capable of that crime. In the Indian state of Tamil Nadu a longtime political boss—the chief minister of the state—known for giving handouts to the poor, is adored by many of her constituents despite her obvious dishonesty. "In 1995, during a period when she professed to earn a salary of 1 rupee per month, she staged an opulent waterfront wedding for her foster son that included 40,000 guests and a formal sit-down dinner for 12,800." When she was eventually sentenced (in 2014) to four years in jail, many of her followers reacted hysterically.

> On the day the verdict was read, a 58-year-old electrician named Venkateshan walked out of the shop where he had been watching the news coverage all morning, soaked himself with gasoline and set himself on fire, shouting, "My *Amma* [meaning 'Mother,' as she is known to her followers] has failed in the court."[8]

Lately, however, elsewhere in India and in other developing countries, citizens have reacted by holding protests and electing a number of officials from anticorruption political parties. In 2015, in response to massive citizen protests, the Guatemalan Congress unanimously voted to strip national president, Otto Pérez Molina, of his office's immunity from charges that he and high-ranking officials in his administration had routinely taken bribes in exchange for lowering tariffs on companies importing large amounts of goods. Within days, Pérez Molina resigned from office—after months of saying he would not—and was promptly arrested. Earlier, the vice president had been detained on the same charges. These developments came in the wake of mass anticorruption demonstrations in a country not far removed from a series of dictatorships during which such protests would have been brutally repressed.

In countries as far-flung as India, Iraq, Mexico, Nigeria, and the Philippines, voters are increasingly supporting anticorruption candidates and joining anticorruption rallies. The issue has become one of the public's major political irritants. Even in dictatorships, the people's revulsion with corruption has forced the government some real or cosmetic action. When he first took office in 2012, China's president Xi Jinping realized that such extensive dishonesty had eroded the ruling Communist Party's legitimacy. He soon unleashed a massive anticorruption campaign that charged and disciplined 72,000 officials in 2014 alone. Their punishment ranged from removal from office, to imprisonment, to the death penalty for some high-ranking officials who had been enormously corrupt. As a result, President Xi's popularity soared, but many Chinese continued to doubt that the campaign would have any permanent or even long-lasting effect.

People have good reason to be skeptical. Many developing countries have held government anticorruption investigations and appointed special prosecutors over the years. In most cases, they turn out to be cosmetic, with a few high-profile cases meant to impress the public. Even when they are real, they usually turn out to be short-lived. And when truly fearless and diligent anticorruption officials do come along, they are often subjected to death threats or actual assassination. Nuhu Ribadu, one of the rare chairmen of Nigeria's anticorruption commission who actually investigated and brought charges against high-ranking politicians, was forced to flee the country after he had received death threats and had survived a drive-by shooting. Later, after he had returned to Nigeria, the government brought false anticorruption charges against him (however, he was acquitted).

The rare success of the Indian state of Bihar shows that pervasive corruption can be brought under control by honest and courageous government leaders. It also demonstrates the benefits that cleaner governments can bring. Bihar, with a population of 103 million, has long been one of the poorest states in India. Moreover, in 2005 TI named it the most politically corrupt of India's twenty-eight states. At the same time, the state economy stagnated, with its **GNP (gross national product)** growing at about half the national rate.

In that year, Nitish Kumar, an anticorruption crusader, was elected Bihar's chief minister. Upon taking office he made public all of his financial assets and required other state ministers to do the same. In 2011, after pushing through a series of other reforms, he enacted a law giving the state government the right "to confiscate any [state official's] ill-gotten property, pending trial, and turn it into a school or health clinic."[9] A number of officials, including the former chief of the state police, lost their property. If an accused official was later found innocent, he/she would get the property back with interest. Whistle-blowers whose tips led to a conviction got rewards of up to $10,000. Because of these reforms and many others like it, TI changed its ranking of Bihar from

India's most corrupt state to its least corrupt. At the same time, the state's economy, which had grown at a sluggish annual rate of 3.5 percent in the five years before Kumar was elected, rose to 7.5 percent growth in his first five years in office, making it the nation's fastest-growing state economy.

Elsewhere in the developing world, LDCs wanting similar success stories will need to create a more educated, more politically aware public, who will elect this type of honest and dedicated government officials.

Some Relationships between the Components of Development

It is logical to assume that political, economic, and social underdevelopment are interrelated. More economically advanced countries can better educate their populations and provide them with superior health care. An educated citizenry, in turn, contributes to further economic growth and participates in politics more responsibly. Responsive and legitimate governments, constrained by competitive elections, are more likely to educate their citizens and to make informed economic decisions. Indeed, these logical intuitions are supported by empirical evidence. Wealthier countries tend to have greater life expectancies, higher literacy rates, and more stable and democratic governments.

However, these correlations are not absolute. For example, a country's literacy and infant mortality rates depend not only on its economic resources but also on government policies in the areas of education, public health, and welfare. Thus, elitist government policies in some countries have contributed to worse social conditions (as measured by their HDIs) than in other nations with comparable or fewer economic resources. "Underachievers" include many petroleum-rich states, such as Saudi Arabia and Kuwait. On the other hand, governments in Cuba and Chile—with strong commitments to social welfare programs—have generated higher life expectancy rates and educational levels than their economic resources alone would lead us to predict ("overachievers").

Both economic and social development tend to correlate with political development. Wealthier, more educated LDCs such as Barbados, Botswana, Costa Rica, and Taiwan tend to have more politically stable, responsive, and democratic governments than poorer nations such as Mozambique, Haiti, and Cambodia. Indeed, developing countries are not likely to become democracies or to maintain democracy unless they have reached a minimal threshold of socioeconomic development.[10] However, as countries undergo the process of becoming more economically developed, there is not necessarily a smooth progression toward greater political stability or democracy. On the contrary, Samuel Huntington has observed that while the most affluent countries in the world (e.g., Switzerland and Canada) are politically stable and the poorest countries (such as Afghanistan and Burundi) are generally politically unstable, countries that are in the mid-stages of economic development often become more unstable as their economies develop.[11] Thus, for example, some of Latin America's most economically advanced countries (including Argentina and Chile) experienced internal conflicts and political unrest in the 1960s and 1970s, resulting in the collapse of their democratic governments and the emergence of highly repressive military dictatorships. In 2001–2002, nearly two decades after the restoration of democratic government, Argentina experienced an economic crisis, urban rioting, and political instability that produced five presidents in the span of less than a month. Huntington explained this political instability in mid-level developing nations by suggesting that as countries modernize, the spread of urbanization, education, and mass media consumption produces an increasingly politically aware and mobilized society, whose citizens make greater demands on the government. All too often, however, political institutions, particularly political parties, are not strengthened quickly enough to channel and respond to this rising tide of demands. Or the government may lack the economic resources to address all these demands. As a result, he maintained, the system becomes overloaded and unstable.

Guillermo O'Donnell posited another theory explaining the rise of extremely repressive dictatorships in South America's more economically advanced nations during the 1960s and 1970s. He suggested that as those countries moved toward a higher stage of industrial growth, they required extensive new investment that they could secure only by attracting foreign capital. Such foreign investment, in turn, would materialize only if the government controlled labor unions and kept down workers' wage demands. In order to achieve those goals, the nations' business leaders and **technocrats** turned to repressive military rule through what he called "bureaucratic-authoritarian states."[12]

Similarly, some scholars have argued that an authoritarian government might be helpful in the early to middle stages of industrialization in order to control labor unions and workers' wages, thereby increasing company profits and attracting new external investment. They point out that the Asian countries that enjoyed the most spectacular economic growth from the 1970s to the mid-1990s—Indonesia, Malaysia, Thailand, Singapore, Taiwan, and South Korea—were all governed by authoritarian regimes during their economic takeoffs. Although these theories have since been challenged, they indicate that the relationships between political, economic, and social development are complex. While, at least in the long run, the three generally go hand in hand, they need not progress at the same rate. Moreover, for some periods of time, they may even move in different directions.

A Major Consequence of Underdevelopment Today: Mass Migration

For much of modern history, international and civil wars, natural disasters, famine, political repression, and the search for a better life have given rise to large-scale human migration. These population movements have happened within individual LDCs, from LDCs to more developed areas (such as Western Europe) and from one developing country to another (such as the migration of many thousands of Afghan refugees to Pakistan). Mass migration is not a defining characteristic of underdevelopment but, rather, a consequence of it.

For over one hundred years, people have emigrated from the developing world to destinations such as the United States, Australia, and Western Europe. But, in the past few decades, migration has become a major issue in world politics. As modern technology and mass media have made millions of the developing world's poor, war-weary, and persecuted or repressed peoples more aware of opportunities elsewhere, millions have embarked on the, often treacherous, path of emigration.[13] And the tide has risen sharply in recent years. As of August, 2015, the number of migrants (mostly from Africa and the Middle East) that had arrived in Greece by sea since the start of that year had reached 158,000; an additional 90,000 had landed in Italy; and perhaps 150,000 more had arrived by land or sea in other countries on Europe's external borders. During that time, over 2,000 had drowned at sea, most of them having embarked on rickety boats sold to them by unscrupulous human traffickers. Once they have reached those countries, they usually try to move on to countries such as Germany, France, and Britain, where they believe there are more economic opportunities. Germany expected some 800,000 asylum seekers to arrive there in 2015.[14] This deluge has been caused by armed conflict and poverty in Northern and Sub-Saharan Africa. It has led to an anti-immigrant backlash in much of the European Union and has raised electoral support for racist and other far-right-wing political parties, such as France's National Front and the Freedom Party of Austria.

Similarly, millions of Latin American immigrants to the United States, mostly from Mexico, have lifted the percentage of Latinos in the U.S. population to more than 15 percent. As in Europe, many Americans have reacted very negatively to illegal immigration, although polls have shown that "more than 7 in 10 Americans (71 percent) say there should be a way for people in the United States illegally to remain in this country if they meet certain requirements."[15] But, the percentage of opponents is much higher among Republicans and backlash against illegal immigration has become a major issue in the Republican run-up to the 2016 presidential elections.

While illegal immigration to the United States, Europe and Australia has attracted substantial attention in the West, the recent, massive migration *within* the LDCs has attracted less consideration, even though it has created a far greater crisis. The cumulative number of Syrian refugees fleeing their country's four-year-old civil war surpassed four million people by mid-2015 (almost 20 percent of that country's entire population). At that time, neighboring Turkey housed about 1.8 million of them, Lebanon (with a native population of less than 5 million) had almost 1.2 million, and Jordan had received over 600,000. Those numbers have placed a tremendous economic burden on all three countries, who have far fewer resources than do Western, industrialized nations. Pakistan has had the only comparable refugee crisis, where millions of Afghans have fled since the Soviet invasion (1978–1989) and the wars since then.

THE CAUSES OF UNDERDEVELOPMENT

Our initial discussion suggested that there is some debate concerning the very *definitions* of political and socioeconomic underdevelopment. Social scientists disagree even more intensely over the underlying *causes* of underdevelopment and the most promising pathways to change. How, for example, do we account for constant military intervention in Pakistani politics, political turmoil in Somalia, government repression in Syria, and periodic financial crises in Argentina? Do these problems originate from internal factors such as authoritarian cultural values, weak political parties, or misguided economic planning? Or, did foreign domination— stretching from the colonial era to today's age of **multinational corporations (MNCs)** and the International Monetary Fund (IMF)—cause many of these difficulties?

Questions about the cause of underdevelopment and pathways to development elicit very different responses from scholarly analysts. Frequently, their evaluations reflect their personal background, country of origin, or ideology. Thus, for example, theories that attribute developing world political unrest or economic backwardness to traditional cultural values generally have emanated from the United States or from other developed nations. On the other hand, approaches such as dependency theory and world systems theory, which view Western exploitation as the root cause of underdevelopment, have been particularly popular among Latin American and African analysts. Similarly, liberal, conservative, and Marxist analysts are each drawn to different explanations.

For years, two competing paradigms shaped scholarly analyses of politics and economic change in LDCs. The first, **modernization theory**, emerged in the early 1960s as American political science's leading interpretation of underdevelopment. The second, **dependency theory**, originated in Latin America in the 1970s and offered a more radical perspective on development, one particularly popular among scholars in developing nations.

Modernization Theory and the Importance of Cultural Values

During the 1950s and 1960s, as the demise of European colonialism produced a host of newly independent nations in Africa, Asia, and the Middle East, Western social scientists began to study politics and economics in the developing world more intensively. That interest produced a complex conceptual model of underdevelopment and development known as modernization theory. Its proponents included some of the most prominent figures in the study of comparative politics. For a decade or more, modernization theory reigned supreme in the study of political and economic development. Though later challenged, it has continued to influence our understanding of developing nations. While there have been variations and disagreement among modernization theorists, they generally share a number of underlying assumptions and perspectives.

Despite the tremendous array of problems facing the LDCs, modernization theorists were initially relatively optimistic about prospects for development. After all, Western industrialized democracies had also started out as underdeveloped countries. Most developing nations, they argued, could—and should—follow a path of political and economic modernization parallel to the one first traveled by the advanced Western countries. To accomplish this, modernization theorists insisted, developing nations had to acquire modern cultural values and create modern political and economic institutions.

Transforming **traditional cultures** was considered the first and, by most accounts, most crucial step in the modernization process. Drawing on the theories of such eminent sociologists as Max Weber and Talcott Parsons, these analysts distinguished between "traditional" and "modern" values. They saw many traditional political and economic values as somewhat irrational, or at least unscientific. For example, the Indian **caste system** assigned people their rank in society at birth, a rank that was difficult to change. Conversely, modern men and women, they maintained, tend to do the following: judge others by universalistic standards (appraise people based on their ability rather than caste, class, or ethnic origins); believe in the possibility and desirability of change; value science and technology; think about issues outside the sphere of the family, neighborhood, or village; and believe that average citizens can—and should—try to influence the political system. At its worst, the theory exhibited elements of ethnocentrism and condescension, implying the inferiority of the developing world's cultures. Thus, one of the founders of Latin American studies in the United States argued,

> There is something in the quality of Latin American . . . culture which
> has made it difficult . . . to be truly modern . . . which has made this part
> of the Western world so prone to excesses of scoundrels, so politically
> irrational in seeking economic growth, and so ready to reach for
> gimmicks.[16]

But how can a traditional society make the transition to modernity? How
does a culture modernize its values? Modernization theorists identified
education, urbanization, and the spread of mass media as central agents
of change. As peasants move to cities, the theory argued, as more children attend schools that teach modern values, and as more citizens access
the mass media, cultural modernization will progress. Another critical
component, it was suggested, was the diffusion of modern ideas from
highly industrialized nations to the developing world and from city to
countryside within the LDCs. Foreign aid and institutions such as the
Peace Corps could help speed up this process.

Gabriel Almond and G. Bingham Powell, depicting modernization
as a rather inexorable force, contended that "the forces of technological change and cultural diffusion are driving political systems in certain
directions, which seem discernible and susceptible to analysis in terms of
increasing levels of development."[17] Others envisioned modernization as
a process of getting developing nations to think and act "more like us"
(i.e., the West). "As time goes on," Marion Levy predicted, "they and we
will increasingly resemble one another. [The] more highly modernized
societies become, the more they resemble one another."[18] Today, as the
forces of modernization have spread McDonald's burgers and fries, computer technology, Hollywood movies, rock music, and democratic values
around the world, that prophecy may seem accurate.

At the same time, modernization theory claimed, developing nations
trying to modernize need to create more specialized and complex political and economic institutions to complement those cultural changes. For
example, whereas a tribal culture might have a council of elders responsible for legislative, executive, and judicial activities, a modern society
needs separate, specialized institutions for each of these tasks. Modernizing societies also need trained bureaucracies, which base professional
advancement on merit rather than personal connections and make decisions according to uniform and consistent standards. Political parties
have to channel citizens' demands and aspirations effectively to government policymakers. Eventually, it was argued, as these cultural and institutional changes progress, a modernizing society can lay the foundation
for a more stable, effective, and responsive political system. During the
decades after World War II, which featured the Cold War against Soviet
communism, modernization theory became far more than an academic
perspective. Its assumptions dominated U.S. foreign policy toward the

developing world, including foreign-aid programs, the Peace Corps, and the tactics used during the Vietnam War.

In time, however, many of early modernization theory's assumptions had to be modified. To begin with, it had been too optimistic and too simplistic in its initial view of change. Its proponents generally expected developing countries to achieve economic growth, greater equality, democracy, political stability, and greater national autonomy simultaneously and smoothly. As Huntington noted, the theory erroneously assumed that "all good things go together."[19] In fact, economic growth proved to be no guarantee of democracy, stability, equality, or autonomy. As we have noted, in nations such as Brazil, China, Mexico, South Korea, and Taiwan, industrialization and economic development originated and advanced for many years under the direction of authoritarian governments.

Analysts were particularly disturbed to find that the very process of social and economic modernization often ushered in political instability and violence. For example, in some of Latin America's most economically developed nations (Argentina, Chile, and Uruguay), industrial growth and greater income inequality unleashed bitter class conflict, causing the collapse of democratic institutions and the rise of repressive military dictatorships.[20] Elsewhere, in much of Africa, Asia, and the Middle East, the hopes once inspired by decolonization gave way to ethnic conflict, military **coups d'état**, and political repression.

Thus, the process of development often turned out to be more difficult and unpredictable than originally imagined. Modernization theory's initial optimism gave way to **conflict theory**. Developing nations, this new perspective argued, would have to make hard choices between seemingly irreconcilable development goals. Concerned about growing political turmoil in many developing nations, some political scientists insisted that political stability was crucial, even if maintaining it sometimes necessitated authoritarian rule for a time. That is to say, democracy might have to take a backseat to stability, at least temporarily. At the same time, many economists and political scientists argued that the early stages of economic growth required wealth to be concentrated so that incipient capitalists could acquire sufficient capital for major investments.

More recently, the experiences of several countries in East Asia and Latin America have produced yet another new perspective. While certainly less naively optimistic than the earliest modernization theories, current analysis is also less pessimistic than conflict theory was. The **reconciliation approach**, offered by contemporary modernization theorists, maintains that, with the right policies, developing nations can simultaneously achieve goals previously thought to be incompatible.[21] Taiwan and South Korea, for example, have shown that it is possible to achieve rapid economic development together with equitable income distribution.

Barbados and Costa Rica have managed to achieve democracy and stability simultaneously. Consequently, current research tries to analyze factors such as state policy, historical traditions, and cultural values that may hinder or contribute to successful development.

One of the major criticisms of modernization theory, at least as originally formulated, was that it was culturally biased, assuming the superiority of Western values. Explicitly or implicitly it suggested that the Western industrialized world was the source of modern ("good") values and attitudes. Therefore, another modification of the theory addresses its initial view of cultural change. First, it recognized that all modern or modernizing cultures are not identical. Indeed, traditional values, which vary from society to society, may influence the nature of the modern culture that emerges positively or negatively. For example, in East Asian countries, such as Japan and South Korea, traditional Confucian and Shinto beliefs help explain why modern citizens of those countries tend to be less individualistic, more concerned with the good of the community or nation, and more family oriented than are Westerners.

Second, scholars now agree that the differences between traditional and modern cultures are not necessarily as stark or clear-cut as originally thought. For example, even though the United States is a highly modern society, many Americans have retained traditional values such as judging others by the color of their skin or their gender. Third, contrary to early modernization theory, it now appears that some traditional values contribute to political and economic development. For example, students of contemporary Japanese culture have argued that traditional religious values have strengthened that nation's work ethic.

Finally, while modern values have indeed swept across the developing world, they have not been universally welcomed. For example in Afghanistan, Iran, Saudi Arabia, and other parts of the Muslim world, many people, including some with advanced educations, have rejected Westernization in favor of Islamic fundamentalism (a highly traditional version of their religion based on literal adherence to the Koran). The September 11, 2001, attacks on New York and Washington and subsequent assaults elsewhere by the Islamic State were violent expressions of many peaceful Muslims' distaste of Western values and lifestyles. Although extremists represent only a very small fraction of the Muslim world, many nonviolent Muslims also reject Western culture, which they view as immoral—sullied, for example, by immodest dress, extramarital sex, and pornography.

Dependency Theory: The Core and the Periphery

During the 1960s and 1970s, social scientists in Latin America and the United States raised more fundamental objections to modernization theory, insisting that the modifications that we have just mentioned had failed to correct the theory's fundamental flaws. Under the banner of dependency theory, they challenged the modernizationists' most fundamental assumptions. A closely related approach was called "world systems theory."[22] Like modernization theorists, dependency scholars differ among themselves, but agree on the theory's fundamental premises.

To begin with, dependentistas (as dependency theorists are known) rejected the contention that LDCs can follow the same path to development as Western nations had, if only because the earliest industrialized nations changed the landscape for those that followed them. When Britain became the world's first industrialized nation, it faced no significant competition from other economic powers. Today, however, newly industrialized countries must compete against well-established industrial giants such as the United States, Japan, and Germany. In addition, argued Brazil's Theotonio Dos Santos, developing countries need to borrow capital and purchase advanced technology from highly developed countries, thereby making them dependent on economic forces beyond their borders and beyond their control.

As we have seen, modernization theory views Western influence over the developing world as beneficial, in that it spreads modern values, technology, and institutions. In contrast, dependency theorists maintain that Western colonialism and economic imperialism are precisely what first turned Africa, Asia, and Latin America into providers of cheap food and raw materials for the developed countries. Moreover, they charge, long after the LDCs had achieved political independence, many First World nations have continued to use their economic power to sustain dependent relationships that disadvantage LDCs. Until recently, the production and export of manufactured goods and technology—the most profitable economic activities—along with major control over world finance remained primarily in the control of **core nations**, the dependentistas label for the industrialized West. Conversely, in the past, LDCs, located in the **periphery**, were generally relegated to the production and export of agricultural goods and raw materials and had to trade for industrial imports on unfavorable terms. This did not mean that the core developed nations controlled every aspect of economic and political development (or misdevelopment) in the LDCs, but rather:

> [Dependency is] . . . a historical condition which shapes a certain structure of the world economy such that it favors some countries to the detriment of others and limits the development possibilities of the subordinate economies . . . a situation in which the economy of a certain group of countries is conditioned by the development and expansion of another economy, to which their own is subjected.[23]

Finally, dependentistas contend that *economic* dependence also had brought about the LDCs' *political* dependence on the core. Within the periphery, the argument went, political, military, and economic elites, backed by the might of the United States and other core nations, maintained a political system that benefited the powerful few at the expense of the many. Dependency theorists have noted, for example, how frequently France used to intervene militarily in its former African colonies to maintain corrupt and unrepresentative governments with which it was allied. Similarly, for many years, the United States has supported friendly, but repressive, regimes such as Egypt's under the long rule of Hosni Mubarak.

As one might expect, many scholars in the developing world embraced dependency theory enthusiastically because it maintained that underdevelopment was not the developing world's "fault," but rather the result of foreign domination and exploitation. Moreover, for a time, dependency theory also challenged or displaced modernization theory in the United States and Europe as the major scholarly paradigm. As Omar Sánchez has observed, this "marks one of those rare instances in which ideas produced in the developing world come to influence the thinking of scholars in the developed world."[24]

However, just as early modernization theory had been overly *optimistic* about the LDCs' prospects for simultaneous economic and political development, early dependency theory turned out to be excessively *pessimistic* about their chances for development. Analysts such as Andre Gunder Frank had warned that less developed nations—largely confined to production of crops, minerals, and other commodities—were ruled by unrepresentative elites and were doomed to face continued backwardness. Some dependentistas believed that radical revolutions were the only solution.

Yet, despite the bleak prognosis of early dependency theorists, it was clear as early as the mid-1960s that nations such as Brazil and Mexico were undergoing substantial industrialization. Some two decades later, China emerged as the world's leading exporters of manufactured goods. Similarly, South Korea, Taiwan, India, Malaysia, and several other Asian nations began to enjoy rapid economic modernization and growth. In his far more sophisticated version of dependency theory, Brazil's Fernando Henrique Cardoso rejected the contention that all developing countries were condemned to underdevelopment and precluded from significant industrialization.[25]

Drawing heavily from the experiences of his own country, Cardoso noted that through the active intervention of the state and the linkage of domestic firms to MNCs, some developing countries had industrialized and experienced considerable economic growth. He referred to this process as **associated-dependent development**.

Cardoso radically altered dependency theory by arguing that countries such as Argentina, Brazil, Colombia, and Mexico could modernize and expand their economies while still remaining dependent on foreign banks and MNCs for loans, investment, and technology. Brazilian industrialization, he noted, had been stimulated largely by a sharp rise in foreign, corporate investment. Still, Cardoso and his colleagues considered associated-dependent development tainted in several important ways. MNCs were making critical economic decisions affecting developing countries, but were outside the developing nations' control. Furthermore, foreign corporations tended to invest in capital-intensive (highly mechanized) production that needed fewer workers than more traditional, labor-intensive firms did. And, these new industries tended to manufacture products for more affluent middle- and upper-class consumers. Hence, unlike most Western firms, they had little incentive to raise wage levels in order to enhance working-class purchasing power. Rather than reduce poverty, dependentistas maintained, associated-dependent development had widened the income gap. At the same time, Peter Evans and others argued, the MNCs' alliances with Latin American economic, political, and military elites helped uphold the power of repressive regimes such as Brazil's military government.

Modernization and Dependency Theories Compared

The dependency approach offered useful corrections to modernization theory. Furthermore, it highlighted important influences over developing world societies that the earlier theory had often neglected—international trade, finance, and investment. In fact, many political scientists now argue that a principal characteristic defining developing nations is their dependence on the core. Consequently, these scholars still consider relatively wealthy nations such as Saudi Arabia as well as stable democracies such as Costa Rica to be part of the developing world because their economic and political systems have not advanced in other important aspects of development.

Regardless of how they view dependency theory, contemporary analysts of underdevelopment now recognize that political and economic modernization requires more than adopting new values or changing domestic political structures (more than modernization theory had postulated). Dependency theory shifted the focus of research from exclusively internal factors to international economic and political relationships. Dependentistas also helped redefine the concept of economic development. Whereas early mainstream research on economic development heavily stressed the goal of economic growth, dependency theorists also emphasized the importance of more equitable economic distribution and greater social justice. When rapid economic growth increases the concentration of wealth and income in the hands of a minority, as it frequently does, it offers limited benefits to the poor, or may even worsen their situation. Influenced by dependency theory and other leftist critiques, establishment pillars such as the World Bank reoriented their focus toward growth coupled with redistribution.

Despite its contributions, however, dependency theory suffered from serious failings. Just as early modernization theorists overemphasized the *internal* causes of underdevelopment, dependentistas erroneously attributed virtually all of the developing world's problems to *external* economic factors—including international trade, foreign investment, and credit—as well as political alliances linking the core nations with the LDCs' economic, political, and military elites. Furthermore, many authors portrayed developing nations as helpless pawns with no way out of their poverty. As Stephan Haggard charged, "Countries are called 'dependent' by virtue of their characteristics and remain so regardless of their action."[26] To be sure, what is striking about much of that literature is its economic determinism and neglect of domestic social or political factors. Its proponents frequently have dismissed governments in the developing world as agents of the local economic elite who colluded with Western- or Japanese-based MNCs. Consequently, there is a disturbing similarity between many of their case studies. The details of Mexican, Nigerian, or Peruvian politics and economic underdevelopment may differ in these works, but too often dependentistas offer identical explanations for each country's problems.

Cardoso refined dependency theory by insisting that the types of constraints imposed by core economies on the periphery varied from one developing nation to another. El Salvador may be extremely dependent—economically and politically—on the United States, while Argentina—a larger country, further from North America—has been better equipped to guide its own course. Furthermore, the effects of external influences emanating from the core are mediated by conditions within each developing country. In other words, he argued, in varying degrees, developing nations have options within the limits imposed by their dependency. For example, a country's class structure and the influence of particular classes on government policy shape the type of associated-dependent development it experiences. As he and Enzo Faletto wrote, "We conceive the relationship between external and internal forces . . . as not [being] based on mere external forms of exploitation . . . but [as] rooted in coincidences of interests between local dominant classes and international ones."[27] In other words, decisions made by governments and business leaders in the developing world *do* matter, and some LDCs have enjoyed notable, if still flawed, economic growth. Combining Cardoso's ideas with elements of modernization theory, Guillermo O'Donnell offered a powerful explanation for the rise of authoritarian military governments in the most developed nations of South America.[28]

However, East Asia's "economic miracle" of rapid and sustained economic growth during the past several decades—most notably in China, South Korea, Taiwan, Hong Kong, and Singapore—has confounded dependency theory. These countries have linked themselves very closely to the industrialized world through trade, credit, investments, and technology transfers. Contrary to what even the more sophisticated dependency scholars had predicted, however, they achieved spectacular economic growth coupled with comparatively equitable income distribution. Countries such as South Korea and Taiwan now have standards of living comparable to a number of Western European countries, along with relatively high income equality. Hong Kong and Singapore have per capita incomes slightly higher than Germany's or Italy's. Moreover, in a further blow to dependency theory, first China and then India (the world's two most populated nations) have become two of the most rapidly growing economies by opening their doors to foreign trade and investment. Even Fernando Henrique Cardoso—dependency theory's most renowned exponent during his career as an academic scholar—later embraced foreign investment, trade, and technology in his second career as Brazil's finance minister and then two-term president.

Contemporary Perspectives

Many political scientists have statistically analyzed the competing theories of underdevelopment and development, drawing on contemporary economic and social data. For example, using regression analysis, they have examined whether there is a correlation between a country's level of economic development and its population's attitude toward science and technology—specifically, "Do societies with more positive attitudes toward science and technology tend to have higher per-capita incomes?" Similarly, others asked whether or not there is a relationship between a country's HDI and its dependence on foreign trade and foreign investment.

The results of this research have been mixed. Depending on which set of countries or what time period scholars examined, their answers to these questions were often quite different. In all, empirical research supports some modernization hypotheses, but not others. One study found that, in accordance with that theory and contrary to dependency theory, the diffusion of technology and communications from highly industrialized nations to developing nations appeared to raise HDI scores.[29] On the other hand, exploring the relationship between several modern attitudes and a country's standard of living, Maria Fernanda Trujillo-Mendoza found that when she used 1990 data there was a positive correlation, but in 1997 the relationship between them was not statistically significant. In all, her analysis indicated that modern values, such as "rational attitudes toward authority . . . [and] openness to ideas . . . do not reflect the underlying differences between developed and developing countries." In other words, she found no evidence that countries with such modern values were more likely to undergo economic or political development.

However, when subjected to empirical testing, dependency theory fared worse. For example, contrary to that theory's predictions, the countries that have experienced the most impressive improvements in per capita income and human development—including China, South Korea, Taiwan, and Chile— tend to be the ones most closely linked to the global economy and its industrialized "core." Conversely, LDCs that have the lowest levels of foreign investment and foreign trade tend to have the poorest record of economic development. Moreover, there is considerable evidence that those developing nations that reduce barriers to free trade, such as tariffs, tend to enjoy faster economic growth than countries that limit international trade.[30]

Similarly, a number of studies suggest that greater foreign investment tends to produce higher economic growth, in part because local firms often adopt technological innovations used by foreign-owned corporations. Using cross-national data over time to analyze the effects of several indicators of dependency—including levels of foreign trade and aid, foreign investment, and foreign debt—Brian Farmer found that there was no correlation between these factors and per capita income, economic growth, income inequality, or HDI. Only one of the measures that he examined supported dependency theory. Countries that relied heavily on primary exports (such as agricultural products, minerals, and even oil) tended to do more poorly on measures of economic and social development.[31] Unfortunately, dependency theory literature rarely uses comparative data and statistical analysis to test its hypotheses. In fact, it often lacks any testable hypotheses that can be confirmed or disproved.

Today, few analysts accept either modernization or dependency theory in their entirety. In their original formulations, both approaches suffered from overgeneralizations that failed to recognize sufficiently the cultural, political, and economic differences among LDCs. Subsequent theories and approaches, such as *bureaucratic authoritarianism* (which attempted to explain the rise of military dictatorships in some of the developing world's more economically developed nations) and neoliberalism (which offered a set of *conservative* economic prescriptions for less developed nations), have avoided global explanations of development and underdevelopment, focusing instead on more specific issues. Indeed, most contemporary analysts reject the very idea of a *single* theory of development. For one thing, the developing world is too diverse and the processes of political and socioeconomic development too complex to be explained by a single theory of change.

This does not mean, however, that the insights offered by dependency and modernization theories have not been useful. Our current understanding of development draws on the strengths of both approaches, while recognizing their limitations. Since the 1990s, several new approaches to the study of LDCs have emerged, but few claim to be explanatory theories. One intellectual approach, postmodernism, has influenced a number of disciplines (anthropology, geography, history, sociology, and literary criticism, among others). Postmodernists charge modernization theory with trying to impose its values on the LDCs. Moreover, they reject the notion that the First World is "developed" and the developing world "underdeveloped." Further, they argue that *all* social science theories are subjective and that both modernization and dependency theories represent deterministic, Western interpretations of the developing world. Rejecting broad, explanatory theories of any kind ("meta-theory"), postmodernists stress local studies that give voice to people without power, most notably the poor and women. They favor "bottom-up" development based on the plans and desires of the underprivileged rather than "top-down" development projects designed by governments, international agencies, or **nongovernmental organizations (NGOs)**.

Other analysts, who stress bottom-up development, reject modernization theory as an externally imposed, elitist ideology that has failed to serve the needs of most people in the LDCs. They refer to their own approach as "another development." Yet another group of scholars label themselves "antidevelopmentalists." They reject the very idea that social, political, and economic development has been beneficial to developing countries. Instead, they argue that modernization, including its current most comprehensive form, **globalization**, has benefited only a small portion of the population and has further impoverished many others. At the same time, they maintain, development has taken power from the rural villages and urban slums and transferred it to a centralized state dominated by the middle and upper classes. Political and economic reforms, they insist, need to respect and value the traditional beliefs and practices of the poor and must transfer state political power back to the grassroots.

While these revisionist critiques of modernization theory (and, sometimes, of dependency theory) offer some useful insights and some necessary modification of existing models of development, they have generally had little influence on political scientists or development specialists in other disciplines. Too often, their arguments are based on abstractions and redefinitions. Their criticisms of modernization, globalization, and development itself frequently are based on isolated anecdotes rather than systematic, empirical evidence. Thus, despite the many challenges they raise to modernization theory, many of them quite legitimate, they have failed to emerge as workable alternatives.

HOW MUCH PROGRESS HAS BEEN MADE?

Since 1980 developing countries have suffered a number of serious economic setbacks. However, despite economic declines in Africa and Latin America during the 1980s and early 1990s, in East Asia in the late 1990s, and in many LDCs from 2008 to 2011, the developing world has enjoyed considerable social and economic development. A number of factors have contributed to these advances. Greater government foreign aid and private philanthropy, especially from the Bill and Melinda Gates Foundation, have contributed billions of dollars of assistance, contributing to the prevention and treatment of malaria, AIDS, tuberculosis, polio, and other diseases. Most importantly, impressive economic growth within many of LDCs has lifted millions of people out of poverty and illiteracy. Indeed, a large portion of those gains have come from China's phenomenal economic growth.

In 2000, all member states of the United Nations and over twenty international organizations pledged to help achieve a number of impressive "Millennium Development Goals" by 2015. These included: combating AIDS, malaria, and other diseases; increasing gender equality; achieving universal primary education; and eliminating extreme poverty and hunger. While some of these objectives seemed impossible to meet, particularly the last one, enormous progress has been achieved in a number of areas. Those goals set benchmarks for development which helped stimulate government and **private sector** foreign aid. Foreign assistance from developed countries increased 66 percent in real terms from 2000 to 2014.

- The number of people . . . living in extreme poverty declined by more than half, falling from 1.9 billion in 1990 to 836 million in 2015. [And, according to the World Bank, the proportion of the population suffering extreme poverty had fallen from 43 percent to 17 percent in that period].
- The number of people in the working middle class—living on more than $4 a day—nearly tripled between 1991 and 2015.
- The proportion of undernourished people in the developing regions has dropped by almost half since 1990.
- The number of out-of-school children of primary school age worldwide fell by almost half, to an estimated 57 million in 2015, down from 100 million in 2000.
- Gender parity in primary school has been achieved in the majority of countries.

- The mortality rate of children under five has fallen to less than half the 1990 rate.
- Since 1990, maternal mortality has fallen by 45 percent worldwide.
- Over 6.2 million malaria deaths were averted between 2000 and 2015.
- New HIV infections fell by approximately 40 percent between 2000 and 2013.
- By June 2014, 13.6 million people living with HIV had been receiving antiretroviral therapy (ART) globally, an immense increase from just 800,000 in 2003.
- Between 2000 and 2013, tuberculosis prevention, diagnosis and treatment interventions saved an estimated 37 million lives.
- Worldwide, 2.1 billion people have gained access to improved sanitation.[32]

In fact, the **UNDP** (United Nations Development Programme) estimates that the level of poverty in the developing world fell faster in the last half of the twentieth century than it had in the previous five hundred years combined. Adult illiteracy is almost two-thirds below its 1965 rate, falling from 59 to about 21 percent. The World Bank recently estimated that improved health care and sanitation have helped reduce infant mortality rates by 60 percent. In turn, lower infant mortality and public health programs have helped raise life expectancy from 53.4 years in 1960 to some 65 years today. In 1950, people living in economically advanced countries could expect to live twenty-five years longer than those in the developing world. By 2008, however, that gap had been halved to about twelve years.

However, despite these gains, many people in the developing world still face a bleak future. Even with significant declines in child mortality, about six and one half million children under the age of five still die annually in the LDCs, nearly 18,000 every day. About one-third of the adults in South and West Asia and in Sub-Saharan Africa remain illiterate. Millions of people have been lifted out of extreme poverty, but many have not and millions more still live in some lesser form of poverty. The UN's World Food Program estimates that "some 795 million people in the world do not have enough food to lead a healthy active life. That's about one in nine people on earth. Hunger kills more people every year than AIDS, Malaria and Tuberculosis combined."[33] In addition, millions more die from civil wars in countries such as Syria, Afghanistan, Congo (Kinshasa), and South Sudan. And, after decades of growth, the indicators of democracy in the world are now falling. More progress in the future will depend on decisions made by governments and at the grass roots.

Practice and Review Online
http://textbooks.rowman.com/handelman8e#ch1

KEY TERMS

Arab States
associated-dependent development
authoritarian government
caste system
conflict theory
core nations
coup d'état
dependency theory
GDP (gross domestic product)
globalization
GNP (Gross National Product)
HDI (Human Development Index)
infrastructure
LDCs (less developed countries)

legitimacy
MNCs (multinational
  corporations)
modernization theory
NGOs (nongovernmental
  organizations)
periphery
private sector
reconciliation approach
Sub-Saharan Africa
technocrats
traditional cultures
UNDP

DISCUSSION QUESTIONS

1. If you wished to examine dependency theory's value in explaining the causes of underdevelopment, how would you design a test of that theory?
2. What is "the Millennium Development Goals"? How successfully have these goals been met? How useful was the setting of these goals? What have been the major reasons many of these goals have been met?
3. What aspects of economic, political, and social underdevelopment contribute the most to recent instances of mass migration?
4. How does economic development affect political development and vice versa?

NOTES

1. Axel Hadenius, *Democracy and Development* (London: Cambridge University Press, 1992).
2. *The Guardian* (England), November 26, 2008.
3. WHO, Global Health Observatory, *Life Expectancy, 1990–2012*.
4. Paul Collier, *The Bottom Billion* (New York: Oxford University Press, 2007), 64–75.
5. Hadenius, *Democracy and Development*; Robert A. Dahl, *Democracy and Its Critics* (New Haven, CT: Yale University Press, 1989).

6. Samuel P. Huntington, *Political Order in Changing Societies* (New Haven, CT: Yale University Press, 1968).

7. Guillermo O'Donnell and Philippe Schmitter, *Transitions from Authoritarian Rule: Tentative Conclusions about Uncertain Democracies* (Baltimore, MD: Johns Hopkins University Press, 1986); Dahl, *Democracy and Its Critics*.

8. "Indian State in Mourning after Graft Conviction," *New York Times*, October 4, 2014.

9. Sudip Mazumdar, "The Battle for Bihar," *Foreign Policy*, January 25, 2012.

10. Mitchell A. Seligson, "Democratization in Latin America: The Current Cycle," in *Authoritarians and Democrats: Regime Transition in Latin America*, eds. James M. Malloy and Mitchell A. Seligson (Pittsburgh, PA: University of Pittsburgh Press, 1987).

11. Samuel P. Huntington, *The Third Wave: Democratization in the Late Twentieth Century* (Norman: University of Oklahoma Press, 1991).

12. Guillermo O'Donnell, *Modernization and Bureaucratic-Authoritarianism: Studies in South American Politics* (Berkeley: University of California Press, 1973).

13. Paul Collier, *Exodus: How Migration Is Changing Our World* (New York: Oxford University Press, 2013), 27–53.

14. Laurence Peter, "Why Is EU Struggling with Migrants and Asylum?" *BBC News*, August 19, 2015, http://www.bbc.com/news/world-europe-24583286.

15. Pew Research Center Poll: "Americans believe undocumented immigrants should stay, but divided on citizenship issue." March 28, 2015, *NBC Latino*, http://nbclatino.com/2013/03/28/poll-americans-believe-undocumented-immigrants-should-stay-but-divided-on-citizenship-issue.

16. Kalman H. Silvert, quoted in J. Samuel Valenzuela and Arturo Valenzuela, "Modernization and Dependency: Alternative Perspectives in the Study of Latin American Underdevelopment," *Comparative Politics* 10, no. 4 (July 1978): 542.

17. Gabriel A. Almond and G. Bingham Powell, *Comparative Politics: A Developmental Approach* (Boston: Little, Brown, 1966), 301.

18. Marion Levy Jr., "Social Patterns (Structures) and Problems of Modernization," in *Readings on Social Change*, eds. Wilbert Moore and Robert Cooke (Upper Saddle River, NJ: Prentice Hall, 1967), 207.

19. Samuel P. Huntington, "The Goals of Development," in *Understanding Political Development*, eds. Myron Weiner and S. Huntington (Boston: Little Brown, 1987).

20. See Juan Linz and Alfred Stepan, eds., *The Breakdown of Democratic Regimes: Latin America* (Baltimore, MD: Johns Hopkins University Press, 1978).

21. Huntington, "The Goals of Development."

22. Immanuel Wallerstein, *World-Systems Analysis: An Introduction* (Durham, NC: Duke University Press, 2004).

23. Theodoro Dos Santos, "The Structure of Dependence," in *Readings in U.S. Imperialism*, eds. K. T. Fann and Donald C. Hodges (Boston: Porter Sargent, 1971), 226.

24. Omar Sánchez, "The Rise and Fall of the Dependency Movement: Does It Inform Underdevelopment Today?" EIAL (Estudios Interdisciplinarios de América Latina y el Caribe) 14, no. 2 (July to December 2003).

25. Fernando Henrique Cardoso and Enzo Faletto, *Dependency and Development in Latin America* (Berkeley: University of California Press, 1979); Peter Evans, *Dependent Development* (Princeton, NJ: Princeton University Press, 1979).

26. Stephan Haggard, *Pathways from the Periphery: The Politics of Growth in Newly Industrializing Countries* (Ithaca, NY: Cornell University Press, 1990), 21–22.

27. Cardoso and Faletto, *Dependency and Development*, 26.

28. O'Donnell, *Modernization and Bureaucratic-Authoritarianism.*

29. Richard Labelle, *ICT Policy Formulation and e-Strategy Development* (New Delhi, India: Elsevier, 2005).

30. Arvind Panagariya, "Think Again: International Trade," *Foreign Policy* (November/December 2003): 20–28.

31. Brian R. Farmer, *The Question of Dependency and Economic Development* (Lanham, MD: Lexington Books, 1999).

32. UNDP, The Millennium Development Goals Report 2015.

33. Works Food Program, *Hunger Statistics*, 2015.

2

The Surge and Partial Retreat of Democracy

Egypt—The Abortive "Arab Spring": As the largest, most influential country in the Arab World, Egypt was considered the most important nation in the Arab Spring of prodemocracy popular uprisings. After mass demonstrations toppled the Mubarak dictatorship, the country held its only democratic election in its history. However, the Egyptian armed forces, which had protected the prodemocracy protesters, ended the country's brief democracy in a subsequent military coup. *AP Photo/Ahmed Ali*

IN THE CLOSING DECADES of the twentieth century, a wave of democracy swept over much of the developing world (and the communist bloc), the so-called **Third Wave**.[1] Never before had so many countries replaced dictatorships with democratic regimes. Since then, although some new **democratic transitions** have occurred, the wave of change has diminished to a trickle. To be sure, the overthrow of dictatorships in Tunisia, Egypt, Libya, and Yemen and the rebellions against autocracies in neighboring states from 2010 to 2013 (known as the **Arab Spring**) gave hope that democratic transitions were at hand in the world region that historically had been the least hospitable to democracy. But, that hope was soon crushed when everywhere but in Tunisia, those uprisings eventually either failed, brought chaos or led to renewed dictatorships.

Since the overthrow in 1974 of Portugal's long-standing, fascist dictatorship, numerous authoritarian regimes in the former Soviet bloc and the developing world have fallen in the face of democratic movements. Most Westerners considered the demise of Soviet and Eastern European Communism to be democracy's most renowned triumph in this era. But in the developing nations, equally dramatic events also deserve our attention. In 1990, Nelson Mandela, the world's most revered political prisoner, left his cell in Pollsmoor Prison and was transported triumphantly to South Africa's capital, Pretoria, ending twenty-seven years of incarceration. There, he and other freed Black leaders of the newly legalized political party, the African National Congress (ANC), eventually negotiated an end to White minority rule. President Mandela's triumph accelerated Africa's "second independence"—a wave of political **liberalization** (easing of repression) that has often led to either electoral or liberal democracy.*

In Asia, Corazón Aquino succeeded her assassinated husband as the result of Filipino "people's power"—massive prodemocracy demonstrations by students, shopkeepers, professionals, businesspeople, and others. Her supporters, backed by the Catholic clergy (from the nation's predominant Church), took to the streets day after day, peacefully challenging government troops. Ultimately, when the nation's dictator, Ferdinand Marcos, tried to deny Ms. Aquino her apparent victory in a hastily called presidential election (1986), the commander of the armed forces along with the defense minister joined the opposition, forcing Marcos to step down. Soon after, student-led demonstrations against South Korea's military regime (partially inspired by events in the Philippines) accelerated that country's transition to democracy. In 1998, "people's power"

---

*Electoral democracies are countries that have free and fair elections, but may violate their citizens' civil rights and liberties and are, therefore, not fully democratic. Liberal democracies are fully democratic political systems that enjoy *both* competitive elections and broad civil liberties.

demonstrations in Indonesia toppled the thirty-year dictatorship of President Suharto. And, since 2011, international pressure has induced Burma's (Myanmar's) military rulers to substantially reduce repression and give the political opposition a limited voice.

But the most sweeping democratic changes took place in Latin America (1978–1990), affecting most countries in the region. Whereas all but a few countries (Colombia, Costa Rica, and Venezuela) had authoritarian or semiauthoritarian governments in the mid-1970s, twenty-five years later, only Cuba and Haiti had failed to establish functioning **electoral democracies** (though since that time civil liberties have eroded in a few countries, including Venezuela and Bolivia). Unlike Asia and Africa, Latin America's democratization process generally lacked charismatic heroes in the molds of Mandela, Aquino, or Burmese Nobel Peace Prize winner Aung San Suu Kyi. Nor did it typically feature mass demonstrations. Instead, democratic transitions often grew out of extended negotiations between the authoritarian government (which had become very unpopular) and opposition leaders, culminated by a relatively peaceful, gradual transfer of power.

Latin America enjoyed two important advantages over Africa and Asia. First, prior to its surge of military takeovers in the 1960s and 1970s, the region had enjoyed the developing world's strongest democratic tradition, most notably in Chile, Costa Rica, and Uruguay. Furthermore, Latin American countries were among the first LDCs to achieve the levels of literacy and economic development that are generally associated with stable democratic governments. Predictably, then, the region's democratic wave has been more sweeping and more successful, ultimately affecting virtually every country in the hemisphere.

In many developing countries, the early years of the twenty-first century were difficult for dictators and quasi-dictators. Augusto Pinochet, Chile's military ruler for nearly seventeen years (1973–1990), fought to avoid a human rights trial in Chile after returning from a humiliating house arrest in England. Former Argentine military dictator Jorge Videla was sentenced to life in prison in 2010 for ordering the torture and execution of political prisoners some thirty-five years previously. Indonesia's long-term dictator, General Suharto, also faced possible detention after he was driven from office by mass demonstrations. Like Pinochet, this aged, once all-powerful leader hid behind the humiliating court plea that he was physically too weak and too mentally incapacitated to stand trial.

Of course, not all democratic movements have been successful. In China, army tanks crushed student demonstrations in Beijing's Tiananmen Square (1989). Similarly, massive prodemocracy street demonstrations in 2009 failed to dislodge Iran's authoritarian government. And even when democracy was installed, it failed to last long in some developing countries.

However, despite these setbacks, most notably in the Arab States, the upsurge of political freedom in the developing world since the 1970s, coupled with the breakdown of communism in the Soviet bloc, has produced history's greatest democratic transition. By the end of the twentieth century, the surge of democratization had largely ended, but many of the new democracies have endured. If this progress can be maintained, it will likely influence many of the aspects of LDC politics discussed in this book. For example, by definition, consolidation of democracy reduces military rule. It also lowers the likelihood of revolutionary movements. And, democracy generally contributes, at least eventually, to a better quality of political and economic life for women, peasants, and the urban poor.

DEMOCRACY DEFINED

Discussions of democratic transformations have frequently been complicated by disagreements over the meaning of democracy. Currently, most political scientists characterize democracy *procedurally*. That is, democracy is measured by the transparency and fairness of the essential procedures governing the election and behavior of government officials. The least-demanding definition focuses almost exclusively on elections. It simply defines democracy as a political system that holds fair, contested elections on a regular basis, with universal (or near-universal) adult suffrage. Political scientists call countries that only meet this minimal standard "electoral democracies." Although this bare-bones definition seems reasonable (most Americans think of democracy in terms of free and fair elections), it allows a number of rather questionable governments to be labeled *democratic*. For example, while they are all electoral democracies, recent governments in Colombia, Turkey, and Sri Lanka have widely violated human rights while battling armed insurgencies. In these countries, government troops have periodically massacred villagers or tortured prisoners. At the same time, in countries such as Thailand and Bangladesh, electoral democracy has been episodic, interrupted periodically by military intervention, often overriding decisions made by elected officials.

As the norm of open elections became more universally accepted in recent decades, the number of electoral democracies worldwide tripled from 1974 (39 nations) to 2000 (120) and has fluctuated near that level since then.[2] But many of these governments still manipulate the mass media and violate their citizens' civil liberties. This chapter uses the term *semi-democracies* (also called *Partly Free* by some human rights groups) to refer to those electoral democracies whose governments regularly repress civil liberties and breach the principles of a free society. Their elections may be relatively free and fair, but their societies are not. These currently include such countries as Pakistan and Haiti. Finally, some semi-democracies have competitive elections but lack adequate mechanisms for holding the government accountable to its citizens between elections.

Consequently, a more stringent definition of "full" democracy (also known as *liberal* democracy) involves more than competitive elections. Instead, it can be defined as a political system that conforms to the following conditions: most of the country's leading government officials are elected*; there is universal or near-universal suffrage; elections are largely free of fraud and outside manipulation; opposition-party candidates have a realistic chance of being elected to important national offices; and civil liberties—including minority rights—are respected, with guarantees of free speech, free assembly, free press (media), and freedom of religion. All these conditions help guarantee that democratic governments are accountable to their citizens in a way that authoritarian regimes are not.[3] Moreover, liberal democracy also includes the rule of law, civilian command over the armed forces, and a vigorous civil society.[†] This definition suggests that competitive elections mean little if unelected individuals or groups who are not accountable to the public (such as military officers, organized crime bosses, business elites, or foreign powers) direct elected officials from behind the scenes. And, free elections do not bring full democracy if elected officials violate their citizens' civil liberties or arbitrarily arrest opposition leaders.

Finally, some observers offer an even more demanding standard for democracy. They argue that any purely procedural definition of democracy, no matter how exacting, is incomplete. Instead, they insist, real democracy requires not only fair elections and proper government procedures, but also fair and just government policy outcomes ("**substantive democracy**"). For example, substantive democracy requires that

---

*Of course, even in some liberal democracies, high-ranking officeholders are appointed, not elected. In the United States, these include Supreme Court justices and cabinet members. But these positions are appointed by a popularly elected president and are subject to Congressional confirmation. But, prior to the 1960s, the United States was not fully a liberal or even a full electoral democracy because large numbers of southern Blacks were barred from voting. And, until the early twentieth century, women also were denied suffrage.

†Civil society is the array of voluntary organizations—including churches, unions, business groups, farmers' organizations, and women's groups—whose members often influence the political system, but are free of government control. Most authoritarian governments weaken civil society, so that it cannot generate a challenge to their rule. Consequently, rebuilding and strengthening civil society are essential tasks for establishing and consolidating democratic governments.

citizens have relatively equal access to public schooling and health care regardless of their social class or ethnicity. Similarly, they insist, any **procedural democracy**—such as Iraq or South Africa—that tolerates gross economic inequalities, ethnic conflicts, or other social injustices is not truly democratic.

These authors make an important point. Procedural democracy alone does not guarantee a just society; it is merely a step in the right direction. But it is a far more important step than its critics acknowledge. Because governments in procedural democracies are accountable to the people, they are less vulnerable to revolution and other forms of civil unrest. They are also very unlikely to make war against other democracies (to be sure, war between two liberal democracies is virtually unknown). Prodded by a free press and public opinion, they are more responsive to domestic crises such as famines (in fact, there has never been a prolonged famine in any procedural democracy), and while some (electoral) democracies have violated their opponents' civil liberties, most of them do respect their citizens' rights.

Mindful of the fact that democratic societies cannot correct all social injustices—the United States, for example, has long endured racial discrimination, poverty, and a high degree of economic inequality—this book defines democracy strictly procedurally. Issues of substantive democracy (reducing poverty, racism, sexism, and the like) are obviously important, but they are a separate matter.

DEMOCRATIC TRANSITION AND CONSOLIDATION

In the discussion that follows, the term *democratic transition* means the process of moving from an authoritarian to a democratic regime. The transition period begins when an authoritarian government shows the first observable signs of collapsing or of negotiating its departure from power. It ends when the first freely elected government takes office. Thus, for example, in South Africa, the democratic transition began in 1990 when the White minority government of President Frederik de Klerk decided to free Nelson Mandela and open negotiations with his ANC party. It concluded four years later when Mandela was inaugurated as the country's first president to be elected through universal suffrage. Even after their transitions are completed, however, many new democracies remain fragile, with a real possibility that they will falter.

Only when democratic institutions, practices, and values have become deeply ingrained in society can we say that a country has experienced **democratic consolidation**. This consolidation is a process through which democratic norms ("rules of the game") become accepted by all politically influential groups in society—including business groups, labor unions, rural landlords, professionals, the church, and the armed forces—and no important political actor contemplates a return to dictatorship. Or, as Juan Linz and Alfred Stepan have put it, democracy is consolidated when it becomes "the only game in town," even in the face of severe economic or political adversity.[4] Consolidation may begin after the democratic transition ends and is completed only when democracy is securely entrenched.

Unfortunately, since 1960 less than half of the transitions to democracy were subsequently consolidated. Many countries have reverted to dictatorship or have remained mired in political disorder. Thus, Kapstein and Converse found that between 1960 and 2004, there were 123 cases in which countries changed from authoritarian to democratic government, of which 98 (nearly 80 percent of the total) were developing countries. A number of nations created democratic governments multiple times only to see them fail. For example, Pakistan established democracy four times in that forty-four-year time span, each of which failed. Of the ninety-eight democratic transitions in the LDCs during that period, less than half (46 percent) survived until 2004. In fact, one-fourth of the democratic governments created during that period collapsed within two years.[5]

Most recently, Egypt enjoyed a transition to democracy when mass demonstrations toppled the Hosni Mubarak's thirty-year dictatorship followed by the first democratic election in the nation's history (2012). But that democracy was never consolidated and the following year the armed forces ousted President Mohamed Morsi to install a military dictatorship that is now more repressive than Mubarak's. Elsewhere during the Arab Spring, the overthrow of the Muammar Qaddafi dictatorship (1969–2011) in Libya eventually led to civil war and chaos. Scholars have identified several internal factors that increased the likelihood that a new democracy would fail (in Arab States and elsewhere), including ethnic divisions (a particular problem in the Middle East, Africa and South Asia) and a failure to build strong political institutions, including institutional checks on the president's powers.

In successfully consolidated democracies, democratic *values* predominate among politically relevant individuals and groups. Even previously antidemocratic political parties and groups, such as the armed forces, former guerrilla groups, and far-right and far-left political parties, have come to accept democracy as the only game in town. This does not mean that consolidated democracies will *never* break down. "Never" is a long time, and in the past, consolidated, developing world democracies in countries such as the Philippines, Chile, and Uruguay weakened, and eventually fell to authoritarian forces. However, consolidated democracies are secure for the foreseeable future. And they will probably endure unless some deep societal divide (such as class or ethnic conflict) emerges to tear them apart.

AUTHORITARIAN BEGINNINGS

With the surge in democratic transitions in recent decades, a global consensus has been emerging in support of democratic government. But this has not always been true. In the decades after World War II, as numerous African, Asian, and Middle Eastern countries achieved independence, many leaders of the LDCs as well as foreign observers believed that these emerging nations were not ready for democratic government. Others argued that democracy was not even desirable at that stage of their socioeconomic development. To be sure, a number of newly independent countries—particularly former British colonies—established democratic political institutions modeled after their former colonial rulers. But only in a few, such as India, did democracy take a firm hold.

Since that time, Middle Eastern nations generally have been ruled by monarchs, all-powerful single parties, or dictatorial strongmen. Many new Sub-Saharan nations also created political systems dominated by a single party, while others established military dictatorships or suffered one-man rule. Democracy fared somewhat better in Asia, but the military in this region frequently aborted the process. Communist revolutionaries toppled corrupt and inept governments in China and Vietnam. Benefiting from greater socioeconomic development and from more than a century of self-rule, Latin America had the most prior experience with democracy. Indeed, during the 1950s, relatively democratic governments predominated in this region. But the armed forces continued to meddle in national politics and in the 1960s and early 1970s a new wave of military takeovers swept the region, often as a result of political and economic instability. Only since the 1980s has democracy again become the norm in Latin America.

JUSTIFYING AUTHORITARIAN RULE

In view of democracy's recent broad advance, it seems hard to believe that many observers once considered freely elected government unattainable or even undesirable in the LDCs. Some modernization theorists believed that the newly emerging African and Asian states were insufficiently economically or socially developed to sustain democracy. And, many dependency theorists declared that democracy was unlikely to emerge because powerful industrialized nations and multinational corporations had allied with LDC elites to bolster unrepresentative governments.

At the same time, other scholars worried that levels of mass political participation in democratic or semidemocratic states often exceeded their governments' capacity to accommodate all the new political demands. Unless developing world political institutions were strengthened, they warned, political unrest threatened to derail economic and political development. Concerned about the dangers of substantial disorder, many analysts and LDC leaders justified authoritarian rule as a necessary stopgap. Only after developing countries experienced sufficient socioeconomic modernization, they argued, could their citizens learn how to peacefully and effectively participate in politics. At the same time, modernizing societies needed to establish political institutions capable of accommodating the people's expanding demands. Developing countries have usually been able to establish stable, democratic governments only when they have raised their per capita incomes and have reached a literacy rate of 50 percent. In addition to raising literacy, modernization also enlarges the size of the middle class and the organized working class, both essential for a more stable and inclusive democracy.

But if socioeconomic modernization was necessary to establish democracy, what type of government could initiate economic and social development? Some experts believed that only a strong and stable authoritarian government—such as General Pinochet's dictatorship in Chile (1973–1990) or South Korea's several military governments (1961–1987)—could jump-start economic modernization and growth. Only authoritarian regimes, they maintained, could limit workers' wages and control labor unrest in order to attract needed multinational and domestic private-sector investment. In East Asia, for example, several repressive governments that had brought about significant economic growth (Indonesia, Singapore, and South Korea) insisted that dictatorial governments could better impose rational, long-term development plans. Thus, the father of Singapore's authoritarian political system and its spectacular economic growth, former president Lee Kuan Yew, stated, "I believe what a [developing] country needs to develop is discipline more than democracy. . . . Democracy leads to indiscipline and disorderly conduct, which are inimical to development."[6] Only later, others said, when a country was "ready," would dictatorships give way to democracy.*

---

*Of course, even defenders of authoritarian governments had to concede that *most* dictatorships are *not* efficient modernizers. Far from it! The developing world has had more than its share of corrupt dictators who have stolen millions, run their country's economy into the ground, and awarded the most lucrative business opportunities to relatives and cronies. What many observers *do* claim, however, is that *efficient* capitalist dictatorships such as Taiwan's or Singapore's offered many countries the best hope for economic modernization. Similarly, supporters of revolutionary dictatorships (such as Cuba and China) believe they are necessary for LDC greater social equality, along with improved literacy and health care.

Using some combination of these justifications, many governments in the LDCs insisted that democracy was inappropriate for countries in the early stage of social and economic development. In Africa, leaders in the struggle for independence often created single-party systems, banning or restricting opposition political parties. Some experts warned that competitive elections in ethnically divided societies would only encourage candidates to organize along tribal lines, thereby further polarizing their country (see chapter 4). In Africa and other LDCs, some founding fathers, influenced by the Marxist-Leninist ideology, asserted that their nations needed an all-powerful state, led by a "vanguard party" (i.e., one that claimed to know what was in the best interests of the masses), if they hoped to combat severe poverty, dependency, class tensions, or ethnic divisions. By 1964, roughly two-thirds of the independent African countries had become single-party states. Subsequently, after many of these governments had failed miserably, military dictators took their place, claiming that civilian rulers were too corrupt or too weak to govern effectively (chapter 8). In the Middle East, similar justifications were used to defend one-party or military rule. Fundamentalist Islamic (also called Islamist) governments in Iran, Sudan, and Afghanistan have also prohibited or restricted political opposition groups.

In contrast, many Latin American nations had enjoyed democratic or semidemocratic governments in the 1950s and 1960s. But, the 1970s and 1980s witnessed the rise of right-wing military dictatorships in much of the region. The new leaders justified their rule by pointing to perceived leftist threats and the need to reinvigorate the economy. Meanwhile, a number of authoritarian rulers in East Asia clung to power long after their countries had surpassed the thresholds of economic and social modernization normally associated with democratic transitions. In Singapore, South Korea, and Taiwan, the governments claimed that their dictatorships were needed to ward off external threats (from Indonesia, North Korea, and China, respectively). Others felt that their Confucian cultures saw political opposition groups as being disruptive to social harmony.

Indeed, in the 1960s and 1970s, democracy was in retreat in the developing world, as countries such as Chile, Nigeria, and the Philippines succumbed to dictatorships. By the mid-1970s, only about thirty-nine of the world's nations were functioning democracies and almost all of those were prosperous, industrialized countries in North America, Europe, and Australia-New Zealand. Thus, Larry Diamond observed,

> The mid-to-late 1970s seemed a low-water mark for democracy and the empirical trends were reified by intellectual fashions dismissing democracy as an artifice, a cultural construct of the West, or a "luxury" that poor states could not afford.[7]

THE THIRD WAVE AND ITS EFFECT ON
THE DEVELOPING WORLD

Since that time, however, developing countries have played a notable role in history's most sweeping transition from authoritarianism to democracy. Writing shortly before the 1991 dissolution of the Soviet Union, Samuel Huntington counted twenty-nine countries throughout the world that had democratized in the fifteen years alone prior to 1991. Of these, twenty were LDCs.[8] Although some of the countries on his list had weak democratic credentials and some subsequently slid back to authoritarian rule, there can be no denying that the global trend toward democracy since the late 1970s was palpable.

He noted that the recent surge of democracy is actually the third such wave that the world has experienced since the early 1800s. In each case, democratic ideals and movements in key countries spread to other nations. The first democratic wave (1828–1926), by far the longest, began under the influence of the American and French Revolutions and ended with the Great Depression of the 1920s–1930s. Democratization during that wave was largely confined to Europe and to former British colonies with primarily European populations (the United States, Canada, New Zealand, and Australia). The second, much shorter, wave (1943–1962) was precipitated by victory over fascism during World War II and the subsequent demise of European colonialism in Africa, Asia, and the Middle East. In that wave, democratic governments emerged in a number of LDCs, though most of these only met the standards of electoral democracy (competitive elections).

It is the Third Wave (from 1974 until about 2000) that most draws our attention because of its pervasive and seemingly lasting reverberations in less developed nations. Of course, the most dramatic Third-Wave transitions were in the Eastern and Central European communist bloc, which brought the Cold War to an end. Pictures of young Germans breaking off pieces of the Berlin Wall and of Boris Yeltsin facing down a military coup in Moscow were among the most powerful political images of the late twentieth century. But in developing nations as diverse as South Africa, the Philippines, and Brazil, years of authoritarian or semiauthoritarian rule also came to an end. Huntington noted that the first two democratic waves were followed by periods of backsliding—reverse waves—during which a number of those countries reverted to authoritarian rule. There has not been a noticeable reverse wave so far, but because the pace of democratization has slowed appreciably since the start of the twenty-first century, many analysts believe that the Third Wave is over, that is, some new countries have made the transition to democracy since that time, but their numbers have been fairly evenly matched by nations seeing democracy collapse.

Table 2.1   The Global Growth of Democracy

Year	Free Countries (%)	Partly Free Countries (%)	Countries Not Free (%)	Number of Countries Rated
1972	29	25	46	151
1985	34	34	33	167
1998	46	28	26	191
2010	45	31	24	194
2014	48	28	26	195

Source: Freedom House, Freedom in the World 2015; Arch Puddington, "Discarding Democracy: A Return to the Iron Fist."

For over forty years, perhaps the most widely used and respected evaluations of global democracy have been published annually by Freedom House, a nongovernmental, research and advocacy group. Each year, its panel of experts evaluates the world's nations on two dimensions of democracy: first, their level of political rights (including the extent of electoral competition and citizen participation); and, second, the quality of civil liberties (such as free speech and freedom of religion) and the prevalence of the rule of law. On the basis of their evaluations, Freedom House's annual reports classify all countries as Free, Partly Free, or Not Free.* As Table 2.1 indicates, in 1972 less than one-third of the world's 151 countries (29 percent) enjoyed fully democratic government and nearly one-half (46 percent) were not free. During the remainder of the twentieth century, the Third Wave swept over Latin America and other parts of the developing world, with the percentage of full democracies (free countries) increasing fairly steadily. Some of the major advances came from the mid-1980s to 2000. These included the fall of the Soviet bloc and the overthrow of extended dictatorships in Chile and the Philippines. During the most recent three periods covered by Table 2.1 (extending from 1998 to 2014), however, the proportion of free countries remained fairly constant. Table 2.1 presents the percentage of free countries in the *entire* world, developed and developing alike. In fact, the LDCs had a lower percentage of free countries. But it is precisely in developing countries that the Third Wave spread most rapidly.

Table 2.2 reveals that democratization has expanded at different rates in the various regions of the developing world. Latin America and the Caribbean now have the highest percentage of free countries (67 percent) and the lowest not free (3 percent). It is followed by Asia and the Pacific

---

*The panel of experts rates each country's level of political rights and civil liberties on a scale of 1 (most free) to 7 (least free). Using the combined score for these two ratings, each country is categorized according to its degree of freedom.

Table 2.2   Democracy by Region

Region	Free Countries (%)	Partly Free Countries (%)	Countries Not Free (%)
Latin America and the Caribbean[a]	67	30	3
Asia and the Pacific	41	36	23
Sub-Saharan Africa	20	37	43
Arab States[b]	6	18	76

Source: Freedom House, *Freedom in the World 2015.*
    [a] Extracted from the Freedom House category "the Americas" by removing the United States and Canada.
    [b] Extracted from the category "Middle East and North Africa" by removing Israel.

(41 percent free), Sub-Saharan Africa (20 percent free), and, well behind the others, the Arab World (6 percent free).

INTERNATIONAL CAUSES AND CONSEQUENCES OF THE THIRD WAVE

Obviously, widespread political changes of this magnitude are inspired and influenced by broad currents that transcend the politics of particular nations. A number of factors contributed to the Third Wave's democratic transitions. For one thing, the economic crises that devastated so many LDCs in the 1980s revealed that most authoritarian regimes were no more effective and no less corrupt than the elected governments that they had contemptuously swept aside (indeed, they were frequently less efficient and more dishonest). Furthermore, because dictatorships lack the legitimacy that free elections bestow on democratic governments, their support depends much more heavily on satisfactory job performance. So when authoritarian governments in countries such as Argentina and Nigeria dragged their country into war (including civil war), economic decay, or rampant corruption, their support rapidly eroded. In Africa, the gross mismanagement and dishonesty of both military and single-party regimes caused their already poor economies to implode, as the continent's per capita GNP declined by some 2 percent *annually* throughout the 1980s. Within Latin America, the economic record of military rulers was relatively strong in Chile and Brazil, but military regimes performed poorly elsewhere. By the 1980s, almost all of that region's authoritarian governments were undermined by a major foreign debt crisis.

By contrast, many East Asian dictatorships (most notably South Korea, Taiwan, Indonesia, and Singapore) enjoyed spectacular economic success from the 1960s through the late 1990s. However, rather than produce wider support for those governments, growth and modernization often generated a burgeoning middle class with democratic aspirations and the political skills to pursue them. As the number of politically informed citizens grew, they increasingly resented government repression, state corruption, and the lack of meaningful political participation.

Throughout the world, no sooner had democratic upheavals occurred in one nation than they spread quickly to neighboring countries. In Eastern Europe, Poland's Solidarity movement inspired democratic challenges in Hungary, East Germany, and Czechoslovakia. Students in South Korea watched television coverage of antigovernment demonstrations in the Philippines and took the lessons of Philippine "people's power" to heart.

As the democratic tidal wave swept forward, some authoritarian leaders began to get the message. Generals in Ecuador and Paraguay watched neighboring military dictatorships fall and decided to abdicate while the going was still good. After more than forty years of authoritarian rule by the Kuomintang Party, Taiwan's government opened up to authentic electoral competition and political freedom. In Africa, a number of single-party states liberalized their political systems, allowing greater freedom and more political space for opposition groups, while a smaller number established liberal democracies.

As we noted earlier, the demise of communist regimes in Eastern Europe exposed the deficiencies of their ideology. As Marxism-Leninism was discredited, even among many of its once-fervent adherents, democracy assumed greater international legitimacy. And, the end of the Cold War permitted the United States to be more consistent in its advocacy of political freedom. That is to say, the United States no longer had any reason to coddle allied developing world dictators—including authoritarian regimes in prerevolutionary Iran and the Philippines—whose friendship it had previously cultivated to thwart the spread of Communism.*

THE PREREQUISITES OF DEMOCRACY IN INDIVIDUAL COUNTRIES

While international influences were catalysts, providing developing countries with incentives and chances to democratize, not all LDCs took advantage of these opportunities. More than thirty years after the start of the Third Wave, some developing countries remain mired in dictatorship, with no openings in their political system. Others either have failed to

---

*There have remained, however, notable exceptions, as the United States has retained close ties with several discredited but strategically important regimes in such countries as Afghanistan, Pakistan, and Saudi Arabia.

complete their democratic transitions or have alternated between authoritarianism and weak democracy. But, some fortunate countries have consolidated democracy.

What accounts for these differences? What determines whether or not a particular country embarks on the road toward democracy, whether it completes that voyage successfully, and whether it eventually consolidates democratic values, practices, and institutions? In other words, how do we know whether or not democracy will take root and survive in Brazil, Indonesia, or Madagascar? Finally, why has democracy advanced further in some regions, such as Latin America, than in other regions, such as Sub-Saharan Africa and the Middle East?

There are no simple answers. But scholars have debated these issues for decades and have identified a number of historical, structural, and cultural variables that help account for democracy's presence in, for example, India and Uruguay, and its absence in countries such as Sudan or Laos. However, political scientists still disagree about the relative importance of those variables. In the discussion that follows, we examine a number of factors that have been widely identified as prerequisites for democracy.

Social and Economic Modernization

Nearly sixty years ago, Seymour Martin Lipset observed that democracy was far more prevalent in industrialized countries such as the United States and Sweden than in poorer nations—a finding congruent with modernization theory (chapter 1).[9] Subsequent political science research has largely supported that claim. The reasoning behind this relationship was that

> industrialization leads to increases in wealth, education, communication and equality; these developments are associated with a more moderate lower and upper class and a larger middle class, which is by nature moderate; and this in turn increases the probability of stable democratic forms of politics.[10]

Social scientists have since identified more precisely the particular aspects of modernization that promote democracy. Philips Cutright determined that when other factors are held constant, there is a strong correlation between the extent of a country's mass communications and its degree of democracy, stronger even than the correlation between economic development and democracy.[11] A free and active mass media and opportunities for citizens to exchange ideas promote a free society. And, Axel Hadenius, examining the influence of dozens of independent variables, found that democracy correlates most strongly with higher levels of literacy and education.[12] Also, educated citizens are more likely to participate in politics and to defend their interests. From 1990 to 2011, the developing world's adult literacy rate rose from 68 percent to 80 percent.[13] This bodes well for democracy in developing countries because, as we have noted, in the recent past, countries whose populations are more than half literate are far more likely to sustain (consolidate) democracy than those that fall below that mark. Today, only about ten countries in the world are less than half literate.

Many analysts have also shown that countries with higher per capita incomes are more likely to be democratic than poorer ones, a finding corresponding to Lipset's observation. Today, for example, most developing countries with per capita incomes that exceed $2,500 (in **constant dollars**) are democracies of some sort, while those with incomes under that figure usually are not.*

This does not mean that countries inevitably become more democratic as their economies develop. In fact, middle-income countries are frequently *less* stable and more prone to dictatorship.[14] For example, even though the World Bank ranked South America's most industrialized countries (Argentina, Brazil, Chile, and Uruguay) as upper-middle-income nations, their democratic governments all fell to repressive, military dictatorships in the 1960s and 1970s. On the other hand, India—a low-income nation—has enjoyed one of the LDCs' strongest records of sustained democracy. But, while these exceptions are important, there is still generally a correlation between economic development and democracy. Although poor countries are as likely as richer ones to make the transition to democracy, they are less likely to *sustain* democratic government. East Asia's rapid economic growth, higher literacy, and expanding middle classes promoted democratic consolidation in South Korea and Taiwan. In Latin America, where levels of modernization are high by LDC standards, the democratic wave since the close of the 1970s has seemingly established consolidated democracies in most of the region. Conversely, Africa, which is home to most of the world's poorest nations, has suffered a number of failed transitions.

Class Structure

Some scholars contend that it is not economic growth per se that induces and consolidates democracy but rather the way in which that growth affects a country's social structure. Specifically, they reason, economic development supports stable democracy only if it induces appropriate changes in the country's class structure.

---

*All dollar figures in the study were expressed in constant dollars, meaning that they are adjusted for inflation, so that per capita "real incomes" of $1,000 in 1960 and in 1990 are equivalent in terms of what they could buy at those times.

Since the time of Aristotle, political theorists have linked democracy and political stability to the presence of a large and vibrant middle class. The middle class, they suggest, tends to be politically moderate and serves as a bridge between the upper and lower classes. Its members also have the political and organizational skills necessary to create political parties and other important democratic institutions. An independent and influential business class (bourgeoisie) also seems essential for developing democracy. So, in those countries where economic growth has failed to create a politically independent and influential bourgeoisie and middle class, modernization does not necessarily buttress democracy and may even weaken it. To be sure, the political independence and the influence of the emerging middle classes have varied among different world regions, depending on the historical period in which those areas industrialized. For example, industrialization and urbanization produced a larger, more powerful, and more independent middle class and bourgeoisie in Northern Europe than it did a century later in Latin America. In the latter case, wealth and income were more concentrated and the middle class was correspondingly weaker and more dependent. Predictably, democracy did not take hold as readily in Latin America as it had in Northern Europe.

Barrington Moore Jr., in his widely acclaimed study of economic and political change, *The Social Origins of Dictatorship and Democracy*, identified three discrete paths to modernization, each shaped by the relative power of the state and the strength of the major social classes. In one path, typified by nineteenth- and early-twentieth-century Germany, modernization was led by a strong state allied with powerful and antidemocratic agricultural landowners and a bourgeoisie that was dependent on the state. There and subsequently in developing countries with similar class configurations, that combination ultimately resulted in the rise of fascist and far-right authoritarian regimes. A second path to modernization, found in countries such as China, was characterized by a highly centralized state, a repressive landowning class, a weak bourgeoisie, and a large and eventually rebellious peasantry. The end result of that alignment was a communist revolution fought by the peasantry.

Finally, Moore's third path, identified most closely with Britain, featured a weaker state and a strong bourgeoisie at odds with the rural landowning elite. Only this alignment of forces, distinguished by the middle class's powerful and independent political role, has led to liberal democracy. "No [strong and independent] bourgeoisie," Moore famously noted, "no democracy."[15] Similarly, in developing nations today, a vibrant middle class and an influential business class have been critical ingredients in the establishment and consolidation of democracy. It should come as no surprise, then, that in countries as diverse as Chile,

Indonesia, the Philippines, South Korea, and, most recently, Iran, middle-class citizens, including university students, have been on the front lines in the struggles for democracy.

Very poor countries, such as Haiti and Afghanistan, whose middle classes are small and dependent on the state, are far less likely to achieve or consolidate democratic governments. But it is also important to remember that even though a strong middle class and bourgeoisie are necessary for democracy, these sectors are not always democratically oriented. For example, in pre-Nazi (Weimar) Germany and in Argentina and Chile during the 1970s, when the middle class felt threatened by social unrest from below, many of its members supported fascist or other far-right-wing dictatorships.

On the other hand, Rueschemeyer, Huber Stephens, and Stephens have focused attention on the role of *organized (unionized) labor* in building democracy. They argue that while the bourgeoisie and the middle class generally fostered democracy in Western Europe, Latin America, and the Caribbean, these groups not only tended to favor a restricted form of democratic government that enhanced their own political strength (vis-à-vis the upper class and the state) but also limited the political influence of the lower class. Consequently, countries have achieved comprehensive democracy only when they also have had a politically potent, unionized working class that has pushed for broader political representation and increased social justice.[16]

In summary, democracy tends to flourish best where economic modernization produces a politically influential and independent bourgeoisie/middle class and where labor unions effectively defend the interests of the working class. When any of these classes are small, weak, or politically dependent on authoritarian actors, such as rural landowners, democracy is less likely to emerge.

Political Culture

In the final analysis, neither a country's level of socioeconomic development nor its class structure can fully explain whether or not it has been able to create or sustain democracy. For example, during the early decades of the twentieth century, Argentina was one of the most affluent nations on earth, with substantial middle and working classes. Yet the country failed to develop into a liberal democracy. Instead, it embarked on a half-century of recurring coups and military dictatorships. Subsequently, Singapore, South Korea, and Taiwan retained authoritarian governments long after they had reached the normal social and economic thresholds for democracy.* And, as we have just seen, economic wealth

---

*South Korea and Taiwan have subsequently democratized, but Singapore still has not.

has not brought democracy to petroleum-rich states such as Kuwait and Saudi Arabia. On the other hand, India has sustained democracy for decades despite its extensive poverty and low literacy rate.

Many scholars have argued that, aside from its level of economic development and its class structure, a nation's democratic potential is also influenced by its **political culture**—that is, its cultural beliefs, norms, and values relating to politics. A country's constitution may call for contested elections, a free press, and the separation of powers, but unless the people, especially elites and political activists, value these objectives, constitutional protections are unlikely to have great weight. Some of the most important values needed to sustain democracy include a belief that the vote and other forms of individual and group political participation are important and potentially productive; trust in government institutions and in fellow citizens; tolerance of opposition and dissenting political opinions and beliefs, even when those views are very unpopular; accepting the outcome of free and fair elections as definitive, regardless of who wins; viewing politics as a process that requires compromise; rejecting violent political action or other circumvention of democratic institutions; and committing to democracy as the best form of government, regardless of how well or poorly a particular democratic administration performs. Obviously, there are no countries in which every citizen subscribes to these values or beliefs, but democracy normally is sustainable only if a large portion of the population supports them.

The recent wave of successful democratic transitions has renewed interest in how a country's political culture affects consolidation of democracy. Robert Dahl, a leading democratic theorist, observes that all political systems eventually confront major crises such as economic decline, ethnic violence, or political stalemate. At those times, many political leaders in unconsolidated democracies are tempted to seek authoritarian solutions such as imposing martial law or restricting civil liberties.* If, however, a broad segment of the population (including members of the political and economic elites) shares democratic values, democracy can survive a crisis intact. Dahl stresses two particularly important democratic values: first, that the armed forces and police must willingly submit to the command of democratically elected civilian authorities; second, government and society must tolerate and legally protect dissident political beliefs.

The first value (civilian control of the armed forces) is taken for granted in industrialized democracies, but not in countries such as

---

*Even in a deeply consolidated democracy such as the United States, civil libertarians charge that the terrorist threat has led to government infringements on civil liberties. These include parts of the Homeland Security Act, monitoring of domestic phone calls, and the treatment of prisoners at Guantanamo Bay.

Guatemala, Thailand, and Bangladesh, where the armed forces have frequently exercised veto power over the policy decisions of elected officials and have often ousted civilian governments. Dahl's second cultural standard—tolerance of dissent—also presents a challenge to many developing nations, where even freely elected governments sometimes silence critics and muzzle opposition leaders. The crucial question, then, says Dahl, is, "How can robust democratic cultures be created in countries where they previously have been largely absent?"[17] He responds that there is no easy answer, but that developing a democratic culture is a gradual process in which socioeconomic modernization and political development need to reinforce each other.

Sometimes, external forces may promote or even impose a democratic political culture on another country, as U.S. occupation forces did in Japan after World War II. Many African and Asian countries were first introduced to modern politics by the colonial powers that ruled them. Analysis of the LDCs reveals that one of the factors most closely related to democratic government is having previously been a British colony. Of course, not all former British colonies became democracies; in fact, during the twentieth century, most of those in Africa and many in Asia did not. However, in general, countries that experienced British colonial rule were significantly more likely to maintain democracy after independence than were nations previously colonized by France, Belgium, the Netherlands, Spain, or Portugal. This pattern suggests that Britain more successfully inculcated democratic values in its colonies than other European powers did. However, apart from those cases, external intervention has had a mixed record of success. For example, recent U.S. interventions in Afghanistan and Iraq have apparently not created democratic cultures.

A country's political culture influences its political system in a number of ways. For example, communities with high levels of mutual tolerance and a politically informed population are more hospitable to democracy than are less tolerant or less knowledgeable societies. But how fixed in a nation's psyche are such values? Is there something inherently more democratic or more authoritarian about Norwegian or Egyptian cultures? Are some religions or philosophies, such as Christianity, more conducive to democracy than, say, Confucianism? Here, scholars disagree strongly. Cultural stereotypes are inherently controversial and often prejudiced. But is it possible that objective analysis could show that countries with certain religions or cultural traditions are more likely to support democratic values, while others are more prone to authoritarianism?

In fact, the data clearly show that predominantly Christian nations, particularly Protestant ones, are the most likely to be democratic, even when other causal factors (such as economic development and literacy) are held constant. That is to say, Protestant nations are more likely to be democracies than are countries that have similar levels of economic development but different religious beliefs. "Protestantism is said to foster individual responsibility and is thereby also more skeptical and less fundamentalist in character."[18]

On the other hand, Islamic countries have had a low level of democracy, especially in the Arab States. Some maintain that Islamic beliefs do not readily support democratic institutions because they fail to separate religion and politics (i.e., church and state).[19] And, when impressive economic growth and increased educational levels during the 1970s and early 1980s were slow to bring democracy to China, Singapore, South Korea, and Taiwan, many experts concluded that cultural (religious) beliefs must have been overriding the positive influences of economic modernization. They argued that Confucian culture promotes rigidly hierarchical societies and encourages excessive obedience to authority, values that are antithetical to democracy.[20]

Not surprisingly, cultural explanations such as these are highly controversial. They are difficult to prove and may simply reflect their proponents' prejudice and ethnocentrism. Catholics may feel uneasy with theories that contrast the traditional strength of democracy in the United States, Canada, and the English-speaking Caribbean with Latin America's authoritarian tradition, leading many analysts to conclude that Catholic values offer less support for democracy than Protestant norms do. Similarly, most Muslims and Confucians reject theories that depict their religions as authoritarian. But do the facts support these hypotheses, however unpleasant some people may find them?

Although Protestant nations are more likely to be democratic than are Buddhist countries and even though democracy has fared poorly in most Islamic nations, it is difficult to ascertain how much these disparities are the result of differing religious values and how much they result from innumerable other historical, economic, and cultural factors that are not easily statistically controlled. We know that several Islamic nations—including Turkey, Lebanon, and, most recently, Indonesia—have achieved some degree of democracy. Moreover, Alfred Stepan and Graeme Robertson demonstrated that while Arab countries, even wealthier ones, have rarely achieved electoral democracy, *non-Arab* Muslim nations are somewhat *more* likely to be democracies than a matched sample of non-Muslim countries with comparable levels of economic and social development.[21]

Furthermore, if Islamic and Catholic cultures inherently promoted nondemocratic values, one would expect that American Catholics would be less democratically inclined than their Protestant counterparts are. In the same way, we would predict that Bosnian Muslims would be less committed to democracy than Bosnian Serbs (Christians) and Indian Muslims would be less likely to have democratic values than Hindus. But there is no evidence to support any of these expectations.

Finally, we need to remember that religious beliefs and political cultures are capable of change and do not permanently mire a country or region in a particular value system. For example, during World War II, the Japanese and German political cultures were considered militarily bellicose and authoritarian. Today, however, these countries are highly consolidated democracies whose citizens have been far less inclined to support armed interventions (such as in Iraq or Afghanistan) than Americans have. Not long ago, many scholars viewed Confucian values as obstacles to East Asian democratization. However, despite such pessimism, Confucianism has apparently not impeded South Korea's and Taiwan's democratic transitions. Nor did the fact that Catholic societies were less hospitable to democracy in the past hinder their democratic transitions during the closing decades of the twentieth century. Indeed, from Portugal and Spain to Argentina, Brazil, and Mexico, democracy has taken root in Catholic nations that not long ago were depicted as culturally authoritarian. Moreover, in recent decades, the church hierarchy itself has been a pivotal voice for democratic change in Catholic countries such as the Philippines and Brazil.

In short, political cultures appear to be more malleable than previously recognized. "This does not mean that the prevalent attitudes . . . within a society have no consequences for the character of its democracy, only that we should not look to unchanging belief systems for their explanation."[22] As Larry Diamond notes, often "democratic culture is as much the product as the cause of effectively functioning democracy."[23] Just as democratic values support democratic consolidation, sustained democratic *institutions* and *behavior* help inculcate democratic values. Many first-time democracies *initially* lack a healthy democratic political culture. In countries such as Russia (where citizens generally accept Vladimir Putin's authoritarian leadership) this has helped cut short democracy in its infancy. But other nations have overcome this obstacle and the longer they continue democratic practices, the better are their chances of acquiring democratic values. In fact, if a country can sustain it for two decades, democracy is unlikely to ever collapse. For example, Robert Dahl's examination of fifty-two countries in which democracy had failed identified only two (Chile and Uruguay) that had enjoyed democracy for more than twenty years prior to that failure.[24] And even these two exceptions subsequently reinstituted democracy more successfully than did neighboring countries such as Bolivia and Ecuador, which lack comparable democratic traditions.

The Curse of Oil

The recent failure of several Arab countries to begin a democratic transition (such as Saudi Arabia and Kuwait) or to consolidate democracy after they had overthrown dictatorships (Egypt, Libya and Yemen) again raises the question of why that region has been so inhospitable to democracy. Scholars often have pointed to the apparent absence of democratic values in Arab culture and other factors. One additional theory is particularly intriguing. Noting that the economies of many Arab nations are heavily dependent on oil exports, some analysts have argued that abundant petroleum production may initially seem like a blessing (since it brings substantial national income), but in the long run, it usually has a pernicious influence on the political system. The distorting effects of excessive economic dependence on oil exports ("the **curse of oil**") have obstructed democracy in countries as diverse as Iran, Russia, and Saudi Arabia. Indeed, almost all countries whose exports and government revenues are dominated by petroleum have been woefully unable to democratize.[25] Larry Diamond has identified twenty-three nations—twenty-one of them in the developing world—that have received 60 percent or more of their export earnings from the petroleum sales. Yet only two of these twenty-one countries have enjoyed a period of liberal democracy in recent decades (Nigeria and Venezuela) and these two have regressed to being only Partly Free.[26]

Why has oil wealth been such an obstacle to democracy? Analysts have suggested a number of reasons. For one thing, currently the petroleum industry in most oil-rich, developing countries is owned or largely controlled by their governments. Consequently, the new oil wealth strengthens the power of the state, providing funds for the armed forces and police and funding large government bureaucracies that offer patronage jobs to government supporters. Also, these nations do not produce the independent bourgeoisie that has historically been crucial for democracy. Similarly, the middle class—another bulwark of liberal democracy—also fails to challenge state power because so many of its members have jobs in the government bureaucracy (including the state petroleum company). And, with little industrialization, a large portion of the working class is employed in the oil industry, making them dependent on the state and, like the middle class and bourgeoisie, unlikely to challenge state power.

Armed with substantial oil and gas revenues, these petroleum states can lower taxes and offer private companies and the general public inexpensive services and goods such as subsidized credit, food, and housing. Although these obviously have their attractions, the consequence is that "people become clients and not citizens," that is, they turn into virtual wards of the state who are not active in the political system.[27] With low taxes and an array of government benefits, the average citizen has little incentive to question government corruption, mismanagement, or repression. To paraphrase a battle cry of the American Revolution, "Without taxation they have no effective representation."

Another curse of oil dependency is massive corruption. Expanding bureaucracies and state enterprises give politicians opportunities to sell jobs. At the same time, businessmen seeking subsidized financial credit from the government and those in the hunt for state contracts routinely bribe public officials. High-level government officials often plunder the national treasury. In the worst example, a former military dictator of Nigeria, General Sani Abacha, is believed to have stolen some $3–$4 billion of government funds prior to his death. Indeed, according to the watchdog organization Transparency International, less developed, oil-centered countries (most of them in the Middle East and Africa) have particularly high rates of government corruption. All of these factors—heavy concentration of economic power in the hands of the state, **clientelism**, bourgeois and middle-class dependency, and corruption—have effectively impeded the growth of democracy.

DEMOCRATIC CONSOLIDATION EXAMINED

It is important to recall that although the breadth of democratic transitions in the developing world has been impressive, political change can occur in both directions. Many countries that have achieved electoral or liberal democracy have seen their new governments fail, followed by a return to authoritarian rule. In 1994, a military coup in Gambia ended years of democratic government. Recent examples of renewed authoritarianism include Pakistan, Bangladesh, and Thailand. Between 1980 and 2000, democracy collapsed in twenty-six countries, though a number of these (such as Ecuador and Turkey) subsequently returned to being Free or Partly Free.[28] What makes democracy endure or falter? Which of the LDC's new democracies have the qualities needed to consolidate democracy?

To answer these questions, Adam Przeworski and his associates analyzed data for 135 countries over a forty-year period. Democracy, they found, is most fragile in poor countries (with per capita incomes of less than $1,000 in constant dollars), and it becomes more stable as national income rises: "Above $6,000 [per-capita real income], democracies are impregnable and can be expected to live forever; no democratic system has ever fallen in a country where per-capita income exceeds $6,055 (Argentina's level in 1976)."[29] Several factors explain why richer democracies are more likely to last. For one thing, they normally have a crucial foundation for democratic government—high educational levels.* For another, class conflict over the distribution of economic rewards is typically less intense in more affluent societies.

Contrary to what many political scientists had believed, Przeworski et al. also found that the faster a nation's economy grows, the more likely it is to sustain democracy. Conversely, democracy is less likely to survive in countries suffering economic decline, high inflation rates, or other forms of economic crisis. However, important as domestic economic factors are, the authors discovered that international political conditions exert a more powerful influence on democratic survivability. Specifically, the more prevalent democratic government becomes in other nations, the more likely any particular LDC is to sustain its own democracy, regardless of its per capita income, literacy rate, or economic growth rate. In other words, as many analysts had suspected, democracy is contagious. Other scholars have noted that developing and maintaining effective political institutions—including representative and responsible political parties, a broad array of interest groups, a representative and influential legislature, a strong but not unlimited executive branch, an honest and independent judicial system—are absolutely critical for sustaining stable and effective democracy. Too often, judicial systems lack independence from the executive branch, do not have adequate legal training, and are corrupt. Consolidating democracies must strengthen their judiciary systems, so that they can stand up to power-hungry presidents or prime ministers and so that court decisions are respected by the electorate. A related problem in many new and reestablished democracies is executive-branch dominance over the national legislature. In Latin America, Russia, and elsewhere, democratically elected presidents have sometimes interpreted their electoral victories to mean that the voters had delegated absolute authority to them. For example, even though they were initially elected democratically, once in office, Presidents Carlos Menem (Argentina) and Alberto Fujimori (Peru) ran roughshod over their nation's congress and court system.

HOW DO DEMOCRACIES PERFORM? PUBLIC POLICY COMPARED

Some of the benefits of democracy are obvious: protecting personal freedom and holding governments accountable to the governed, to

---

*In other words, countries that are more economically advanced normally have higher literacy and education rates, and countries with higher literacy rates are more likely to be democratic. There are several petroleum-producing countries (such as Saudi Arabia and Angola) that, although wealthy, do not have particularly high literacy rates. None of these are democracies.

name but two. Nonetheless, academics have long debated whether democratic governments also better provide for the economic and social welfare of their citizens. As we noted earlier, during the closing decades of the twentieth century, many international agencies, journalists, and scholars maintained that certain dictatorships—in countries such as Chile, Indonesia, Singapore, and South Korea—had imposed the efficiency and discipline necessary to generate rapid economic growth.[30] The dramatic economic growth these authoritarian regimes produced into the 1990s was often compared to the less impressive performance at that time of democratic governments in countries such as India and Uruguay.

But, the passage of time and a closer examination of more than one hundred developing nations have dispelled such claims. Those who have insisted that authoritarian rule is likely to produce economic development have usually based their argument on the accomplishments of a few successful authoritarian cases. But for every authoritarian regime that has had an impressive economic record—including Chile, China, South Korea, Singapore, and Taiwan—there were far more cases of authoritarian governments with disastrous economic records—such as Burma, Haiti, North Korea, Tajikistan, and Zimbabwe. In fact, "between 1960 and 2000, 95 percent of the world's worst economic performances . . . were overseen by nondemocratic governments."[31] Furthermore, prior to its market-oriented reforms begun in the late 1980s, China's communist regime had a much more erratic record of economic growth. Chile's rate of growth was generally strong under its military dictatorship, but growth improved when the country restored democracy. Finally, in recent decades, the once-stagnant economy of India—the world's largest democracy—became one of the most dynamic in the world.

Analyzing annual economic growth data from more than 150 countries during each year from 1960 to 2001, Halperin, Siegle, and Weinstein compared the performance of democratic nations with those of autocracies (dictatorships). They found that in every one of the more than forty years studied, the democratic nations as a group grew faster than the autocracies. Furthermore, "citizens of democracies live longer, healthier lives, on average, than those in autocracies [with comparable per capita incomes]."[32] It is true that when they examined only the world's poorest nations, they observed no difference in the economic growth rate of democracies versus dictatorship. Still, even among the poorest countries, economic growth was less volatile in democracies than in autocracies (less subject to sharp ups and downs).

Similarly, Dani Rodrik used regression analysis to examine data for more than eighty countries over a span of twenty-four years (1970–1994).

He found that there was no appreciable difference between the long-term economic growth rates of democracies and authoritarian governments. But, democracies outperformed authoritarian regimes on several other important economic indicators. Their economies were less volatile, were more predictable, paid better wages to workers, and could "handle adverse shocks [like the Asian financial crisis or severe jumps in oil prices] much better."[33] Finally, another recent study comparing democracies with nondemocracies found that democratic countries spent more on public education, had higher school enrollments, higher literacy rates, and greater public access to health-care services.[34]

Democratic governments are not necessarily superior in all areas of governance. In theory, freely elected government officials should be less corrupt than authoritarian administrators because they are held accountable in the next election. But in countries that have simultaneously switched from command economies to capitalism, in nations that have enormous sources of natural resource wealth (such as oil revenues) linked to the government, and in countries with a historical tradition of corruption, democratization may not improve government honesty and may actually make things worse. Thus, for example, Russia's transition to capitalism and to democracy in the 1990s opened up the floodgates for corruption. In Cambodia, the communist regime has been replaced by a government of competing "mafias."

Nigeria has both extensive petroleum reserves and a tradition of deep government corruption. The military governments that had ruled the country were enormously dishonest, even by LDC standards, and turned their leaders into billionaires. But, the 1999 transition to democracy brought little improvement. The Nigerian government is still considered one of the most corrupt in the world. Governors of the country's thirty-six states "get a check each month that represents their state's cut of Nigeria's booming oil fortune, and have almost no one to answer to for how they spend that money."[35] Not surprisingly, a significant portion of that money ends up in the pockets of the governors and their cronies. Small wonder that some governors, when faced with serious electoral opposition in their bids for reelection, have threatened the lives of their opponents and, in some cases, have had them murdered.

IMPROVING THE QUALITY OF DEMOCRACY

More than three decades after the start of the Third Wave, its reach has become far broader than the previous two waves, and, equally importantly, to date there has not been a reverse wave. In all, the number of countries categorized as "free," "partly free," and "not free" has remained fairly steady since the turn of the century.* The fact that democracy is now widely accepted as the best form of government is cause for satisfaction.

On the other hand, *Freedom in the World 2015*, "finds an overall decline in [world-wide] freedom for the ninth consecutive year." This deterioration is the longest since Freedom House began its evaluations in 1972. "A troubling number of countries moved backward . . . Venezuela, Egypt, Turkey, Thailand, Nigeria [and] Kenya."

At the same time, in many developing countries, democratic governments have failed to meet the needs of their citizens. Free and fair elections, improved civil liberties, and civilian command over the armed forces are important achievements. But too often the public has been disappointed by the failures of democratic rule: continued or increased economic inequality, an unjust judicial system, and widespread corruption (which may actually be less pervasive than during authoritarian rule, but is now more visible because of a free press).

Consequently, many political scientists have turned their attention from studying the consolidation of democracy to examining the *quality* of democracy and are looking for ways to improve it.[36] Public opinion surveys in both advanced industrial democracies and developing world democracies have indicated that citizens are becoming more distrustful of government and suspicious of political parties and politicians. Frequently, they consider government officials corrupt and self-serving. Thus, any search for higher-quality democratic governments has two important objectives: first, it is a moral imperative (fair, effective, and honest governments are obviously a desirable objective); second, more effective and honest democratic governments normally increase support for democracy and, thereby, increase democracy's longevity. Slightly modifying Larry Diamond and Leonardo Morlino's model, we can evaluate the *quality* of democracy in terms of seven dimensions, which, in turn, can be grouped into three broad categories[37]:

1. **Procedural Dimensions** The procedures used to elect government officials and the procedures that public officials use to govern must be honest, fair, and equitable. These procedures can be divided into four categories:
   a. *Participation*: All (or nearly all) adult citizens must have the right to vote as well as to participate in the political system in other ways. Powerful groups should not intimidate the poor or ethnic minorities about participating. A politically aware citizenry should not allow apathy to restrict their own participation.

---

*That is because the number of countries that ceased to be free has about equaled the number of countries that became free.

b. *Competition*: There should be free and fair elections between competing political parties, and the incumbent party should not have any built-in advantage in gaining access to state funds or to the media. The electoral system should not give any party a built-in advantage.

c. *Accountability*: A democratic electoral system must guarantee that government officials are fairly elected. But officials must also be held accountable for their actions between elections. Vertical accountability refers to procedures that allow citizens or independent groups to challenge or criticize a government official's behavior. Horizontal accountability refers to the ability of one government body to check the power of another branch, such as the Supreme Court overruling a decision by the president or the parliament removing a prime minister.

d. *The Rule of Law*: The legal system must apply equally to all citizens and all laws must be publicly known and clear. The judiciary must be neutral and independent.

2. **Substantive Dimensions**   Beyond adhering to proper procedures, quality democracies must pursue policies that advance:

a. *Respect for Civil Liberties and the Pursuit of Freedom*: This includes respect for individual liberty, security, and privacy; freedom of information, expression, and religion; and due process.

b. *Reductions in Political, Economic, and Social Inequalities*: In order to attain political equality, where there is substantial social and economic inequality, governments need to reduce sharp income gaps. Scholars such as Terry Karl and Dietrich Rueschemeyer maintain that political equality and democracy have been difficult to achieve in the face of glaring income inequalities in Latin America and parts of Africa.[38] Different analysts, however, disagree on how much equality is possible or perhaps even desirable.

3. **Result Dimensions**   This final category includes only a single dimension—*responsiveness*. A democratically responsive government is one in which "the democratic process induces the government to form and implement policies that the people want."[39] In order to achieve this, there needs to be a stable political party system, with parties that offer coherent and distinguishable programs.

CONCLUSION

Too frequently, democratic transitions have produced unfulfilled economic aspirations, corrupt governments, and widespread dissatisfaction with government institutions. Hence, even though most citizens in the LDCs have an abstract preference for democracy as a form of government, many of them are cynical about the *performance* of democratic regimes. In a 2013 survey of eighteen Latin American nations by *Latinobarómetro*, 56 percent of those polled agree with the abstract statement that "democracy is preferable to any other form of government," but only 40 percent were satisfied with the actual way that democracy was working in their own country.[40]

A recent Afrobarometer survey of thirty-four Sub-Saharan African nations revealed that despite the scarcity of democratic governments in that continent, about 70 percent of those surveyed agreed that "democracy is preferable to any other form of government." But only about half considered their own country a democracy. A similar percent favored limits to presidential terms.

If the citizens of current democracies become more critical of their government's performance in the future, it does not necessarily mean these countries will revert to authoritarian rule. In countries where the political and economic elites continue to support democratic regimes, those governments may be able to survive considerable grassroots discontent. Furthermore, even if there is considerable support for a return to military rule, the armed forces may not be interested. In fact, in many countries, most notably in Latin America, the failures of recent military governments caused the armed forces so much internal discord and loss of prestige that the generals were reluctant to seize power again. Moreover, despite growing citizen discontent with democratic performance, in only a small number of cases have many people supported revolutionary or other authoritarian alternatives. Still, in many fragile democracies, the elites' commitment to democracy is soft and should there be substantial mass discontent over the government's performance, those democratic regimes might collapse.

To date, it appears that even among the many inhabitants of the LDCs who have been dissatisfied with their government's performance under democracy, most have unwittingly accepted Winston Churchill's argument that "democracy is the worst form of government except for all the others that have been tried." But, without future improvement in social and economic conditions, democratic governments may cease commanding widespread support. In Latin America, where income inequality is higher than in any region of the world, the gap between the "haves" and "have-nots" has widened since its transition to democracy. Likewise, income inequality has soared in post-communist Eastern Europe and the former Soviet Union. From Colombia to the Philippines and from Pakistan to Peru, the poor suffer from highly unequal land and income distribution, pervasive poverty, rising crime rates, inadequate public health service, and corrupt police and judicial systems. Until such injustices are addressed, democracy will remain incomplete and often precarious.

Practice and Review Online
http://textbooks.rowman.com/handelman8e#ch2

KEY TERMS

Arab Spring
clientelism
constant dollars
curse of oil
democratic consolidation
democratic transition
electoral democracy

liberal democracy
liberalization (of the political
    system)
political culture
procedural democracy
substantive democracy
Third Wave

DISCUSSION QUESTIONS

1. Discuss the differences between electoral democracy, liberal democracy, and substantive democracy. In what way does each of these definitions provide a useful measure of democracy in a range of countries?
2. What is the evidence supporting the belief that some religions support democracy better than others? What is the contrary evidence? Discuss the hypothesis that, while a society's religion does not *determine* its level of democracy, some religions make it more difficult for a society to democratize.
3. Why do you think the Third Wave of democracy has not been followed so far by a reverse wave like those that followed the First and Second Waves? How likely is this to change in the future?
4. How does the "Arab Spring" of 2010 illustrate the difficulty of getting from democratic transitions to democratic consolidations?

NOTES

1. Samuel P. Huntington, *The Third Wave: Democratization in the Late Twentieth Century* (Norman: University of Oklahoma Press, 1991).
2. These figures come from Freedom House (discussed later in the chapter).
3. There has been a long, ongoing debate over what conditions, and how many of those conditions, a country must meet in order to be called a democracy. The definition offered in this textbook draws from several sources, including Philippe C. Schmitter and Terry Lynn Karl, "What Democracy Is and Is Not," *Journal of Democracy* 2, no. 2 (Summer 1991): 75–88; Robert A. Dahl, *Democracy and Its Critics* (New Haven, CT: Yale University Press, 1989).
4. Juan Linz and Alfred Stepan, "Toward Consolidated Democracies," in *Consolidating the Third Wave Democracies*, eds. Larry Diamond, Marc F.

Plattner, Yun-han Chu, and Hung-mao Tien (Baltimore, MD: The Johns Hopkins University Press, 1997), 15.

5. The statistics cited here are drawn from Ethan B. Kapstein and Nathan Converse, *The Fate of Young Democracies* (New York: Cambridge University Press, 2008), 39–40. I adjusted Kapstein and Converse's statistics to remove European countries.

6. Quoted in Morton H. Halperin, Joseph T. Siegle, and Michael M. Weinstein, *The Democracy Advantage* (New York: Routledge and the Council on Foreign Relations, 2005), 25.

7. Larry Diamond, "Introduction: In Search of Consolidation," in *Consolidating the Third Wave Democracies*, xv.

8. Huntington, *The Third Wave*, 271.

9. Seymour Martin Lipset, *Political Man* (Garden City, NY: Anchor Books, 1960).

10. Dietrich Rueschemeyer, Evelyne Huber Stephens, and John D. Stephens, *Capitalist Development and Democracy* (Chicago, IL: University of Chicago Press, 1992), 14.

11. Philips Cutright, "National Political Development: Measurement and Analysis," *American Sociological Review* 28, no. 2 (April 1963): 253–64.

12. Axel Hadenius, *Democracy and Development* (New York: Cambridge University Press, 1992).

13. UNESCO *Institute for Statistics, May 2013.*

14. Huntington, *Political Order in Changing Societies*. On the rise of repressive authoritarian regimes in Latin America's most industrialized nations, see Guillermo O'Donnell, *Modernization and Bureaucratic Authoritarianism* (Berkeley: Institute of International Studies, 1973).

15. Barrington Moore Jr., *The Social Origins of Dictatorship and Democracy* (Boston: Beacon Press, 1955), 418.

16. Rueschemeyer, Huber Stephens, and Stephens, *Capitalist Development and Democracy*.

17. Robert Dahl, "Development and Democratic Culture," in *Consolidating the Third Wave Democracies*, 34.

18. Hadenius, *Democracy and Development*, 118–19. Of course, there are many branches of the Protestant religion and some of them are quite fundamentalist.

19. Amr G. E. Sabet, *Islam and the Political* (Ann Arbor, MI: Pluto Press, 2008), 251–52.

20. Samuel P. Huntington, *The Clash of Civilizations and the Remaking of World Order* (New York: Simon & Schuster, 1996).

21. Alfred Stepan with Graeme B. Robertson, "An 'Arab' More than 'Muslim' Electoral Gap," *Journal of Democracy* 14, no. 3 (July 2003): 30–44.

22. David Beetham, "Structural and Cultural Preconditions for Democracy," in *Democracy and Development*, ed. Bernard Berendsen (Amsterdam: KIT Publishers, 2008), 178.

23. Larry Diamond, "Three Paradoxes of Democracy," in The Global Resurgence of Democracy, eds. Larry Diamond and Marc F. Plattner (Baltimore, MD: The Johns Hopkins University Press, 1993), 104.

24. Robert A. Dahl, "The Newer Democracies: From the Time of Triumph to the Time of Troubles," in *After Authoritarianism: Democracy or Disorder?* ed. Daniel N. Nelson (Westport, CT: Greenwood Press, 1995), 7.

25. Michael Ross, "Does Oil Hinder Democracy?" *World Politics* 53 (April 2001): 328–56.

26. Larry Diamond, *The Spirit of Democracy* (New York: Times Books, 2008), 74–79.

27. Ibid., 75.

28. Halperin, Siegle, and Weinstein, *The Democracy Advantage*, 71.

29. Adam Przeworski et al., "What Makes Democracies Endure?" in *Consolidating The Third Wave Democracies*, 297.

30. See, for example, M. G. Quibria, *Growth and Poverty: Lessons from the Asian Economic Miracle* (Asian Development Bank, Working Paper No. 33, 2002); more broadly, Huntington's *Political Order* argues that countries in the early stages of development often need authoritarian government.

31. Halperin, Siegle, and Weinstein, *The Democracy Advantage*, 13.

32. Ibid., 35. See also, 29–43. Data were collected from the Polity IV project, an interuniversity project that collects a wide range of data on all of the world's nations with populations exceeding 500,000. Polity ranks each country on a scale of 1–10 based on its degree of democracy.

33. Dani Rodrik, "Democracy and Economic Performance" (Cambridge, MA: Unpublished Paper, Harvard University, December 14, 1997), 2.

34. Iñias Macías-Aymar, "Does Income Inequality Limit Democratic Quality?" in *An Unequal Democracy?* eds. Carlo Benetti and Fernando Carillo-Flórez (Washington: Inter-American Development Bank, 2005), 84–85.

35. *New York Times*, "Money and Violence Hobble Democracy in Nigeria" (November 24, 2006).

36. For example, Maxwell Cameron and Eric Hershberg (eds.), *Latin America's Left Turns: Politics, Policies & Trajectories of Change* (Boulder, CO: Lynne Rienner, 2010).

37. This section is based on Larry Diamond and Leonardo Morlino, eds., *Assessing the Quality of Democracy* (Baltimore, MD: The Johns Hopkins University Press, 2005). But, I have combined their "vertical and horizontal accountability" into one category.

38. Terry Lynn Karl, "Economic Inequality and Democratic Instability," *Journal of Democracy* 11 (January 2000): 149–56; Dietrich Rueschemeyer, "Addressing Inequality," in *Assessing the Quality of Democracy*, 41–61.

39. G. Bingham Powell Jr., "The Chain of Responsiveness," in *Assessing the Quality of Democracy*, 62.

40. *The Economist*, November 2, 2013.

3
Religion and Politics

Pope Francis before enthusiastic crowds in Quito, Ecuador. The developing world's two largest religions are Islam and Catholicism. Pope Francis has headed the Roman Catholic Church since 2013 and has stood out for his strong position on several major political issues. He has taken a "liberal" position on climate change and on income inequality and a "conservative" position on same-sex marriage and on the possibility of women in the priesthood. *AP/Dolores Ochoa*

IN HIS INFLUENTIAL BOOK *The Secular City*, Harvey Cox, a Harvard theology professor and Baptist minister, discussed the privatization of religion in modern urban society, particularly the separation of religion and politics.[1] While this trend was not yet apparent in the LDCs, many social scientists were convinced that as those societies modernized, the role of religion in politics (and of politics in religion) would diminish, just as it had in the West.

Indeed, in Latin America, the Catholic Church no longer exercises nearly as much control over education or reproductive rights as it once did. Following independence, the Indian government tried to ameliorate the injustices of the caste system, a cornerstone of Hindu religious practice. And at various times Muslim countries such as Turkey established relatively secular political systems. Accordingly, one leading authority observed, "Political development includes, as one of its basic processes, the secularization of politics, the progressive exclusion of religion from the political system."[2]

For the most part, early modernization theorists viewed traditional religion as an impediment to political and economic development, while dependency theorists scarcely mentioned it in their writings (see chapter 1). Yet, contrary to those expectations, developing world religions have been a resilient, growing political force that has withstood the onslaughts of modernization. In some instances, such as prerevolutionary Iran, rapid and destabilizing modernization has even stimulated a militant religious backlash. As David Little has observed, "Modernization was supposed to mean the gradual decline and eventual disappearance of religion from public life, but, as we know, that hasn't happened. Religion is very much alive as a part of politics."[3] In fact, since the 1970s, much of the developing world has experienced a religious resurgence, which has intensified the role of religion in the political arena. At the same time, even the most conservative religious group has incorporated elements of modernity. Currently, the Islamic State (IS) enforces medieval practices in the territories it has conquered while effectively using modern technology including videos and the social network to recruit new members and disseminate propaganda.[4]

Nowhere is the importance of religion more apparent than in the Middle East and parts of Africa and Asia, where there is a resurgence of Islamic **fundamentalism**, also called **Islamism** or Islamic **revivalism** (referring to its desire to revive the "true faith"), terms preferred by many scholars. This revival, along with deepened sectarian violence between Sunnis and Shi'ites (the two major branches of Islam), has destabilized Iraq, Syria, Yemen, and Lebanon. The 1979 seizure of American hostages in Iran and Lebanon, the assassination of Egyptian president Anwar Sadat (1981), the terrorist assault on U.S. Air Force barracks in

Saudi Arabia (1983), the bombing of two U.S. embassies in East Africa (1998), and, above all, the 9/11 attacks on the World Trade Center and the Pentagon (2001) all concentrated Western attention on "religion and politics."

Subsequent **Islamist** (Islamic fundamentalist) terrorist attacks in Europe, Africa, and Asia, along with religiously related civil wars in Iraq, Syria, and Afghanistan, all deepened that focus. In fact, since the end of the Cold War, *radical* Islamic fundamentalism has supplanted Soviet Communism as the most widely perceived threat to Western security. This concern has persisted with continued Islamist terrorism—most notably, in recent years, the military advances and brutality of the so-called Islamic State (IS, also called ISIS or, less commonly, ISIL).

THE MEETING OF CHURCH AND STATE

Many preconceptions about religion and politics emerge from misinterpretations, both of American politics and of political systems elsewhere. Americans accept a constitutional separation of church and state as the normal state of affairs (though some wish to blur this line). This formal barrier, however, does not exist in numerous industrialized democracies and developing nations. Many Western European nations, though generally less religious than the United States, lack legal walls between religion and politics. In England, for example, the Church of England (the Anglican Church) is the official state religion and Norway's government provides housing and financial support for Lutheran ministers. Moreover, even in the United States, religious organizations and beliefs continue to influence political behavior. Black Baptist churches, for example, were in the forefront of the American civil rights movement. Ministers from Martin Luther King and Jesse Jackson—on the left—to Jerry Falwell and Rick Warren—on the right—have been deeply involved in U.S. politics. Since the 1980s, the so-called Christian right has been an influential force within the Republican Party. Indeed, in recent decades, conflicts over issues such as abortion, school prayer, and stem-cell research led one expert to observe that "far from rendering religion largely irrelevant to politics the structure of [American] government may actually encourage a high degree of interaction."[5]

Religion is even more firmly embedded in many Third World cultures, and its impact on politics is correspondingly more pronounced. In fact, it is so central to traditional values that we often identify national or regional cultures by their predominant religion: Buddhist culture in Burma and Thailand, Catholic culture in Latin America, Confucian culture in China and Korea, Hindu culture in much of India and Nepal, and Islamic culture in North Africa and the Middle East.[6]

The blending of religion and politics is most apparent in **theocratic states** (political systems dominated by religious leaders and institutions) such as Iran, where the Shi'a clergy have been the final arbiters of public policy since that country's 1979 Islamic revolution. Similarly, when the Taliban ruled Afghanistan (1996–2001), their government became an extension of the fundamentalist clergy. But it is also very significant in anti-Western, outlaw Islamic countries such as Sudan, as well as in some American allies, most notably Saudi Arabia. In Latin American nations like Brazil and Nicaragua, the **"Theology of Liberation,"** espoused by radical Catholics, has motivated many priests and nuns to mobilize the poor in their struggle against economic and political injustices. Although not a "liberationist" himself, Pope Francis's (the first Pope ever from Latin America) strong commitment to the underprivileged, to social justice, and toward protecting the environment has been strongly influenced by that theology. And in India, the Bharatiya Janata Party (BJP), which currently heads the country's governing coalition, has carried the torch of Hindu revivalism.

GREAT RELIGIONS OF THE DEVELOPING WORLD

Four of the world's "great religions" predominate in the LDCs. Catholicism, the only major religion to have penetrated extensively into both industrialized democracies and the developing world, is preeminent in the Philippines and Latin America and is also the faith of significant minorities in various Sub-Saharan African countries. Islam, the world's second largest religion (now estimated to include 23 percent of the world's population), prevails across a broad span of Asia, the Middle East, and Africa—from Indonesia and Malaysia in the east through Pakistan and Bangladesh in the Indian subcontinent to the Middle East, and North Africa. It also represents about half the populations of Nigeria, as well as substantial minorities in countries as far-flung as the Philippines, Tanzania, and Trinidad and Tobago. Buddhism is a major religion in East Asia, Southeast Asia, and parts of South Asia (including Thailand, Burma, Tibet, Vietnam, and Japan). Finally, Hinduism is the dominant religion only in India and neighboring Nepal. However, there are also Hindu populations exceeding 1 million persons in nearby Bangladesh, Indonesia, Sri Lanka, Pakistan, and Malaysia, as well as significant immigrant communities in South Africa and Trinidad and Tobago.

To be sure, not everyone in the developing world belongs to one of these major religions. Protestantism is the leading religion in the English-speaking islands of the Caribbean and represents important minorities in a number of other LDCs. Confucianism (perhaps more a philosophy and way of life than a religion) still influences Chinese society (even after the communist revolution), as well as Japan, South Korea, and Taiwan. Christian Orthodox minorities are significant in Lebanon and Egypt, while many Africans believe in traditional local religions. The impact of these religions on politics, however, is generally limited. Consequently, this chapter restricts its analysis to the four global religions just discussed, particularly emphasizing Islam and Catholicism.

None of the developing world's major religions is monolithic, though the Catholic Church, with its doctrine of papal infallibility on matters of faith and its hierarchical structure, comes closest. Buddhism is divided into two major traditions. But, Islam has the most consequential internal divisions, with intense and exceptionally violent conflict in the Arab World.

The most important division within Islam is between its two major branches, Sunnis and Shi'ites. The split between them, dating to the decades following the death of the Prophet Muhammad (570–632 AD), centered on the issues of "who should succeed him and the nature of the successor's [spiritual and political] role[s]."[7] The Shi'ites have a more hierarchical clergy than the Sunnis, and they revere their most prominent politico-religious leaders, particularly the Imams (the Guides). Religious practices and beliefs of the two branches differ somewhat, although, in truth, the similarities of their faith outweigh the differences. Yet, many Sunnis do not consider the Shi'ites to be authentic Muslims, and, in several countries, Shi'ites resent political and economic domination by Sunnis. In spite of these differences, in the past the two groups have often lived together peacefully. Since at least the 1980s, however, animosities and violence between the two have erupted in many parts of the Arab World and in a number of other countries in Asia and Africa. Chapter 4 will examine their political conflicts in Iraq, Syria, and Lebanon.

Currently, 85–90 percent of the world's nearly 1.6 billion Muslims are Sunnis, while Shi'ites account for only 10–15 percent (there is also a small Sufi branch). Shi'ism is the majority faith only in Iran, Iraq, and the small nations of Azerbaijan, Oman, and Bahrain. But its adherents are significant minorities (15–35 percent of the population) in Afghanistan, Kuwait, Pakistan, Saudi Arabia, Syria, Turkey, and Yemen.

Countries such as Iraq, Lebanon, Bahrain, and Syria, with significant population of both Sunnis and Shi'as, have suffered from sharp political and cultural tensions between the two. In most Arab countries with that division, Sunnis have had greater political power and higher social status than Shi'as, even when they are in the minority. Consequently, Shi'ites see themselves as "champions of the downtrodden," and they glorify suffering and self-flagellation.*

---

*In Syria, however, the Alawites, a Shi'a sect, have dominated the Sunni majority since the early 1970s.

Other religions that lack such formal divisions may still have competing theological or ideological perspectives. For example, even though they are united by a single church hierarchy, Latin American Catholics span the ideological spectrum from the ultraconservative members of Opus Dei to leftist believers in the Theology of Liberation. In the name of God and anti-Communism, some Latin American Catholics have supported fascist movements, rightist death squads, and repressive military regimes. Conversely, in the name of God and social justice, other Catholic priests and nuns have supported the Sandinista Revolution in Nicaragua, fought as Marxist guerrillas in Colombia, and organized the slum dwellers of Brazil and Peru.

RELIGION, MODERNITY, AND SECULARIZATION

We have already observed that social and economic modernization does not necessarily reduce religious observance, at least not in the short run. What about the reverse side of this relationship? That is, what is the impact of religion on modernity? Here again, most early analysts felt they were largely incompatible. "It is widely, and *correctly*, assumed," said one scholar, "that religion is in general an obstacle to modernization."[8] In the realm of politics, this interpretation suggested that the intrusion of religious institutions into government impedes the development of a modern state. At times, other analysts linked Catholic, Islamic, and Hindu beliefs to authoritarian values.

Subsequently, political scientists have developed a more nuanced understanding. Religious institutions may inhibit development in some respects, while encouraging it in others. For example, all of the great religions have legitimized the state's authority at some point in their history, a necessary step for state building. No longer facilely dismissing organized religion's contributions to development, many scholars now credit Confucianism with facilitating East Asia's rapid modernization in the second half of the twentieth century. Specifically, they credit the Confucian work ethic and its spirit of cooperation.

The argument that political modernization requires **secularization** has two bases—one empirical and the other normative. The *empirical* component notes that as Western societies modernized (i.e., became more literate, urban, institutionally organized, and industrialized), their political systems invariably became more secular. In effect, modern, Western societies developed a specialization of functions. Increasingly, the state-controlled politics, while the church oversaw religion, and each usually has refrained from interfering in the other's realm. Political scientists anticipated that as the LDCs modernized, they would experience the same division of responsibilities. The related *normative* argument holds that secularization is not only a common trend, but it is also desirable because it increases religious freedom, reduces the likelihood of state persecution of religious minorities, and permits the state to make more rational decisions free of religious bias.

We have noted the weakness of the first assumption. To be sure, modernization has induced political secularization in many developing countries, such as Turkey (at least until recently) and Mexico. But elsewhere it has not altered church-state relations; in fact, modernization frequently has precipitated a religious backlash when pursued too rapidly. Saudi Arabia and Iran offer two examples of reactions to the forces of modernization. In Iran, the last two Shahs—emperors—(1925–1979) imposed rapid Western-style socioeconomic development (including "unveiling" women), which destabilized society and helped precipitate a radical Islamic revival. In contrast, the Saudi royal family has controlled the pace of modernization in order to preserve a very traditional Islamic culture and maintain close links between Islam and the state.

At an individual level, many people in Africa, Asia, and the Middle East have defied the notion that more educated and professionally trained citizens will be less religiously orthodox. For example, Hindu and Islamic fundamentalist activists in India and Egypt are frequently professionals, not uneducated peasants. Most of the terrorists who attacked the Pentagon and the World Trade Center on September 11, 2001 (9/11) were relatively well educated and middle class. So too are many current recruits and leaders of the IS. Church-state relationships are more varied and complex than early development theory had assumed.

Some religious influences contradict accepted norms of modernity, as when they induce political leaders to violate the rights of religious minorities (or majorities). Similarly, many religiously inspired restrictions on women are clearly antithetical to modernization. But need there always be a strict wall between politics and religion or between clerics and politicians? Sometimes, analysts offer contradictory answers prompted by their own political ideologies. Many of those who lamented the political activities of leftist priests in Nicaragua and the clerically led Taliban in Afghanistan may have cheered political involvement by Dr. Martin Luther King Jr. or the Reverend Jerry Falwell in the United States.

Not surprisingly, most evaluations of religiously based political participation are influenced by how much this involvement furthers the goals and policies that the observer favors. Perhaps this is as it should be. The recent histories of Iran and Tibet illustrate this point. Iran has been a theocracy (politics are controlled by religious authorities) since its 1979 revolution, just as Tibet had been prior to its absorption by China in the 1950s. Each has had a political system "in which the political structures are clearly subordinate to the ecclesiastical establishment."[9] Yet most Westerners judged them quite differently.

Iran has become an international outcast because of its repression of civil liberties, its persecution of religious minorities, its support for international terrorism, and its nuclear program. And, until the late 1950s, Buddhist clerics dominated Tibetan politics. Viewed as divine by his people, the Dalai Lama had been the country's secular and spiritual leader. But because of Tibetan Buddhism's record of pacifism and tolerance, theocratic rule aroused no foreign indignation. Indeed, the Dalai Lama's long struggle to free his people has won him worldwide admiration and the Nobel Peace Prize. All of this suggests that the issue of separation of church and state may matter less to outside observers than the way in which the church uses its political influence when it holds power.

STRUCTURAL AND THEOLOGICAL BASES OF CHURCH-STATE RELATIONS

The extent to which religions influence political attitudes and behavior as well as the degree of political involvement by various organized religions vary considerably from place to place. Just as the separation of church and state in Western Europe is historically stronger in predominantly Protestant nations than in Catholic ones, the political impact of the LDCs' four major religions also differs. Two factors help define a particular religion's political involvement: its theological views regarding the relationship between temporal and spiritual matters and the degree to which its clergy are hierarchically organized and centrally controlled. From its inception in seventh-century Arabia, Islam has been a "religio-political movement in which religion was integral to state and society."[10] Today, the bond between religion and politics remains strong in most Muslim societies, though there is considerable variation. Turkey has been the most notable secular state in the Islamic world. In the early 1920s, Mustafa Kemal Ataturk ousted the sultan (the political and religious leader of the Ottoman Empire), emancipated women, and established a firm wall between church and state. In recent years, the governing Islamic government has rolled back a number of these measures, but important elements of the secular state remain in place. At the other end of the spectrum, *Islamic states* (not to be confused with the terrorist IS) base their governing philosophies on the **Koran** and Islamic law. Iran and Saudi Arabia are among the best-known examples. But, these regimes can be quite distinct from each other. These states may be Sunni (Saudi Arabia) or Shi'a (Iran), anti-Western (Iran and Sudan), or pro-Western (Saudi Arabia).

More than any other major religion, Catholicism has a well-defined and hierarchical ecclesiastical structure that enables it to have a considerable impact on the political system. At the church's apex is the Pope, whose religious authority is unchallenged and whose official pronouncements on matters of faith and morals are accepted by believers as infallible. Consequently, papal declarations can carry considerable political importance. For example, note the great controversy over Pope Francis's recent pronouncements indicating the obligation of Catholics to combat climate change. Within each country, the church hierarchy is headed by cardinals or bishops, who often have substantial political influence in Latin America and in other Catholic LDCs such as the Philippines.

Like Islam in the Middle East, Catholicism once was the state religion in a number of Latin American countries. Today, however, countries in the region either have ended official state religions or have rendered that link unimportant. Still, church doctrine has generally supported the established political regime and helped legitimize it. This does not mean, however, that the church has always supported the government. There have been periodic clashes between the two, particularly when the state has challenged church authority in areas such as education or when the state has violated human rights. Thus in the Philippines, church support of Corazón Aquino's democratic reform movement helped topple the dictatorship of Ferdinand Marcos. Similarly, Catholic authorities opposed conservative military dictatorships in Brazil and Chile during the 1970s and 1980s.

Unlike the Catholic Church, Asia's major religions—Hinduism and Buddhism—have a weak or nonexistent religious hierarchy. Hence, the clergy are relatively unorganized as an institution and are, therefore, less directly involved in politics than have the clergy in Catholicism and Islam. To be sure, India's BJP, until recently led by Hindu fundamentalists, are a major political force (a more moderate faction now heads the government). But the party has no linkage to the Hindu "clergy". In Burma, Buddhist clerics recently have led attacks on the Muslim minority. But, these have been localized.

Buddhism grew out of the Hindu religion in the sixth century BC, emerging from the teachings of a Nepalese prince, Siddhartha Gautama, the Buddha (Enlightened One). Though greatly influenced by Hinduism, Buddhism rejects one of its basic tenets, the caste system. It also differs from Hinduism in that it does have an organized ecclesiastical organization, its monastic orders. And in some countries, such as Burma, each religious community has its own leader, providing a hierarchical structure. Still, when compared to the Roman Catholic Church or to Shi'ite Islam, Buddhism's religious structure is much less centralized and, thus, less able to impact the political system. Hence, the remainder of this chapter centers on the political impact of Islam and Catholicism in the LDCs.

RELIGIOUS FUNDAMENTALISM AND ISLAMISM

No expression of religious influence on developing world politics has attracted more attention or inspired more fear and loathing than Islamic fundamentalism, particularly terrorist groups like the Taliban, al-Qaeda, and the IS. While 9/11 confirmed the world's worst nightmares about Islamic fundamentalist terrorism, experts on Islam insist that it is unfair to blame a major world religion, with more than 1 billion adherents, for the actions of a small minority. President George W. Bush and other leading U.S. public officials went out of their way to make this very point in the days after the attacks. Some people have noted that blaming the Islamic religion for Al Qaeda's actions would be as misguided as holding Christianity responsible for violent actions taken in its name. For example, a self-styled Christian on a mission recently killed nearly eighty people in Norway.

Others point out that not even all Islamists (fundamentalist Muslims) support violence. Moreover, many scholars reject the very term *fundamentalism* to describe current militant revivals. Instead, these analysts prefer such terms as *revivalism, militancy*, or *Islamist movements* rather than *Islamic fundamentalism*. Still, a number of leading authorities accept and even use the label *fundamentalism* in their writings. Fred Halliday notes that "there are some problems with applying the term fundamentalist to Muslim movements, but with the necessary caveats it can legitimately be so used."[11] In this chapter, I will use the term *fundamentalism* because of its common usage in contemporary political discourse. However, I also employ the terms *revivalism* or *Islamism* to refer to Islamic fundamentalism. Finally, the term *Islamists* refers to believers in Islamism.

Many scholars warn against the widespread belief that most or all Muslims are fundamentalists. Islamic scholars, such as John Esposito and Halliday, note that Westerners are usually unaware of the long tradition of liberal theology within Islam, which has advocated religious tolerance, progress for women, and democratic values.[12]

> At the very core of this supposed [Islamic] challenge or conflict lie confusions: the mere fact of peoples being "Islamic" . . . [has been confused] with that of their adhering to beliefs and policies that are . . . "Islamist" or "fundamentalist." It has been assumed . . . that most Muslims seek to impose a political program supposedly derived from their religion. The fact that most Muslims are not supporters of Islamist movements is obscured.[13]

On the other hand, periodic Islamist terrorism in Israel, Western Europe, the United States, Indonesia, Morocco, and other parts of the world indicate that although it is mistaken to speak of an "*Islamic* threat," it is surely reasonable to talk of a "radical *Islamist* threat." Hopefully, this chapter's discussion of Islamic revivalism conveys this distinction. In short, when this text discusses Islamic revivalism at some length— because of its obvious political importance—two caveats should be kept in mind: most Muslims are not fundamentalists and not all fundamentalists are repressive at home or violent abroad.

Defining and Explaining Fundamentalism (Revivalism)

Fundamentalism is the . . . effort to define the fundamentals of a religious system and adhere to them. One of the cardinal tenets of Islamic fundamentalism is to protect the purity of Islamic precepts from the adulteration of speculative exercises. . . . Behind all this is a drive to purify Islam in order to release all its vital force.[14]

The precise meaning of fundamentalism varies somewhat from religion to religion. But its adherents do share certain points of view across religious lines. To begin with, they all wish to preserve their religion's traditional worldview and resist the efforts of religious liberals to reform it. They also want to revive the role of religion in private and public life, including politics, lifestyle, and dress.

In the developing world, revivalism often appeals particularly to people who are disgusted by the inequalities and injustices in their country's political and economic systems. This disgust reflects popular revulsion against unjust, local political and economic elites, against pervasive corruption, and against repression. In Lebanon, the radical Hezbollah (Party of God) grew out of Shi'a resentment against the economically powerful Christian community, as well as anger toward Israel and the West. And in Algeria, Egypt, and Sudan, militant fundamentalists expanded their support as a result of government repression directed against them. Mohammed Ayoob notes that Islamists seek "to re-create a future based on . . . a romanticized notion of a largely mythical golden age" of Islam (under the Prophet and his earliest successors).[15]

Radical fundamentalists also tend to be nationalistic or chauvinistic, rejecting "outside" influences that they feel challenge or pollute their culture and their true faith. Islamists view Western culture as particularly insidious, associating it with imperialism, immodest dress, and scandalous films and music that promote promiscuity and drugs. But they reject Western values for another reason as well. For years, repressive government leaders, such as the Shah of Iran and Egypt's president Anwar Sadat, promoted Western-style modernization as the route to economic modernization. But, after decades of failed development in the Middle East, North Africa, and Asia, many people have felt deceived and have looked elsewhere for answers to their problems.

Indeed, many analysts argue that the most powerful force behind radical Islamic fundamentalism, even more than religious faith, has been nationalism and resentment toward Western-backed dictatorships—in countries such as Egypt (under Mubarak), Pakistan, Saudi Arabia, and prerevolutionary Iran. Moreover, Ahmed Rashid argues that most of the earliest volunteers for worldwide *jihad* (holy war) in the 1990s were primarily motivated by a desire for adventure. "The young men who trained in these [jihadist] camps were not educated in the Islamic schools called madrassas and they were inspired less by extremist Islamic ideology than by their desires to see the world, handle weapons, and have a youthful adventure."[16] Today, many of the volunteers for the IS are also motivated by this search for adventure. Jihadism seems also to appeal to young people unhappy with their social status.

Fundamentalists: Radical and Conservative

Any analysis of revivalism must distinguish between radical and conservative fundamentalists. Radicals, inspired by a "sacred rage," feel that they are conducting a "holy war" against enemies that threaten to corrupt their fundamental religious values. As a Hezbollah manifesto declared, "We have risen to liberate our country, to drive the imperialists and the invaders out of it, and to take our fate in our own hands."[17] Indeed, contemporary Islamism first arose from resistance to nineteenth- and twentieth-century Western intrusions into the Muslim world. In recent times, it has been nurtured by hatred of Israel and resentment against the American-led invasions of Iraq and Afghanistan. Islamist **mujahideen** ("holy warriors") in Afghanistan first waged jihad in the 1980s against that country's Marxist government and the occupying Soviet troops who supported it. Iran's Ayatollah Khomeini and Al Qaeda's Osama bin Laden both declared jihads against the United States ("the great Satan").

Elsewhere, other Islamist groups have waged battles against domestic enemies as well. Having been denied an almost certain electoral victory in 1991, when the military canceled the second round of the parliamentary elections, Algeria's fundamentalist movement, the Islamic Salvation Front (FIS or French-Front Islamique du Salut), attacked the nation's armed forces, the police, secular politicians, and foreigners. Soon, more violent militant organizations, most notably the Armed Islamic Group (GIA), launched a war of terror against Algerian civilians and the government, often mixing banditry with religious warfare. From 1992 through early 2001, the GIA, the Algerian military, and government-supported civilian militias massacred more than 100,000 Algerians between them. In recent years, Muslim extremists have killed innocent civilians in New York City, London, Madrid, Tel Aviv, Baghdad, Mumbai, Paris, and elsewhere.

Hindu fundamentalists have periodically launched bloody mob attacks against India's Muslim minority as well (see chapter 4).

Such radical militancy contrasts with the views and behavior of non-violent fundamentalists, such as Hasidic Jews or the leaders of India's BJP, who do not see themselves in such a battle. To be sure, heads of many nonviolent, fundamentalist groups also wish to shield their flocks from unwanted outside influences. But they do not view adherents of other religions or nonfundamentalist members of their own faith as mortal enemies.

For years, radical Islamic fundamentalists have been a major political force in Middle Eastern and North African countries such as Algeria, Egypt, Lebanon, and Sudan as well as in Afghanistan, and Pakistan.[18] Afghanistan's Taliban regime (1996–2001) was surely the world's most rigidly fundamentalist (until the IS). For example, it prohibited girls and women from attending school or working outside the home. Similarly, the Ministry for the Prevention of Vice and Promotion of Virtue banned television, sports events, dancing, and secular music. The prohibition on female employment meant that the country's estimated fifty thousand widows (the legacy of years of war) and their dependents—numbering several hundred thousand—were denied any legal means of support.[19] The Taliban also has sheltered bin Laden and al-Qaeda. Until the 1990s and the emergence of al-Qaeda and ISIS onto the world scene, however, Western observers viewed Iran's Islamist regime as the greatest threat to global stability. It is a concern that has revived as Iran seems to be developing a nuclear weapons capability.

The Iranian Revolution: Radical Shia' Islamism as a Reaction to Western-Style Modernization

The origins of the Iranian Revolution can be traced to the early decades of the twentieth century and the Muslim clergy's resistance to a government program of secular modernization imposed by the royal family.[20] Military, political, and economic intervention by a series of foreign powers—Czarist Russia, Britain, and the United States—turned the country into "a virtual protectorate" and made the ruling Shahs (emperors) appear to be tools of the great powers. Years later, resentment against foreign domination became an important component of the Islamic revolution.

Starting with the reign of Shah Reza Pahlavi (1925–1941), the imperial government antagonized the Shi'a mullahs (Muslim clergy and/or religiously learned men) with a series of modernizing reforms that included unveiling women, mandatory Western dress, and transferring control over various economic, educational, and political resources from the clergy to the state. The Shah's son, Mohammed Reza Pahlavi, ruled from 1941 to 1979 as a close ally of the United States. His so-called

White Revolution of the 1960s and 1970s expanded women's rights, extended general literacy, and promoted a land reform program that included the transfer of land from Islamic institutions to the peasants.

As a result, land was redistributed to some three million peasants, educational levels rose substantially, and oil wealth doubled the size of the middle class.[21] By 1976, Iran had the developing world's highest GNP per capita. However, the gap between the rich and the poor widened, widespread government corruption alienated the population, and many suspected opponents of the government were brutally suppressed. Because of his close ties to the U.S. government, many Iranians saw the Shah as a tool of American **neocolonialism**. At the same time, the Islamic clergy and other devout Muslims objected to the secularization of society and the intrusion of Western values and customs. As tension between the government and the mullahs intensified, a revered religious leader, the Ayatollah Ruhollah Khomeini, emerged as one of the Shah's leading critics.* In 1964 Khomeini was sent into exile for nearly fifteen years. The effect was to turn him into a martyr in a Shi'a culture that greatly admires martyrdom, thereby greatly enhancing his influence over the masses. In January 1979, with much of Iran's urban population involved in strikes and demonstrations against the regime, the Shah went into exile.

Three interrelated developments set the tone for the Islamic revolution. First was the merger of the country's religious and political leadership. The new "Islamic republic," declared the Grand Ayatollah, is "the government of God."[22] While nonclerical figures have since held important government posts—including the presidency—ultimate power resides in the hands of the Supreme Leader (currently Ayatollah Ali Khamenei)—a cleric to whom all government officials are beholden—and the Guardian Council (dominated by Islamist **mullahs**), which screens candidates for political office and has the power to overrule parliamentary votes.

The second important development was the revival of traditional Islamic observances. Women now must be veiled in public and are strongly encouraged to wear the chador, the shapeless shroud that conceals all parts of the body.† Highly intrusive Revolutionary Guards have penetrated all aspects of Iranian life, policing possible violations of "correct" Islamic behavior. During the 1980s, in the Shi'a tradition of martyrdom, many thousands of young volunteers died in a holy war against (then Sunni-ruled) Iraq. Assuring their families that it was a privilege to

---

*The title of Ayatollah is bestowed on the highest and most respected Shi'ite religious authorities.

†But, unlike the Taliban, who barred females from attending school at any level when they governed Afghanistan (and who currently violently attack girls' schools and female students), Iran's Islamic government doubled the female literacy rate from 36 to 72 percent in its first two decades in office.

die for the faith, the Ayatollah Khomeini proclaimed, "We should sacrifice all our loved ones for the sake of Islam. If we are killed, we have performed our duty."[23]

Finally, Iran's radical revivalism has embraced an aggressive foreign policy that has supported kindred Islamist groups abroad—such as Lebanon's Hezbollah and Palestine's Hamas—and has been highly antagonistic toward countries that it perceived as enemies—especially, Israel and the United States. Currently, it is one of the major military suppliers to the repressive, Syrian regime of Bashar al-Assad. The country's hostility toward the outside world was illustrated by several events. Shortly after the Islamist regime came to power, revolutionary students seized the U.S. embassy in Tehran, taking diplomats and embassy staff hostage, in an extraordinary breach of diplomatic protocol and international law, then held them for 444 days. In 1980, Iraqi president Saddam Hussein sent troops into Iran following a number of border disputes. Saddam was motivated by Iranian support for Iraq's repressed Shi'a majority. Once the conflict began, "both sides . . . portrayed the war as a noble crusade: Iraq saw the conflict as a historic defense of Arab sovereignty . . . against the marauding Persians [Iranians]; Iran depicted it as a holy war against the [Iraqi] infidels."[24] Before the war finally ended eight years later (with no victor), it cost the two nations a combined total of some 1 million lives.

Since that time, the government has periodically been less repressive at home and has sometimes moderated its confrontational foreign policy, particularly following the election of two reform-oriented presidents— Mohammad Khatami (1997–2005) and Hassan Rouhani (in office since 2013).* Since 2009, the Rouhani government has engaged in negotiations with the United States (and four other nations) aimed at reducing international economic sanctions on Iran, in return for its halting (for at least ten years) its nuclear weapons program.

al-Qaeda and Militant Islamism

While Shi'a Iran has continued to intervene in Iraq, Lebanon, and Syria, since the attacks, probably the greatest threat to the West has come from two Sunni terrorist groups, al-Qaeda and ISIS. Although officially founded in 1988, al-Qaeda's roots trace back to 1979, the year of the Iranian Islamic revolution and the Soviet invasion of Afghanistan. When Afghan mujahideen resisted the Soviet occupation, they were joined by a growing number of foreign volunteers drawn primarily from the Middle East. Among the earliest arrivals was Osama bin Laden, the Saudi-born

---

*While the only presidential candidates allowed to run must support the Islamic revolution, the Supreme Leader has allowed more moderate candidates to run against—and even defeat—hardliners.

son of a self-made construction tycoon. He used his enormous wealth, international contacts, and magnetic personality to recruit large numbers of foreign volunteers. Ironically, because they were fighting the Soviet army, the mujahideen also received weapons and encouragement from their future enemies, the United States and Saudi Arabia (as well as Pakistan).

In 1984, bin Laden and Ayman al-Zawahiri established the Afghan Service Bureau (MAK) which

> played a decisive role in the anti-Soviet resistance. . . . In addition to recruiting, indoctrinating, and training thousands of Arab and [other] Muslim youths, MAK distributed $200 million of [Arab], American, and British [state] aid destined for the Afghan jihad. Osama also channeled substantial resources of his own to the cause, a gesture that resonated with his fighters, [increasing] his own credibility.[25]

Eventually, the foreign mujahideen (primarily Saudis, Egyptians, Yemenis, and Algerians) numbered between 25,000 and 50,000 fighters, who helped their more than 200,000 Afghan colleagues to drive the Soviets from Afghanistan in 1989. One year earlier, bin Laden, together with Ayman al-Zawahiri, had created al-Qaeda, built largely out of MAK.* Like other Islamist militant groups, one of its goals has been to topple their so-called near enemy—despised Arab national governments in countries such as Egypt and Lebanon, whom they consider too pro-Western or too irreligious. But unlike those other Islamist groups at that time, al-Qaeda also has had far broader objectives. It seeks to destroy the "far enemy," the United States and its Western allies, whom it detests for their support of Israel and their backing of corrupt and unrepresentative governments in a number of Muslim nations.

With the Soviets vanquished in Afghanistan and many of the Arab Afghans (as the Arab volunteers were called) returning home, bin Laden and Zawahiri looked for new worlds to conquer. They widened their original objective of defending Islamic nations against conquest by "infidels" (those who do not believe in Islam) to include toppling religiously "derelict" Islamic regimes (such as Egypt) and supporting the struggles of Muslims against non-Islamic governments. In addition, the mujahideens' underdog victory over the Soviets in Afghanistan convinced Al Qaeda's leaders that they were capable of defeating the world's remaining superpower, the United States.

Western intelligence agencies were slow to realize that al-Qaeda existed. And even today, experts differ regarding the extent of its

---

*Zawahiri was an Egyptian surgeon who subsequently became Al Qaeda's leader after bin Laden was killed in 2011.

involvement in high-profile terrorist strikes and the degree of top-down control its leaders have exerted over its tactical operations. There is general agreement, however, that in addition to 9/11, al-Qaeda was directly or indirectly responsible for a number of major terrorist acts, including the following: a 1993 truck bombing of the World Trade Center in New York; an attack on American military barracks in Saudi Arabia (1996); the nearly simultaneous bombing of the U.S. embassies in Tanzania and Kenya, which killed 258 people and wounded more than 5,000 (1998); an attack on the naval ship, USS *Cole* in the port of Aden (2000); the deadly bombing of a nightclub in Bali, Indonesia (2002); bombings of commuter trains in Madrid (2004) that killed nearly 200 people; subway and bus bombings in London (2005); and a major share of the suicide bombings in Iraq. Major al-Qaeda affiliates in Nigeria (Boko Haram), Somalia (Al Shabaab), and other African countries have slaughtered thousands of civilians, kidnapped or killed hundreds of school students, and raped scores of women.*

Still, many experts do not see it as a centrally controlled, tightly knit unit whose every move was controlled by bin Laden or, subsequently, al-Zawahiri. Rather, they argue that it is a loosely linked network of organizations, many of which operate independently as "terrorist entrepreneurs" who come to al-Qaeda (the name means "the base" or "base of operation") for financial or logistical support. In the words of one observer,

> Although bin Laden and his partners . . . create[d] a structure . . . that attracted new recruits and forged links among preexisting Islamic militant groups, they never created a coherent terrorist network. . . . Instead, Al Qaeda functioned like a venture capital firm—providing funding, contacts, and expert advice to many different militant groups and individuals from all over the Islamic world.[26]

The destruction of the group's home base following the allied invasion of Afghanistan and the death or capture of many of its leaders after 2001 have contributed to further decentralization. Consequently, "some analysts have suggested that the word al-Qaeda is now used to refer to a variety of groups connected by little more than shared aims, ideals and methods." This decentralization of command has accelerated in the wake of bin Laden's death. The most deadly terrorist attacks in Europe since 9/11—London and Madrid—were carried out by young, European-born Muslims inspired by al-Qaeda, but acting independently. In the eyes of many analysts, such as Britain's International Institute of

---

*Boko Haram, probably Africa's most powerful and frightening radical Islamist group, has since changed its affiliation from al-Qaeda to the Islamic State.

Strategic Studies, this decentralization has made it even more elusive, "more insidious [than] and just as dangerous" as it was at the time of 9/11.

Despite Al Qaeda's unbending theology and its own brutal attacks on civilians, opinion polls initially indicated that the organization, and especially bin Laden, once had considerable support in the Islamic world. But, that support has evaporated subsequently. Thus, a 2003 Pew Center survey revealed that a solid majority of Muslims in the Palestinian territories (72 percent), Indonesia (59 percent), and Jordan (56 percent) said they had confidence in bin Laden. But, by 2009–2010 that confidence had dropped to 52 percent in Palestine, 25 percent in Indonesia, and 14 percent in Jordan.[27] By 2014, the IS had eclipsed al-Qaeda as the most powerful and popular Islamist terror organization.

It should also be noted that most orthodox Islamic scholars and most Arabs, even some of those supporting Al Qaeda's and IS's "defensive jihad" against the West, still condemn their terrorist tactics. The Koran, they insist, explicitly prohibits suicide (including suicide bombers) or killing civilians in war. Thus, Ahmed Rashid argues that Al Qaeda's "tactics had hardly anything to do with religion and everything to do with gaining political power and influence."[28] Other Islamic scholars and clerics have passed similar judgments on ISIS.

With bin Laden's death, the leadership of al-Qaeda passed to al-Zawahiri, a far less charismatic and dominant leader, and the organization has become more decentralized. But its "local franchises" in Somalia, Nigeria, Syria, and elsewhere—inspired by Al Qaeda's example and ideology, but largely independent of al-Zawahiri's command—continue to wreak havoc. Indeed collapse or near-collapse of several authoritarian Arab regimes in the region and the power vacuum that this has created may present new opportunities for terrorist and other Islamist groups. In Yemen, for example, the general chaos allowed al-Qaeda in the Arabian Peninsula (one of Al Qaeda's most powerful affiliates) to seize control of much of the country's south. Al Qaeda's affiliate has conquered considerable territory in Libya as well. Elsewhere in Africa, Nigeria's Boko Haram (meaning "Western education is forbidden") has killed thousands of civilians and kidnapped (or killed) hundreds of students at non-Muslim schools. And Somalia's Al Shabaab conquered much of that country before it was driven back by a combined force of the Somali army, the Kenyan and the Ethiopian militaries, and international troops from the African Union. It continues to launch terrorist attacks at home and in neighboring Kenya. By 2014–2015, however, ISIS had absorbed Boko Haram and reached out to Al Shabaab. And, as we have noted, it has overtaken al-Qaeda as the most prominent jihadist group in the Arab World and elsewhere.

Islamic State: The Terror State

The origins of ISIS and the IS date back to 2004, when "al-Qaeda in Iraq" (AQI) was organized as one of the many Sunni, jihadist guerrilla groups formed after the United States' invasion of that country the year before. Initially, its indiscriminate use of force, even against fellow Sunnis, lost it considerable support. But its prospects were revived by the 2011 outbreak of the revolution against the Assad dictatorship in neighboring Syria. AQI successfully moved into the power vacuum in that country and soon held considerable territory in both Syria and back home in Iraq, while changing its name to ISIL and then ISIS. At the same time, schisms developed between that group and Al Qaeda's new worldwide leader, Zawahiri (who felt that the ISIS's extreme brutality in the territories it had conquered was alienating the local population).

In early 2014, ISIS left al-Qaeda, changed its name again to the IS, and soon fought Al Qaeda's newly formed Syrian branch for control of the jihadist campaign in that country. Several months later, having built up its military capabilities, it swept out of Syria and quickly conquered huge swaths of Iraq, quickly routing the incompetent, Shi'a-led, Iraqi army. At the same time, much of the group's military leadership consists of former Sunni officers in Saddam Hussein's armed forces, who were swept out of their positions by the U.S. occupation. Unlike al-Qaeda, which functions purely as a military and terrorist group, IS has conquered and governed large swaths of territory.

In the territories it controls in Syria and Iraq it has provided improved public services (like medical care, electricity, and potable water) along with unspeakably brutal behavior. It has carried out beheadings, crucifixions, amputation of limbs, mass executions of non-Muslims and Shi'a Muslims, rapes of large numbers of young women, and abduction of other women and girls as sex slaves or into forced marriage of women to IS militants.[29]

Islamist Terrorists in Western Europe: A New Frontier

Most Islamist terrorists live in the Middle East or in other Muslim countries. However, since the start of the twenty-first century, there has been an alarming rise in terrorist attacks in Western Europe, carried out by Muslim immigrants—or, more often, their children. Swelled by a surge in immigration from the Arab World and Turkey from the 1940s to the 1990s, family reunifications, and higher birth rates, the current Muslim population of Western Europe had already reached approximately eighteen million before the current surge of immigrants, with over two-thirds of that total living in Germany, France, Britain, Italy, and Spain.[30]

In the decades after World War II, many European nations welcomed developing world immigrants as a source of unskilled, low-wage labor. As with Muslims worldwide, the vast majority of these immigrants and their children have rejected violence. Many of them have become European citizens and have integrated into their new homes. However, a number of dramatic terrorist attacks carried out by immigrants or, more often, by children of immigrants born on European soil have created security concerns and contributed to a backlash against the entire Muslim population. These have included the bloody bombings of Madrid commuter trains and mass transit in London, an attempted attack on the Glasgow (Scotland) airport, and the murder of Dutch filmmaker Theo van Gogh. In 2015, Islamist extremists gunned down over 100 people in Paris and killed 14 in San Bernardino, California. And currently, thousands of young Muslims living in Western Europe have traveled to Syria or Iraq to join the forces of IS. Perhaps one-third of IS's approximately thirty thousand troops today are foreign recruits, with about three thousand coming from Western Europe.

What accounts for the "European jihadist"? Surprisingly, many of the future holy warriors were former university students, who were either born in Europe or arrived there without being particularly devout or militant but were soon alienated by elements of Western culture (such as its much wider role played by women), felt culturally isolated, or were stung by real or perceived racial and religious sights. "Indeed, radical Islam in Europe . . . appears increasingly to have become an ideology of desperation, driven by frustration, helplessness and a sense of impotence."[31] Some analysts have speculated—based on the fact that foreign recruitment seems to rise after each IS beheading or after some atrocity appears on TV—that it is precisely the group's brutality that attracts many disaffected youths.

THE PROGRESSIVE CATHOLIC CHURCH

At roughly the same time that numerous Muslims were becoming more conservative and traditional, important sectors of Latin America's Catholic Church embarked on a progressive path. From the time of Spanish colonialism through the first half of the twentieth century, the church had supported the political and economic status quo, thereby legitimizing Latin America's elite-dominated governments. Provoked by the anticlerical positions of the French Revolution and of European and Latin American liberals, the Catholic hierarchy allied with conservative political parties and factions in Europe and, especially, in Latin America.

In the decades after World War II, however, many Catholic clergy, particularly at the parish level, began to abandon the church's erstwhile conservatism. This accelerated in the 1960s, when Pope John XXIII moved the "Church universal" in a more liberal direction, placing greater emphasis on social concerns. "The Second Vatican Council" [convened by Pope John between 1962 and 1965, also called Vatican II] moved international Catholicism from a generally conservative and sometimes authoritarian position to one that was more concerned with democracy, human rights, and social justice."[32] Catholics were encouraged to address pressing social issues and to begin a political dialogue with liberals.

In 1968, the Latin American Bishops Conference (CELAM) met in Medellín, Colombia, to apply the lessons of Vatican II to their own region. Challenging the status quo, their ideas reflected the influences of reformist theologians from the so-called **progressive church**. The theme of liberating Latin America's poor echoed through many of CELAM's pronouncements. The clergy, said the bishops, must heed the "deafening cry . . . from the throats of millions asking their pastors for a liberation that reaches them from nowhere else."[33] To do so, the church must "effectively give preference to the poorest and the neediest sectors." In short, an institution historically allied with the region's power elite was in some ways becoming the church of the poor.

The CELAM conference must be understood in the broader context of political change that was shaking Latin America at the time. In 1959, the triumph of the Cuban Revolution highlighted the poverty and oppression afflicting so many Latin Americans. Cuba's far-reaching educational, health, and land reforms impressed and radicalized many Catholics. Although left-leaning Catholic priests almost universally rejected violence, many accepted elements of Marxist political and economic analysis, while they identified with the plight of their underprivileged parishioners and helped organize and politicize peasants and slum dwellers.

Though always a minority within the church, leftist clergy had an important influence in Central America during the 1970s and 1980s, most notably in Nicaragua, El Salvador, and Guatemala. Many Nicaraguan priests and nuns supported the Marxist-leaning Sandinista Revolution in the 1970s. So, when the Sandinistas came to power, the president's cabinet contained four priests, more than any other government in Latin America.

For most of Latin America, however, the 1970s and 1980s were not years of revolution. Instead, much of the region came under the control of right-wing military dictatorships. Reacting to a perceived radical threat, repressive military regimes replaced civilian democracies in Argentina, Brazil, Chile, and Uruguay. At the same time, the rule of armed forces continued in much of Central America and the central Andes, where democratic traditions had never been strong. Ironically, right-wing repression spurred the growth of the progressive church more effectively than the Cuban or Nicaraguan revolutions had.

Many radical clergy and laity were outspoken in their criticism of the military regimes and, consequently, suffered severe reprisals. Dozens of priests and nuns were murdered and many more persecuted in countries such as Brazil, El Salvador, and Guatemala. In El Salvador, for example, a far-right death squad called the White Warriors distributed handbills stating, "Be a Patriot, Kill a Priest."[34] But such repression only radicalized many moderate Catholics. "When committed Catholics were imprisoned, tortured, and even killed, bishops in a significant number of cases then denounced the state, setting off a spiral of greater repression against the Church, followed by new Church denunciations of authoritarianism."[35]

In Chile, Brazil, El Salvador, and Peru, the church became a leading critic of government human rights violations. The most celebrated example was El Salvador's Archbishop Oscar Romero, its highest-ranking cleric, who had begun his tenure as a conservative. Increasingly appalled by the military's widespread human rights abuses, in 1980, he wrote President Carter asking him to terminate U.S. military aid to the ruling junta until human rights violations had ended. Later, he broadcast a sermon calling on Salvadorian soldiers to disobey orders to kill innocent civilians. "No soldier is obliged to obey an order against God's law," he declared. "In the name of God and in the name of this suffering people, I implore you, I beg you, and I order you—stop the repression."[36] The following day Romero was assassinated as he said a requiem mass, murdered by a death squad linked to the military. Pope Francis has recently started the first step in naming him a saint.

Like Romero, Latin America's progressive clergy have far more commonly been reformers rather than radicals. At times, their political rhetoric and analysis have found some common ground with the Left. For example, the progressive church shares the Marxists' indignation over the plight of the poor, and many of its clergy identified dependency and U.S. domination as root causes of Latin American underdevelopment. But almost all Catholic activists rejected revolutionary violence and the Leninist state as solutions. Reform, not revolution, was also the prescription of CELAM's bishops when they suggested progressive Catholic theology as an alternative to both capitalism and Marxism.

A number of the bishops' pronouncements originated with a radical Peruvian priest, Gustavo Gutiérrez, the father of "liberation theology." Writings by him and other liberation theologians influenced the progressive church in Latin America and other parts of the world. The Theology of Liberation calls on Catholic laity and clergy to become politically active and to direct that activity toward the emancipation of the poor. Drawing on Marxist analysis, Gutiérrez preached the notion of nonviolent class struggle. The poor, liberation theologians argued, should organize themselves into **Ecclesial (or Christian) Base Communities (CEBs)** where they can recognize the need to transform society through their own mobilization. CEBs spread through much of Latin America, most notably in Brazil along with Chile, Peru, and Central America.

Since the early 1980s, the influence of Latin America's progressive church has diminished considerably. One cause, ironically, was the region's transition from military dictatorships to democracy. Absent massive human rights violations and open assaults against the poor, Catholic clergy have generally been less motivated to enter the political arena. Furthermore, without a common foe, moderate and radical priests no longer have a common cause. And, many political activists who had used the church as a protective "umbrella" during the military dictatorships (since those regimes had been less likely to persecute church-affiliated radical groups) were now able to participate in politics through other political organizations.

Perhaps more importantly, for some thirty-five years (1978–2013), the Vatican under Popes John XXIII, Paul II, and Benedict XVI was quite unsympathetic to political activism among priests and nuns, particularly when related to the CEBs and liberation theology. But, although Pope Francis (2013) has not encouraged that theology itself, he has been a major force in promulgating many of its ideas and reviving the ideas of the progressive church as he passionately calls for the Catholic Church to be "the church of the poor."

THE FUTURE OF RELIGION AND POLITICS IN THE DEVELOPING WORLD

The hold of religion on the human heart and spirit, and its consequent impact on the political process, has been frequently misunderstood by Western observers. As we have seen, the initial error of both modernization and dependency theorists was to undervalue the significance of religion. Several factors account for the unanticipated resurgence of fundamentalism and other forms of religiously based politics in recent decades. In many countries, rapid modernization has left people psychologically adrift, searching for their cultural identity. The breakdown of village life and the erosion of traditional customs and values often create an emotional void not filled by the material rewards of modern life. In the Middle East, the indignities of colonialism and neocolonialism, resentment against Israel and the West, and dismay over decades of failed development since independence have all contributed to the region's religious revival. However, contrary to Western stereotypes, the appeal of Islamic fundamentalism is by no means limited to the poor and uneducated, who are less familiar with modern ideas and lifestyles. For example, most of the 9/11 terrorists had university educations and had lived outside the Muslim world. A biographical study of 173 jailed jihadists—from nearly a dozen countries—found that most were middle or upper class, most had received secular educations in primary and secondary schools, nearly two-thirds had at least some college or university education, and more than 40 percent were professionals (including physicians, architects, teachers, and preachers).[37] And many of the holy warriors operating in Europe and current volunteers for the IS have been young men, raised in the West, who feel like outcasts, isolated from both European lifestyles and their own culture.

Turning to Latin America, the progressive church offered a shield against political repression and a voice for the poor. As vastly different as they are, Islamic revivalism and the progressive Catholic Church have a few similarities. For example, both were grounded in revulsion over poverty and over government repression and corruption. Thus, the resurgence of religion often was linked to a yearning for social and political justice, even if that vision of justice is sometimes unpalatable to those outside the movement. Other religious movements, not discussed in this chapter, have different worldviews. For example, the most rapidly growing religious movement in Latin America today is Pentecostal and other Evangelical Christianity.* The number of Pentecostals and Charismatics in the region has exploded from under 13 million in 1970 to perhaps 170 million or more today, most of whom have left the Catholic Church.[38] Unlike progressive Catholics, these converts generally are conservative politically and in their lifestyles.

Having previously underestimated the impact of religion on Third World politics, analysts now risk overstating its importance. To begin with, the political weight of the movements that have attracted the most attention—Islamic revivalism and progressive Catholicism—must be put into perspective. Influential as they have been, they are not representative of the religions from which they have sprung. This point requires particular emphasis in relation to Islam, because a militant minority has left many Westerners with an extremely negative image of the entire Muslim world. They consider Islam to be backward and intolerant when, actually, like all religions, it encompasses a range of outlooks, some reactionary and some progressive. For example, the media sometimes suggest that all Muslim women are repressed and confined, yet there are many Islamic feminists and professional women in countries such as Egypt, Lebanon, and Malaysia. It is worth remembering that four Muslim nations—Bangladesh, Indonesia, Pakistan, and Turkey—have had female prime ministers or presidents, something the United States has yet to achieve (as of

---

*The Pew Center notes that "Pentecostals share many beliefs with other evangelical Protestants, but they put more emphasis on the 'gifts of the Holy Spirit,' such as speaking in tongues, faith healing and prophesying."

the writing of this book). Similarly, contrary to stereotype, some Muslim countries, including fundamentalist Saudi Arabia, are on good terms with the West. Lastly, when fundamentalist parties (Muslim or Hindu) have assumed power, no matter their original intentions, their behavior in office has often been moderated by their need for parliamentary coalition partners, their desire to appeal to a wide range of voters in future elections, and the dangers of offending powerful secular actors, such as the Turkish military.

When evaluating the current religious revival, we cannot assume that current trends will continue long into the future. History reveals that "religious resurgence is a cyclical phenomenon."[39] Consequently, Jeffrey Haynes argues that "there is no reason to doubt that the current wave of religion-oriented political ideas and movements will in time give way . . . to [a] partial resurrection of secular ideologies."[40] For the foreseeable future, however, religion will continue to be an important influence in the politics of many developing nations.

RELIGION AND DEMOCRACY

The relationship between institutionalized religions and democracy has been complex and varied. Traditionally, the leaders of influential religions have tended to ally with their country's political and economic elites, becoming pillars of the status quo. Haynes's explanation of why most local Christian religious leaders, from the 1960s through the 1980s, failed to speak out against Africa's authoritarian rulers applies equally well to other religions in the LDCs:

> Church and state developed mutually supportive relationships. . . . [Frequently] it was in . . . the interests of both Church and state for there to be social and political stability, even if it required authoritarian rule to achieve it.[41]

Speaking out against a dictator, at the very least, would cut off government financial support for the church and, at worst, would subject the clergy and perhaps their parishioners to persecution. Sometimes, church leaders actually held official positions in their ruling regimes. For example, for many years, the Catholic archbishop of Kigali (Rwanda's primary city) was a member of the central committee of the country's only legal party. The thirty-two-year-old dictator of Congo (Kinshasa), President Mobutu Sese Seko, gave Cardinal Malula a mansion to live in and subsequently gave a Mercedes to every Catholic and Protestant bishop in the country.[42] While there were also some prominent clergymen who demanded social justice and criticized government repression and corruption, it was not until the 1990s that the Congolese church became a prominent voice for democracy.

In Latin America and southern Europe, the Catholic Church hierarchy also had supported authoritarian regimes in years past. As we have noted, historically, Latin American churches had close links with the landholding elite (and were themselves major landowners). Europe's Catholic Church frequently supported right-wing, antidemocratic parties and movements as well. But, as we have seen, many organized religions became more progressive in the closing decades of the twentieth century, supporting democratization and greater social and economic justice. Indeed, the Latin American Catholic Church was a leading voice for democratic change during the Third Wave. The Philippine Church and its leader, Cardinal Jaime Sin, also lent critical support to Corazón Aquino's "people's power" movement, which brought democracy to that country. In South Korea, social movements led by several Protestant churches as well as the smaller Catholic Church also played an important role in the country's transition to democracy. Looking beyond these cases, two important questions come to mind regarding the relationship between religion and democracy. First, "Does liberal democracy require the separation of the church from a secular political system?" Second, "Are the cultural values of some religions more supportive than others of democracy?" In his classic work, *Democracy in America*, the French author Alexis de Tocqueville suggested that a linchpin of democracy in the United States was the separation of church and state.

> I learned with surprise that [the clergy] filled no public appointments . . . [and] I found that most of its members seemed to retire from their own accord from the exercise of power, and that they made it the pride of their profession to abstain from politics. . . . They saw that they must renounce their religious influence if they were to strive for political power.[43]

Today, many analysts still believe that maintaining the pluralist values and the tolerance underlying democracy requires limiting the influence of religion on politics. But others reject the notion that democracy can only exist under a strict separation of church and state. In their book, *Religion and Democracy*, David Marquand and Ronald Nettler insist,

> Even in the absence of a . . . bargain keeping church and state apart, religion and democracy can coexist. Communities of faith do not necessarily imperil the foundations of pluralist democracy by seeking to pursue essentially religious agendas through political action.[44]

But, they add, there is a necessary restriction if this intermingling of religious political action and democracy is to work. "A degree of mutual tolerance, or at least of mutual self-restraint, is indispensable. Religious groups have to accept the right of other religious groups—and . . . the right of the nonreligious—to abide by their own values."[45] Many countries and religions uphold this tolerance, but in some fundamentalist religions—Islamic or otherwise—it is absent.

Our second question has been the subject of intense debate—whether certain religious cultures are more supportive than others of democratic values. We saw in chapter 2 that empirical studies have shown that Protestant countries are significantly more likely to be democratic than are Catholic or Muslim nations. In contrast, Islamic nations have had a rather poor record of democracy, leading some scholars to conclude that Islam has authoritarian underpinnings. John Anderson looked at countries that have one predominant religion (i.e., countries where over 60 percent of the population nominally adheres to a single faith) and correlated them with their Freedom House ratings. The twenty-three Protestant countries ranked by Freedom House had the best average level of freedom. Catholic countries (fifty of them) ranked next, not far behind. The two Hindu countries (India and Nepal) followed, while the four predominantly Buddhist countries came next and thirty-nine Muslim nations had the lowest rate of democracy. But, as Anderson notes, this correlation may be spurious since it may be explained by other factors such as their level of socioeconomic development.[46]

One problem with such arguments is that, while they may have an element of truth, they fail to take into account differences within religions. Not all religious Catholics or priests, for example, have the same political values. Militant Islamic fundamentalist cultures that have flourished in Afghanistan and Sudan are surely unacceptable environments for democracy. Yet, most analysts agree that Islamic values can be quite compatible with democracy in a more moderate Muslim setting such as Indonesia or Malaysia. Indonesia, the largest Muslim country in the world, encompasses a range of Muslim believers, from Islamists (only a small portion of whom are active in terrorist groups) through very progressive clerics and laity.

Traditionally, Indonesians have practiced a more moderate form of Islam than is normally found in Middle Eastern or North African countries. The streets of its cities feature many unaccompanied women on motor scooters, and women have been free to choose whether or not they wished to wear the *hijab* (the Islamic headscarf), though in some areas pressure to wear it has mounted in recent years. Perhaps the country's most influential cleric during the country's democratic transition (in 1998) was Abdurrahman Wahid, then head of Indonesia's largest Muslim organization, the Nahdlatul Ulama (NU). While religiously conservative, the NU preached tolerance toward Indonesia's Christian and Hindu minorities and was an important actor in the campaign against the Suharto dictatorship. In Indonesia's first democratic presidential election (1999), Wahid was chosen by parliament to lead the country. In office, he continued to demonstrate the tolerance so essential to democracy. Criticizing the frequent local violence against Indonesia's Christian minority, he insisted that Christians were equal to Muslims in the eyes of God. Moreover, in a rather dramatic departure from most Islamic heads of state, he publicly and enthusiastically supported Zionism and one of his first presidential visits was to Israel.

Another important factor limiting generalizations about the compatibility of particular religions with democracy is that, like most institutions and value systems, religions change over time. At one time, there was solid empirical evidence that Protestant countries were most likely to sustain democracy and economic growth, while Catholic and Confucian nations were less supportive. Today, neither relationship (political or economic) seems to hold. Confucian East Asia and Catholic Southern Europe both achieved rapid economic growth in the second half of the twentieth century, faster growth than in many Protestant countries. And more recently, as democracy has spread to various Catholic and Confucian nations (including Spain, Portugal, Poland, Brazil, Mexico, Taiwan, and South Korea), the suggested linkage between religions and democratic norms has faded. This isn't to deny that some religions are more tolerant or more authoritarian than others. Rather, it does mean that we need to avoid sweeping generalizations and consider differences within religions as well as changes over time.

Practice and Review Online
http://textbooks.rowman.com/handelman8e#ch3

KEY TERMS

CEBs (Christian Base
   Communities)
Islamist
Jihad (Jihadist)
Koran
mujahideen
mullahs

neocolonialism
progressive church
revivalism
secularization
theocratic state
Theology of Liberation

DISCUSSION QUESTIONS

1. Why did early analysts of religion in the LDCs think that modernization would lead to a diminished political role for organized religion? Has this happened and, if not, why not?

2. What factors caused the growth of the progressive church in Latin America, and what is distinct about its followers' beliefs? Why has the progressive church lost so much of its influence in recent times?
3. What factors have led to the resurgence of Islamic fundamentalism (or revivalism) in Afghanistan, Iran, Syria, and other parts of the Muslim world? Why do you think so many people in that part of the world supported Islamism?
4. What are the major similarities and differences between the IS and al-Qaeda?

NOTES

1. Harvey G. Cox, *The Secular City* (New York: Collier Books, 1990).
2. Donald Eugene Smith, *Religion and Modernization* (New Haven, CT: Yale University Press, 1974), 4.
3. Quoted in Timothy D. Sisk, *Islam and Democracy* (Washington, DC: United States Institute of Peace, 1992), 3.
4. Abdel-Bari Atwan, *Islamic State: The Digital Caliphate* (London: Saqi, 2015).
5. Kenneth D. Wald, "Social Change and Political Response: The Silent Religious Cleavage in North America," in *Politics and Religion in the Modern World*, ed. George Moyser (New York: Routledge and Kegan Paul, 1991), 240.
6. One of the most influential and controversial books using the framework of these allegedly clashing, religiously based cultures is Samuel P. Huntington, *The Clash of Civilizations and the Remaking of World Order* (New York: Simon & Schuster, 1996).
7. Latif Abul-Husn, *The Lebanese Conflict: Looking Inward* (Boulder, CO: Lynne Rienner Publishers, 1998), 35.
8. Donald Eugene Smith, *Religion and Political Development* (Boston: Little, Brown, 1970), xi, italics added.
9. Ibid., 70.
10. John L. Esposito, *Islam and Politics*, 2nd ed. (Syracuse, NY: Syracuse University Press, 1987), 1.
11. Fred Halliday, *Islam and the Myth of Confrontation: Religion and Politics in the Middle East* (London: I. B. Tauris Publishers, 1996), 233, fn. 1.
12. John L. Esposito and John O. Voll, "Islam and Democracy," *Humanities* (November/December 2001).
13. Halliday, *Islam and the Myth of Confrontation*, 107.
14. Dilip Hiro, *Holy Wars: The Rise of Islamic Fundamentalism* (New York: Routledge and Kegan Paul, 1989), 1–2.
15. Mohammed Ayoob, *The Many Faces of Islam: Religion and Politics in the Muslim World* (Ann Arbor: The University of Michigan Press, 2008), 2.
16. Ahmed Rashid, "Jihadi Suicide Bombers: The New Wave," *The New York Review of Books* 55, no. 10 (June 10, 2008), http://www.nybooks.com/articles/21473; For similar assessments, see Omar Nasiri, *Inside the Jihad: My Life with Al Qaeda, A Spy's Story* (New York: Basic Books, 2006).

17. Quoted in Mats Wärn, *Staying the Course: the "Lebanonization" of Hizbullah* (online).

18. See Robert D. Lee, *Religion and Politics in the Middle East* (Boulder, CO: Westview Press, 2010); Peter Mandaville, *Islam and Politics* (New York: Routledge, 2014).

19. Brian R. Farmer, *Understanding Radical Islam* (New York: Peter Lang, 2007), 115.

20. Useful sources on the origins and course of the revolution include Robin Wright, *The Last Great Revolution: Turmoil and Transformation in Iran* (New York: Vintage Books, 2001); Hiro, *Holy Wars*, chap. 6.

21. Cheryl Bernard and Zalmay Khalilzad, *The Government of God: Iran's Islamic Republic* (New York: Columbia University Press, 1984), 12–13.

22. Wright, *In the Name of God*, 65.

23. Ibid., 87.

24. Gary Sick, "Trial by Error: Reflections on the Iran-Iraq War," in *Iran's Revolution*, ed. R. K. Ramazani (Bloomington, IN: Indiana University Press, 1990), 105.

25. Rohan Gunaratna, *Inside Al Qaeda: Global Network of Terror* (New York: Columbia University Press, 2002), 18–19.

26. Burke, "Think Again: Al Qaeda," *Foreign Policy*, May/June 2004.

27. Pew Research Center, "Osama bin Laden Largely Discredited among Muslim Publics in Recent Years," May 2, 2011.

28. Rashid, "Jihadi Suicide Bombers."

29. Michael Weiss and Hassan Hassan, *ISIS: Inside the Army of Terror* (New York: Regan Arts, 2015).

30. Pew Center for Research, Religion and Public Life, *The Future of the Global Muslim Population, Region: Europe* (January 27, 2011). The 2015 data I present are extrapolated from the Pew Center's 2011 data.

31. Alison Pargeter, *The Frontiers of Jihad: Radical Islam in Europe* (Philadelphia, PA: University of Pennsylvania Press, 2008), viii.

32. Paul Sigmund, *Liberation Theology at the Crossroads* (New York: Oxford University Press, 1990), 19.

33. Ibid., 29–30.

34. Jennifer Pearce, "Politics and Religion in Central America: A Case Study of El Salvador," in *Politics and Religion in the Modern World*, 234.

35. Scott Mainwaring and Alexander Wilde, eds., *The Progressive Church in Latin America* (Notre Dame, IN: University of Notre Dame Press, 1989), 13.

36. Philip Berryman, "El Salvador: From Evangelization to Insurrection," in *Religion and Political Conflict in Latin America*, ed. Daniel H. Levine (Chapel Hill, NC: University of North Carolina Press, 1986), 58–78, 114.

37. Marc Sageman, *Understanding Terror Networks* (Philadelphia, PA: University of Pennsylvania Press, 2004), 74–78.

38. The Pew Forum on Religion and Public Life: Surveys (July 7, 2007); The Pew Research Center, "Why has Pentecostalism grown so dramatically in Latin America?" (November 14, 2014).

39. Donald Eugene Smith, "The Limits of Religious Resurgence," in *Religious Resurgence and Politics in the Contemporary World*, ed. Emile Sahliyah (Albany, NY: State University of New York Press, 1990), 34.

40. Jeff Haynes, *Religion in Third World Politics* (Boulder, CO: Lynne Rienner Publishers, 1994), 155.

41. Jeff Haynes, "Religion and Democratization in Africa," in *Religion, Democracy and Democratization*, ed. John Anderson (New York: Routledge, 2006), 68.

42. Ibid., 69.

43. Alexis de Tocqueville, *Democracy in America*, ed. Alan Ryan (London: Everyman's Library, 1994), 309–12.

44. David Marquand and Ronald L. Nettler, "Forward," in *Religion and Democracy*, eds. David Marquand and Ronald L. Nettler (Oxford, England: Blackwell Publishers, 2000), 2–3.

45. Ibid., 3.

46. John Anderson, "Does God Matter, and If So Whose God? Religion and Democratization," in *Religion, Democracy and Democratization*, 204–05.

4

The Politics of
Cultural Pluralism
and Ethnic Conflict

★ ★ ★

Myanmar (Burma)—Buddhist vigilantes, armed with sticks: While Buddhism is perhaps the most nonviolent of the major world religions, Burmese Buddhist priests recently led violent attacks against the country's Muslim minority, killing several hundred people and forcing hundreds of thousands more to flee. *AP/Gemunu Amarasinghe*

FOR MANY YEARS, much of the developing world has suffered from ethnic, racial, and religious clashes periodically punctuated by outbreaks of brutality and carnage. Progress in one location has repeatedly been followed by deterioration in another. Today, the Middle East is devastated by intense hostility and ongoing warfare between the two main branches of the Muslim religion. And in some cases, that conflict has taken on international ramifications.

Since the overthrow of Iraqi dictator, Saddam Hussein, by American and allied forces, that country's fate has been largely defined by the bloody clashes between the Shi'a majority and Sunni minority. Similarly, the uprising against Syrian dictator Bashar al-Assad and the ensuing civil war have centered on hostilities between the Alawite (a Shi'ite sect) Assad regime and the Sunni-dominated opposition. And in Yemen, the Arab World's poorest country and the last to participate in the Arab Spring, the overthrow of President Ali Abdullah Saleh (who ruled from 1990 to 2012) led to civil war as well. This battle has pitted the country's rebel-Shi'a minority (called Houthis) against the national government as well as the al-Qaeda rebels (both Sunni).

These conflicts have been aggravated by the intervention of the Middle East's richest Sunni nation (Saudi Arabia) and the dominant Shi'a power (Iran). Most prominently, Yemen's civil war has been turned into a "proxy war" between Iran, which is arming the Houthis, and Saudi Arabia, which has been bombing Houthi-controlled areas mercilessly. In Iraq, the Shi'a-led government has invited in Iranian troops to train Shi'a militias in the fight against the IS. And in Syria, President Assad's government has been supported by aid from Iran and by the entry into the war of several thousand Hezbollah (Shi'a) troops from Lebanon.

Appalling ethnic confrontations are not new. A century ago (1915–1917), in the midst of World War I, Turkey's embattled Ottoman government launched a genocidal campaign against the country's Christian, Armenian population that left perhaps 1–1.5 million dead. Some thirty years later, as Britain relinquished power over India, it divided its former "jewel in the [imperial] crown," into two nations—largely Hindu India and mostly Muslim Pakistan. But the religious communities in each country then savagely turned on each other, with a resulting death toll of approximately 1 million. Millions of Hindu and Sikh refugees fled Pakistan to India, while millions of Muslims fled India to Pakistan. More recently, Hutus in the African nation of Rwanda massacred some 800,000 of their Tutsi countrymen. During the twentieth century, religious clashes (e.g., in India, Iraq, and Lebanon), tribal animosities (e.g., Nigeria and Rwanda), racial prejudice (e.g., in South Africa), and other forms of ethnic rancor frequently produced violent riots, civil wars, and genocidal brutality. Continuing ethnic clashes and tensions in the early years of the

twenty-first century—for example, in the South Sudan and Burma—
seem to confirm the prediction—that wars between "peoples" (ethnic,
religious, racial, or cultural groups) will continue to far outnumber wars
between nation-states.

> Classic accounts of modernization, particularly those influenced by
> Marx, predicted that the old basis for divisions, such as **tribe** and
> religion, would be swept aside. As hundreds of millions of people
> poured from rural to urban areas worldwide, during the nineteenth
> and twentieth centuries, it was expected that new alliances would be
> formed, based on social class in particular.[1]

But, significant as class conflict has been, no cleavage in modern times
has more sharply and oftentimes violently polarized nations than has
ethnicity. "**Cultural pluralism** [i.e., ethnic diversity]," notes Crawford
Young, "is a quintessentially modern phenomenon." It has been closely
linked to the growth of the middle class and the emergence of politicians
who articulated nationalist or other ethnic aspirations while mobilizing
workers and peasants behind that ideal.[2] Scholars point out that hostility
toward other ethnic groups is far older and often more entrenched than
modern principles of tolerance or equality under the law. "No matter
how we may wish for it otherwise, we did not leave violence against outsiders behind us as our nations became modern and democratic."[3] To be
sure, ethnic minorities have been victimized for hundreds of years. So,
such struggles are not new. One need only look to the nineteenth-century
frontier wars between White settlers and Native Americans in the United
States and Chile.

Still, the level of ethnically based *internal* conflict has grown since
the 1980s, in marked contrast to the dramatic decline in wars *between*
nations in the same period. Indeed, the most frequent settings for violent
confrontation over the past fifty years have not been wars between sovereign states, but rather internal strife tied to cultural, tribal, religious,
or other ethnic animosities. Between 1989 and 2004, there were 118
military conflicts in the world. Of those, only seven were between nation-
states and the remaining 111 occurred within a single state, a large portion of which involved ethnic conflict.[4] According to another recent
estimate, "nearly two-thirds of all [the world's] armed conflicts [at that
time] included an ethnic component. [In fact], ethnic conflicts [were] four
times more likely than interstate wars."[5] Another study claimed that 80
percent of "major conflicts" in the 1990s had an ethnic element.[6]

Any contemporary listing of the world's most bloody wars would
include ethnically based **internal warfare** or massacres in Syria, Rwanda,
Congo (Kinshasa), Ethiopia, Sudan, Lebanon, Sri Lanka, and Indonesia.
Between 1945 and 1998, an estimated fifteen million people died

worldwide as a result of ethnic violence (much of that total from war-related starvation and disease).[7] In the years since then, ethnic battles in Congo (Kinshasa) alone have resulted in some five million additional deaths, while many thousands more have died in Sudan, Ethiopia, Iraq, Syria, and elsewhere.

Warfare between Serbs, Croats, Bosnian Muslims, and Kosovars in the former Yugoslavia, along with separatist movements by French-speaking Québécois, racially based riots in Los Angeles, Basque terrorism in Spain, and Protestant-Catholic clashes in Northern Ireland, all demonstrate that ethnic friction and violence can erupt in developed countries. But such battles have been particularly widespread and cruel in Africa, Asia, Arab States, and other regions of the developing world—in part because LDCs tend to be more ethnically diverse and in part because their political systems frequently lack the institutions or experience needed to resolve such tensions peacefully. One study determined that at the start of this century there were approximately 275 "minorities at risk" in the world (i.e., ethnic groups facing actual or potential repression), with a total population exceeding one billion people (about one-sixth of the world's populations at that time) scattered in 116 countries. Approximately 85 percent of the at-risk population lived in the LDCs. Although Asia has the highest *absolute* population of such minorities, Sub-Saharan Africa has the highest *proportion* of its population at risk (about 36 percent), followed by the Arab World (26 percent).[8]

The intensification of ethnic, racial, and cultural hostilities during the twentieth and twenty-first centuries undercut several assumptions of modernization theory; it also contradicted an influential social psychology theory called the "contact hypothesis." Its hypothesis predicted that as people of different races, religions, and ethnicities came into greater contact with each other, they would better understand the other groups' common human qualities, causing prejudice to decline. Although the contact hypothesis frequently describes *individual*-level attitudes and behavior (i.e., as individuals of different races or religions come to know each other better, their prejudices tend to diminish), increased interaction between different ethnic *groups*—occasioned by factors such as migration—often *intensifies* hostilities. Moreover, in some cases such as Rwanda and Bosnia, despite years of close interethnic contact and intermarriage, neighbors and even relatives by marriage viciously turned against each other once group violence had taken on a momentum of its own. This is particularly true when the political and economic systems are biased in favor of one ethnic group or when ethnic leaders play on their followers' prejudices to advance their own political agendas.

Neighboring ethnicities that lived peacefully side by side for decades may also confront each other when new, valuable natural resources are discovered on their common lands. Thus, for example, in Nigeria, the upsurge of oil production in the Niger Delta sparked unrest by tribal minorities in the region, who perceived that great wealth was being extracted from the delta while the local population was left in poverty. Similar ethnic violence has arisen in the neighboring country of Niger after the discovery of substantial uranium deposits.

This chapter focuses on the most protracted and intense ethnic group conflicts in the developing world. In doing so, it runs the risk of conveying the erroneous impression that all LDCs are aflame with violent ethnic clashes. In truth, most ethnic tensions do *not* lead to violence and many developing nations have been comparatively free of such conflict. Ethnic warfare is most pronounced in the Indian subcontinent, the Middle East, Southeast Asia, and much of Africa. It is less common in Latin America and the Far East. A number of developing countries—Uruguay and Korea, for example—are fairly ethnically homogeneous, eliminating the possibility of such struggle. Others have developed a fairly stable, if not necessarily just, relationship between ethnicities, including Ghana and Taiwan. A number of Latin American countries are multiracial and have varying degrees of racial discrimination and tension. But rarely do those conflicts now become violent. So, although this chapter focuses on the most difficult and vicious cases in order to illustrate the obstacles that ethnic confrontations may present to political and economic development, it *does not* imply that most LDCs are riddled with ethnic violence.

DEFINING ETHNICITY

Many scholars have maintained that human beings have a deeply rooted social and psychological need to identify with a group that protects them from outsiders and gives them a sense of belonging (i.e., to create an "us" to protect ourselves from "them"). Although it is challenging to define ethnicity precisely, certain common qualities set ethnic groups apart. Most analysts agree that ethnic identity is usually a *social construction*—a way that certain groups have come to view themselves over time as distinct from others—rather than an inherent or primordial characteristic. Each ethnicity "share[s] a distinctive and enduring collective identity based on a belief in a common descent and on shared experiences and cultural traits."[9] While they frequently have some basis in fact, these identities and histories are typically created or embellished by entrepreneurial politicians, intellectuals, and journalists who gain some advantage by "playing the ethnic card." The real or imagined common history, tradition, and values not only unite the group, but also distinguish it from neighboring ethnicities, sometimes giving rise to ethnic conflict. Thus, J. E. Brown's cynical definition of a "nation" can be applied to ethnic identities generally: "A group of people united by a common error about their ancestry and a common dislike of their neighbors."[10] In times of great uncertainty or crisis, intellectuals and politicians are likely to create historical myths that give their ethnic group a sense of security in the face of perceived external challenges. In the words of Vesna Pesic, a Serbian peace activist, ethnic conflict is caused by the "fear of the future, lived through the past."[11]

Chinese in Malaysia, Hmong in Laos, and indigenous peoples (Indians) in Peru often form their own political organizations or business groups. However, ethnic groups are usually not socially homogeneous or politically united. Frequently, class, ideology, or religion divides them. For example, Indian Muslims and Nigerian Ibos are internally divided by class. South Koreans may be Buddhist or Christian (or both). Still, the factors that bind these ethnic groups are more powerful than elements that divide them. Thus, Ibo peasants normally identify more closely with businesspeople from their own ethnicity than they do with fellow peasants from the Hausa or Yoruba communities. Indeed, Cynthia Enloe notes that "of all the groups that men [or women] attach themselves to, ethnic groups seem the most encompassing and enduring."[12]

Often, outside observers erroneously assert or assume that certain contemporary ethnic identities and ethnic clashes are deeply rooted in history. For example, during the bitter civil war between Bosnian Muslims and Serbs (in the former Yugoslavia), many Western journalists and political leaders claimed that violence could be traced to centuries-old religious tensions and conflicts (dating to the Middle Ages) between Orthodox (Christian) Serbians, Muslim Bosnians, and Catholic Croatians. But actually, prior to the breakup of Yugoslavia in the early 1990s, the three groups had lived together in harmony for many years, and intermarriages were somewhat common. "In the 1970s, ethnicity played a minor and, compared to earlier realities, diminishing part [in Bosnian life]. The vast majority of Bosnians . . . were up to the 1990s determined to keep the significance of the ethnic factor to a minimum." Only after nationalist politicians [particularly Serbs] used ethnic appeals to replace the previous influence of Communism were people forced to choose an ethnic identification.

Some ethnic classifications were initially imposed by outsiders. The classification of "**Colored**," once used to denote racially mixed or Asian South Africans, was an artificial construct established by the White regime. And although Mexicans feel little in common with Cubans, Ecuadorians, or Nicaraguans when they live in their home countries, all of these nationalities have become an ethnic group called "Latinos" or "Hispanics" after they immigrated to the United States—viewed as a homogeneous mass by their "Anglo" neighbors. Once individuals begin to accept the group label imposed on them, however, even artificially created ethnic classifications become politically relevant.

Ethnic groups may have their own social clubs, soccer teams, schools, or cemeteries. For an insecure Peruvian Indian recently arrived in Lima from her rural village, or a Hausa migrant seeking a job in Lagos, ethnically based social clubs are invaluable for finding employment, housing, and friendships in an otherwise cold and inhospitable city. In the threatening environment associated with modernization and social change, "fear, anxiety, and insecurity at the individual level can be reduced within the womb of the ethnic collectivity."[13] At the same time, however, ethnic consciousness normally creates barriers *between* groups. Relatives, friends, and neighbors tend to frown upon interreligious or interracial marriages, for example. Usually, when two or more ethnic groups live in close proximity to each other, there will be some tension or apprehension. But the way in which society handles these relationships varies considerably from place to place. Countries such as Canada, Malaysia, and Trinidad and Tobago have managed ethnic divisions fairly amicably and peacefully. More frequently, however, ethnic divisions lead to tensions or even conflict. In multiethnic countries such as Angola, Indonesia, and the United States, a common consciousness and culture unite certain religions, castes, tribes, or races, while generating distrust or even hostility toward other ethnicities.

ETHNIC AND STATE BOUNDARIES

If the world were composed of fairly homogeneous countries such as South Korea or Iceland, ethnically based wars might continue between nation-states, but there would be no ethnic tensions or strife *within* individual countries. In other words, the underlying cause of most internal ethnic conflict is that boundaries for *nations*—distinct cultural-linguistic groups such as Kurds, Ibo (Igbo), or Palestinians—and other ethnicities frequently fail to coincide fully with boundaries for *states* (self-governing countries). Indeed, the world's nearly two hundred countries are home to approximately five thousand ethnic groups, most of whom do not have their own nation-state and some of whom seek that goal. For example, Sikh militants in the Indian state of Punjab have demanded the creation of a Sikh nation-state. Iraqi Kurds have had similar aspirations. When ethnic groups feel that they have been denied their fair share of political and economic rewards, they will frequently mobilize to demand their rights.

At least 80 percent of the world's countries today contain two or more ethnic groups. Furthermore, in at least one-third of the world's countries, no single ethnic group accounts for even half of the total population. This pattern is most striking in Sub-Saharan Africa, where nearly every country is composed of several ethnic (tribal) groups. For example, it is estimated that Nigeria, the most populous African state, has more than two hundred linguistic (tribal) groups.

Many Africans attribute their continent's legacy of tribal conflict to the European colonizers who divided the region into administrative units little connected with ethnic identities. In some cases, antagonistic groups were thrown together into a single colony, while elsewhere individual ethnic groups were split between two future countries. In Africa, Asia, and the Middle East, colonial powers regularly exacerbated ethnic tensions by favoring certain groups over others and by using "divide and conquer" strategies to control the local population. Yet colonialism was but one of many factors contributing to ethnic discord. Given the thousands of tribal groups in Africa, even if the European powers had shown greater ethnic sensibility, it would be impossible to have created that many viable states.

At the same time, however, the *breakdown* of European colonialism also led to a number of extremely unhappy ethnic marriages. When the Portuguese withdrew from the small Southeast Asian colony of East Timor in 1975, neighboring Indonesia annexed it against the local population's will. In its efforts to crush the organized Timorese opposition, the Indonesian military killed or starved approximately 150,000 people (about 25 percent of the region's population). Elsewhere, following years of Italian colonial rule and a brief British occupation, the East African colony of Eritrea was forcibly merged with Ethiopia in the early 1950s. The Eritrean people (who have different religions and cultures than the Ethiopians) resented the Ethiopian takeover and soon embarked on a long struggle for independence. Three decades of civil war resulted in thousands of deaths. The collapse of the Ethiopian military dictatorship in 1991 allowed Eritrea to finally achieve independence. But the two countries fought a bloody border war during 1998–2000 and relations between them remain tense.

TYPES OF ETHNIC AND CULTURAL DIVISIONS

In order to better grasp the range of ethnic tensions that currently pervade much of the developing world, I will classify all types of ethnicities into a set of somewhat overlapping categories: **nationality**, tribe, race, and religion.

Nationality

In ethnic analysis, the term *nation* has a specialized meaning distinct from its more common usage designating a sovereign country (as in the

United *Nations*). It refers, instead, to a population with its own language, cultural traditions, historical aspirations, and, sometimes, its own geographical home. Frequently, nationhood is associated with the belief that the interests and values of that nation supersede any competing interests.

Unlike other types of ethnic groups, nationalities usually claim sovereignty over a specific geographic area. But, as we have seen, these proposed *national* boundaries frequently do not coincide with those of *sovereign states* (independent countries). For example, India and Sri Lanka are both sovereign states that encompass several distinct *nationalities* (cultural identities). In each case, members of at least one of those nationalities—Muslim Kashmiris (India) and mostly Hindu Tamils (Sri Lanka)—have waged long struggles for independence. On the other hand, the Chinese are a nationality that, through migration, has spilled over to several East Asian countries and to other parts of the world. The approximately thirty million Kurds are one of the largest ethnic groups in the Middle East, residing primarily in Turkey, Iraq, and Iran. Unlike the Chinese, however, so far they have been a nation without a state of their own.

As with other types of ethnicity, the political significance of national identity is related to a number of subjective factors. Nationality becomes politically important only when its members believe that their common history and destiny greatly distinguish them from other ethnicities in their country. The most critical basis for national identification is the preservation of a distinct spoken language. Because French Canadians, Turkish Kurds, and Malaysian Chinese have maintained their "mother tongues," their national identities remain politically relevant. Chinese speakers in Southeast Asia have maintained their own cultural and political organizations and feel strong emotional ties to China. On the other hand, because most immigrants—including Chinese, Italians, and Germans—to countries such as the United States, Canada, and Australia have largely assimilated into their new language and culture, usually dropping their language of origin after one or two generations, their original national identity loses much of its political and social impact.

When multilingual countries throughout Africa and Asia gained their independence from the 1940s through the 1970s, they needed to choose which language or languages would be their official state language. In some of these countries—such as, Cameroon, India, Indonesia and Nigeria—hundreds of different languages are spoken. As we will see in Sri Lanka, the choice of the official language(s) or a change in the official language is often very contentious and may become the source of the intense ethnic conflict. This is particularly true if the government chooses the language of the political-economic elite rather than the most widely spoken tongue. One way that many multilingual countries have tried to avoid such conflict is to pick a language that is not native to any of the language groups, but is widely known across ethnic groups, as a means of interethnic communication (a lingua franca). Frequently, the choice is the language of the former colonial power (such as English or French).[14] In other cases, it is a language or dialect that is used for commercial purposes (such as Tagalog in the Philippines or Swahili in Kenya and Tanzania).

In their more limited manifestations, nationalist movements simply seek to preserve the group's cultural identity and promote its economic and political interests. For example, the large Lebanese community in Brazil, East Indians in Guyana, and Irish-Americans in the United States take pride in their distinctive cultures, but none has entertained visions of self-governance. On the other hand, nationalist movements become more provocative when they seek to create a separate nation-state of their own. Such separatist movements can arise when an ethnic minority is concentrated in a particular region of the country and represents a majority of the population in that area. Those conditions exist in Sri Lanka, where the Tamil-speaking population is concentrated in the country's northern and eastern provinces, particularly the Jaffna Peninsula region in the far north. Even before the intrusion of European colonizers, the Tamils kept themselves apart from other ethnicities inhabiting Ceylon. The British conquest and colonization of the entire island produced a nationalist reaction among the majority Sinhalese (Sinhala-speaking) population, which, in turn, provoked friction between them and the Tamil minority.

Since independence in 1948, political power has been concentrated in the hands of the Sinhalese (who constitute about three-fourths of the country's population). As in most nationality-based ethnic clashes, language issues were at the heart of the conflict. Eight years after independence, Sinhala replaced English as the country's official language, giving the Sinhalese population a significant advantage in securing government jobs. As one Tamil political leader put it, "Not until 1956 did we really believe that we were second-class citizens. Until then all we engaged in were preventive measures, which we thought would hold."[15] From that point forward, however, the battle for Tamil self-rule intensified. Conversely, when Tamil acquired equal legal status in 1978, many Sinhalese felt victimized. Religious differences between the largely Hindu Tamils and the predominantly Buddhist Sinhalese augmented their language and cultural divisions, though religious issues remained secondary.

Since independence (1949), Tamil leaders (representing almost one-fifth of the population) have demanded a federal system that would grant their regions substantial autonomy (some degree of self-rule) within Sri Lanka. Sinhalese nationalists, in turn, tried to impose their language on the entire nation. In 1958, Sinhalese mobs attacked Tamils in various parts of the country, and in 1964, the central government signed an agreement with India calling for the eventual return to India of 525,000 Tamils whose families had migrated from that country. Faced with these threats, Tamil nationalism became increasingly strident and violent. Early calls for autonomy were superseded by demands for secession and the creation of a sovereign Tamil state. By the early 1980s, the most powerful political force in the country's predominantly Tamil areas was the Liberation Tigers of Tamil Eelam (also known as the Tamil Tigers or the LTTE), a secessionist force engaged in guerrilla warfare, terrorism, and, ultimately, conventional war.

In 1987, following a major national government offensive against the LTTE, India (concerned about demands for autonomy from its own Tamil minority) intervened militarily in Sri Lanka. The resulting Indo-Lanka Peace Accord called for a multiethnic, multilingual Sri Lankan state with increased regional autonomy for the Tamil areas. Though signed by the Indian and Sri Lankan governments, the accord was rejected by many Sinhalese, particularly the ultranationalist National Liberation Front (JVP). From 1987 to 1989, the JVP launched its own campaign of strikes, boycotts, and terrorism, resulting in thousands of deaths. A brutal government campaign eventually crushed the JVP, but the war against the Tamil Tigers continued. Although many Tamils welcomed the Indo-Lanka accord, the Tigers rejected it as inadequate. Instead, they expanded their guerrilla war, first against India's sixty-thousand-man occupation force and then, after the 1990 withdrawal of foreign troops, against the Sri Lankan government and moderate Tamils.

The Tamil Tigers were responsible for the 1993 assassination of the country's president and hundreds of suicide bombings. Human rights groups condemned the Tigers for using young girls as suicide bombers, who were more likely to get past police and army checkpoints with bombs strapped to their bodies. By 2000, about 62,000 people had been killed in the civil war, out of a total Sri Lankan population of only twenty-one million. Although a cease-fire temporarily halted the fighting, by 2005, the truce broke down as more militant factions of the Tamil Tigers emerged. Soon, the armed forces launched a major offensive against the LTTE stronghold in the Northeast, driving them into an increasingly smaller area. Thousands of civilians died and many more fled the region as the Tigers regularly used the local population as human shields, while the government shelled and bombed the enclave with little concern for civilian lives.* In May 2009, the rebels were

---

*In a 2011 report, the United Nations accused the Sri Lankan military of having massacred some forty thousand Tamil civilians in the closing stages of the war. The military allegedly invited many of these civilians into supposedly "safe zones" and then shelled the zones.

forced to abandon their twenty-five-year struggle. With the war's end, up to 300,000 Tamil civilians, who fled the war zone, were held for months (or, in some cases, for years) in "displacement camps," often in deplorable conditions.

Tribe

The very use of the category *tribe*—especially when applied to African cultures—is quite controversial. Many anthropologists and political scientists find it arbitrary and unhelpful. Instead, they prefer the terms *ethnicity* or *ethnolinguistic group*. This chapter, however, still refers to *tribes* or *tribal groups* because this term is familiar to most readers and has long been used by many scholars of ethnic politics and by numerous political leaders in Africa and Asia. It describes *sub*national groups that share a collective identity and language and believe themselves to hold a common lineage.

Tribal conflict has frequently sparked violence in Sub-Saharan Africa, affecting more than half the countries in that region at one time or another. Ethiopia, Rwanda, Burundi, Uganda, Sudan, Congo (Kinshasa), and the Central African Republic, among others, have been torn apart by civil wars that were primarily or partially ethnically based. In Liberia, Angola, and Mozambique, conflicts begun about other issues were aggravated by tribal divisions.

From the time of its independence, Nigeria experienced enmity between the Muslims in the north and the populations of the south and east. With approximately half the country's population, the Hausa-Fulani (primarily Muslim) and other northern tribes were a dominant political force, resented by southerners and easterners such as the Ibo (largely Christian), who considered themselves more advanced than northerners. Northerners, in turn, feared the influence of the more modern and commercially successful Ibo people. Each of the three major ethnic groups (Hausa-Fulani, Ibo, and Yoruba) prevailed in one region of the country, casting a shadow over smaller tribes in their area. Each major group, in turn, feared domination by the others. Two coups in 1966 intensified friction between military officers of differing ethnic backgrounds and sparked violence against the large number of Ibos who had migrated to the North. As many as thirty thousand Ibos were killed, while one to two million more, fearing for their lives, fled back to their homeland. In May 1967, Colonel Chukwuemeka Ojukwu, an Ibo military leader, declared that eastern Nigeria was withdrawing from the country to become the independent nation of Biafra. But the Nigerian national government was determined to prevent the secession and was able to cut off food deliveries to the area. As many as one million Ibo civilians died of starvation before the war ended in 1970. Since that time, the Ibos have been successfully reintegrated into Nigerian society, but intertribal tensions and periodic religious violence between Christians and Muslims persist.

Unfortunately, these events were followed by a large number of ethnically based civil wars that have plagued the African continent since that time. Some of the most intense and prolonged tribal conflicts took place in the former Belgian colonies of Burundi and Rwanda in the Great Lakes region of central Africa. Since they gained power in the early 1970s, Burundi's ruling Tutsi minority has crushed a series of uprisings by the Hutus—who constitute about 85 percent of the population—massacring some 100,000 people in 1972 alone. In 1993, when a Tutsi soldier assassinated the country's first freely elected president, a Hutu, new bloodshed erupted. One year later, in the neighboring country of Rwanda, a Hutu president's death in a plane crash set off an orgy of violence. A government-directed massacre led by Hutu extremists was aimed at the minority Tutsis and, to a lesser extent, at moderate Hutus. During the next hundred days, local Hutu militia and allied villagers hacked or beat to death approximately 750,000 Tutsis and 50,000 Hutus. Eventually, a well-trained Tutsi revolutionary army, supported by neighboring Uganda, gained control of the country and jailed thousands of Hutus. An additional several hundred thousand fled to nearby Congo (Kinshasa), where many of them starved to death or were massacred by the anti-Hutu regime of then-President Laurent Kabila.

In other conflicts, such as the Angolan and Mozambican civil wars (which had both ideological and ethnic origins), major world powers supported one side or the other, thereby intensifying the struggles and adding to the bloodshed. For example, acting in consort with the Soviet Union, Cuba provided military assistance to the leftist governments of Ethiopia, Angola, and Mozambique. The United States covertly armed UNITA, the Angolan rebel force, while the South African military supported Mozambique's RENAMO guerrillas. Belgium and France armed Rwanda's Hutu-led government prior to its genocidal attacks on the Tutsi population. In each of those countries, hundreds of thousands perished from warfare or starvation. The end of the Cold War has reduced such external intervention. But horrendous civil wars in countries such as Congo (Kinshasa), Sierra Leone, and the Central African Republic indicate that tribally based violence will likely continue in the region for some time. Moreover, the intervention of neighboring African countries in Congo (Kinshasa) added to the enormous loss of lives in that country's ethnically based civil war.

Race
We have noted that cultural identity involves a common set of values and customs and a shared sense of history and destiny. Race, while normally

the most visible of ethnic distinctions, is a more recent source of group identity. Only when people live in *multiracial* settings do individual racial groups use race to define themselves and distinguish themselves from "others." Indeed, Crawford Young indicates that "there was no common sense of being 'African,' 'European,' or 'Indian,' prior to the creation of multiracial communities by the population movements of the imperial age."[16]

South Africa was the most notorious example of race-based political conflict. From its colonization by the British until its 1994 transition to majority rule, the country was ruled by a White minority constituting only about 15 percent of the population. Meanwhile, Blacks, the majority population, were denied fundamental legal and economic rights, including the right to vote or hold political office. Until the government renounced it in 1991, the legal centerpiece of South African racial policy was *apartheid* (separateness). This system rigidly segregated employment, public facilities, housing, marriage, and more, envisioning a day when most Blacks lived in eight allegedly self-ruling "homelands." In fact, these homelands, consisting of desolate rural territories, could not possibly support the country's Black population. Moreover, because important sectors of the South African economy, most notably its mines, were dependent on Black labor, the geographical segregation envisioned by apartheid was implausible even from the perspective of the White business community. Meanwhile, Blacks were denied fundamental civil liberties, including the right to own property.

Apartheid officially created racial classifications for the entire population that defied international standards and frequently fell victim to its own logical contradictions. *Blacks*, by far the largest racial group, constituted 70–75 percent of the national population and were subjected to the greatest amount of legal discrimination. *Coloreds*—mostly people of mixed race—totaled about 10 percent of the population, primarily concentrated in Cape Town and Cape Province. Asians (mostly Indians and Pakistanis) represented another 3 percent. Both Coloreds and Asians enjoyed a higher socioeconomic status and greater legal and political rights than Blacks did, but still ranked considerably below Whites. Finally, *Whites* (some 15 percent) dominated the political and economic systems.

Despite international disapproval, South Africa's minority government was determined to maintain apartheid indefinitely. In time, however, the country came under intense domestic and international pressure to end White domination. South Africa became an international outcast—particularly after several massacres of peaceful Black protesters—subject to diplomatic, economic, and cultural isolation. Though slow to take effect, these sanctions eventually impaired the country's economic growth. Growing protest and unrest in the Black townships (outlying urban slums) added to the country's international isolation. Finally, a growing number of powerful voices within the White economic, legal, and intellectual elites pressed the government for racial reform.

By the start of the 1990s, President F. W. de Klerk's government, recognizing that apartheid was no longer viable, legalized the African National Congress (ANC), the leading Black opposition group, after decades of banishment. The ANC's legendary leader, Nelson Mandela, the world's most celebrated political prisoner, was released from jail (after twenty-seven years of imprisonment) along with hundreds of other political prisoners. These changes, coupled with the ANC's suspension of its armed struggle, opened the door to a new constitution enfranchising the Black majority and ending White minority rule.

In December 1991, the Convention for a Democratic South Africa (CODESA) brought together the government, the ANC, and seventeen smaller groups for discussions of the new political order. In a 1992 national referendum called by de Klerk, nearly 70 percent of all White voters endorsed negotiations with the ANC and other Black groups. The following year, the government and the ANC agreed to the election of a constitutional assembly that would create a new political system with equal rights for all South Africans. Universal suffrage ensured an ANC parliamentary majority and in 1994 that body elected Nelson Mandela president of the new, majority-ruled South Africa.

In the years since that time, South Africa has established itself as one of the most democratic nations on the continent. However, significant challenges to democratic consolidation remain. Blacks have discovered that although majority rule has established greater social justice and human dignity, many of them remain mired in poverty. To be sure, government housing programs have benefited numerous urban slum dwellers and the Black middle class has swelled. On the other hand, with most farmland still owned by Whites and limited funds available for schools and clinics in the countryside, the Black rural population remains impoverished. Faced with high unemployment, high crime rates, and one of the world's greatest incidences of AIDS, the urban poor also continue to struggle. Until now, at least, the government has pursued moderate economic policies to reassure the White business community. These policies have brought economic growth but have been slow to alleviate poverty. The ANC remains popular and still dominates all national elections. Over time, however, if Black living conditions do not improve and if there is not a sizable redistribution of economic resources, the ANC's base may demand more radical policies.

Religion

Because it involves deeply felt values, religion has frequently been the source of bitter "communal strife" (i.e., conflict between ethnic communities). In chapter 3, we examined the influence of religious *beliefs* on political attitudes and behavior, particularly those of fundamentalists and others favoring close links between church and state. We saw that a group's religious orientation often shapes its political beliefs and behavior.

In this chapter, we look at a related but distinct aspect of religion, namely the degree to which coreligionists identify strongly with each other and try to enhance their political and economic power relative to other religious groups. In other words, we are concerned here, not with the political ramifications of religious beliefs (considered in chapter 3) but with conflict *between* religious groups (defined here as one type of *ethnic community*). Such discord may pit one religion against another or may involve conflict between two branches of the same religion. Two factors influence the likelihood of tensions between religious groups: first, the extent to which one religious community feels ill-treated by another; and second, the degree to which any religion regards itself as the only true faith and rejects alternate theologies. Thus, Catholics and Protestants coexist rather harmoniously in the United States and Germany because neither of those conditions applies. On the other hand, in Northern Ireland, where Catholics have resented the Protestants' political and economic powers and Protestants have feared political domination by the Catholic community, paramilitary groups representing both sides engaged in a nearly forty-year armed struggle.

In 1992, thousands of Hindu fundamentalists destroyed a sixteenth-century Muslim mosque in the northern Indian town of Ayodhya. Like many such clashes, the incident grew out of centuries-old beliefs and hostilities. Many Hindus believe this to be the spot where their god Ram had been born ages before. To the BJP, the leading Hindu political party, and to the more militant World Hindu Council, the mosque was a symbol of Islamic domination during the three hundred years of Mogul rule prior to the British colonial era. Within days of the 1992 assault, rioting in northern and central India left about two thousand dead. Ten years later, Hindu mobs in the city of Ahmedabad murdered over one thousand Muslims, burning some of them alive. In neighboring Islamic countries, Pakistani crowds attacked Hindu temples and Bangladeshis assaulted Hindu-owned shops.

In fact, India and Pakistan were born of communal violence, and neither has been free of it since. Although both countries had been part of a single British colony, when negotiations for independence advanced in the late 1940s, the Muslim League insisted on the creation of a separate Muslim state. Using language that classically defines an ethnic group, League leader Mohammed Ali Jinnah declared, "We are a nation with our own distinctive culture and civilization, language and literature . . . customs . . . history and tradition."[17] In 1946, as independence approached, political tensions between the Muslim League and the dominant Congress Party (a nonreligious party led largely by secular Hindus) touched off communal violence that left thousands dead. Finally, the British reluctantly divided their most important colony into two countries: India, with roughly three hundred million Hindus and forty million Muslims; and Pakistan, with approximately sixty million Muslims and twenty million Hindus, at that time. No sooner had independence been declared (August 15, 1947), when horrendous religious massacres began in both countries. Whole villages were destroyed, twelve million refugees of both faiths fled in both directions across the border, more than seventy-five thousand women were abducted and raped, and somewhere between 500,000 and one million people were killed in one of the twentieth century's worst ethnic conflagrations. Two decades later, Pakistan itself split in two, as geography, language, and cultural differences rather than religion divided its population. With support from India, the Bengali-speaking eastern region broke away from the dominant, primarily Urdu-speaking, west to form the country of Bangladesh.

In recent years, Muslim separatists in the Indian-controlled portion of Kashmir have waged guerrilla warfare aimed either at Kashmiri independence or at unification with Pakistan. In 2001, Islamic fundamentalists attacked the Indian parliament, once again bringing India and Pakistan (both of them nuclear powers) to the brink of war. Since early 2004, the two countries have engaged in a series of peace talks and confidence-building measures. But basic differences over Kashmir and ingrained suspicions keep that region volatile, as have recent terrorist attacks on India. In November 2008, an Islamist terrorist group named Lashkar-e-Taiba or LeT ("Army of the Pure") launched a deadly attack on the center of Mumbai (formerly Bombay, one of India's largest cities and its financial capital), killing nearly two hundred people and wounding more than three hundred. Based in Pakistan, that group is committed to "liberating" the Indian-controlled portion of Kashmir. Like the Afghan Taliban, the LeT and other Islamist groups have received assistance from Pakistan's intelligence service (the ISI), and they likely still receive help from ISI hard-liners.

But the most notorious religiously based conflict today does not pit two religions against each other, but rather sees the Sunni and Shi'a branches of Islam at war. It is in Iraq that this struggle escalated in the 1980s and it is from there that it spread to neighboring countries. Like many of the ethnic clashes in the LDCs, the origins can be traced, in part, back to its colonial past. When Iraq received full independence in 1932, the outgoing British rulers transferred power to the Sunni Arab elite. For more than seventy years, the relatively small Sunni community (about 15 percent of the total population) dominated both the Arab Shi'a majority (about 60 percent) and the Kurdish minority (close to 20 percent). Although most Kurds are Sunnis, they consider themselves a separate nationality, have their own language, customs, and traditions, and have long opposed Arab control by either Sunnis or Shi'ites. After taking control of the government (in 1979), President Saddam Hussein intensified persecution of the Shi'ites. After the United States defeated Iraq in the First Gulf War (1991), the Shi'a heartland in southern Iraq, like the Kurds in the north, rose up in an unsuccessful attempt to overthrow Saddam, but both revolts were crushed. Towns across the south were razed and tens of thousands of Shi'ites were massacred. Over time, moved by persecution and by economic necessity, many Shi'ites migrated to the country's Sunni-dominated central region. In greater Baghdad, large Shi'a enclaves created more extensive, tense contacts with the Sunnis.

Because of Saddam's relentless persecution of the Shi'ites, they rejoiced in his overthrow by U.S. and allied forces in 2003 and eagerly anticipated the dawn of a new government, which they would dominate. At the same time, the Sunni community was hostile toward American and allied occupation forces for purging government officials and military officers who belonged to Saddam Hussein's Ba'ath Party, the primary avenue of Sunni political power. Most of all, the Sunnis, not surprisingly, feared retaliation by the Shi'ites whom they had so long dominated and mistreated.

Within a year of Saddam's fall, Sunni elements were attacking both American troops and Shi'a neighborhoods, using roadside bombs and suicide bombings. In the face of these attacks, many Shi'ites turned to their own extremist militias that killed and tortured in return. When the American military completed its pullout in 2011, conflict between these ethnic communities intensified. The Shi'a-dominated government—the first ever in the Arab World—has distrusted the Sunnis and has excluded them from important posts in either the national government or the armed force.* Sunni communities and regions also have received inferior government services, including electricity and sanitation. Often, the government retaliated for Saddam's persecution of the Shi'a and for the post-2003 Sunni unrest by arresting and mistreating Sunni citizens. That conflict continues to take a heavy toll through suicide bombings and the like.

That intrareligious struggle soon spread to neighboring Syria, where a prodemocratic uprising against the Assad dynasty's dictatorship (backed by the ruling Shi'a minority) transformed into a sectarian battle. Once again the clashes within the two neighboring countries were

---

*Iran, of course, already had a Shi'a government before Iraq did, but that country is Persian, not Arab.

intertwined. As neither Western-backed rebels nor al-Qaeda was able to topple the Assad regime, IS stepped into the vacuum, quickly becoming the most powerful force in that country. In 2014, when IS troops swept into Iraq (the country where it had originated), they quickly conquered large portions of the north—including Mosul, the country's second largest city and the major city in northern Iraq—with only 1,500 men. Despite having twenty times as many combatants as the IS invaders and despite a huge advantage in heavy armaments (supplied by the United States), thirty thousand government troops fled without a fight, leaving their guns and heavy weapons behind for IS fighters to pick up. Many government troops also exchanged their uniforms for civilian clothing in order to blend in with the local population. Indeed, in spite of years of American training and billions of dollars of weapons from the United States, the Iraqi military showed little ability to fight anywhere in the north, due in part to its highly corrupt officers' corps and the resulting low morale of its troops. Today, a large portion of IS's weapons and equipment consists of material taken from government troops in Syria and Iraq. In their conquest of Mosul and other parts of northern Iraq, the IS captured an estimated $1 billion worth of American-supplied Humvee armored vehicles from fleeing government troops.[18]

The ease with which the IS was able to conquer large parts of the Sunni-populated north of the country so easily also reflected the fact that many Sunni civilians, even if they were not IS supporters, preferred its control over that of the Shi'a-dominated national government. Since then, IS brutality in the areas they control has been directed primarily at non-Muslims (including the small Christian communities and their off-shoots), Shi'a, and the minority of Sunnis who disobey their commands. For the majority of the Sunnis in these areas, as long as they "keep their noses clean," they escape persecution and benefit from the improved government services (electricity, water, etc.) that the IS conquerors provide (compared to what the Iraqi government had provided).

DEPENDENCY, MODERNIZATION, AND ETHNIC CONFLICT

Western analysts once assumed that improved education and communications break down ethnic clashes. Because of their country's experience as a "melting pot" for immigrant groups, Americans in particular have supposed that socioeconomic modernization enhances ethnic integration and harmony.* Yet in Africa and Asia, early modernization has

---

*Yet, even America's image as a successful melting pot has often been overstated. For example, prejudice, though much diminished, continues to divide Blacks and Whites. Furthermore, many of today's Hispanic immigrants are not well integrated into society.

frequently politicized and intensified ethnic antagonisms. In fact, Crawford Young observes that "cultural pluralism [and ethnic strife] as a political phenomenon" was not significant in traditional societies but, rather, emerged "from such social processes as urbanization, the revolution in communications and spread of modern education."[19] Early modernization theorists, who were quite optimistic about the positive effects of literacy, urbanization, and modern values, clearly underestimated the extent to which these factors might mobilize various ethnic groups and set them against each other. Dependency theorists, on the other hand, provided a rather superficial analysis of ethnic issues, tending to blame these conflicts on colonialism or neocolonialism.

During the era of European colonialism, ethnic divisions in Africa and Asia were often kept in check by the struggle for independence, which encouraged a common front against the colonial regime. After independence, however, previously submerged ethnic rivalries frequently rose to the surface. In the new political order, religious, racial, tribal, and nationality groups competed for state resources such as roads, schools, and civil service jobs. Furthermore, rural-to-urban migration brought previously isolated ethnic groups into closer contact with each other for the first time. Indeed, urbanization, increased education, and the spread of mass communications have frequently mobilized sectors of the population along ethnic lines. The spread of higher education, rather than generating greater harmony, frequently produces a class of ethnically chauvinistic professionals and intellectuals, who become the ideologists of ethnic hostility. Eventually, as these groups come to know each other, these tensions may diminish. For now, however, ethnic tensions remain high in much of the developing world.

LEVELS OF INTERETHNIC CONFLICT

Although most countries are ethnically heterogeneous, there are wide variations in how ethnicities relate to each other. In some cases, different races or religions interact amicably; in others, deep resentments inspire shocking atrocities. Having examined the various types of ethnic communities, we will now consider the *nature* and *intensity* of relations between them. In theory, these relationships can be measured by the frequency of interethnic friendships and marriages, by the degree to which political parties, trade unions, and other civic organizations are either heterogeneous or ethnically based, and by the extent to which ethnic divisions are reinforced by other social cleavages such as class. In any particular country, relations between ethnic communities may range from minimal levels of conflict (Brazil) to systematic violence (Sudan).

Minimal Conflict

As we have seen, modernization frequently intensifies ethnic antagonisms in the short run, but usually ameliorates them in the longer term. Consequently, affluent democracies are more likely than LDCs to enjoy amicable ethnic relations. Although First World countries are not exempt from racial, religious, or linguistic conflict, such tensions are more likely to be resolved calmly. In Switzerland, for example, German-, French-, and Italian-speaking citizens have lived together peacefully for centuries. In Brazil and the island nations of the Caribbean, relations between Blacks and Whites are generally more harmonious than in the United States. For instance, interracial dating and marriages are quite common, particularly among lower-income groups. Still, this harmony is relative, because even those countries have maintained a social hierarchy between races. For example, although there are many people of color in the Dominican, Brazilian, and Panamanian middle classes, most Blacks remain mired in the lower class, and few make it into the political and economic elites.

In short, even the countries classified as harmonious are only categorized that way relative to other, more sharply divided societies. In Brazil and Cuba, for example, despite a long history of interracial marriages and more recent government efforts to promote racial equality, Blacks have yet to attain their proportional share of government leadership positions. But ethnic tensions are limited and rarely lead to violence.

Uneasy Balance

In countries such as Trinidad and Tobago and Malaysia, relations between the principal ethnic groups are somewhat more strained. Although still generally peaceful, ethnic relations are in an *uneasy balance*, in which different groups predominate in specific areas of society. For example, in Malaysia, the Muslim Malay majority dominates the political system, including the parliament and the government bureaucracy, while the Chinese minority dominates the business community. Ethnic riots in 1969 led the Malaysian government to introduce new policies designed, in part, to redistribute more of the country's wealth to the Malays. Fearful of Chinese economic domination, the Malays have received ethnic preferences in education and the civil service. Since 2009, however, the government has begun to eliminate some ethnic quotas.

The Caribbean nation of Trinidad and Tobago offers another example of uneasy balance. During the second half of the nineteenth century, British colonial authorities encouraged the migration of indentured plantation workers from India who joined the Black majority and small White elite. Contrary to the normal Caribbean practice of extensive racial mixing, there were fewer interracial marriages between Blacks and

East Indians. Each of these groups currently constitutes about 40 percent of the population, with the remaining 20 percent made up of Chinese, Whites, Arabs, and others. Following Trinidadian independence in 1962, ethnic frictions increased as Blacks and East Indians competed for state resources. Most of the important political, civil service, military, and police positions since that time have been held by Blacks, who predominate within the urban middle and working classes. Whites still predominate in the upper ranks of the business community. Traditionally, most East Indians have been small- to medium-sized businesspeople or poor farmers and farmworkers.

Trinidadian politics do not feature the same overt ethnic appeals that characterize many LDCs, but most of its political parties and unions have primarily represented one race. During the first parliamentary elections after independence, each of the major parties received 80–90 percent of its votes from a single ethnic group. For twenty-four years (1962–1986), the People's National Movement (PNM), the party that led the independence movement, headed the national government. While drawing votes from various races, the PNM's leadership and base have been mostly Black. During that time the opposition was led by various Indian-dominated parties. Major labor unions also tended to be either predominantly Black or East Indian. Only in 1986 did the newly formed National Alliance for Reconstruction (NAR) finally dislodge the PNM from power by forging the first electoral alliance between the two dominant ethnic groups.

Black and Indian political and labor leaders cooperate periodically and in 1995 a party representing both races elected Trinidad's first prime minister of East Indian origin. At the same time, however, the two communities continued to maintain their social, political, and economic distance. And, in 1990, a radical Black Muslim movement, the Jamaat al Muslimeen, briefly captured the parliament building and held the prime minister and members of parliament hostage for six days while many poor Blacks rioted in the capital. Jamaat's manifestos reflected the antagonism that many Black Trinidadians feel toward East Indians, but their violent behavior was an aberration in the nation's racial relations.

Enforced Hierarchy (Ethnic Dominance)

One important factor permitting ethnic balance in countries such as Malaysia and Trinidad and Tobago has been the division of political and economic powers between the competing ethnicities. Typically, one ethnicity predominates in the political arena and the other is more influential in the economy. But, in *enforced hierarchies*, both forms of power are concentrated in the hands of the ruling ethnic group. South African apartheid represented the most blatant example of such a relationship.

Until the 1990s, Whites dominated both the private sector and the state, including the courts, police, and armed forces. Blacks were denied the most basic rights.

Latin American nations with large Native American (Indian) populations—including Guatemala, Bolivia, Ecuador, and Peru—have a less overt, but still significant, form of hierarchy. Since the Spanish conquest, most Indians in those countries have been poor peasants at the bottom of the social and political ladder. Even today, despite important recent gains in Indian rights, most positions of political and economic influence remain in the hands of Whites or Mestizos.* At the same time, however, unlike the United States, racial classifications in Latin America tend to be culturally rather than biologically defined. Consequently, they are more flexible and open up opportunities for at least some people of color. If a young Indian villager moves to the city, adopts Western dress, and speaks Spanish, he or she becomes a Mestizo (or *Cholo*), a higher social status. And in the rural highlands of Ecuador and Peru, entire peasant communities that spoke Quechua a generation ago have switched to Spanish and changed to Western clothing in a process called *mestizaje* (and are then considered to be Mestizos) has increased, with a corresponding decline in the number identified as indigenous (Indian). This, more flexible, cultural definition has obvious advantages, but an important disadvantage as well. Although it facilitates individual upward social mobility, until now it only affords that mobility to Indians who largely abandon their own culture.

Since the 1980s, however, Indians have begun to assert their cultural rights and political influence in several Latin American countries through grassroots political movements and through the election of Indian government officials, sometimes at the highest levels. In Bolivia, where 60 percent of the population is indigenous, Indian social movements organized mass protests against the government's free-market (neoliberal) economic policies. These protests brought down the nation's president and subsequently led to the 2006 election of Evo Morales, the country's first indigenous president. In Ecuador, a national Indian federation (CONAIE) joined the military in a 2000 coup, which installed a ruling junta that included the CONAIE president. Peru elected its first president of Indian descent in 2001 and Ollanta Humala, a former army colonel of partial Indian extraction, took office in 2011. Finally, in the Mexican state of Chiapas, a group known as the Zapatistas staged a 1994 peasant rebellion in behalf of Indian rights. Though it never had a chance to seize national power (nor did it intend to), the group received a remarkable

---

*Persons of mixed Indian and White racial origin, often applied to an Indian who adopts much of White culture.

amount of national support from Mexicans of all ethnicities and social classes.

In all these cases of enforced hierarchy, racial and class distinctions are closely intertwined. Those higher up the social ladder tend to be lighter skinned; those at the lower ranks of society are generally darker. Unlike South Africa's old apartheid system, Latin America's racial hierarchy is enforced informally, not legally, and is far less repressive. Even so, during some forty years of revolutionary upheaval and intense government oppression, the Guatemalan armed forces viewed rural Indian communities as breeding grounds for Marxist guerrillas. Consequently, successive military regimes massacred tens of thousands of Indian peasants in a policy bordering on genocide. Fortunately, since the 1990s, a peace treaty with the guerrillas has curtailed such violence.

Systematic Violence

In the worst-case scenario, deep ethnic resentments have led to mass violence or even civil war. As we have seen, in a number of countries—including India, Bangladesh, Ethiopia, Rwanda, and Sudan—*systematic violence* has resulted in thousands or hundreds of thousands of deaths and huge numbers of displaced refugees and rape victims. Often, violence develops when ethnic divisions are reinforced by class tensions. In Bahrain, the Shi'a majority chafes under the domination of the Sunni monarch.

Ethnic bloodshed also occurs when one ethnicity seizes political power and then takes reprisals for real or imagined past indignities. Thus, when General Idi Amin seized power in Uganda, he ordered the slaughter of Langi and Acholi soldiers who were identified with the regime of ousted president Milton Obote. In both Rwanda and Burundi, the deaths of Hutu presidents opened the floodgates to violence between Hutus and the long-dominant Tutsis.

OUTCOMES AND RESOLUTIONS

Whether ethnic antagonisms arise from competition over government resources, resentment over the division of political and economic powers, or an ethnic community's demands for greater autonomy, there are a number of possible results. Although some outcomes are peaceful, others may spawn intense violence. And while some resolutions are successful, others do not endure. In seeking a peaceful and lasting resolution, government and ethnic leaders are constrained by the history and intensity of their ethnic cleavages, by the degree of previous ethnic cooperation, and by the country's political culture. Nonetheless, within these constraints, the creativity and statecraft of national leaders and outside mediators can contribute to successful solutions. Thus, political elites may seek reasonable, negotiated solutions or they may choose to play on ethnic tensions for their own advantage.

Unfortunately, all too often chauvinistic political leaders inflame ethnic relations in order to inflate their own political power. For example, although Bosnian Serbs and Muslims had enjoyed rather amicable relationships for many years, after the breakup of Yugoslavia extremist leaders—such as then-Serb president Slobodan Milosevic—promoted ethnic hatred and mass murder in order to build their own political power base. In the end, Milosevic brought both Bosnia and Serbia to ruin. Similarly, the 1994 massacres in Rwanda were orchestrated from above. Government officials pressured Hutu villagers to attack their Tutsi neighbors, with whom most of them had been living peacefully for years.

When more responsible elites are willing to resolve bitter ethnic conflicts through negotiations, they may arrive at one of several types of resolutions. In the next section, we examine those possible outcomes and also look at several options that have been tried when negotiations have failed. Although the alternatives presented here are not exhaustive, they cover a wide range of experiences.

Power Sharing: Federalism and Consociationalism

Power-sharing arrangements seek to create stability by dividing political power among major ethnic groups. These settlements generally follow protracted negotiations and constitutional debate. If power sharing is introduced into the constitution at the time of independence, it may head off ethnic violence before it gets started. Unfortunately, however, many such arrangements later break down.

Federalism, the primary form of power sharing, is "a system of government [that] emanates from the desire of people to form a union without necessarily losing their various identities."[20] It may involve the creation of autonomous or semiautonomous regions, each of which is governed by a particular ethnicity. But it is only possible in situations where contending ethnic groups are concentrated in different regions of the country. For example, prior to its collapse, Yugoslavia consisted of six autonomous republics mostly governed by individual nationalities, including Serbs, Croats, and Slovenes. The constitution mandated power sharing between the various republics at the national level. But, this compromise began to unravel in the 1970s following the death of Marshal Joseph Broz Tito, the country's long-term strongman. It collapsed completely in the early 1990s when the Communist Party lost its grip on several republics.

Industrialized democracies have had greater success with ethnically based federalism. Each of Switzerland's 22 cantons is dominated by one of the country's three major language groups, with German-, French-, and Italian-speaking cantons coexisting harmoniously. Canada's federalism, though not based on ethnic divisions, has allowed the primarily French-speaking province of Quebec a substantial amount of autonomy regarding language and other cultural matters. Although the country's constitutional arrangement has not satisfied many Québécois nationalists, it has accommodated many of their demands and convinced the province's voters to reject independence in two separate provincial referendums.

In the developing world, power sharing has been less successful. Following independence, Nigeria tried to accommodate its ethnic divisions through federalism. As we have seen, the country's north was dominated by the Hausa and Fulani, the east by the Ibos, and the west, to a lesser extent, by the Yoruba. This union came apart when the Ibos tried to secede. Although the Biafran war took a terrible toll, a new federal solution has subsequently taken hold. On the other hand, Pakistani federalism failed to overcome the antipathy between the country's more powerful western region (populated largely by Urdu speakers) and the Bengali-speaking east. In 1971, relations between the two regions broke down completely, resulting in the massacre of 500,000 Bengalis by western Pakistani troops. When India went to war with Pakistan, the eastern region was able to secede and form the new nation of Bangladesh.

Consociationalism offers another potential solution to ethnic conflict. It is frequently used where major ethnic groups reside in close proximity and lack a distinct "homelands," making a federalist solution impossible. Its power, designed to protect the rights of all participants, involves the following components*:

1. The leaders of the major ethnic groups form a ruling coalition at the national level.
2. Each group has veto power over government policies that affect them.
3. Public employment, such as the civil service, is divided between ethnicities, with each receiving a number of posts roughly proportional to its population. Often the most important government positions—such as prime minister, president, and parliamentary leader—are reserved for specific ethnicities.
4. Each ethnic group is afforded a high degree of autonomy over its own affairs.[21]

---

*Consociationalism can exist among competing groups other than ethnicities, but we confine this discussion to ethnically based consociationalism.

Thus, consociational democracy consciously rejects strict majority rule. Instead, it seeks to create a framework for stability and peace by guaranteeing minorities a share of political power—even veto power—to protect them against the majority. It has been tried in several developing nations, including Cyprus (where it failed) and Malaysia (where it has generally succeeded). Some mutual trust and cooperation between the leaders of contending ethnic groups is the key to effective consociational arrangements. Sadly, trust is difficult to establish in times of ethnic hostility and becomes ever more problematic after that hostility has erupted into bloodshed. Iraq's current consociational arrangements involve the division of leadership posts between the three major ethnic groups and the use of parliamentary election rules that indirectly guarantee a bloc of seats for the Kurds and Sunnis. But, continued mistrust between the three major ethnic groups has stalemated the national parliament.

Secession

When power sharing or other forms of compromise do not succeed, disgruntled ethnic minorities may attempt to secede (withdraw) from the country in order to form their own nation or join their ethnic brothers and sisters in a neighboring state. As one author put it, "Secession, like divorce, is an ultimate act of alienation."[22] It offers a potential way out of a "failed marriage" between ethnic groups within a nation-state. Unfortunately, however, like divorce, secession or the threat of secession frequently provokes bitterness and hostility. It is possible only when the group seeking to secede predominates in a clearly defined territory.

Given the large number of ethnically divided developing countries, we should not be surprised to find many secessionist movements. Central governments, faced with such breakaway efforts, almost always try to repress them because they are unwilling to part with some of their country's territory or resources, just as the United States was unwilling to part with the Confederate states. This chapter has previously discussed secessionist movements by Blacks in southern Sudan, Tamils in Sri Lanka, Eritreans in Ethiopia, and Sikhs in northern India. Other secessionist movements have included the Karen in Burma, Moros in the Philippines, and Muslims in Indian Kashmir. In 2015, there was hope that negotiations may finally bring an end to the sixty-seven-year civil war between the Karen ethnic minority and the Burmese government (believed to be the longest ongoing war in the world).

Following the two Gulf wars, the world briefly focused its attention on Saddam Hussein's persecution of Iraq's Kurdish population. A decade later, Kurdish militia supported American-led coalition forces in the war to topple Saddam. But Kurdish separatism in Iraq and elsewhere date to the collapse of the Ottoman Empire at the close of World War I. Residing in a mountainous region that they call Kurdistan, perhaps thirty million Kurds live in adjacent areas of Turkey (home to about half of all Kurds), Iran, and Iraq, with a smaller community in Syria. Over the years, the Kurds have been persecuted in all of those countries. But as a result of America's two wars with Iraq, that country's Kurds have achieved virtual autonomy and currently exercise considerable influence in that country's national government.

Although many aggrieved nationalities would like to secede, few have accomplished this goal. In Africa, we have noted that Eritrea attained independence from Ethiopia in 1993 after three decades of civil war and South Sudan has recently seceded from Sudan following a twenty-one-year-old struggle. While in Asia, Bangladesh (formerly East Pakistan) withdrew from Pakistan in 1971 with the help of the Indian armed forces and East Timor finally gained independence from Indonesian occupation in 2002. But successful secession movements have been few and far between in the developing world and they have been achieved at a tremendous cost in human lives. During East Timor's struggle for independence, one-fourth or more of its total population (about 600,000 people) were killed or starved to death. Estimates of the number of lives lost in Bangladesh and South Sudan run into the millions. Elsewhere, the best outcome that secessionist movements have achieved is greater autonomy and many (like Tibet) fail to gain even that.

Noting the spread of secessionist conflicts in the 1970s and 1980s and the breakup of the Soviet Union, Yugoslavia, and Czechoslovakia into many smaller, ethnically based states in the 1990s, many analysts predicted that Eastern Europe and portions of the developing world would see the disintegration of an ever-growing number of nation-states. But, in fact, the number of secessionist wars has actually declined significantly since the start of the 1990s. From 1991 to 1999, sixteen such wars were settled and eleven others were held in check by cease-fires or continuing negotiations. Thus, as this century began, only eighteen secessionist wars continued worldwide, fewer than at any time since 1970.[23]

Outside Intervention

We have already seen how outside intervention by Iran and Saudi Arabia *intensified* religious conflicts in Yemen, Syria, and Iraq. Elsewhere, outside actors seeking to *end* ethnic conflicts have often faced a moral and practical dilemma. On the one hand, they may feel morally compelled to somehow intervene on behalf of a victimized minority. Such intercession can span the gamut from simply agreeing to take in refugees all the way to armed intervention aimed at putting a stop to the bloodshed. At the same time, however, outside nations are constrained from interference by international laws regarding national sovereignty, or international power alignments, or lack of public support at home. Even the nonaggressive act of offering refuge to the victims of ethnic strife may seem too costly or too risky. Indeed, the outside world has stood by as millions died in ethnic massacres in such countries as Indonesia, Congo (Kinshasa), Rwanda, and Sudan. Looking at the world's prolonged inaction regarding the Serbs' and Croats' bloody "ethnic cleansing" in Bosnia, military strategist Edward Luttwak asked, "If the Bosnian Muslims had been needle-nosed dolphins, would the world have allowed the Croats and Serbs to slaughter them by the tens of thousands?"[24] His blunt question raises important ethical and pragmatic questions about the world's obligations and limitations under those circumstances.

Except for the rare instance when outside forces are invited in by a country's own government (as when Sri Lanka asked India's armed forces to quell its civil war), external involvement violates the principle of national sovereignty, raising a number of difficult issues. At what point do other nations or international organizations (such as the United Nations, NATO, or the **African Union**) have the right to violate a country's sovereignty in order to save innocent lives? For example, should the United Nations or the West have sent troops into Rwanda, Congo (Kinshasa), or Darfur, even without the permission of their governments, in order to stop the massacres of hundreds of thousands? Many analysts would answer affirmatively. But if those interventions are justified, wouldn't the same moral principles have given the United Nations the authority to send troops into Birmingham, Alabama, and rural Mississippi in the 1960s in order to protect the lives of Blacks who were being terrorized by the Ku Klux Klan and the local police? Who is to decide in which situations outside intervention is legitimate?

Furthermore, there are also pragmatic questions regarding the likely effectiveness of intervention. Under what circumstances does outside interference (including military involvement) prevent ethnic persecution and impose a durable solution, and when is it futile or counterproductive? Will countries such as Norway, India, or Nigeria be willing to commit their soldiers and economic resources on a sustained basis to support future peacekeeping operations? How many casualties among their own soldiers are peacekeeping nations prepared to accept?[25]

In the end, governments contemplating humanitarian interventions have to weigh their own national interests and the costs of intervention against their commitment to sustaining human rights abroad. Most nations are reluctant to risk their soldiers' lives for humanitarian purposes. A fairly small number of American soldiers (eighteen) brutally killed in 1993 during a mission to restore order and distribute food in war-torn Somalia shocked U.S. public opinion and caused President Bill Clinton to withdraw the remaining American troops. Only a year later, government leaders in Washington, Paris, and other Western capitals were warned that an ethnic massacre was likely to unfold in Rwanda. Sobered by the recently failed intervention in Somalia and unsure how well they could prevent genocide, they decided against interference. Some analysts insist that the United Nations or the United States or France could have saved thousands of lives if they had quickly sent a military force to quell the violence.[26] Indeed, President Clinton subsequently said (after he left office) that his greatest regret of his presidency was his failure to take preventive action in Rwanda. Others disagree, arguing that the Rwandan genocide took place so quickly (most of the deaths occurring within a few weeks) that intervention could not have arrived in time to save that many victims.[27]

In recent years, the United Nations, the African Union, and the Western powers have lamented the genocidal warfare unleashed against non-Arab minorities in Darfur. Only after nearly one to two million people had fled Darfur to squalid and dangerous refugee camps and perhaps as many as 200,000 had died (largely of starvation) did the African Union send a small and ineffective military force, with the acquiescence of the Sudanese government. The United Nations was even slower in taking action. Several thousand UN peacekeeping troops were finally dispatched to Darfur in 2007 in a joint operation with African Union troops already on the ground. But the joint UN and AU peacekeeping force was hampered by the Sudanese government and has been rather ineffective in protecting Darfur's population.

Even when world opinion has forced the host government to accept external intervention, such as UN intervention in East Timor and Sudan, troops have normally been sent in only *after* the worst outrages had already been committed. To be sure, outside forces occasionally *have* imposed solutions on a few seemingly intractable ethnic conflicts. In such cases, the intervening power is usually a neighboring state that either has ties to one of the warring ethnic factions or has a strategic interest in the country it invades. Such was the case with India's intercession on behalf of the Bengalis in East Pakistan. Without that intervention, the nation of Bangladesh could not have been born.

More frequently, international interventions come too late and often end badly. While the Iraqi Kurds have benefited greatly from America's wars against their oppressor, Saddam Hussein, a prior U.S. intrusion had devastating results. Some two decades earlier, the United States and Iran supported a Kurdish rebellion against the Iraqi government. But, for Washington, Kurdish interests were secondary to its own policy objective—supporting the Shah's government in Iran, which was then America's ally and Iraq's enemy. The following year, however, when the Shah withdrew his support for the Kurdish insurrection, the CIA also terminated its assistance and the rebellion collapsed. Thousands of Iraqi Kurds were killed or driven from their homes. To be sure, most countries only assist persecuted ethnic groups when that help furthers their own national interests. And some of those interventions have even intentionally intensified ethnic conflicts. For example, from the late 1990s to 2003, as many as nine African nations, particularly Rwanda and Uganda, intervened in Congo (Kinshasa)'s ethnic conflict, which pitted the Congolese government against its own Hutu population and some two million Hutus who had fled Rwanda. In what some have called "Africa's World War," several million people died in a conflict that went largely unnoticed in the West. While the loss of life would have been horrifying in any event, outside intervention clearly added to the death toll. And, as we have seen, India's attempt to settle the Tamil-Sinhalese conflict in Sri Lanka ended disastrously.

Finally, sometimes minority groups wishing to secede from their country receive help from neighboring countries with whom they share an ethnic identity. Somali rebels in the Ethiopian region of Ogaden have received help over the years from neighboring Somalia. In South Asia, the Pakistani military has aided Islamic secessionists in the Indian, predominantly Muslim, state of Kashmir.* In all these cases, outside intervention may merely have thrown gasoline on the fire of existing ethnic strife.

In short, outside interventions frequently fail to resolve ethnic conflicts. Furthermore, even when they are well intentioned, outside powers are often unwilling or unable to "stay the course." Thus, Glynne Evans notes,

> A half-hearted [outside] military response [to ethnic conflict] without any underlying political action is a poor option. . . . Conflicts with a high degree of ethnic mobilization last for generations rather than years, and are intense in their impact as neighbors turn on neighbors. An intervention for humanitarian purposes in such cases becomes a major military commitment, and one of long duration.[28]

Events in countries such as Congo (Kinshasa), Rwanda, and Sudan suggest that this is a commitment that outside powers are rarely prepared to make.

The most common type of outside intervention has come from neighboring countries that support an ethnic rebellion, generally intensifying the conflict rather than containing it. A recent study of ethnic uprisings involving violence found that nearly 80 percent involved ethnic groups located along an international border.[29] In fact, ethnic minorities that

---

*Kashmir, lying between India and Pakistan, is divided into two regions, one controlled by Pakistan and the other by India.

reside along such borders are far more likely to rebel than are groups living in the interior. If nothing else, proximity to a neighboring country allows rebel soldiers and their supporters to take refuge from pursuing government troops. Often, the rebelling ethnicity lives on both sides of the border and it gains support from their fellow tribesmen or nationals. The neighboring government sometimes also offers sanctuary or even military support. This chapter offers several examples. Kurdish rebels in Turkey were able to gain refuge and material support from the Kurdish-controlled regions of northern Iraq. Muslim rebels in Kashmir, as we have seen, have often been supported by the neighboring Pakistani armed forces and intelligence service. Rwanda's Tutsi-dominated government long supported Tutsi rebel forces in Congo (Kinshasa).

Settlement through Exhaustion

Finally, many ethnic conflicts have been resolved, not through statecraft, constitutional arrangements, or external intervention, but rather through the exhaustion of the warring parties. Although the Ugandan government continues to clash periodically with the Acholi and Langi tribes, conflict has been held in check because Ugandans do not want to return to the ethnically based bloodshed of the Amin and Obote eras. And, in Sudan, a similar process contributed to the end of a twenty-one-year war between the Arab-dominated national government and the Black (non-Muslim) population of the south.

Toward a Peaceful Resolution of Conflict

If developing nations are to avoid the horrors of civil war, secession, and foreign intervention, they must arrive at legal, political, and economic solutions that can reduce ethnic tensions. This goal, though clearly reasonable, is more easily said than achieved. More difficult still is the task of repairing the damage done to plural societies that have been torn apart by bloody conflict (e.g., Rwanda, Iraq and Kashmir) or by decades of prejudice and segregation (South Africa). Not long after South Africa's new, multiracial government was installed in 1994, President Mandela's administration created a Truth and Reconciliation Commission, before which perpetrators of racially based violence and injustices were invited to confess their crimes in return for amnesty. The goal of the Commission was to further unearth the crimes of apartheid and, more importantly, to allow the nation's races to live together more harmoniously. Yet, as some observers of the Commission's hearings have suggested, in countries that have experienced systematic repression or extensive ethnic violence, reconciliation—the creation of harmony between formerly hostile parties—may be too much to hope for. A more realistic goal, they suggest, is establishing the basis for *coexistence* between these groups.

ETHNIC PLURALISM AND DEMOCRACY

Crafting peaceful scenarios for multicultural societies remains one of the greatest challenges facing Third World leaders. During the 1970s and 1980s, increased ethnic violence in the developing world and the former communist states of Eastern Europe frequently coincided with the spread of democratic government. This raised two questions about the relationship between democracy and ethnic politics: First, "Are multi-ethnic countries less likely to maintain democracy than are culturally homogenous societies?" Second, "Do the growth of citizen participation and the creation of democratic governments intensify conflict between ethnic communities?"

The first question can be answered quite easily. Democracy *is* clearly harder, though far from impossible, to establish and maintain in multi-ethnic countries. We have seen, for example, how Lebanon, long considered the most democratic Arab country, was devastated by ethnic civil war. Looking at democracy's failure to take root in most of Africa and Asia from the 1960s to the 1980s, Rabushka and Shepsle concluded that ethnic antagonisms had created important obstacles to democratization. Democracy, they argued, "is simply not viable in an environment of intense ethnic preference."[30] Here, they referred to societies in which powerful ethnic groups receive special privileges, while others suffer discrimination.

An examination of both developed and developing countries reveals that democracy has fared best in nations that are most ethnically homogeneous (such as Botswana, Uruguay, and Japan) or in countries of "new settlement" (including the United States, Canada, New Zealand, and Australia), populated primarily by immigrants and their descendants who have created a new common culture. In Africa, Asia, and the Middle East, where many countries labor with strong ethnic divides, the growth of democracy and mass political participation may unleash communal hostilities, sometimes intensified by opportunistic politicians who use group fears to build a political base.

Ethnic pluralism poses a particular obstacle to democracy in poorer countries, where various groups must contend for limited government resources in the "politics of scarcity." But although democracy is more challenging to achieve in plural societies, it is not impossible even in very poor nations. Despite its history of religiously based violence, India, one of the world's most ethnically diverse countries, has maintained democratic governments for all but two of its more than sixty years of independence. Similarly, Trinidad and Tobago, a country divided by religion and race, is among the developing world's most democratic nations.

To be sure, the initial transition to democracy frequently intensifies existing ethnic animosities. Newly formed political parties often base their support in competing ethnic communities. Politicians, even those opposed to violence, are tempted to use ethnic appeals as a means of gaining public support. As public resources are distributed through more transparent legislative decisions, ethnically based interest groups and political parties fight for their fair share. Some analysts warn that "the opening of democratic space throws up [so] many groups pulling in different directions, that it causes demand overload, systematic breakdown and even violent conflict," a danger particularly relevant in societies with deep ethnic tensions prior to their democratic transitions.[31] This danger is greatest in strict **majoritarian democracies**, where a single ethnic group or allied ethnicities can dominate parliamentary or presidential elections without affording constitutional or other institutional protections to minority groups. Thus, the Carnegie Commission on Preventing Deadly Conflict concluded:

> In societies with deep ethnic divisions and little experience with democratic government and the rule of law [a common phenomenon in Africa, Asia and the Middle East], strict majoritarian democracy can be self-defeating. Where ethnic identities are strong and national identity weak, populations may vote largely on ethnic lines. Domination by one ethnic group can lead to a tyranny of the majority.[32]

But this merely indicates the importance of limiting majority rule in democratic, multiethnic societies. It does not suggest that authoritarian government is preferable in such situations. Indeed, in the long run, the only way ethnicities can resolve their differences is through open discussion and bargaining in a reasonably democratic political arena, as long as majority rule is tempered by constitutional guarantees of human rights, consociational arrangements, or other institutional protections for minorities.

Although dictatorships in Yugoslavia and the Soviet Union were able to repress ethnic conflicts for many years, in the long run, they actually intensified these grievances by denying their existence, silencing them, and failing to deal with them. As we have seen, after the fall of Saddam Hussein, long-repressed antagonisms burst to the surface, producing civil conflict. Elsewhere, dictators such as Laurent Kabila (Congo-Kinshasa), Suharto (Indonesia), and Saddam Hussein (Iraq) presided over ethnic massacres that would have been unthinkable in a democracy monitored by public opinion and a free press.

Conversely, democratic politicians are open to interest group pressure from ethnic minorities and, hence, seem more likely to settle disputes peacefully before they degenerate into violence. Indeed, the recent study of "minorities at risk" throughout the world revealed that democratic regimes are more likely than dictatorships to negotiate peaceful settlements of ethnic warfare. Political discrimination and, to a lesser degree, economic discrimination against ethnic minorities were more likely to decline in democracies than under authoritarian governments.[33] In short, to accommodate ethnic pluralism and resolve tensions, what is needed is democratic, mature, and enlightened political leadership, a spirit of compromise, and the implementation of politically negotiated solutions such as federalism and consociational democracy.

Unfortunately, some ethnic conflicts, most notably the Shi'a-Sunni civil wars, seem particularly entrenched and are, therefore, likely to devastate parts of the developing world for many years to come.

Practice and Review Online
http://textbooks.rowman.com/handelman8e#ch4

KEY TERMS

African Union
colored(s)
cultural pluralism
internal warfare

majoritarian democracy
nationality
tribe (tribal)

DISCUSSION QUESTIONS

1. What are the differences and similarities between ethnic tensions and conflict in the United States and ethnic divisions in the developing world?
2. Discuss the effect that modernization has had on ethnic identification and ethnic conflict.
3. What are some reasons that might explain why major civil strife related to ethnicity has declined in the last ten to fifteen years?
4. How have some recent movements for democracy in the Arab World (the Arab Spring) been influenced by ethnic divisions?

NOTES

1. Quoted in Yueh-Ting Lee, Fathali Moghaddam, Clark McCauley, and Stephen Worchel, "The Global Challenge of Ethnic and Cultural Conflict," in *The Psychology of Ethnic and Cultural Conflict*, ed. Y. Lee, C. McCauley, F. Moghaddam, and S. Worchel (Westport, CT: Praeger, 2004), 3.
2. Crawford Young, *The Politics of Cultural Pluralism* (Madison, WI: University of Wisconsin Press, 1976), 23.

3. Patrick Inman and James Peacock, "Conclusion: Ethnic and Sectarian as Ideal Types," in *Identity Matters*, eds. James Peacock, Patricia Thornton, and Patrick Inman (New York: Berghahn Books, 2007), 208.

4. Jennifer De Maio, *Confronting Ethnic Conflict* (Lanham, MD: Rowman & Littlefield Publishers, 2009), 23.

5. Monica Duffy Toft, *The Geography of Ethnic Violence: Identity, Interests, and the Indivisibility of Territory* (Princeton, NJ: Princeton University Press, 2003), 3.

6. David Bloomfield and Ben Reilly, eds., *Democracy and Deep-Rooted Conflict: Options for Negotiations* (Stockholm: International Institute for Democracy and Electoral Assistance, 1998), 4.

7. "By the Numbers: Ethnic Groups in the World," *Scientific American* (September 1998), http://www.sciamdigital.com.

8. Ted Robert Gurr, *Peoples versus States: Minorities at Risk in the New Century* (Washington, DC: United States Institute of Peace Press, 2000), 10–11.

9. Ibid., 5.

10. Quoted in Francine Friedman, *The Bosnian Muslims: Denial of a Nation* (Boulder, CO: Westview Press, 1996), 1.

11. Quoted in David A. Lake and Donald Rothchild, "Spreading Fear: The Genesis of Transnational Ethnic Conflict," in *The International Spread of Ethnic Conflict*, ed. David A. Lake and Donald Rothchild (Princeton, NJ: Princeton University Press, 1998), 7.

12. Cynthia Enloe, *Ethnic Conflict and Political Development* (Boston: Little, Brown, 1973), 15.

13. Young, *Politics of Cultural Pluralism*, 20.

14. Amy H. Liu, *Standardizing Diversity: The Political Economy of Language Regimes* (Philadelphia: University of Pennsylvania Press, 2015).

15. Appapillai Amirdhalingam, quoted in Jack David Eller, *From Culture to Ethnicity to Conflict* (Ann Arbor, MI: University of Michigan Press, 1999), 123.

16. Charles W. Anderson, Fred R. von der Mehden, and Crawford Young, *Issues of Political Development*, 2nd ed. (Upper Saddle River, NJ: Prentice Hall, 1974), 21.

17. Cited in T. Walker Wallbank, *A Short History of India and Pakistan* (New York: Mentor, 1958), 196.

18. *The International Business Times* (online), "ISIS Has $1B Worth of US Humvee Armored Vehicles," June 1, 2015.

19. Young, *Politics of Cultural Pluralism*, 65.

20. J. Isawa Elaigwu and Victor A. Olorunsola, "Federalism and the Politics of Compromise," in *State versus Ethnic Claims: African Policy Dilemmas*, eds. David Rothchild and Victor Olorunsola (Boulder, CO: Westview Press, 1983), 282.

21. Arend Lijphart, *Democracy in Plural Societies* (New Haven, CT: Yale University Press, 1977), 25–40.

22. Ralph R. Premdas, "Secessionist Movements in Comparative Perspective," in *Secessionist Movements in Comparative Perspective*, eds. Ralph R. Premdas, S. W. R. de A. Samarasinghe and Alan B. Anderson (London: Pinter Publishers, 1990), 12.

23. Gurr, *People versus States*, 276.

24. Edward Luttwak, "If Bosnians Were Dolphins . . .," *Commentary* 96 (October 1993): 27.

25. See Samantha Power, "Bystander to Genocide," *The Atlantic Monthly* 288, no. 2 (September 2001): 84–108; Romeo Dallaire, *Shake Hands with the Devil: The Failure of Humanity in Rwanda* (Toronto: Random House Canada, 2003).

26. David Carment and Frank Harvey, *Using Force to Prevent Ethnic Violence* (Westport, CT: Praeger, 2001).

27. For example, Alan K. Kuperman, *The Limits of Humanitarian Intervention: Genocide in Rwanda* (Washington, DC: Brookings Institution Press, 2001).

28. Glynne Evans, *Responding to Crises in the African Great Lakes* (New York: Oxford University Press, Adelphia Paper 33, 1997), 75.

29. Idean Salehyan, *Rebels Without Borders: Transnational Insurgencies in World Politics* (Ithaca, NY: Cornell University Press, 2009), 86–87, 91. I subtracted the nonviolent cases from Salehyan's total.

30. From *Politics in Plural Societies* (Columbus, OH: Merrill, 1972) quoted in Larry Diamond and Marc F. Plattner, eds., *Nationalism, Ethnic Conflict, and Democracy* (Baltimore, MD: Johns Hopkins University Press, 1994), xix.

31. Quoted in Claude Ake, "Why Humanitarian Emergencies Occur: Insights from the Interface of State, Democracy and Civil Society," *Research for Action* 31 (1997): 8.

32. Quoted in Robin Luckham, Anne Marie Goetz, and Mary Kaldor, "Democratic Institutions and Democratic Politics," in *Can Democracy Be Designed: The Politics of Institutional Choice in Conflict-Torn Societies*, eds. Sunil Bastian and Robin Luckham (London and New York: Zed Books, 2003), 43.

33. Gurr, *People versus States*, 152–63, 169, 204.

5

Women and Development

President of Liberia, Ellen Johnson Sirleaf. She is the first woman ever elected as president in Africa (2005). A graduate of Harvard University and a former official in the World Bank and the United Nations, she was reelected in 2011. In that same year she was named a cowinner of the Nobel Peace Prize for having advanced peace and reconciliation in her country after it had suffered two horrendously brutal civil wars. *European Pressphoto Agency BV/Alamy Stock Photo*

A CHINESE PROVERB OBSERVES that "Women hold up half the sky." Yet for many years, scholars, governments in the LDCs, and Western development agencies appeared strangely oblivious to women's role in the modernization process. Most early studies of political and economic change in the LDCs said little or nothing about women's issues. In recent decades, however, increased political empowerment of women in many parts of the developing world and the advance of gender-related research have heightened awareness of how women play a distinct and important role in development. For example, women in the LDCs are concentrated in certain occupations—including agriculture, domestic service, street vending, and teaching—and face barriers to entering others—such as management and higher-paid professions. Distinctions between "women's work" and "men's work" have obvious economic implications, with women's jobs usually earning lower wages or salaries and wielding less power. Moreover, women are also greatly underrepresented in the political arena. Not only do they hold far fewer government posts than men do, but their share diminishes as one moves up the pyramid of power.

Although gender inequality and exploitation exist in most societies, the problems are more severe in the LDCs. In its most horrifying form, the list of injustices includes painful and dangerous female genital mutilation (so-called female circumcision) in parts of Africa, the Middle East, and Southeast Asia; the sale of child brides for dowries in Bangladesh; wife beatings in Zambia and Peru; the murders of several thousand Indian women annually by husbands who were dissatisfied with the size of their dowries; courts that condone "**honor killings**" of women suspected of extramarital relations or even dating unapproved partners; and economic deprivations that drive many women into prostitution, often involuntarily.

Recently, a village chief in rural West Bengal, India learned that a young woman had accepted a marriage proposal from a man outside the village. He and the village council ordered her to stop the marriage and fined her and her family the rupee equivalent of a few hundred dollars (a huge amount in that setting). When they refused to pay, he ordered villagers to gang-rape her, which a number of them did.[1] Nor are such incidents confined to backward, rural villages. In Delhi, the nation's capital, Bhawna Yadav, a third-year university student, was strangled by her parents for having married outside her caste. In a landmark six-nation survey of ten thousand men in Asia and the Pacific, a UN study reported that nearly one quarter of those interviewed said they had raped a woman or girl at some time. "Half of those who admitted to rape reported their first time was when they were teenagers."[2] In the Congo (Kinshasa), during its long and unusually brutal civil war (in which over five million people were killed), rape was used as a weapon of war designed to force residents of contested villages to flee. In 2011, the *New York Times* reported that a woman was raped in that country, on average, every minute, for an annual total of over 500,000 victims.

Nor is the legal system of any help in many cases and often it adds injury (and insult) to injury. In Saudi Arabia, a woman who was kidnapped and raped by seven men was sentenced to two hundred lashes for having placed herself in a vulnerable position. Until recently (2006), Pakistani law required a woman to produce four *male* witnesses to substantiate her claim of having been raped, an obviously impossible task in almost all situations. Worse yet, if she could not produce those witnesses, she could be charged with adultery. If convicted, she might be flogged, imprisoned, or even stoned to death.

Other acts of violence toward women include female genital mutilation, primarily practiced in Africa on girls and young women. The World Health Organization estimated (in 2014) that about 125 million women then living in twenty-nine countries had suffered this procedure, whose aim is to reduce female sexual desires. Beyond traumatizing young women, the practice has no health benefits and sometimes results in heavy bleeding or infection, which can be fatal. While a number of African nations have officially outlawed this practice, the laws are rarely enforced. For example, Guinea outlawed these "female circumcisions" in 1965. But forty years later, 99 percent of that country's women continued to be mutilated and not a single violation of the law had been prosecuted by the authorities. Less chilling, but no less significant, examples of gender inequality in many developing countries include divorce laws that greatly favor husbands; barriers to women seeking commercial credit for small businesses; the "double day" that working women typically face (coming home after a day's work and having to do most of the housework and child care); and few opportunities for women in government, the professions, and better-paid, blue-collar jobs.

But the study of women in the developing world is by no means confined to issues of inequality and victimization. After years of neglect, many international agencies and government planners have begun to recognize women's special status and particular needs in economic development projects. At the same time, increasing numbers of women are refusing to be mere subjects who are victimized or "acted upon." Their political activity has ranged from the quiet subversion common to many oppressed groups to a more vigorous assertion of their political, economic, and social rights. A growing body of scholarly literature now focuses on women's *empowerment*. Throughout Latin America, for example, women have played a decisive role in independent, grassroots political organizations known as "**new social movements (NSMs)**," which have burst upon the scene since the 1970s. Focusing on gender issues, human rights, poverty, and a range of other concerns, NSMs have provided an important alternative to political parties, labor unions, and other mainstream political organizations that are typically dominated by men. Elsewhere, revolutionary movements in countries such as El Salvador, Nicaragua, and China opened up opportunities for female activism and leadership that had not existed previously. In nations as diverse as Argentina, Bangladesh, Brazil, India, Liberia, Pakistan, the Philippines, and Thailand, women have headed their national governments. And a growing number of developing countries have **reserved seats** for women in national, state, and local legislatures, while other nations have introduced more indirect gender quotas governing candidates for these positions. These measures have frequently increased the number of female office holders dramatically.

THE POLITICAL AND SOCIOECONOMIC STATUS OF WOMEN IN THE LDCs

One problem in many LDCs is that women have fewer educational opportunities than men do. In the most extreme case, Afghanistan's Taliban government (1996–2001) prohibited females from attending school and Taliban rebels continue to attack girl students and schools. Because education significantly affects income, health, and political participation, this **gender gap** influences other important facets of political and economic life. We know, for example, that as women's educational levels rise, birth rates and family size decline.

The first two columns in Table 5.1 compare literacy rates for women and men in the major regions of the developing world as of 1990 and 2015. They show how impressively the rates for both sexes have improved in the last twenty years, with the sharpest gains coming among women in South and West Asia (from 33.6 to 60.8 percent literate) and in the Arab States (from 47.9 to 71.4 percent). But women in both regions started from a very low base and they are still among the least educated groups. On the other hand, Central Asia and East Asia have essentially eliminated the gender gap, while Latin America and the Caribbean are only slightly behind.

The last column, the **Gender Parity Index (GPI)**, which is calculated from the previous two columns—indicates how the female literacy rate in each region compares to the male rate. So, for example, the 2015 GPI for South and West Asia is 0.76 and for Latin America and the Caribbean it is 0.99. This means that today the percentage of females in South and West Asia who are literate is only 76 percent as high as the male literacy rate. On the other hand, the current Latin American and Caribbean GPI of 0.99 shows that the two sexes have nearly equal rates of literacy.

Table 5.1   Women's Literacy Rates Compared to Men's

Region	Female Adult Literacy Rate (%)		Male Adult Literacy Rate (%)		GPI[a]	
	1990	2015	1990	2015	1990	2015
Arab States	47.9	71.4	67.9	86.6	0.62	0.83
Central Asia	97.0	99.6	99.0	99.6	0.98	1.00
East Asia	74.4	94.0	89.0	97.6	0.84	0.96
Latin America and Caribbean	84.4	92.4	87.0	93.3	0.97	0.99
South & West Asia	33.6	60.8	58.9	79.7	0.57	0.76
Sub-Saharan Africa	43.2	55.8	63.6	71.6	0.68	0.78

Source: UNESCO Institute for Statistics, Data Centre.

[a] The GPI (Gender Parity Index) indicates the percentage of females attaining literacy (or any other variable) to the percentage of males attaining it. Thus, if the percentage of females is 0.60, it means the percentage of females in that region who are literate is only 60 percent as high as the male literacy rate. A GPI of 1.00 means that the percentage of females in that region who are literate is the same as the male percentage. In short, the higher the GPI, the more equal female and male literacy rates are. These do not represent the actual rate of literacy. Thus, a country in which only 45 percent of both males and females are literate has a GPI of 1.00 (since male and female literacy rates are equal). Another country that has much higher literacy rates for both men and women—80 percent for females and 100 percent for males) would have a GPI of 0.80.

The first column in Table 5.2 presents **Gender Inequality Index (GII)** ranks and raw scores for each country. The GII is a composite index comparing men and women on three dimensions—political and economic empowerment, participation in the work force, and measures of health. The raw scores (listed here in parentheses) can theoretically range from 0.000 (*most* equality) to 1.000 (*least* equality). The number preceding the score indicates how that country ranks compared to the 148 nations that have calculated GIIs. Generally, inequality is highest in the LDCs such as Mozambique, Egypt, and India. However, some developing nations in the table have comparatively low gender inequality, including Singapore and China, which have, respectively, the 15th and 37th least inequality.

The remaining columns compare recent adult literacy rates for women and men in each country. During the last decade or two, the gender gap in literacy has narrowed considerably in most developing countries, as girls have enrolled in primary schools at rates approaching, and occasionally even surpassing, boys. In fact, as the last column indicates, Singapore and China have achieved full or nearly full gender equality in literacy. Brazilian women are very unusual in that women have a *higher* literacy rate than men do (even though their actual literacy rate of 92.9 percent (data column 2) is not as high as Singapore's or China's. On the other hand, women in India, Egypt, and, especially, Mozambique not

Table 5.2   GII and Comparative Gender Literacy Rates

Country	Gender Inequality Index (GII) Rank (and raw score)	Female Adult Literacy Rate (%)	Male Adult Literacy Rate (%)	Female Literacy as a Percent of Male
Switzerland	2 (0.030)	99.0	99.0	100
Singapore	15 (0.090)	95.0	98.6	96
China	37 (0.202)	94.5	98.2	96
Brazil	85 (0.441)	92.9	92.5	>100
India	127 (0.563)	60.6	81.3	75
Egypt	130 (0.580)	65.4	82.2	80
Mozambique	146 (0.657)	45.4	73.3	62

Source: UNDP, *Human Development Reports*, 2014; CIA, *The World Fact Book*, 2015.

only have relatively low literacy rates, but their rates are considerably lower than men's. In this respect, they are typical of the countries in their regions.

Finally, Table 5.3 offers data on women's socioeconomic status. The first column presents the country's score for the **Gender-Related Development Index (GDI)**, which is a composite score that compares female life expectancy, education, and income with those of men. It ranges from 1.04 in Sweden (meaning Swedish women have a higher combined score for those measures than men do) to 0.847 in Iran (indicating a large GDI gap between the sexes). The numbers in parentheses following the GDI scores indicate each nation's ranking among nearly 150 countries in the world. Developed European countries—such as Sweden (ranked 6th)—tend to have the highest rankings. Colombia's rank (46th) puts it ahead of most LDCs as well as Italy (ranked 61st) and Austria (91st), not in the table. This means that although Italian and Austrian men and women both have much higher GDIs than their counterparts in Colombia, the gaps *between* the sexes are smaller in Colombia. Egypt's and Iran's very low GDI rankings are typical of many, though not all, Muslim countries.

Women in the Economy: Rural and Urban

Turning to columns 2 and 3, we find that even in a very egalitarian, developed country, such as Sweden, women are less likely to be in the workforce and earn less than men. As expected, in developing countries, gender gaps are much wider than in economically advanced countries. For example, in Egypt, the rate of female participation in the workforce is less than one-third as high as the men's (23.6 versus 74.6 percent) and women, on average, earn only about one-fourth (26 percent) of what men do. These employment and income gaps are even greater in Islamist

Table 5.3   **Measures of Gender Empowerment**

Country	Gender-Related Development Index (GDI) (ranking in the world)	Percentage of Women and Men in the Workforce		Average Women's Income as a Percent of Men's
		Women	Men	
Sweden	1.004 (6)	60.2	68.1	79
Egypt	0.855 (125)	23.6	74.6	26
Colombia	0.972 (46)	55.7	79.7	50
Iran	0.847 (128)	16.4	73.1	18
South Korea	0.940 (85)	49.9	72.0	56
Sri Lanka	0.961 (66)	35.0	76.4	37

Source: UNDP, *Human Development Report*, 2014; Inter-Parliamentary Union, *Women in Parliament: 20 years in review*, 2014.

Iran, where women participate in the workforce less than one-fourth as often as men do and earn only 18 percent as much. On the other hand, in relatively economically advanced South Korea, women earn over half as much as men and are employed at over two-thirds the men's rate.

It is in the comparatively traditional countryside, rather than in modern cities, where women play the most vital economic role. A few years ago, the United Nations' Food and Agriculture Organization (FAO) estimated that women constitute over 40 percent of the agricultural labor force in the developing world, with this number reaching about 60 percent in some countries.[3] In time, international agencies (particularly nongovernmental organizations) and LDCs' governments began to recognize women's role in rural development. The percentage of the agricultural workforce that is composed of women ranges from about 20 percent in Latin America and the Caribbean to nearly 50 percent in East and Southeast Asia, Africa, and the Middle East. In parts of Asia and Africa, this percentage has grown in recent decades as many men migrate to find better-paying jobs in the urban economy, leaving their wives behind to work the family farm. While many developing-world governments and international development organizations have become more sensitive to the special problems of poor, women farmers, gender blindness persists: farmers have been widely perceived as "male" by policymakers, development planners, and agricultural service deliverers. Therefore, women often find it more difficult to gain access to crucial resources such as credit, agricultural inputs, technology, and training that would enhance their productivity.

During the past half-century in most LDCs, there has been an enormous population shift from the countryside to the cities (see chapter 6). Modernization theorists had expected that urbanization—often accompanied by increased industrialization, literacy, and exposure to the mass media—would offer women greater occupational and educational opportunities, thereby enhancing their status. In many Latin American nations, the majority of the migrants to urban centers have been women. But while many of them have benefited from their move, others have been left behind. Once settled in the city, most women are only able to secure low-end jobs. Indeed, in many Latin American countries, the most common type of employment among female migrants is as cleaning ladies or maids, for which they generally earn the legal minimum wage or lower. Another major source of employment is the so-called **informal sector**—including street peddling, some small businesses, employment in "sweatshops," and doing "piece-work" at home for contractors. These activities are "unregulated by the institutions of society [most notably the state], in a legal and social environment in which similar activities are regulated" by the government (e.g., safety standards) and taxed. Many men also work in this sector, but the majority of the informal-sector labor force is female (including the vast number of market and street vendors).[4] Although some informal-sector workers earn higher incomes than blue-collar laborers in the modern economy do, many others fall below the poverty line. Finally, in newly industrializing countries, women are often employed in low-wage manufacturing. Over time, as factories become more technologically sophisticated and as wages rise, the percentage of female employees tends to decline.

East Asia's industrial boom since the 1980s has created many new jobs for women, particularly in **labor-intensive industries** such as apparel and electronics. Often these firms prefer hiring young unmarried women for several reasons: the jobs frequently require manual dexterity, a skill that employers associate with women; because they are not the principal breadwinners in their families, young women are frequently willing to work for lower wages; and, finally, women are less likely to join unions or participate in strikes. During economic downturns, women are commonly the first fired because employers believe that men need their jobs more in order to support their families.

Because women in the majority of developing countries have fewer educational opportunities than men (see Table 5.1) do and face other forms of discrimination, their occupational prospects are more limited. All too often, poverty and a lack of vocational skills force women into prostitution. Despite Thailand's economic boom since the mid-1960s, continuing rural poverty has driven many young female migrants into Bangkok's thriving "sex tourism" industry. One study of Bangkok and Manila (Philippines) revealed that 7–9 percent of female employment in these two major cities was "prostitution related." Some desperately poor families in that region have sold young daughters to brothels or given them as collateral for loans. A study of Southeast Asia by the International Labour Organization estimated that the number of sex workers in the mid-1990s was 140,000–230,000 in Indonesia and 200,000–300,000 in Thailand, where the number of prostitutes grew tenfold, between the early 1970s and the 1980s. In the economically depressed Philippines, "the estimated 400,000–500,000 prostitutes in the country *approximated the number of its manufacturing workers.*"[5]

While some sex workers enter the trade voluntarily, many others (including underage girls) do not. A State Department report notes that a survey in Cambodia "found that 40 percent of women and girls who work[ed] as prostitutes [did] so voluntarily, while 60 percent had been forced to work as prostitutes or [had] been deceived into prostitution."[6]

While these studies document the severe problems that frequently accompany Third World modernization, it is important to recognize that long-term economic growth, most notably in East Asia, has improved the incomes of millions of other underprivileged women newly employed in the modern sector of the economy. This is particularly true in the countries where female educational opportunities have also improved. Among middle- and upper-class women, the advantages of higher-class status usually mitigate the educational and career disadvantages of being female. In Asia and Latin America, the number of women professionals and businesswomen has increased rapidly in recent decades. Still, through most of the developing world, "women [remain] vastly underrepresented in government, business, political and social institutions."[7]

WOMEN AND POLITICS

The same traditions and prejudices that have undermined women's social and economic positions have also disadvantaged them politically. In Latin America, for example, women won the right to vote considerably later than they did in industrialized democracies. Whereas the United States and most European democracies legalized female suffrage in the first two decades of the twentieth century, only seven of twenty Latin American countries allowed women to vote before the close of World War II. Ecuador was the first nation in that region to extend the franchise (1929) and Paraguay the last (1961). In Africa and Asia, the situation was different. Because most of the countries in those regions did not become independent until the decades after World War II, when female suffrage was a universally accepted principle, women were normally enfranchised from the start of self-rule. However, the Arab Gulf State of Bahrain enfranchised women only in 2001, while Kuwait did it in 2005. Today, women in the LDCs generally still vote at a lower rate than men do, but this gender gap is narrowing.[8]

In much of Africa, Asia, and the Middle East, traditional cultural values have limited women's political participation and activism. Lower-income women generally have few educational opportunities, which effectively limits their level of participation. Indeed, social class correlates particularly strongly with female political participation. In some LDCs, highly educated and Westernized women, many of them born to elite families, are nearly as likely to hold important political offices as women in the West are. For example, although the countries of the Indian subcontinent have some of the world's lowest levels of female literacy and empowerment, Bangladesh, India, Pakistan, and Sri Lanka all have had women prime ministers. The first woman president of the United Nations General Assembly and the first female chair of the Security Council were both from Africa, rather than advanced, industrial countries.

Because developing countries encompass so many cultural traditions, and because social change has impinged so differently on each nation's social classes and sectors, there are no simple generalizations about the way in which modernization has influenced women's political status. Modernization theory would lead us to expect that more socially and economically developed countries would be quicker to grant political rights to women. If we look at Latin America, however, we find little correlation between a country's literacy rate or per capita income and the year in which it granted suffrage to women. Thus, the spread of education alone does not guarantee women greater political equality. At the same time, governments of countries such as Rwanda, Mozambique, South Africa, Argentina, Costa Rica, and Cuba have made conscious efforts in recent times to change traditional values regarding gender. More recently, many countries have increased women's political representation by creating reserved seats and other types of quotas for women in parliament (discussed later).* This has given a number of developing countries a higher percentage of female representatives in parliament than many developed nations have. In fact, countries such as Argentina and Rwanda now have much higher proportions of women in their national legislatures than France or the United States do.

Women's Political Activism at the Grassroots

Perhaps, women have exerted the greatest influence on the politics of the developing world when acting through grassroots organizations in their own neighborhoods and villages. Community-based groups afford them opportunities for participation and leadership which are usually absent at the national or regional level. Furthermore, these organizations typically

---

*"Parliament" is the generic term for a national legislature, even in countries where that body is called "Congress" or some other name.

focus on issues that are of immediate importance to underprivileged women—housing, health care, nutrition, and education. Finally, neighborhood and village organizations are more accessible to poor women, who have no day care for their young children and usually cannot travel far from home. In short, many women who have been excluded from mainstream political parties, interest groups, and government institutions are attracted to community groups because of their accessibility and relevance to their own lives.

In recent decades, a range of grassroots organizations representing poor and middle-class women have emerged in many developing countries. Some represent women exclusively, while others include members of both sexes but are led by women or contain women's wings. Jana Everett examined several Indian community organizations in urban and rural settings, finding important similarities and differences. Both urban and rural groups were first led by politically experienced, middle-class women committed to organizing the poor. But, as low-income women became more involved in community activities, their political awareness and confidence grew, stimulating, in turn, greater participation in the broader political system.

However, the goals and tactics used by these groups varied. For example, Everett found that the rural grassroots groups were more likely than urban organizations to stage demonstrations and other types of protest. They were also more prone to demand redistributive economic remedies such as land reform. In comparison, urban women's groups were generally more moderate in their goals and tactics. Armita Basu's study of female rural protests in the Indian state of Maharashtra also noted their militancy. In one case, when a woman villager complained that the local police had ignored her charges against a landlord who had beaten her severely, a crowd of 300 women and 150 men "smeared [the landlord's] face with cow dung . . . and paraded him through the surrounding villages."[9] The rural women's greater aggressiveness likely resulted from the more hostile political atmosphere they confronted. Because village political and economic elites are usually less willing than their urban counterparts to redress the grievances of the poor through normal political channels, these women were forced to use more radical tactics.

In Latin America, opposition to the authoritarian military governments that governed much of the region during the 1970s and 1980s was a major catalyst for grassroots political activity. In Argentina, Brazil, Chile, and Uruguay, military dictatorships suspended elections, banned many political parties and unions, and arrested, tortured, or killed suspected "subversives." At the same time, a major debt crisis in the 1980s, coupled with harsh government economic remedies, produced the worst recession in the region since the Great Depression of the 1930s and a precipitous decline in living standards. Women played an important role in antiauthoritarian social movements, which helped pave the way for the restoration of democracy in the 1980s and 1990s.

The women's movement incorporated three types of political organizations, all largely urban based. First were feminist groups, primarily consisting of middle-class women. They included many professionals who previously had been active in leftist political parties, but had become disillusioned by the left's disinterest in women's issues at that time. A second type, neighborhood organizations, represented women from the urban slums. In the face of the region's severe economic crisis, poor women organized self-help groups to run communal kitchens, infant nutrition centers, and other antipoverty activities. Though not highly politicized originally, many of these groups radicalized over time as they demanded more equitable distribution of state expenditures and the restoration of democracy.

Finally, a third strand of the women's movement was devoted to human rights. Argentina's "Mothers of the Plaza de Mayo" regularly marched in defiance of government restrictions to demand an accounting of their missing children and grandchildren, who had disappeared at the hands of the police or armed forces. Responding to state-sponsored imprisonments, torture, and assassinations, women's groups in Brazil, Chile, and Uruguay became major components of the human rights movement. This was one of the few instances in which women's organizations had an advantage over similar groups led by men. Because the military governments viewed women as inherently less political than men and, hence, less dangerous, they allowed women's human rights groups greater freedom than they gave other protest movements. Furthermore, this was the most socially integrated branch of the women's movement, bringing together participants from the middle and working classes. In many cases, they also joined forces with other human rights activists in the Catholic Church (chapter 3).

Ironically, the restoration of democracy reduced the need for unity among the disparate wings of the women's movement. Furthermore, as female leaders and militants became increasingly involved in the restored democratic system, many of them returned to party politics and lost their close ties to community groups representing the urban poor. Thus, the return of democratic governments actually demobilized many lower-income women and weakened their movements. More recently, however, the explosion of **NGOs** in developing areas worldwide has created new opportunities for women's grassroots political participation. As their name suggests, NGOs are issue-based organizations, independent of government control. Many try to influence public policy in areas such as democratization, human rights, women's rights, environmental protection, housing, health care, and education. The best-known and financed groups operate internationally, including the Catholic Relief Services, Amnesty International, Greenpeace, and Oxfam. On the other hand, most NGOs are limited to the local or, at most, the national level, where many of them try to mobilize popular support and influence government policy. In India, for example, it is estimated that national and local NGOs number in the tens or likely hundreds of thousands. Throughout the developing world, they have contributed enormously to the expansion of civil society, particularly in democratizing societies, where they often provide a political voice to women and otherwise powerless groups seeking reform.

Women as National Political Leaders
Women Heads of Government
Throughout the developing world, women are severely underrepresented in political leadership positions. For the most part, women still have not nearly achieved equal representation in important government offices, including seats in the national parliament and national cabinets. Slowly this has begun to change. In Asia—especially South Asia—and in Latin America, a number of women have risen to the top of the political ladder in recent decades. Four nations in South Asia have been led by women prime ministers.* The most prominent member of this group was Indira Gandhi, who served four terms as prime minister (1966–1977 and 1980–1984) and dominated Indian politics for eighteen years, until her assassination in 1984. In Sri Lanka, a woman president and a female prime minister controlled the country's politics for many years. And in Bangladesh, one of two women rivals—Begum Khaleda Zia and Sheikh Hasina Wajed—has been prime minister for most of the time since 1991. Elsewhere in Asia, women have been presidents of the Philippines (twice) and Indonesia as well as prime ministers of Thailand and Pakistan.

Nine of the thirty-three countries in Latin America and the Caribbean have elected female presidents or prime ministers, the largest proportion of any region in the developing world. They include the current presidents of two of the most important countries in the area—Argentina's Cristina Fernández de Kirchner and Brazil's Dilma Rousseff. In addition, Chile's President, Michelle Bachelet, is now serving her second (nonconsecutive) term in office. Previously, Costa Rica, Panama, and Nicaragua all had women presidents.

---

*Many countries have both a president and a prime minister and the relative power of each leader varies from country to country. In Latin America, East Asia, and Africa, the president is normally the more powerful figure. In the rest of Asia, the Caribbean, as well as Europe, the prime minister is usually the major governmental leader.

Although several Sub-Saharan parliaments have among the highest percentages of women in the world (discussed later), that region has had far fewer women heads of government or heads of state than either Asia or Latin America. Only recently have two female presidents been elected (in Liberia and Malawi), while women have been prime ministers in at least six African countries.

Several caveats must be raised regarding the political success of women leaders in Asia. First, most of them emerged from the tiny elite of highly educated, upper-class women in powerful families. Thus, they were not at all representative of women's societal status generally. For example, Pakistan's Benazir Bhutto attended Oxford and Harvard Universities. Corazón Aquino belonged to a powerful, Filipino landowning family. Thailand's Yingluck Shinawatra was a successful businesswoman with an MA in Public Administration from the United States.

Second, many of the most influential women leaders everywhere, but particularly in Asia, have been the widows, wives, or daughters of charismatic national leaders: Indira Gandhi was the daughter of India's legendary first prime minister, Jawaharlal Nehru; former Indonesian president Megawati Sukarnoputri is the daughter of President Sukarno, that country's first president and founding father; Filipino president Gloria Macapagal Arroyo's father had also been president; and Benazir Bhutto's father preceded her as Pakistani prime minister. Most recently, Thailand's prime minister, Yingluck Shinawatra, was, in effect, a stand-in for her brother, a former prime minister. In Latin America and the Caribbean, most of the first women presidents also were all the wives or widows of former presidents.

Indeed, a shocking number of female government leaders in developing countries, most notably in Asia, have been the widows or daughters of assassinated political leaders. Sri Lankan prime minister Sirimavo Bandaranaike was the widow of a slain prime minister, while that country's former president, Chandrika Kumaratunga, endured the political assassinations of both her father and her husband (thirty years apart). Former president Corazón Aquino, hero of the Filipino democracy movement, was the widow of an assassinated opposition leader. Bangladesh's two long-standing female prime ministers are, respectively, the widow of a slain national president and the daughter of Bangladesh's founding father and first president. Benazir Bhutto's father, a former prime minister, was ousted by the Pakistani armed forces and hung. And in Latin America, former Nicaraguan president Violeta Chamorro was the widow of a famed newspaper editor whose assassination sparked the Nicaraguan Revolution.

This does not imply that these women lacked political ability or leadership qualities. Indira Gandhi was recognized as one of the world's most accomplished political leaders, and Violeta Chamorro helped heal the wounds of her country's civil war. After Sri Lanka's Sirimavo Bandaranaike succeeded her assassinated husband as prime minister, she dominated that country's political system for the next three decades.* Still, no matter how highly skilled they have been, until recently most female government leaders have been able to reach the top of their political system only as heirs to their fathers or husbands.† That blueprint seems to be changing in Latin America and, to a lesser extent, in Africa, where several women have been elected presidents in the twenty-first century (in Chile, Brazil, Costa Rica, Liberia, and Malawi) without having inherited their husband's or father's political following.

Women Cabinet Ministers

Another important gage of women's political empowerment is the number and type of ministerial posts they hold in their nation's cabinet. In many countries these are the next most influential government positions after the president or prime minister. Although women continue to hold a low share of cabinet posts in most LDCs, their numbers have increased from a mere 3.4 percent in 1987 to over 17 percent in 2015. Because cabinet ministers are appointed by the president or prime minister, the percentage of women in that institution (in any particular country) is more volatile than their percentage in parliament. The proportion of women may change unpredictably (may go up or down from year to year) depending on which political party or which president/prime minister is in office. In general, however, the percentage has grown over time worldwide and in the LDCs. Some developing nations have a substantial portion of women in their cabinets. For example, as of early 2015, women were about half the ministers in Cape Verde (in Africa) and Nicaragua. And they held between 35 percent and 40 percent of the cabinet posts in South Africa, Rwanda, Burundi, Costa Rica, and Chile. But, in the majority of LDCs, women held fewer than 20 percent of their ministers and the percentages in Turkey, Thailand, Pakistan, and Saudi Arabia was less than 5 percent.

Beyond a simple head count of the number of women appointed to ministerial positions, it is interesting to consider the *types* of cabinet positions that women have held. Most frequently, they headed ministries such as education, women's affairs, and health and social welfare—areas traditionally believed to be suited for women's **"nurturing role."**[10] At the

---

*On the other hand, some widows who succeed to leadership, such as Argentina's Isabel Perón, were not capable.

†Until the 1970s a similar pattern held in the United States, where the majority of women who served as governors or in either house of Congress were the widows of men who had held these positions. This pattern has obviously changed tremendously since then.

same time few women (none in most countries) held such key cabinet ministries such as defense, economics, or foreign affairs. Only since the start of this century have a small number of women held these posts (e.g., the current president of Chile, Michelle Bachelet, had been appointed Chile's first female defense minister in 2002).*

Reserved Seats and Quotas: Female Representation in Parliament

The participation of women in national legislatures has been more complex. Since women normally account for approximately half the national population, gender-neutral political systems would presumably produce a corresponding percentage of female representatives in those institutions. However, few regions or countries come close to such parity. Table 5.4 shows that, although the percentage of women in parliament worldwide doubled from 1995 to 2015—and grew in every world region—women still constitute only 22.5 percent of all MPs (Members of Parliament) today. As the second data column reveals, of all world regions, only the Nordic nations (Norway, Sweden, Denmark, Finland, and Iceland), with 41.3 percent, come close to having women fill half the seats.

We might expect women to hold a larger share of parliamentary seats in more modern and more educated countries. But looking at the major regions in the table, we see that this is not necessarily so. While it is true that the Nordic region—with the highest rate of women MPs in the "lower house" of the national legislature—is very socioeconomically advanced, the rest of Europe has a lower percentage of women in that chamber (25.7 percent) than does Latin America and the Caribbean (27 percent).† Moreover, of the eight parliaments with the highest percentage of women in the world (all over 40 percent female), seven are LDCs from either Latin America (Bolivia, Cuba, and Ecuador) or Africa (Rwanda, the Seychelles, Senegal, and South Africa).‡

---

*Interestingly, in the United States, no woman has ever been Secretary of Defense or Secretary of the Treasury. The first female Secretary of State, Madeleine Albright, took office in 1997 (there have been two more since then—Condoleezza Rice and Hillary Clinton).

†In a parliament or congress with two chambers (bicameral legislatures), the "lower house" refers to the larger chamber, whose entire membership is elected at the same time (usually every two to four years), as with the U.S. House of Representatives.
Despite its name, the lower house has greater power than the so-called upper house in most countries (but not in the United States). The upper house (often called "the Senate") is normally a smaller chamber, whose members have longer terms of office and run in staggered years (like the U.S. Senate). Some national legislatures are unicameral (they have only one chamber) and in Table 5.4 they are grouped together with the lower house of bicameral legislatures.

‡As of June 1, 2015. These rankings change when there are new elections.

Table 5.4   **Percentage of Women in National Parliaments: Regional Averages**

Region	1995	2015
Nordic Countries	36.4	41.5
Europe excluding Nordic Countries	13.2	25.7
Latin American and the Caribbean	12.7	27.0
Sub-Saharan Africa	9.8	22.2
Asia	13.2	19
Arab Countries	4.3	19
World Average	11.3	22.5

Source: Inter-Parliamentary Union, *Women in National Parliaments* (online—as of June 1, 2015).

Thus, a country's or region's percentage of women MPs may be determined as much by its history, culture, and politics as it is by its level of modernization. Most African and the Middle Eastern countries did not gain independence until the 1940s or later, when the importance of female political participation had greater currency in the world's political culture and practices. Some of the LDC governments with high representation of women in parliament (such as South Africa, Eritrea, Cuba, and Nicaragua) came to power after revolutionary struggles in which traditional values had been open to challenge, and women often played an important part in the struggle. As we have previously seen, the East African nation of Rwanda experienced a genocide in 1994 when 500,000 to one million people (mostly men) were killed in approximately one hundred days, depleting the country's male population. After peace was restored, women, by necessity, took on a far greater role in the country's government, including holding more than half the seats in parliament.

Elsewhere, several social, economic, and cultural factors help account for women's underrepresentation in most of the world. Pippa Norris and Joni Lovenduski have argued that the number of women in elected office depends on various factors affecting "supply and demand."[11] Supply refers to the number of women who meet the socioeconomic standards of public officeholders in their country. Because women in many LDCs have lower levels of education, lower status, and, most important, fewer economic resources than men—all factors closely related to political success—they are able to "supply" fewer viable candidates for office. In fact, Rae Lesser Blumberg's research in several regions of the world indicates that "the most important variable . . . affecting the level of [political] equality [or inequality] between men and women is economic power" as defined by their relative incomes and control of economic resources.[12] On the "demand" side (i.e., society's acceptance of female political leaders), widespread cultural prejudice in some regions against the empowerment of women, most notably in the Islamic world, has also restricted the number of women from holding public office.

In the past two decades, as women's educational levels have risen in most developing countries, as they have entered the professions in greater numbers, and as cultural prejudices have diminished in many places, both the supply of and demand for women officeholders have increased. The most important change in recent years has come from the demand side—the introduction of **gender quotas** for parliament. Since 1991, the number of countries implementing this electoral mechanism has climbed sharply, and today about one hundred countries, primarily in the developing world, have some form of gender quota. Although the intent of all of these gender quotas is to enhance the number of women in parliament, we will see that some countries have made only token efforts and achieved few gains, while others have sharply increased the number of women MPs. Latin America, though often associated with *machismo* (male chauvinism), has been the world leader in effecting reform measures. Across that region, the number of female representatives has jumped from 12.7 percent in 1995 to over 27 percent in 2015 (a higher percentage than in Canada or the United States).[13]

Legislated and voluntary attempts to raise the proportion of women in national parliaments have taken several forms. The most direct and certain method is to *reserve* a designated number of parliamentary seats for women. The basic justification for reserving seats is that because many cultures have deeply ingrained gender prejudices, the only way a significant number of women can gain office is by setting aside a bloc of seats for them. In fact, many of the reserved seats systems were introduced in Arab States, South Asia, and in parts of Africa, where prejudices against women officeholders are generally strongest. Two of the recent countries introducing this form of gender quota are Afghanistan (an extremely religiously conservative Muslim country) and Iraq (also Muslim) and they have about 25 percent of their lower house's seats reserved. But in both cases, this was only because the US occupying forces had pressured the two governments to insert quota provisions in their new constitutions.

Unfortunately, in some countries, creating reserved seats seems to have created a "glass ceiling," blocking further electoral gains for women. Although women are allowed to contest parliamentary seats beyond the number reserved for them, the use of reserved seats often signals voters that women have gotten their "fair share" and do not deserve to be elected beyond their guaranteed quota. Also, many political parties in more traditional societies have similar attitudes and see no need to include women in their regular slate of parliamentary candidates.[14]

However, some countries have set aside a substantial number of reserved seats for women and have also elected a significant number of women beyond that quota in contests that are open to both sexes. Thus, in Rwanda, 30 percent of the seats (twenty-four out of a total of eighty) in the Chamber of Deputies are reserved for women candidates. In addition, in the last parliamentary election, women candidates won almost half of the nondesignated seats, which were open to both male and female candidates. This gave them a total of fifty-one seats (i.e., 64 percent of the entire chamber), the highest portion in the world. It is now one of only two lower chambers of parliament in the world where women are in the majority—the other is Bolivia.

Another means of reducing gender underrepresentation is to establish quotas for the slates of parliamentary *candidates* in general elections. Such quotas may take two forms. First, individual political parties may voluntarily guarantee that their slate of parliamentary candidates will contain a certain percentage of women. In Europe, for example, Scandinavia enjoyed the first major gains in female parliamentary representation when that region's socialist parties (frequently the largest parties in those countries) agreed to gender quotas. In the LDCs, the most successful example of voluntary quotas has been in South Africa's dominant party, the African National Congress (ANC).

The second type of candidate quota is legislated (or sometimes included in the constitution) and is binding on all political parties. Both voluntary and legislated candidate quotas commit political parties to nominate a stipulated percentage of women candidates on their tickets. In many quota systems, women must constitute at least 30 percent of their party's list of parliamentary candidates. This number reflects the "critical mass" of female MPs commonly needed to produce government policies friendly to women's interests. A dozen Latin American countries and a number of other developing nations passed some form of a gender candidate quota during the wave of democratic transitions in the 1990s. Argentina was a pioneer in this area and by 2006 dozens of countries, mostly LDCs, had some sort of quota system.[15]

The goal of candidate quotas is purportedly to give women a greater opportunity to hold regularly elected seats rather than fill seats specially reserved for them. But candidate quotas, particularly when legislatively imposed, are frequently ineffective because their objective is easily circumvented if major political parties nominate most of their women candidates in races that the party has little chance of winning. Many countries (including Britain and a number of its former colonies) have electoral systems with **single-member districts (SMD)** in which voters elect only one MP in each parliamentary district. This is the system used to elect the U.S. House of Representatives. In such countries, most electoral districts usually lean heavily toward one party or another. So, political parties that want to satisfy the letter of the quota laws, but wish to circumvent their spirit, can simply nominate most of their women candidates in districts where they had little chance of winning the general elections. For example, imagine that the United States had a 30 percent gender quota for congressional candidates and that party officials, rather than voters in primary elections, were the ones who selected the candidates.* If Democratic Party leaders wanted to circumvent the quota law, they could nominate men in districts that are safely theirs and nominate most of their women congressional candidates (30 percent of the total) in heavily Republican states ("Red States"), such as Alabama or Utah, where they would stand little chance of beating the Republican candidates in the general election. Similarly, the Republicans could run their male candidates in Red States, while fielding the women candidates in Democratic strongholds such as Boston, New York, and San Francisco.

While some developing nations elect their parliaments in SMDs, most use an electoral system called **proportional representation (PR)**. To understand how PR works, let us imagine a country with a five hundred-seat parliament divided into twenty-five electoral districts, each of which elects twenty MPs. The national parties each nominate a "party list" of twenty candidates in each district, with candidates ranked from one through twenty (closed lists). Rather than select a single candidate, as American voters do when they cast their ballots for the House of Representatives, voters in PR elections generally choose an entire party list (e.g., the Christian Democratic Party list of twenty candidates or the Socialist Party list). Seats are then allocated in proportion to the percentage of votes that each list receives. Thus, if the Christian Democrats' list received 40 percent of the votes in "district A," they would win 40 percent of the twenty seats in that district (i.e., eight seats). But which eight of that party's twenty listed candidates would go to parliament? It would be those who were ranked first through eight on the party's list prior to the election. If we further imagine that a quota law requires that at least 35 percent of each party's candidates be women (i.e., at least seven candidates in each district), the number of women who actually are elected would depend on where they had been *ranked* on the party list. Thus, even with the 35 percent quota requirement, if all of the female candidates had been ranked in the bottom half of the party list, all eight of that party's victorious candidates would still be men.†

---

*The United States is one of the few countries in the world that hold primary elections to select party candidates. In most countries, candidates are named by party officials in conventions, caucuses, or other types of meetings.

†Actually, there are many varieties of PR elections. I have described just a simplified, generic version.

To put teeth into a legislated quota system and prevent dumping of women candidates into hopeless positions at the bottom of the party lists (in PR systems) or in districts that the party knows it cannot win (in SMD systems), countries such as Argentina passed electoral laws requiring so-called **zipper-style quotas**. This means that each party must not only meet its quota of female candidates, but also alternate male and female candidates, according to that quota percentage from the top of the list downward. For example, if a country such as Argentina has a zipper-style gender quota of 33 percent, women candidates have to occupy every third position on the list from the top rank on down. So, if a party won nine of the thirty seats in a particular multimember district, the nine winning candidates would include three women. In general, elections through zipper-style proportional representation with closed lists (i.e., where voters cannot select individual candidates on the list) benefit women candidates more than quotas in SMD elections do.

Since 1991, the spread of legally mandated quotas, of any type, has been a major factor in the worldwide increase in female MPs. For example, in ten Latin American countries that enacted quotas between 1991 and 1997, the number of women in parliament rose by an average of 8 percent in the very next national election.[16] However, results have been most impressive when electoral laws mandate zipper-style quotas or their equivalent. For example, when Costa Rica's Supreme Court strengthened that country's quota law by insisting that women be proportionally included in *competitive* races, the percentage of women in Congress rose from 19 percent in 1997 (already higher than in the U.S. Congress at that time) to 35 percent in 2002. Also, when the ANC took power in South Africa and voluntarily adopted a gender quota, the percentage of women MPs rose from 141st in the world in 1994 to 7th highest today.*

Ultimately, the issue of reserved seats and candidate quotas raises another fundamental question. How much difference does increased female representation have on government policy? The evidence suggests that legislatures with significantly higher female membership (in either LDCs or developed nations) are more prone to address issues such as gender bias, child care, education, rape, domestic violence, and divorce law and are more likely to produce legislation in these areas that is beneficial to women. However, most analysts agree that even a substantial increase in female representation from a very low base—for example, the Arab World's huge jump in female MPs from 4.3 percent in 1995 to

---

*The African National Congress is the only South African party to impose a gender quota. But since it holds almost two-thirds of the seats in parliament, its quota obviously affects the nature of the entire legislature.

19 percent today—is usually not sufficient to affect government policy on those issues because there are still too few female MPs to influence policy. Indeed, when women hold fewer than 30 percent of parliamentary seats, they tend to be co-opted or are simply ineffective in pressing "women's issues." As female representation approaches that 30 percent level, however, parliaments are more likely to pass "women-friendly" legislation. As of 2015, there were forty-four countries that had reached that threshold, over half of them developing nations.*

Earlier, we noted the growing number of women prime ministers and presidents in the LDCs, most notably in South Asia. While we might assume that gains for women at the pinnacle of government would either reflect or cause broader political or socioeconomic advances for women generally—as they do, for example, in the Nordic countries—this has not necessarily been true in the LDCs. Sri Lanka and Bangladesh most glaringly demonstrate that point. Women have served for extended periods as Sri Lanka's president (eleven years) and prime minister (eighteen years). Yet, they currently constitute only 5.3 percent of that nation's MPs, less than one quarter of the international average. Similarly, although Bangladesh has been led by either of two female prime ministers for fifteen of the past eighteen years, it still ranks seventy-five among all nations that have recorded GII scores.

Although electoral mechanisms such as quotas and reserved seats are the most important factors responsible for greater female representation in parliament, social, cultural, and historical forces also play a role. At the same time, these factors also help explain why a particular country introduces quotas or reserved seats in the first place. For example, in Scandinavia, the culture's strong emphasis on gender and class equality produced a very high number of female MPs even before those countries' major parties adopted voluntary quotas. Denmark's parties abandoned gender quotas in 1996 (after enforcing them for nearly two decades) yet, even without the benefit of quotas, women currently hold 38 percent of their country's parliamentary seats, one of the world's highest percentages. In Africa, the countries with the highest proportion of women in parliament are often "postconflict states," which have come through bloody internal conflicts (Rwanda, Burundi), long wars of independence against their colonial masters (Angola, Mozambique), or struggles against minority White rule (South Africa). While these conflicts took a terrible toll in lives and suffering, they also opened up new opportunities for women who were involved in them.

---

*A number of these countries—such as Cuba—are not democracies and in those countries it is unclear how much women MPs exert independent influence on legislation or to what extent all MPs—including women—normally vote as the ruling party dictates.

The Effect of Reaching a Critical Mass on Policy Outcomes

We noted earlier that it seems that in order to be effective agents of change in advanced industrial societies (Europe, North America, Japan etc.), women seem to need to hold at least 30 percent of the legislative seats. What about the LDCs that have reached that threshold (usually with the help of gender quotas) or come close? Has that helped advance "women's issues," such as medical and nutritional care for mothers and their small children? Mala Htun and Jennifer M. Piscopo have found that, in Latin America, countries with gender quotas (and, therefore, higher percentages of women) are likely to pass gender-related legislation that does not conflict with their countries' cultural values, such as laws that protect women against violence. They are unlikely to change culturally or religiously sensitive laws, such as easing restrictions on abortion.[17]

In Asia and the Arab World, gender quotas are less likely to lead to any kind of gender-friendly legislation. In a number of cases, they have adopted quotas to satisfy the United Nations, Western countries, or other possible aid donors. And in two nations where gender quotas were introduced as a result of American invasions—Afghanistan and Iraq—these quotas are very unlikely to produce policies that help women.

Women and Revolutionary Change

Both because of their ideological commitment to gender equality and because they needed military recruits, some revolutionary armies heavily recruited women and offered them greater opportunities for upward mobility. For example, women constituted an estimated 20–30 percent of the revolutionary guerrilla forces in Eritrea and Nicaragua and held high leadership positions in El Salvador's FMLN.

More generally, the political, economic, and social changes brought about by revolutions in the LDCs often present women with unique opportunities. Revolutionary regimes in countries such as China, Vietnam, and Cuba have tried to transform traditional cultural values through education and propaganda. Combating society's conventional restrictions on women has been a part of that process. When the Chinese communists came to power, they eliminated the last vestiges of foot binding for young girls and prohibited the sale of women and girls as wives, concubines, or prostitutes. New institutions, such as the Cuban Federation of Women (FMC)—officially representing 70 percent of the country's women—and China Women's Federation were created to mobilize women in support of the revolution and to give them some voice in the political process.

In Cuba, longtime FMC leader, Vilma Espín, was a particularly effective force for gender equality because she was married to (now-President) Raúl Castro and was Fidel Castro's sister-in-law. The federation was instrumental in creating the nation's Family Code (the law governing family relations), which requires both spouses to contribute equally to domestic chores (child care, cooking, cleaning, etc.). Today, women make up about two-thirds of all university graduates and a similar proportion of all professionals, including lawyers and judges.[18]

But even revolutionary societies find it difficult to eradicate long-standing sexist attitudes and they are no panacea. In many cases, radical rhetoric exceeds actual accomplishments. In China, women generally still hold less-skilled, lower-paying jobs. While women have advanced professionally in both China and Cuba, in neither country do they have a significant share of high-level positions in government or in the Communist Party. Although the Cuban Family Code requires husbands to do half of the house work, few men do.

In rural China (where half the population lives), the country's stringent population control policies limit most families to two children.* While this program has lowered the nation's birth rate impressively, the policy has had disturbing, unanticipated consequences. Worldwide, the gender ratio of babies at birth is around 106 or 107 males to 100 females.† But in China the ratio was as high as 121:100 in 2004 and is currently about 117:100. Consequently, males exceed the number of female newborns by well over one million each year. China's huge gender gap (the largest in the world) raises the question of "what happened to the missing girls?"

As in many Asian countries, the Chinese—particularly in rural areas—have a strong cultural and economic preference for sons. Because the population control program limits the number of children that they can have, villagers are concerned that one of those be a boy. Therefore, many prospective parents who can afford prenatal gender tests—ultrasounds, though officially illegal, can be rather easily secured for as little as $12—opt for abortions of female fetuses. And in an unknown, but significant, number of cases, girls who are born fall victim to "gendercide," the murder of female babies by parents who want their child to be a boy (though this practice has decreased in recent years). In addition, many newborn girls are sent to orphanages, where more than 95 percent of the children who are put up for foreign adoption have been female. At the same time, the cumulative effect of the one-child policy has made it harder for young men to find women whom they can marry. In recent years, the Chinese government's growing concern over the gender imbalance has led it to relax some population control measures.[19]

---

*Urban families are limited to one child.

†While one might imagine that half of all newly born babies would be female, male births worldwide normally exceed female births by about 6–7 percent (i.e., a male to female ratio for newborns of 106:100 or 107:100).

MODERNIZATION AND THE STATUS OF WOMEN

Our discussion has revealed that the political and economic status of Third World women varies considerably from region to region and from country to country. Two factors are particularly influential: a country's dominant cultural values and its level of socioeconomic modernization.

A nation's or region's culture—including its religious values—sets baseline boundaries for most women, affecting both the opportunities available to them and the restrictions they face. This is most obvious in fundamentalist Islamist countries such as Afghanistan, Iran, and Saudi Arabia. Political leadership in all these fundamentalist countries is an exclusively male preserve. Cultural restraints are more subtle in East Asia, but even in a relatively modern society such as South Korea women are underrepresented in politics and have a significantly lower income and development indices than do men.

Contrary to modernization theory—but in accordance with radical feminist analysis—socioeconomic modernization has often adversely affected women in the LDCs in the short term. In Africa, for example, the commercialization and mechanization of agriculture have benefited male cultivators disproportionately, frequently at the expense of women farmers. In East and Southeast Asia, rapid industrialization based on cheap labor frequently has given many female laborers higher wages than they earned in their previous jobs, but often has exploited many others. But although modernization often harms poor women initially, its longer-term effects are mostly positive. A growing middle class, wider educational opportunities, and higher rates of literacy make women more aware of their rights and opportunities, while increasing their capacity to defend any gains. Socioeconomic development also tends to create more egalitarian values within society. It is not coincidental that women in Europe and in more modernized Latin America generally enjoy greater political and economic equality. In recent decades, the feminist movement has spread from the world's economically advanced democracies into the LDCs through the media and the demonstration effect. In many developing nations, women's rights movements have emerged where none had existed, or were even conceivable, a decade or two earlier. Educated women in more traditional countries, such as Bolivia and Jordan, are frequently influenced by the women's movements in more progressive neighboring nations such as Chile and Lebanon. The women's movement in economically advanced countries only took off about fifty years ago, and one can only speculate about its influence in the developing world several decades from now.

Given that full gender equality does not exist even in the most advanced industrialized democracies (only small, northern European democracies come close), it seems unlikely that socioeconomic modernization or the spread of democratic norms will automatically bring gender equality to the developing world. Future economic development can be expected to produce both negative and positive consequences. In countries suffering severe economic downturns, such as the recent global financial crisis, or those experiencing civil conflict, women will doubtless continue to bear a disproportionate share of the burden. And the spread of Islamic fundamentalism in many parts of the Middle East and Africa bodes poorly for women's rights in those nations. In the long term, however, economic modernization, higher educational levels, and modern values seem to offer women their best hope.

DEMOCRACY AND THE ROLE OF WOMEN IN SOCIETY

Because democratic ideology endorses equal opportunity and equal rights for *all* citizens, we might expect the Third Wave of democracy to have advanced gender equity. Yet our discussion of revolutionary societies revealed that some nondemocratic governments have promoted women's rights more effectively than comparable democracies have. A number of revolutionary regimes have raised the number of women in the national legislature, improved the legal status of women, banned oppressive traditional customs, and, to some degree, infused respect for women's rights into the new political culture. Thus, there is much evidence that revolutionary governments in China, Cuba, and Mozambique advanced the cause of gender equality more successfully than such democratic governments as Colombia or India. It is also true that the Eastern European transition from communism to democracy brought a precipitous drop in the percentage of women elected to parliament. But most authoritarian governments are neither radical nor committed to women's rights. These rights have fared poorly under both religious fundamentalist regimes and right-wing military dictatorships.

How did women's groups influence the wave of democratization that has swept across the developing world since the 1970s, and how did the emergence of democracy affect women's economic and political standing? In a number of Asian and Latin American nations (such as Argentina and South Korea), women's social movements helped topple repressive regimes. Yet, the return to center stage of male-dominated political parties and interest groups during the subsequent democratic transitions frequently marginalized those grassroots political groups and NGOs in which women had played a major role. Thus, the restoration of democracy had contradictory effects on women's political participation. As Mala Htun has observed,

> The return to civilian rule and the consolidation of democratic governance created many more opportunities for women to be politically

active, but also reduced the comparative advantage of gender-specific organizations as conduits for social demands. As a result, many women, who had entered politics during the struggle against authoritarian rule, left gender-specific organizations for political parties and other "traditional" organizations like labor unions.[20]

In general (looking at *all* developing countries), however, it appears that democratic governments tend to have more gender equality than authoritarian regimes do. No doubt this is because women's groups in liberal democracies are able to mobilize politically, lobby government officials, and otherwise voice their concerns through democratic channels. At the same time, women's advocacy groups are more likely to be heard by a free press and by politicians who want to be reelected. To be sure, some authoritarian regimes, such as Cuba, have a strong record on gender equality. Yet in authoritarian governments, women's rights depend on the will of the (heavily male) political leadership. In most authoritarian governments this will is lacking.

Practice and Review Online
http://textbooks.rowman.com/handelman8e#ch5

KEY TERMS

GDI (gender-related development index)
gender gap
gender quotas
GII (gender inequality index)
GPI (gender parity index)
honor killings
informal sector
labor-intensive industries

NGOs (nongovernmental organizations)
NSMs (new social movements)
nurturing role
PR (proportional representation)
reserved seats
single-member districts
zipper-style quotas

DISCUSSION QUESTIONS

1. If Hillary Clinton is elected U.S. president in 2016, how much of an effect do you think that it would have on women's rights and opportunities in this country? Have LDCs with women prime ministers or presidents made greater progress toward gender equality? What might explain why some governments headed by women made greater progress on "women's issues," while others did not?
2. What are some of the reasons (hopefully including some not mentioned in the chapter) that democracy seems to contribute to greater

gender equality? Under what circumstances might greater democracy end up *diminishing* women's rights in some countries?

3. What is the value of having women serve as UN peacekeepers?

NOTES

1. *The New York Times*, "Village Council in India Accused of Ordering Rape," January 23, 2014 online.

2. UNDP, "UN survey of 10,000 men in Asia and the Pacific reveals why some men use violence against women and girls," September 10, 2013 online.

3. Agricultural Development Economics of the FAO, "The role of women in Agriculture," Working Paper No. 11-02 (March, 2011).

4. Ruth Pearson, "Reassessing Paid Work and Women's Employment: Lessons from the Global Economy," in *Feminisms in Development*, eds. Andrea Cornwall, Elizabeth Harrison, and Ann Whitehead (London: Zed Books, 2007), 202–03.

5. Cited in Alan Gilbert and Josef Gugler, *Cities, Poverty and Development: Urbanization in the Third World*, 2nd ed. (New York: Oxford University Press, 1992), 104, fn. 29. Italics added.

6. *Women and Human Rights*—U.S. Department of State report (released by the Bureau of Democracy, Human Rights and Labor, U.S. Department of State, February 2001).

7. Sonia Nunes Jorge, "Gender-Aware Guidelines for Policy-Making and Regulatory Agencies" (Geneva: ITU Telecommunication Development Bureau Task Force on Gender Issues), 1.

8. World Bank, *Engendering Development* (New York: Oxford University Press 2001), 57.

9. Armita Basu, *Two Faces of Protest: Contrasting Modes of Women's Activism* (Berkeley, CA: University of California Press, 1992), 3.

10. Jane L. Parpart and Kathleen A. Staudt, "Women and the State in Africa," in *Women and the State in Africa*, eds. Jane L. Parpart and Kathleen A. Staudt (Boulder, CO: Lynne Rienner Publishers, 1989), 8.

11. Pippa Norris and Joni Lovenduski, *Political Recruitment: Gender, Race and Class in the British Parliament* (Cambridge, England: Cambridge University Press, 1994).

12. Rae Lesser Blumberg, "Climbing the Pyramids of Power: Alternative Routes to Women's Empowerment and Activism," in *Promises of Empowerment*, eds. Peter Smith, Jennifer Troutner, and Christine Hnefeldt (Lanham, MD: Rowman and Littlefield, 2004), 60.

13. Unless otherwise cited, all of this chapter's statistics on the number of women in the world's parliaments come from two web sites, which are frequently updated: the Inter-Parliamentary Union, Women in National Parliaments, www.ipu.org; and IDEA (the International Institute for Democracy and Electoral Assistance), Quota Project: Global Database of Quotas for Women, http://www.quotaproject.org.

14. All of the data on reserved seats comes from IDEA, *Quota Project: Global Database of Quotas for Women*, http://www.quotaproject.org/.

15. Mona Lena Krook, *Quotas for Women in Politics* (New York: Oxford University Press, 2009), 161–206.

16. Mala Htun, "Women and Democracy," in *Constructing Democratic Governance in Latin America*, eds. Jorge L. Domínguez and Michael Shifter (Baltimore, MD: The Johns Hopkins University Press, 2003), 122.

17. Mala Htun and Jennifer M. Piscopo, "Presence without Empowerment? Women in Politics in Latin America and the Caribbean," Paper prepared for the Conflict Prevention and Peace Forum of the (GIGR), originally presented in 2010, updated in 2015.

18. American Association of University Women (AAUW), "Gender Equality and the Role of Women in Cuban Society," (whitepaper online: February 2011).

19. "Why is China relaxing its one-child policy?," *The Economist*, December 10, 2013; Cristina Larson, "In China More Girls are on the Way," *Bloomberg Business*, July 31, 2014; Gwynn Guilford, "China's ratio of boys to girls is still dangerously high," *Quartz* (online—no date).

20. Htun, "Women and Democracy," 125.

6

The Politics of the Rural and Urban Poor

A group of Haitian women with their children doing their family wash in an urban shantytown. As in the rest of the developing world, many Haitians have migrated from the countryside to the cities, where a large percentage of them live in poor, self-built housing such as this. *Eye Ubiquitous/Alamy Stock Photo*

IN MANY DEVELOPING COUNTRIES, the rural and urban poor are the two largest segments of the population. At the same time, however, they are usually the least influential politically because they lack the power resources—wealth, education, professional skills, organizational ability—available to the middle and upper classes and to skilled workers. To be sure, in times of revolutionary upheaval or even moderate political and economic reform, they may wield considerable influence, but even then they generally need outside leadership and organization. This chapter will begin with a discussion of the rural poor and then examine their urban counterparts, many of whom began life in the countryside.

THE RURAL POOR: THE PEASANTRY IN THE DEVELOPING WORLD

For millennia, mankind lived primarily in the countryside. As recently as 1960, two-thirds of the world's population was rural, with a much higher percentage in developing nations. It is in the countryside where some of the worst aspects of political and economic underdevelopment prevail. In nations as distinct as China and Mexico, rural annual incomes are only 20–30 percent as high as average urban earnings. Wide urban-rural gaps also persist in literacy, health care, and life expectancy. Finally, rural villagers are less likely than their urban counterparts to have clean drinking water, electricity, or schools.

While the proportion of the LDCs' population living in the countryside is usually substantially greater than in highly industrialized nations, this percentage varies greatly from country to country: from over 80 percent in Nepal, Sri Lanka, and Uganda to about 10 percent in Argentina and Chile. Almost everywhere, the rural rate of poverty far exceeds the urban rate. Peasants generally suffer from inadequate housing, widespread illiteracy, malnutrition, and high rates of infant mortality.

In most of the developing world, political and economic power are concentrated in the cities. Consequently, government policies—on issues ranging from social expenditures to agricultural pricing—have a predictable urban bias. As noted in chapter 1, modernization theory argues that as countries develop, modern values and institutions will spread from the cities to the countryside, and the gap between the two will narrow. Conversely, dependency theorists maintain that the links between urban and rural areas replicate the exploitative international relationship between the industrialized core (the industrialized world) and the periphery (the LDCs). What is certain is that resolving the political and economic tensions *between* urban and rural areas, reducing the vast inequalities *within* the countryside, and dealing with urban-to-rural migration remain among the most difficult and important challenges facing developing nations today.

RURAL CLASS STRUCTURES

Within the countryside, there are generally substantial disparities in land-ownership. Often, agricultural property is concentrated in a relatively small number of hands. These inequalities have contributed to rural poverty and produced rigid class systems in countries such as Colombia, the Philippines, and parts of India. Landownership is most concentrated in Latin America, while East Asia (excepting the Philippines) has the most equitable distribution of farmland among the less developed regions. Land concentration in Africa varies considerably between countries. In recent decades, the spread of plantations (mostly growing produce for export) has increased agricultural concentration in a number of nations.

At the apex of the rural class system stand the large and powerful landowners, sometimes known as "the oligarchy." Major Filipino sugar growers and Argentine cattle barons, for example, have historically exercised considerable political power in national politics. In El Salvador, the most influential coffee producers dominated the country's political system for much of the twentieth century. Land concentration in Latin America dates back to the Spanish colonial era with its tradition of large estates (*latifundia*). In the Philippines, Sri Lanka, Pakistan, and Bangladesh, along with parts of India, Indonesia, and Thailand, reactionary landed elites have also contributed to rural backwardness and poverty.

Since the middle of the twentieth century, the economic and political powers of rural landlords have declined considerably in numerous LDCs. In the most dramatic cases, radical revolutions in countries such as China and Vietnam stripped landlords of their property. Revolutionary governments sometimes killed many big landowners and sent others to prison camps for "political reeducation." Elsewhere, nonrevolutionary and relatively peaceful **agrarian reform** undermined the rural elites of countries such as Peru and South Korea.* In industrializing nations such as Brazil and Thailand, the economic importance of agribusiness at the national level has diminished relative to the industrial and commercial sectors. Therefore, numerous wealthy, landowning families have diversified into those economic sectors or have left agriculture entirely.

At the local and regional levels, however, landlords in much of Latin America, Asia, and Africa continue to exercise considerable power. For example, upper-caste farmers in the Indian state of Bihar and large cattle ranchers in the Brazilian interior retain virtually unchallenged local supremacy. At times, they have intimidated, or even murdered, **peasant**

---

*The terms *agrarian reform* and *land reform* are often used interchangeably. However, as discussed below, *land reform* refers only to the redistribution of land to needy peasants or farm laborers. *Agrarian reform* is a broader process encompassing financial and technical aid, which must support land redistribution if it is to be effective.

organizers and union leaders without fear of the legal consequences. Such was the fate of Chico Mendes, the celebrated Brazilian union leader who had organized Amazonian rubber-tree tappers against the powerful ranchers who were clearing the forest and destroying the local habitat. Despite Mendes's impressive international stature (the Turner broadcasting network and various U.S. senators had honored him, for example) and despite his links to influential American environmental groups, local landlords hired gunmen to assassinate him. Hundreds of lesser-known Brazilians have been killed on orders from powerful landlords—crimes that often go unpunished.

On the rung beneath the landed elite, we find midsized landlords and more affluent peasants. The latter group consists of peasants who, unlike small landlords, still work on the land themselves. However, unlike poorer peasants, they can afford to hire additional peasant labor to work with them. While neither midsized landlords nor richer peasants belong to the national power elite, they usually exercise considerable political influence locally in countries such as India and Pakistan. Indeed, in much of Asia, where the biggest agricultural holdings are not nearly as large as those in Latin America, these two groups are a potent political force. Extended family networks typically magnify their influence.

Finally, at the bottom of the socioeconomic ladder, the rural poor—including peasants who own small plots of land, tenant farmers, and farmworkers—are generally the LDCs' most impoverished and powerless occupational group. Peasants are defined as family farmers who work small plots and maintain a traditional lifestyle that is distinct from city dwellers. Because they are typically poor and poorly educated, peasants often lack the means to transport their crops to market themselves, ready access to credit, and the knowledge or resources to deal with the legal or bureaucratic proceedings that they periodically have to deal with. As a result, they depend on the services of merchants, moneylenders, lawyers, and government bureaucrats, many of whom exploit them. Their links to the world—including the government, the military, the church, and the market economy—are largely dependent upon individuals and institutions outside the peasants' community.[1] Thus, as Eric Wolf has noted, "Peasant denotes an asymmetrical structural relationship between the producers of surplus [peasants] and controllers [including landlords, merchants, and tax collectors]."[2]

We may further subdivide poor peasants into two subgroups: those who own small amounts of land for family cultivation (**smallholders**) and those who are landless. The ranks of the landless, in turn, include tenant farmers (who enter into various types of rental arrangements with landlords) and wage laborers. However, these categories are not mutually exclusive. Smallholders, for example, may also supplement their incomes by working as farm laborers or renting additional land as tenants. Usually, it is the landless who constitute the poorest of the rural poor. While they represent a mere 10 percent of all agricultural families in countries such as Kenya and Sierra Leone, their numbers rise to 50–70 percent in India, Pakistan, the Philippines, and Brazil. Not surprisingly, in Latin America and parts of Africa and Asia, where concentrated landownership and associated peasant landlessness have been particularly notable, the issue of land reform has often been at the center of rural politics.

PEASANT POLITICS

Despite their vast numbers, peasants often play a muted role in the politics of developing countries. Because most LDCs did not have competitive national elections until recently and because, even where there have been elections, powerful groups have often controlled the peasant vote, the rural poor have not readily converted their numbers into corresponding political influence. The peasantry's political leverage is also limited by poverty, lack of education, dependence on outsiders, and physical isolation from the centers of national power and from peasants elsewhere in the country. Cultural values stressing caution and conservatism may further constrain peasant political behavior. In his classic study of peasants, Robert Redfield argued: "In every part of the world, generally speaking, peasants have been a conservative factor in social change, a brake on revolution."[3]

Indeed, over the years, anthropological writings frequently have depicted peasant political culture as fatalistic and isolated. Hence, it was claimed, most of them doubt that collective political action can better their own fate. Discussing the reaction of Indian villagers to local government authorities, Phyllis Arora describes a sense of powerlessness resulting in political apathy. "Helplessness is . . . evoked by the presence of the district officer. The peasant tends to feel that all he [or she] can do before such authority . . . is petition for redress of grievances. . . . In the ultimate analysis, however . . . the peasant feels at the mercy of the whims of the [political] authorities."[4]

No doubt, peasants typically *are* wary of radical change and respectful of community traditions. To some extent, this conservatism reflects a suspicion of outside values—distrust frequently grounded in religious beliefs and other long-standing traditions. Indeed, the maintenance of a distinct peasant culture depends, to some extent, on the rejection of external influences. But peasant suspicion of social change is frequently understandable and rational. Struggling on the margins of economic survival, the rural poor have found that the commercialization and mechanization of agriculture, as well as other aspects of rural modernization, have often impacted their lives negatively. In rural Pakistan, for example, the introduction of tractors improved the output and income of the farmers who could afford them. As a consequence, however, many of poorer tenant farmers who could no longer compete were forced off their plots, thereby concentrating land into fewer hands. Political changes may also be threatening. For example, when outside activists have organized the rural poor to challenge local injustices, these peasants have often been ruthlessly repressed. Small wonder, then, that they are frequently suspicious of change, including any challenge to the power structure.

This does not mean, however, that they are incapable of standing up to landlords and government authorities who wrong them. Far from it! Examples of peasant resistance are commonplace, ranging from the most restrained to the most radical. James C. Scott has demonstrated that peasants in Southeast Asia who appear to accept the established order actually often engage in unobtrusive "everyday forms of resistance," such as theft and vandalism against their landlords, "foot dragging, and false deference."[5] Elsewhere, peasants have presented their political demands more openly and aggressively. The allegedly conservative peasantry was a critical actor in most twentieth-century revolutions, including communist upheavals in China, Vietnam, and Cuba, as well as in less radical insurgencies in Bolivia and Mexico.[6] More recently, they have been the backbone of guerrilla movements in Colombia, El Salvador, Peru, Cambodia, Nepal, the Philippines, and parts of India. And, in scores of other LDCs, ranging from India to Ecuador, well-organized peasant groups have also become influential actors in democratic political systems.

We will examine the role of the peasantry in revolutionary movements in greater detail in chapter 7. For now, however, suffice it to say that peasants are neither inherently conservative nor intrinsically radical. Rather, they vary considerably in their ideological propensities and their capacity for collective political action. To understand why peasants so often accept the political status quo, while others choose to resist or even rebel, we must first examine the relationship between the powerful and the weak in the countryside. Although traditional landlords frequently exploit their tenants or neighboring smallholders, mutually understood boundaries usually limit the extent of that exploitation. Links between landlords and peasants are usually grounded in long-standing **patron-client relationships** involving reciprocal obligations. Despite the landlords' superior power, these relationships are not always exploitative. For example, landowners frequently provide their tenants with land and financial credit in return for labor on their estate. And, they may fund religious festivals or serve as godparents of their tenants' children.

As long as landlords fulfill their obligations, peasants generally accept the traditional order despite its many injustices. However, should rural modernization and the commercialization of agriculture induce rural patrons to cease discharging their traditional responsibilities, the peasantry may conclude that the previously existing **"moral economy"** has failed them.[7] In some cases, rural modernization may also give landlords (who can afford farm machinery and irrigation pumps) a competitive advantage over peasants (who cannot) and eventually force the smallholders off the land. Eric Wolf has noted that the transition from feudal or semifeudal rural relations to capitalist economic arrangements often strips peasants of the certainty and protection afforded to them by the old order (even an unjust old order). Frequently, the result is rural upheaval. Thus, he argued, revolutions in China, Vietnam, Cuba, Mexico, and other developing nations originated with the threats to the peasants' traditional way of life posed by the rise of rural capitalism.[8]

This in no way suggests that rural modernization and the transition to capitalism *always* radicalize the peasantry or drive them to revolutionary activity. But when peasants feel that their way of life is threatened, they will resist change or at least try to channel it into forms more beneficial to their interests. How effectively they engage in collective political action and how radical or moderate their demands are depend on a number of factors: the extent to which they perceive themselves to be exploited; how desperate their economic condition is; the degree of internal cohesion and cooperation within their communities; their ability to form political linkages with peasants in neighboring villages or in other parts of the country; the extent to which they forge political ties with nonpeasant groups and leaders; the type of outside groups with whom they ally (be it the Catholic Church in the Philippines or Maoist revolutionaries in Nepal); the responsiveness of the political system to their demands; and the types of political options that the political order affords them.

The last two factors suggest that the probability of radical peasant insurrection depends as much on the quality of the political system as it does on the nature of the peasantry. Given a meaningful opportunity to secure change by working within the existing political system, few peasants will choose to join revolutionary movements, since that would endanger their lives and those of their families. In short, revolution is an act of desperation normally entered into only when other options are unavailable. It is perhaps for this reason that no democratic political system (offering alternatives to radical action) has ever fallen to revolutionary insurgency.

In recent decades, the spread of the mass media throughout the countryside, increased rural educational levels, and the broadening of voting rights in numerous LDCs (such as extending the vote to illiterates) have greatly increased the political influence of peasant voters in electoral democracies. In countries such as India, Bolivia, and Thailand, politicians must now consider the interests of the rural poor more seriously. Still, voting power is of little use in many nondemocratic nations in Africa, the Middle East, and Asia. And even in competitive party systems, the peasantry's political power is usually not proportional to their numbers.

On the whole, the range of peasant political activity runs the gamut from the far Left to the far Right, from peaceful to violent. As Samuel Huntington has noted, "The peasantry . . . may be the bulwark of the status quo or the shock troops of revolution. Which role the peasant plays is determined by the extent to which the existing system meets his immediate economic and material needs as he sees them."[9] In India, for example, many peasants support the BJP—a conservative, Hindu fundamentalist party (see chapter 3). In Latin America, on the other hand, peasants often vote for moderately left-of-center candidates. And, in countries such as China, Vietnam, Nicaragua, and Colombia, still other peasants have supported revolutionary insurrections. Whatever their political inclinations, the peasants' economic and political concerns usually revolve around four broad issues: the prices they receive for their crops, the prices of goods they buy, taxes, and the availability of land. The issue of land has been the most volatile and the most critical to the political stability of many developing nations, and it is to this issue that we now turn our attention.

THE POLITICS OF AGRARIAN REFORM

In those areas of the LDCs where landownership is highly concentrated, agrarian reform has long been an issue in the national political debate. Agrarian reform is composed of two components. First, the most important element is land reform, which involves the redistribution of agricultural land—generally from large landowners or from public property—to land-hungry peasants, either as family plots or as **collective farms**. Second, in order for land recipients to farm their plots successfully, the government usually must provide them with some mix of technical assistance, credit, improved access to markets, and social services (such as health care). To be sure, the pressure for agrarian reform has waxed and waned and other models of rural development have become more popular in recent years. Still, the issue lingers in numerous LDCs.

Patterns of Land Concentration
In much of the developing world, especially Asia, landless peasants constitute a large portion of the rural population. For example, about half of Bangladesh's rural population and 40 percent of India's are landless. In addition, millions of peasant smallholders own plots too small to support their families adequately.

Concentrated land ownership is most pronounced in Latin America, where large estates control a substantial proportion of the region's farmland. In Brazil, for example, slightly over 3 percent of the nation's farms, each exceeding five hundred hectares (about 1,250 acres),* control 56 percent of the nation's farmland.[10] Since 1995, several government administrations have introduced modest agrarian reforms that have distributed land to thousands of landless or land-hungry peasant families. To some extent, these programs have been a response to the emergence of the MST (the Landless Workers' Movement). Founded in the mid-1980s, the MST represents landless workers throughout the country and, with a membership of some 1.5 million people (the largest social movement in Latin America), it has placed substantial pressure on the government. Since the mid-1980s, through various government land reforms, the MST has won titles to 7.5 million hectares of land, which 370,000 families currently farm. In addition, 150,000 other families live on land whose ownership is contested. But, at the same time, about 90,000 peasant farms are being purchased or grabbed by agribusiness annually, mostly aimed at exports. In fact, government studies suggest that land concentration has actually increased in the last two decades.

With different historical traditions and far higher population density, Asia does not have agricultural units as large as Brazil's or Argentina's. In nations such as Indonesia, India, and Pakistan, farm holdings have rarely exceeded fifty hectares. In Bangladesh, one of the world's most densely populated countries, the largest farms are relatively small, rarely exceeding five to ten hectares. Yet less than 3 percent of these units controlled more than 25 percent of the country's agricultural land. In the Philippines, similar data showed 3.4 percent of the country's farms accounting for 26 percent of the land.

Patterns of land ownership vary widely in Africa, depending in part on how extensively European colonial rule concentrated land in the hands of white settlers. But, a study of Ethiopia, Kenya, Mozambique, and Rwanda noted that approximately one-quarter of their total farm population was either landless or virtually landless (making them dependent on the landlords for either wage labor or tenancy).[11]

The Case for Agrarian Reform
Facing powerful landed elites and their political allies, who oppose land redistribution, proponents of reform have defended their position on several grounds, including social justice and equity, greater political stability,

---

*A hectare, rather than an acre, is the standard measurement of farmland area in most parts of the world. One hectare is equivalent to 2.47 acres.

improved agricultural productivity, economic growth, and preservation of the environment.

Some governments, such as El Salvador's and the Philippines's,' have redistributed farm land to the rural poor in order to reduce the likelihood of peasant unrest. Huntington starkly linked land reform to political stability:

> Where the conditions of land tenure are equitable and provide a viable living for the peasant, revolution is unlikely. Where they are inequitable and where the peasant lives in poverty and suffering, revolution is likely, if not inevitable, unless the government takes prompt measures to remedy those conditions.[12]

Similarly, a recent study by the World Bank warns that "social costs of failing to [implement agrarian] reform often have included peasant uprisings and civil wars."[13]

Opponents of agrarian reform maintain that land redistribution lowers agricultural output, thereby diminishing food supplies for the cities and curtailing export earnings. Citing **"economies of scale,"** they argue that large agricultural units are generally more productive than smallholdings because they are more easily mechanized and use rural infrastructure (such as irrigation and roads) more effectively.

Advocates of agrarian reform counter that, in fact, smallholders are more efficient producers of domestic food than larger landlords. Many empirical studies have found that when small and large farm units are compared *within* Latin American, Asian, and African countries, labor-intensive smallholders (peasants who devote large amounts of physical labor on small land units) usually have higher yields per acre than large-scale, capital-intensive (mechanized) producers.* Peasant landholders tend to farm their plots very intensively because their families' living standards depend on raising productivity. This does not mean that small peasant-run units are *always* more efficient. Smaller farm units tend to outperform larger farms in growing vegetables and legumes (important components of the local diet), which are best cultivated by hand labor. But ranching and cultivation of crops suitable for mechanical harvesting—such as sugar, wheat, and rice (grown largely for export)—are usually more efficiently farmed on large plantations.

In underdeveloped rural societies with a surplus of labor (i.e., many underemployed people who are willing to work for low wages), it is

---

*If we measure productivity in terms of output per (farm) worker, then large farms are usually more efficient. Advocates of land reform insist, however, that in most LDCs, where farm land is scarce and labor is abundant and cheap, productivity per acre (or hectare) is the most relevant measure of productivity.

often more cost-effective to use family or hired labor intensively rather than invest in machinery. Out of economic necessity, peasant cultivators work hard, exploiting their own family labor. On the other hand, most large, mechanized estates are farmed by hired laborers, who do not gain directly from raising productivity. Long ago, the president of the Overseas Development Council argued that "a land and capital scarce (but population plentiful) country should favor 40 two-and-a-half acre farms over a single-owner 100-acre farm in order to make optimum use of available land, labor, and capital."[14]

Finally, another value for agrarian reform relates to environmental protection. For example, Brazilian ranchers and farmers deliberately burn tracts of the Amazonian rainforest to clear land for agriculture, annually destroying a forest area equal to the size of New Jersey. The fires are so vast that they contribute to the *greenhouse effect* on world climate. Although large landowners create a substantial portion of this burn-off, peasant settlers also contribute. Driven out of the nation's poorest regions by desperation, land-hungry peasants colonize the jungle in search of a better life. Once there, however, they discover that cleared jungle soil quickly loses its nutrients. So, they must soon move on, clearing yet more forest land. Land reform in Brazil's unforested regions would reduce landlessness and give tenant farmers a greater stake in the land they farm, thus reducing migration to the Amazonian basin.

The Decline of Agrarian Reform

Despite these benefits, the number of extensive agrarian programs has remained limited. Usually, the extent of land redistribution is not determined by factors such as agricultural productivity. Rather it is most influenced by the balance of political power between peasants and landlords, by the government's perception of whether land redistribution would help or hurt it. Perhaps the most successful agrarian reform programs were initiated in East Asia in the years following World War II. Fearing the spread of Chinese-style peasant revolutions, the U.S. occupation forces introduced far-reaching land redistribution in Japan, and Washington strongly endorsed reform in South Korea and Taiwan, both facing external communist threats from North Korea or China.

In all three of these countries landlords were in an unusually weak position: Japanese landlords were in no position to oppose the U.S. military occupation; Korean landlords were discredited at home because most had supported the Japanese invasion in World War II; and in Taiwan, the former landed elite had just fled from their defeat on the Chinese mainland. All three nations were heavily dependent on the United States, which was pressuring them to implement reform. The resulting agrarian reforms were very extensive and very successful: agricultural production increased, peasant living standards rose, peasant consumption helped fuel industrial growth, and the rural poor became pillars of support for the government.

Many experts as well as institutions such as the FAO have continued to support expanded agrarian reform in the developing world.

> While globalization, industrialization, and (often subsidized) commercial agriculture are creating wealth for some, they are also dramatically increasing the socio-economic disparities within and between countries, further exacerbating land concentration. . . . Investment has tended to favor the development of the industrial, urban and service and often military sectors, at the expense of agriculture and rural development.[15]

Yet, there have been few extensive land redistribution programs in recent decades. Often, landed elites have had enough political and economic power to water down reform efforts. At the same time peasants are usually poorly organized and unable to exert much pressure on their governments. And the United States has generally lacked the leverage or desire to push for major agrarian reform, as it did in East Asia in the postwar years.

Revolutions and Rural Reform

The most comprehensive agrarian reform programs have been introduced by revolutionary movements and governments. These include Bolivia, China, Cuba, Mexico, Nicaragua, and Vietnam. In all of these, peasants were an important, sometimes dominant, part of the revolutionary struggle. At the same time, the revolutions destroyed the landlord's political and economic powers, thereby eliminating a roadblock that so often has limited or derailed reform efforts. But, the outcome of revolutionary change often was not what most peasants had fought and died for. They had hoped or expected the large estates to be divided into peasant family farms. Instead, the new revolutionary governments pressured or forced the peasantry to join collective farms of some sort—principally cooperatives or state farms. In China, Ethiopia, Russia, and Vietnam, tens of thousands of peasants died resisting **collectivization**. In fact, in most cases, collective farms were not efficient. Indeed, China's forced collectivization during the Great Leap Forward (1958–1961) caused such a sharp drop in food production and distribution that perhaps twenty-five million people died of starvation.

Eventually, several communist regimes (including China, Vietnam, and, more recently, Cuba) have recognized these failures and have essentially privatized (de-collectivized) many or all farm units—breaking up communes, collectives, state farms, and other government-imposed production units—returning the land to peasant-controlled family plots.

In both China and Vietnam, the de-collectivization of agriculture resulted in greater food production and significant improvements in the peasantry's standard of living.

THE FUTURE OF THE RURAL POOR

For decades, development policies have emphasized industrial growth and urban modernization, often to the detriment of the rural sector. Frequently, the result has been stagnant agricultural production, growing food imports, rural poverty, and heavy rural-urban migration. Most notably in Africa and Latin America, government bias in favor of urban areas, along with the forces of capitalist modernization, have driven many peasants into the urban slums in a process known as *proletarianization*. In some instances, rural poverty has led to peasant insurrections. Pessimistic scholars have predicted the inevitable spread of large, mechanized farms to the detriment of peasant family farming.

More recently, however, research in countries such as Bolivia, Ecuador, and Colombia has revealed that, in at least some regions, innovative peasants have adapted skillfully to the forces of rural capitalism and modernization, taking advantage of new commercial opportunities to compete successfully in the marketplace. In Africa and Asia, peasant smallholders remain an even more important component of rural society. Rather than abandoning the peasantry as a relic of history, governments and international agencies need to promote balanced economic and political development that gives proper weight to the rural poor. Since the 1990s, recurring hunger and malnutrition in the LDCs have led some important foreign-aid donors to rethink their attitudes toward peasant farming. Despite the large landholders' financial advantages and widespread government neglect of peasant farming, smallholders still produce about 60 percent of the food consumed in the developing world. Coming into the 2009 G8 summit of the world's major economic powers, its participants pledged $15 billion in contributions over three years to aid food production, largely by peasants, in Africa and in very poor developing nations outside Africa.* At the forum itself, President Obama convinced the members to raise that pledge to $20 billion. The purpose of this aid would be to "transform traditional aid beyond simply donated [food to alleviate famines] to assistance building infrastructure and training farmers to grow their own food and to get it to market more efficiently."[16]

---

*The G8 or Group of 8 referred to the world's seven leading democratic industrial powers (including the United States, Germany, France, and Japan) and Russia, whose leaders met annually to discuss world economic, security, and energy issues. In 2014, following the Russian invasion of Ukraine, that country was suspended from the group and it now calls itself the G7.

Several months later (October 2009), Bill Gates announced that the Bill and Melinda Gates Foundation would be changing its philanthropic focus from fighting diseases in the LDCs to aiding the poor farmers, whom he described as the key to eradicating world hunger.

While many analysts hailed this new emphasis on food production, some respected NGOs, such as Oxfam, reacted skeptically. To begin with, they considered the $20 billion totally inadequate, particularly because the developing world had lost far more than that amount in the current global financial crisis. Second, G8 countries (and G7) had a notoriously poor record of coming through with the aid pledged at previous meetings. In a worst-case example, Italy has delivered only three percent of all the aid it had pledged in previous summits. Furthermore, too many of the countries targeted for such aid have notorious records of government corruption that siphons off large portions of the foreign assistance. Finally, a significant portion of foreign aid is grabbed by the most politically well-connected larger farmers, rather than by those who need it the most or can best use it. Still, at the very least, many developed nations have come to realize that advancing peasant agriculture is crucial to the LDCs' development. Finally, until the vast gaps between rural and urban incomes, education, housing, sanitation, and health care are reduced, large portions of the rural poor will continue to flood into the cities.

RAPID URBANIZATION AND THE POLITICS OF THE URBAN POOR

Every day, in the villages of Bangladesh, China, Kenya, Egypt, and Brazil, thousands of young men and women pack up their meager belongings and board buses, trucks, or trains for the long trip to, respectively, Dhaka, Shanghai, Nairobi, Cairo, or Rio. Often they travel alone, sometimes with family or friends. They are a part of the largest and most dramatic tidal wave of human migration in world history. Despairing of any hope for a better life in the countryside and seeking new opportunities for themselves and their children, millions of villagers leave the world they have known for the uncertainties of the city. In Africa, refugees fleeing civil wars and famine have augmented the legions of migrants. At the same time, as migration adds to the size of the LDCs' cities, urban populations are also growing as a result of "natural increase"—the annual total of births minus deaths—among those already living there.

THE DEVELOPING WORLD'S URBAN EXPLOSION

As the world approached a new century (1997), the United Nations Population Fund (UNFPA) predicted that "the growth of cities will be the single largest influence on development in the 21st century." In 2008, the number of people living in cities throughout the world exceeded the rural population for the first time in human history. In developing countries, the proportion of city dwellers will cross 50 percent by 2017.

Most migrants maintain close links with their rural roots long after they have left the countryside. Some of them intend to accumulate savings and eventually return to their villages. Indeed, in various parts of West Africa and Southeast Asia, more than half of the urban migrants are temporary, including those who repeatedly circulate between village and city. In China prior to the 1980s, government restrictions made it difficult to migrate. Even now, most urban migrants live in a bureaucratic limbo without assurance of permanence. Known as China's "floating population," they currently number more than 150 million and this figure is expected to double by 2025.* Some stay permanently, but most do not because of their marginal legal status. Although not officially counted as part of the urban population (because their government supposedly restricts their residence to their home villages), they actually account for about one-fifth of China's urban residents. In Shanghai, China's largest city and its economic hub, six million migrants constitute one-third of the population. In contrast, Latin America's cityward migrants tend to settle permanently. Whatever be their initial aspirations, migrants continue to crowd the urban slums and **shantytowns** that they have come to call home.

Swelled by the influx of migrants and by natural increases, urban populations have ballooned and will continue to grow rapidly in the coming years. Currently, eight to nine of the world's ten largest metropolitan areas are in the LDCs.† Table 6.1 shows that between 2000 and 2050, the urban population of the world's *developed* nations is expected to grow by about 230 million, an increase of approximately 26 percent. By contrast, cities in the developing world will expand by 163 percent (from under 2 billion people to almost 5.2 billion). During the first half of this century, urban growth will slow down in both regions, but cities in developing nations will continue to grow about five to six times faster than in industrialized nations. As of 2000, less than one-half of the

---

*In order to reduce further mass, "illegal" migration to China's established cities, the government has begun to create new cities (with projected populations of several million each) in rural areas. These are designed to create jobs for villagers in the surrounding areas.

†Different sources have widely varying populations for the world's largest cities and for their rank. In large part this depends on whether they are measuring just the official population of the city in question or whether they are reporting the much larger population of the "metropolitan areas" ("urban agglomerations") that includes suburbs and more. The urban populations and rankings discussed in this chapter mostly refer to the metropolitan areas.

Table 6.1   Urbanization in Developed and Less Developed
             Countries

	2000	2025 (Estimate)	2050 (Estimate)
	Urban Population		
Developed Countries	869,233,000	1,013,700,000	1,099,730,000
Less Developed Countries	1,968,198,000	3,522,225,000	5,186,151,000
	Percentage Urban		
Developed Countries	72.7	79.4	86.2
Less Developed Countries	40.0	52.3	65.9

Source: United Nations Population Division, *World Urbanization Prospects.*

Table 6.2   Percent of the Developing World's Population in Urban
             Areas

Region	1975	2015	2050
The United States	73.7	81.6	87.4
Sub-Saharan Africa	20.3	37.9	54.8
North Africa	39.4	51.6	63.3
East Asia	25.5	60.0	77.9
South Asia	21.3	34.8	52.5
Latin America and the Caribbean	60.7	79.8	86.2

Source: United Nations Population Division, *World Urbanization Prospects.*

LDCs' population (40 percent) lived in cities, but by midcentury, this figure will increase to 65.9 percent.

The magnitude of this expansion has placed tremendous strains on public services, housing, public health, and personal safety in these large cities. In Latin America, the rate of growth was most rapid in the middle of the twentieth century, when some primary cities such as Bogotá and Lima nearly doubled their populations in a single decade (1950–1960). While the *rate* of growth in the region's largest cities has slowed, many have continued enormous growth in absolute terms. African cities, starting from a smaller base, expanded at an even faster pace. Between 1960 and 1983, Kinshasa (Congo) grew by nearly 600 percent and Abidjan (Côte d'Ivoire) by more than 800 percent. Today, a number of major cities in LDCs are still doubling their populations in two decades or less.

As Table 6.2 indicates, Latin America and the Caribbean is by far the most urbanized region in the developing world, having reached 60.7

Table 6.3   Populations of Developing World Metropolitan Areas, 1975–2025 (in millions)

Metropolitan Area	1975	2015	2025
Mexico City (Mexico)	10.7	19.0	21.0
São Paulo (Brazil)	9.6	18.8	21.4
Cairo (Egypt)	6.4	11.9	15.6
Istanbul (Turkey)	3.6	10.1	12.2
Mumbai (India)	7.1	19.0	26.4
Karachi (Pakistan)	4.0	12.1	19.1
Dhaka (Bangladesh)	2.2	13.5	22.0

Source: United Nations Population Division, *World Urbanization Prospects.*

percent of the national population in 1975 and projected to be 86.2 percent by 2050. In 1975, Sub-Saharan Africa's (20.3 percent) and East Asia's urban population (25.5 percent) constituted a far lower portion of the national total. On the other hand, cities in those two regions are now growing far more rapidly than in the Americas and by 2025, they will have closed the gap with Latin America and the Caribbean considerably (especially East Asia).

Table 6.3 demonstrates the incredible growth that many of the developing world's largest cities will have experienced in one-half century (1975–2025). In 1975, Latin America, the developing world's most urbanized region, had two of the world's largest megacities—Mexico City (10.7 million) and São Paulo, Brazil (9.6 million). They have continued to grow and by 2025 will have about doubled their populations in fifty years. On the other hand, two of the largest cities in South Asia— Mumbai (Bombay) and Dhaka—trailed well behind their Latin American counterparts at the start of this era. But, by 2025, their populations will increase between fourfold (Mumbai) and tenfold (Dhaka), putting both South Asian cities ahead of São Paulo and Mexico City. Indeed, Dhaka, which started with the smallest population in the table ("only" 2.2 million), will be the second largest megacity in the groups by 2025 (22 million).

Of course, *within* each region, the proportion of people residing in cities also varies considerably. As Table 6.4 indicates, Indonesia (4.5 percent urban), Mozambique (9.6 percent), and China (17.4 percent) were far less urbanized in 1975 than Argentina (81 percent) or Brazil (60.8 percent). But, by 2050, China's percent urban will have multiplied by over four times, Mozambique's will have multiplied close to fivefold, and Indonesia will be over fifteen times as urbanized as it was at the start of that period.

Table 6.4   Percent of the Population Living in Urban Areas

Country	1975	2015	2050
Mozambique	9.6	32.2	49.1
Egypt	43.3	43.1	56.5
China	17.4	55.6	77.9
India	21.3	32.7	50.3
Indonesia	4.5	53.7	70.9
Argentina	81.0	91.8	94.7
Brazil	60.8	85.7	91.0

Source: United Nations Population Division, *World Urbanization Prospects.*

THE POLITICAL CONSEQUENCES OF URBAN GROWTH

This chapter examines two important aspects of urban politics. First, it looks at the challenges that exploding urban populations present to political leaders and government planners. Specifically, it asks how poor countries can provide city dwellers with needed jobs, housing, sanitation, and other basic services, while also protecting them from crime. What is the government's role in those areas, and how do state policies interact with private-sector activities and self-help efforts? Second, we examine the political attitudes and behavior of the lower classes, who account for the majority of the urban population. To what extent do the inhabitants of urban shantytowns and slums have political orientations that are distinct from those of the rural poor and those of the urban middle and upper classes? Is rapid urbanization likely to contribute to political development, or does it carry the seeds of political instability?

THE SEARCH FOR EMPLOYMENT

It is worth remembering that just like today's LDCs, Western nations experienced an urban explosion from the 1870s to the start of World War I (1914). But rapid urbanization in Europe and North America occurred during an era of unprecedented industrialization and economic growth. As capitalism came of age, it needed the giant wave of migrant and immigrant laborers. By contrast, most contemporary developing countries are unable to provide sufficient employment to their rapidly expanding urban workforce.

To be sure, many people do find factory jobs, and some low-income workers achieve impressive upward mobility, but they are the exception. Most of the urban poor must engage in an ongoing struggle for economic survival. The severe recessions that gripped Africa and Latin America in the 1980s, parts of Asia in the late 1990s, and much of the world from 2008 to at least 2010, all exacerbated urban poverty, as industrial employment plummeted in scores of countries. Furthermore, at times, various countries in Latin America and Africa have suffered from high rates of inflation, making it difficult for many people, even those who were regularly employed, to support their families adequately.

Many of the urban poor who are unable to find work in the so-called *formal* segment of the urban economy (the government and modern, private-sector enterprises) turn to the *informal sector* for jobs. As noted in chapter 5, this sector is defined as the part of the economy that is "unregulated by the institutions of society [most notably the state], in a legal and social environment in which similar activities are regulated" and taxed.[17] Most of the workers in that sector are self-employed (an estimated 70 percent) in occupations ranging from garbage recyclers to shoeshine boys, street vendors, mechanics, electricians, plumbers, and drivers of unlicensed taxis. Others work in "underground" factories or other businesses that operate outside the law.

Of course, even cities such as New York, Los Angeles, and Milan in the industrialized world have informal sectors, including unlicensed street vendors, underground sweatshops, and other endeavors that are "off the books." In the LDCs, however, this sector provides a substantial proportion of urban jobs. According to the World Bank, the informal sector may generate as much as 70 percent of urban employment and 30 percent of the LDCs' GDP.

In the vast garbage dumps of Cairo and Mexico City, hordes of entrepreneurs sift through the refuse looking to recycle marketable materials. On the commercial boulevards of Manila (Philippines) and Nairobi (Kenya), an army of street vendors sells food, household appliances, and bootleg videos. In Lagos and Lahore (Pakistan), shoemakers and carpenters, working out of their homes, sell their wares to appreciative clients. All belong to the informal sector. While outside observers once assumed that people working in this sector were particularly impoverished, we now know that their earning power varies greatly and that in some countries they have average higher incomes than the typical factory worker does.

Over the years, government planners and social scientists have debated the informal sector's merits and faults. Critics point out that its workers are not protected by minimum-wage laws and do not have access to government health and welfare programs such as Social Security. Proponents respond that the sector not only employs vast numbers of people who would otherwise have no work, but also contributes a substantial proportion of the developing countries' consumer goods and services. Consequently, these analysts argue, governments should cease trying to regulate and license the informal sector and instead should allow it to flourish and expand.

Another source of employment is the public sector. The governments of less developed nations employ significant numbers of white-collar workers and bureaucrats. These jobs are a boon to the urban middle class since there is not enough work in the private sector. In addition, many governments own various economic enterprises (parastatals)—including petroleum fields and refineries, railroads, electric power plants, and steel mills—which provide relatively well-paid, blue-collar jobs in economies plagued by high unemployment.

Unfortunately, there are two major problems with public-sector employment. First, in their efforts to gain popular support, the government or the ruling party has often padded bureaucratic and parastatal payrolls with unneeded employees. While this creates badly needed jobs, it adds to government budget deficits and makes these institutions highly inefficient. Second, public-sector employment is frequently treated as a political plum, with jobs going to activists in the ruling party and government supporters, rather than to the most qualified applicants. In many countries, government bureaucracies and parastatals hire unneeded white-collar workers as a form of political patronage. In fact, many employees never show up except to collect their paychecks. At one time, some 40 percent of Sierra Leone's government bureaucrats and state workers were "ghosts"—employees who were paid but never worked.

In recent decades, faced with spiraling government spending and large external debts, most LDCs have been forced to reduce the size of their state sectors substantially. Although these cuts were usually necessary in order to cut huge government budget deficits and reduce inflation, they have imposed a heavy burden on white- and blue-collar workers who have been laid off and on young workers who faced more limited opportunities for future employment.

Only in communist countries such as China and Cuba has the state been a major employer of blue-collar workers. Those governments have commonly considered employment to be a fundamental workers' right and an important source of legitimacy for the system. Until recently, some communist governments created as many jobs as necessary to achieve full, or nearly full, employment, no matter how economically inefficient many of these jobs might be. Under China's "iron rice bowl" policy, factory workers were essentially guaranteed a job for life. But as the country has moved toward a capitalist economy, it has closed many inefficient plants and no longer guarantees workers permanent employment. In recent years, millions of workers have been laid off from state-owned enterprises. Similarly, Cuba has announced plans to shed up to one million government employees in the coming years.

Encouraged or pressured by the IMF, the World Bank, and private foreign banks, many heavily indebted African and Latin American countries have adopted macroeconomic policies, designed to reduce inflation rates. These measures seek to lower large budgetary and trade deficits by lowering government spending—including cuts in public-sector employment and the privatizing of many state enterprises (selling them to private investors). These policies—officially called structural adjustment and monetary stabilization programs, but widely known as austerity programs—are often successful in curtailing high inflation rates (which sometimes had exceeded 100 percent annually). Curbing rampant inflation obviously helps consumers, especially the poor. But at the same time, stabilization entails major cutbacks in government and private-sector employment. For example, when the Mexican government privatized the previously state-owned steel industry, the new owners laid off half of the workforce.

THE URBAN POOR'S STRUGGLE FOR HOUSING

Of all the challenges facing the urban poor, particularly the wave of new migrants, few are more pressing than finding adequate housing. With many cities doubling in size every ten to twenty-five years, private-sector housing cannot possibly expand fast enough to meet the need. Besides, most of the new homes and apartment houses constructed for private sale or rental are built for the middle and upper classes, since there is little profit to be made in building low-income housing. At the same time, although many governments have invested in public housing, their rents are commonly too high for low-income families to afford. So, lacking adequate options in both the private and state sectors, many of the urban poor live in **squatter settlements** and other forms of "self-help" (occupant-built) housing, called "**spontaneous housing.**"* Others crowd into existing urban slums (decaying tenements). The poorest city dwellers, lacking the resources to rent or build, are often homeless, residing in doorways, unused construction material, or the like. In the "City of the Dead"—a series of huge cemeteries on Cairo's outskirts—hundreds of thousands of the city's poor (largely migrants) live among the cemeteries' tombs. They are allowed to live there rent-free (but with no basic services) in return for guarding and maintaining the tombs.

In all, the total population of slum dwellers, those living in squatter settlements and homeless persons account for close to half the population

---

*While squatter settlements (also called shantytowns) are poor neighborhoods, not everyone living in them is poor. A minority of shantytown residents are white-collar workers or well-paid blue-collar workers. Some of them achieved upward mobility since first settling there, but have remained there because of attachments to friends and their community.

of the developing world's cities. About 30 percent of the urban population in North Africa, Latin America, and the Caribbean live in slum (substandard) housing. This number rises to nearly 60 percent in South Asia and more than 70 percent in Sub-Saharan Africa. Looking at individual nations, about 40 percent of the urban populations live in slums or squatter settlements in Brazil, Egypt, and Turkey. This figure rises to about 55 percent in India, 70–80 percent in Kenya, Pakistan, and Nigeria, and over 90 percent in Afghanistan.[18] Millions of the LDCs' urban poor, including many of them who have built their own homes, have no direct access to clean water or sanitation facilities.

In recent decades, some countries have reduced their slum population by upgrading the quality of housing for many inhabitants and by providing drinking water and sanitation. Thus from 1990 to 2010 four North Africa countries (Egypt, Morocco, Libya, and Tunisia) cut their slum dwelling population in half, from 20.8 million to 11.8 million. Throughout the LDCs, housing upgrading enabled 227 million people to escape urban slums between 2000 and 2010. But, at the same time, some 282 million people were added to the slum population, meaning that the total number of slum dwellers actually increased by 55 million during that decade.[19]

Today, the availability of basic urban services in low-income neighborhoods varies considerably from region to region. For example, a survey of eight low-income neighborhoods in Latin America—located in Rio de Janeiro and Aracaju (Brazil) as well as Santiago and Temuco (Chile)—found that nearly all of the inhabitants had running water and electricity. On the other hand, a parallel study of eight poor African neighborhoods—in the cities of Abidjan and Man (Côte d'Ivoire) along with Nairobi and Kisumu (Kenya)—revealed that almost all the residents had to buy their drinking water. Similarly, very few homes in any of the eight African neighborhoods studied had electricity.[20] In light of these glaring needs, developing nations frequently have searched for appropriate state responses.

Public Housing and the Role of the State

Throughout the developing world, many governments have constructed public housing to alleviate housing shortages. In China, workers in state enterprises are commonly assigned apartments linked to their employment. Cuba's revolutionary government has built large apartment blocks, some of them housing 25,000–40,000 persons on the outskirts of its largest cities. During Venezuela's petroleum boom in the late 1970s and early 1980s, the government constructed as many as 34,000 urban housing units annually.[21] Hugo Chávez's populist government has built many additional units during its oil boom years. In the 1960s and 1970s, various African governments established housing agencies with far fewer resources.

In time, however, it has become clear that public housing cannot provide sufficient shelter for the poor, and, in some cases, it actually worsens their plight. In the capital cities of India, Senegal, and Nigeria, for example, government housing projects have often been designed to eradicate "urban blight," that is, "unsightly," low-income slums built near the city center. To make the central city more aesthetically pleasing to upper- and middle-class residents, and foreign tourists, the government has sometimes removed those slums and replaced them with government buildings or government-built middle-class housing. Only a small portion of the poor families who had been evicted from their homes have subsequently secured a replacement in low-income public housing projects. Even those who received alternate housing were usually relocated on the edges of town, far removed from their workplace. Zimbabwe's government periodically ousted the same squatters from their settlements in different parts of the nation's capital, in effect "chasing them around town." Instead, the urban poor often turn to self-built housing, generally in sprawling shantytowns located in remote parts of the town. Many government planners, viewing these shacks from a middle-class perspective, believed that unless the squatters can afford "decent" urban housing with plumbing and multiple rooms for their families, they would be better off returning to the countryside.

In fact, many of the public housing projects do not serve the poor at all, housing lower-middle-class families instead. In order for a government to recoup its construction costs, it must sell or rent the new housing units at higher rates than the urban poor can afford. Consequently, the state faces two options: it can subsidize rents and mortgages to bring their cost down to a level within the reach of the poor or it can rent or sell the dwellings to those who have enough money to live there without state subsidies, namely the middle class.

Although many governments provide some subsidized housing to the poor, these programs have several drawbacks and by their nature must be limited. First, even when a government wants to subsidize substantial numbers of low-income units, it is too costly for most developing nations to sustain. For example, following the Cuban revolution, the government committed itself to providing new homes for the urban lower class. To demonstrate its generosity and gain public support, it poured funds into a number of large housing projects, while recouping only a fraction of the costs out of the low rents that the new tenants paid. Projects such as Santiago's José Martí provided schools, day-care centers, theaters, clinics, and stores for its forty thousand inhabitants. However, by lavishing excessively "luxurious" housing on early recipients, the government soon ran out of funds for the many others needing shelter. Thus, the East Havana project, planned for 100,000 dwelling units, ultimately contained only 1,500.

But even though the state lacked the resources to meet the country's housing needs, it limited private ownership to families who owned their homes at the time of the revolution (1959). People could not build new private homes and those who already owned them were not allowed to sell them. To alleviate the country's severe housing shortage, the government has allowed the sale of existing private homes since 2011.

Elsewhere, another problem is that (subsidized) public housing is often allocated to supporters of the ruling party or the government rather than on the basis of need. Because political patronage plays such an important role, police officers, government bureaucrats, and teachers are often among the first served.[22] Consequently, residents in state housing are frequently from the middle class. They have enough political connections to secure access to public housing and can also afford to pay higher rents than low-income families can.

With the exception of Hong Kong, Singapore, and several small, oil-rich Gulf states, the governments of other developing countries lack the resources to provide housing for a large segment of the urban poor. Consequently, many analysts believe that the state should not try to provide relatively costly, completed housing units to poor families, but instead should support cheaper alternatives that can serve far more people. With most LDCs cutting back government spending since the 1980s, the case for cheaper, but more widely disbursed, housing solutions has become even stronger.

Spontaneous Housing

For years, many social scientists and urban planners have maintained that the most effective remedy for urban housing shortfalls is to allow or encourage spontaneous (self-built) housing—that is, the very shanty-towns that have been considered urban blight. In cities throughout the developing world, the poor have built their own homes, sometimes with hired or volunteer assistance. While living in these dwellings, many proprietors, particularly in Africa, also rent part of their home to others. In some cases, the property owners are squatters, living on land that has been occupied illegally, often with the compliance of government authorities.

Spontaneous housing settlements range in size from a few isolated homes to communities of many thousands. For example, on the dried-up marshlands outside Mexico City, the municipality of Netzahualcóyotl began as an illegal squatter settlement in the 1940s. By 1970, it housed 600,000 people.[23] Organized protests eventually persuaded the national government to provide badly needed urban services and to grant the squatters legal titles to their homes. Elsewhere, up to 40 percent of Nairobi's population and one-fourth to one-third of the inhabitants of Jakarta, Karachi, and Lima live in squatter settlements. These homes, many analysts contend, often have been erroneously viewed by politicians and planners as a problem, when, in fact, they are a major part of the solution to urban housing needs. Rather than building public housing, they argue, governments can serve many more people by removing the legal and political obstacles to spontaneous housing settlements, giving squatters titles to their land and helping residents upgrade the dwellings that they have built.

Self-built homes have several important advantages over public housing. First, they actually serve the poor, whereas public housing generally does not. Second, they afford occupants the opportunity to upgrade their homes continuously. For example, in Lima's vast network of shantytowns, one can observe many wood and straw shacks whose owners are building brick walls around them, slowly constructing a better home as funds become available. Third, precisely because they are self-built, these homes better address the needs and desires of their owners than do units built by government planners. Finally, squatter settlements have the churches, bars, and neighborhood stores that help create a sense of community, which is too often lacking in large, impersonal public housing projects. Accepting these arguments, over the years, the governments of Peru, Brazil, and other nations have given millions of illegal squatters titles to their plots of land and provided public services such as sewage and drinking water.

Sites-and-Services Programs

Other analysts who favored a more active role for the state view this perspective as a convenient excuse for governments that do not wish to spend much on the poor. Championing self-help housing, these critics charged, merely perpetuated the status quo and allowed the state to direct its limited housing resources toward the middle class.

Ultimately, many developing world governments, the World Bank, and many foreign-aid donors have pursued a middle-ground policy that falls between providing expensive, fully built public housing units and a hands-off policy that leaves the government with little role to play. In countries as diverse as Colombia, India, Malawi, and Turkey, the state has sold or rented parcels of land to the poor that come with basic services such as running water, sewage, and electricity. Buyers then build their own homes on the sites as they do with spontaneous housing. In some cases, governments provide credit, technical assistance, or low-cost construction materials.

These "sites-and-services" programs have several obvious advantages. First, they allow the government to steer self-built housing to locations that are safe and environmentally sound. By contrast, unregulated spontaneous shelters in Caracas illustrate the dangers of unzoned squatter settlements. There, more than half a million people live on precarious hillsides in shacks that are sometimes washed away by mudslides during the rainy season. Second, in contrast to many sprawling squatter communities, inhabitants of sites-and-services settlements have electricity, sanitation, and other basic services from the outset. Furthermore, although occupants must purchase their sites, the lots are far more affordable than are fully built, state housing units.

THE PROBLEM OF URBAN CRIME

Escalating crime is a major problem in Latin America (with the world's highest homicide rate) and in many African cities. On the other hand, Asia's murder rate is lower than Western Europe's. In fact, it is the lowest of any region in the world. In places such as San Salvador and Nairobi, large, well-armed youth gangs escalate the level of violence. In many developing countries, crime is more than a personal concern. It has become an important political issue, eliciting mass demonstrations and angry demands for better protection from robbery and violent crime. As in the United States and other industrialized nations, the origins of criminal activity often lie in poverty, discrimination, income inequality, inadequate schools, and broken families. Its victims, of course, come from all social classes, rich and poor alike. However, the urban poor make up a disproportionate share of both the perpetrators *and* the victims.

Although violent crime rates generally are associated with poverty, there are some important exceptions. For example, homicide and rape rates are significantly higher in the United States than in a number of developing countries such as Chile, Egypt, and Senegal. And, as we have noted, Asia—with severe poverty in a number of countries—has the lowest violent crime rate of any world region. One possible explanation for such anomalies is that income *inequality* may be a more important factor influencing the crime rate than the *absolute* rate of poverty is. A number of cross-national studies have found a positive correlation between inequality and violent crime.[24] Countries such as the United States, South Africa, and Brazil—all with high income inequality—tend to have higher violent crime rates than other countries with comparable or lower per capita incomes, but greater equality. Conversely, although Asian countries such as Bangladesh, India, and Laos suffer from extensive and acute poverty, they also have low income inequality when compared to either affluent or developing countries. And all three have relatively low homicide rates.

Latin American and African cities (largely poor *and* unequal) suffer from high crime rates. For example, Honduras and South Africa, with some of the world's most extreme income inequality, have among the world's highest urban homicide and rape rates. Of course, the association between inequality and crime is not absolute. For example, while income is very unequally distributed in Chile, its cities have low levels of violent crime. Similarly, both Hong Kong and Singapore, though having moderately high income concentration, are among the safest cities in the world. In some of these exceptional cases, other factors likely influence crime rate. These include cultural values, the strength of nuclear families, and the likelihood of being caught and punished by the criminal justice system. For the most part, however, a country's degree of income equality is a strong predictor of its crime rate.

In addition to normal criminal activity, residents of many cities must deal with "government crime" in the form of corruption or intimidation. In polls conducted in a range of locations, only 0.1 percent of British residents (one in a thousand) and 0.2 percent of Americans responded that they had been asked to pay a bribe to a government official (including police) during the year preceding the survey or expected to be asked to pay one before the end of the year. That proportion increased to 19.5 percent in Kampala (Uganda) and 29.9 percent in Jakarta (Indonesia).[25]

Police shakedowns and solicitation of protection money are common in many LDCs, but in some countries, police corruption is far more serious. In Mexico, many national and municipal policemen support major drug cartels and are involved in kidnappings, extortion, and murder. In early 2011, when mass graves containing at least 145 bodies were found not far from the Texas border, sixteen local policemen were arrested for links to the brutal Zeta cartel and for involvement in those killings. In Argentina, one sociologist observed:

> Each division [of the Buenos Aires police department] dedicates itself to the area of crime that it is supposed to be fighting. The robbery division steals and robs, the narcotics division traffics drugs, auto theft controls the stealing of cars and the chop shops, and those in fraud and bunko, defraud and swindle.[26]

Not surprisingly, the Argentine public had the lowest level of trust in their police of any of the twenty-six countries surveyed in the Western Hemisphere.[27] In many other developing countries, rampant crime and, especially, extensive police corruption not only threaten the security of all city dwellers (regardless of economic status) but also undermine the government's legitimacy.

THE POLITICS OF THE URBAN POOR: CONFLICTING IMAGES

How do the urban poor react politically to their daily struggles for jobs, shelter, and personal safety? As with discussions of peasant politics, social scientists have presented sharply contrasting images of the politics of the urban poor. When political scientists and sociologists first noted the flood of migration and urban growth, many viewed the sprawling slums and squatter settlements as potential hotbeds of unrest or revolution. In a highly influential early work on the LDCs, James Coleman warned that "there exist in most urban centers elements predisposed to anomic activity [that is, behavior caused by alienation, often lacking societal or moral constraints]."[28] Huntington maintained that the first generation of urban migrants was unlikely to challenge the existing order, but their children often would: "At some point, the slums [and shantytowns] of Rio and Lima are likely to be swept by social violence, as the children of the city demand the rewards of the city."[29] And economist Barbara Ward, taking note of shantytown poverty and the rise of radical urban movements, insisted that "unchecked, left to grow and fester, there is here enough explosive material to produce . . . bitter class conflict . . . erupting in guerrilla warfare, and threatening, ultimately, the security even of the comfortable West."[30]

As we will see, the urban poor have, indeed, contributed to several revolutions in LDCs. Yet, the urban conflagrations that many analysts had once expected have been rare. For the most part, the poor have shunned radical political activity and violence. Even at the ballot box, they have been as likely to vote for right-wing or centrist political candidates as for radical ones. It now seems clear that initial expectations of a violent or radicalized urban lower class were based on erroneous premises. Many social scientists had assumed that urban migrants, coming to the cities with raised expectations and heightened political sensitivities, would surely turn militant when these expectations were not satisfied. Instead, although the slums of Cairo, Calcutta, and Caracas may appear horrendous to outside observers, most migrants find them preferable to their previous life in the countryside. For example, the urban poor are far more likely than their rural counterparts to have access to electricity, sewage, tap water, and nearby schools. In many countries, urban migration provides an escape from semifeudal social controls or ethnic civil war. Small wonder that early surveys of migrants to Ankara, Baghdad, Bogotá, Mexico City, Rio de Janeiro, and other cities have indicated that most respondents feel better off in their urban hovels than they had in their rural villages.[31] Periodic economic downturns have lowered urban living standards for a while and have undoubtedly embittered some of the poor. Yet, surveys over the years have shown that urbanites generally remain optimistic about the future, particularly their children's future.

When early expectations of urban radicalism and political violence generally failed to materialize, some scholars jumped to the opposite conclusion. For example, on the basis of his studies of low-income neighborhoods in Mexico and Puerto Rico, anthropologist Oscar Lewis concluded that most of the urban poor are prisoners of a "**culture of poverty.**" By this he referred to an underclass that lacks class consciousness, economic and political organization, and long-term aspirations. While distrustful of government, they feel powerless and fatalistic about effecting change. The culture of poverty, Lewis argued, is inherently apolitical and, hence, quite unlikely to generate radical activity or, for that matter, great pressure for any change.

Related scholarship describes the urban poor as marginal—outside the mainstream of their nation's political and economic life. This suggests a vicious circle in which the exclusion of the poor magnifies their political apathy, which, in turn, isolates them further. They demonstrate a "lack of active participation due to the fact that . . . marginal groups make no decisions; they do not contribute to the molding of society."[32] Like the victims of Lewis's culture of poverty, these "marginals" allegedly show little class consciousness or capacity for long-term collective action.

While it may be true that many poor city dwellers feel incapable of advancing their own lives or influencing the political system—often with good reason—they do not necessarily suffer from the apathy or helplessness that many scholars ascribed to them. Levels of fatalism or optimism vary from place to place and from time to time, depending on both the community's cultural values and its socioeconomic experiences. When poor slum dwellers in Côte d'Ivoire and Kenya—low-income African countries—were asked whether they believed that "when a person is born, the success he/she is going to have is already decided" (an obvious measure of fatalism), nearly 60 percent of them strongly agreed and an additional 11 percent agreed somewhat. In Brazil, a much more economically developed country with one of the world's most unequal income distributions, only about 15 percent strongly agreed, but some 30 percent agreed somewhat. Finally, in Chile, which since the start of the 1990s has experienced the most rapid economic growth in Latin America, with a sharp decline in urban poverty, a mere 4 percent of the respondents strongly agreed, while only 15 percent agreed somewhat.[33] In short, the level of fatalism or optimism among the urban poor varies considerably across nations and seems to correspond more to objective economic conditions than to culturally embedded values.

Just as initial predictions of radicalism and political violence among the urban lower class have turned out to be greatly exaggerated, so too have the reverse assertions that the poor are invariably apathetic and fatalistic. To be sure, low-income communities generally are not highly politicized. In his early study of the poor in Guatemala City, Bryan R. Roberts found that "they claim to avoid politics in their local work, and to them the term *politician* is synonymous with deceit and corruption."[34] Yet, these assessments often do not originate in the slum dwellers' innate apathy or fatalism. Rather, they come from their accurate perception that they have little chance of changing the political and economic order. On the other hand, when given the opportunity to organize (i.e., when their political activity is not repressed) and when there is a realistic chance of attaining some benefits from the political system, many low-income communities have seized the opportunity. The slums and shantytowns of Caracas, Lima, and Rio, for example, have spawned numerous well-organized and politically effective community groups. Furthermore, their leaders often have a keen understanding of how to operate within the political system and manipulate it.

In time, many social scientists questioned the concepts of marginality and the culture of poverty. In the previously mentioned survey of poor neighborhoods in four African cities (in Côte d'Ivoire and Kenya) and four Latin American cities (in Brazil and Chile), political attitudes, levels of political interest, and political knowledge varied considerably. In all four countries, a majority of the people (ranging from 51 to 63 percent) surveyed responded that they were *not* interested in politics.[35]

Yet, despite their professed disinterest, many of these slum dwellers were well informed and communicative about politics. In Chile, Côte d'Ivoire, and Kenya, roughly half of them reported talking occasionally with other people "about the problems which [their] country has to face today." This proportion rose to almost two-thirds in Brazil. Moreover, although over half of them professed to have no interest in politics, about half of those surveyed in Chile and Côte d'Ivoire claimed that they regularly followed political news. When asked to name important government leaders, most were quite knowledgeable. In all four nations, at least two-thirds were able to name the president of their country (reaching 94 percent in Kenya and 96 percent in Chile). Moreover, about half the respondents in Chile and Kenya and two-thirds in Brazil and Côte d'Ivoire could name the mayor of their town. Most impressively, more than 70 percent of these poor Kenyans and Ivorians could name the president of at least one *other* African country, while almost half the Chileans could name the president of another Latin American country (Brazilians were less knowledgeable). One suspects that these figures exceed the percentage of Americans who can name the president of Mexico or the prime minister of Canada. In short, these low-income city dwellers seemed to have a greater interest in politics than they were willing to admit. Perhaps the question on their level of political interest meant something different to them than it did to the people conducting the survey.

Unfortunately, however, in all four countries the urban poor tended to take a rather dim view of their political system and their elected representatives. More than 80 percent of those surveyed in each of the four countries believed that "those we elect to parliament lose touch with people pretty quickly," with this number reaching 94 percent in Chile. When asked whether they believed that "public officials care what people like me think," a significant majority in all of the eight cities said "no." Surprisingly, Ivorians, living in a country that was not then democratic, were most positive about their public officials. On the other hand, Chileans, who live in the most democratic and politically responsive of the four nations, were least likely by far to believe that their government officials care about them and were also least likely to believe that their parliamentary representative keeps in touch with low-income constituents. Perhaps Chileans had harbored unrealistically high expectations of their new political leaders following the restoration of democracy in 1990 after a seventeen-year military dictatorship. Another important factor may be that Chilean parties, renowned for their strong linkages to the lower classes prior to the dictatorship, had become more elitist and distant during their years in exile.

Thus, there seems to be a wide variety of political attitudes among the urban poor. Moreover, their attitudes may vary over time in response to changes in national politics. Although the slums of Santiago (Chile) or Tehran (Iran) once boiled with unrest, the same neighborhoods were largely tranquil or even passive years later. Clearly, a more nuanced view of urban politics requires us to ask: Under what circumstances do the poor organize politically? What goals do they seek, and how do they pursue them? What factors determine whether their political organization is peaceful or violent, conservative or radical, reformist or revolutionary?

FORMS OF POLITICAL EXPRESSION
AMONG THE URBAN POOR

Political scientists have long understood that the urban poor tend to be better informed and more politically active than their rural counterparts. Indeed, early scholarship on LDCs used a nation's level of urbanization as an indirect indicator of its level of political participation. Lower-income city residents have higher levels of literacy than peasants do, greater exposure to the mass media, and more contact with political campaigns and rallies. This does not mean, however, that most of them are highly politicized. To the contrary, as we have noted, many of them are indifferent, apathetic, or fatalistic about political events (just as many Americans are). Nor does it mean that political activists in the community are necessarily radical or indignant about local living conditions or prone to violent protest. What it does mean is that the urban poor generally vote in higher numbers and follow politics more closely than the peasantry does. Furthermore, it appears that many low-income neighborhoods carefully calculate what benefits they can secure from the political system and then organize to secure them. Contrary to initial expectations that the disoriented and frustrated urban poor would riot and rebel, they have tended, instead, to be rather pragmatic and careful in their political behavior.

Individual Political Behavior

For most slum and shantytown dwellers, opportunities for individual political activity are rather restricted. In the many developing countries ruled by military or single-party dictatorships, voting is meaningless. And even in electoral democracies, where many candidates court the support of the urban poor, political officials tend to forget these voters until the next election.

An alternate, often more fruitful, type of individual political activity takes the form of clientelism (patron-client relationships). Members of the urban lower class often advance their interests by attaching themselves to a prominent patron within the government, an influential political party, or an organized political movement. Clientelism involves "the dispensing of public resources as favors by political power holders/seekers . . . in exchange for votes or other forms of popular support." While it does offer concrete advantages to the less powerful partner (i.e., the client), it is at its heart "a strategy of elite-controlled political participation fostering the status quo."[36] Potentially frustrated or radicalized individuals and groups are thereby co-opted into the political system with the lure of immediate, though limited, gains.

Of course, patron-client relations were also common tools of America's urban political bosses in the late nineteenth and early twentieth centuries. Big-city political machines aided recently arrived immigrants by supplying jobs, access to local government authorities, and Christmas turkeys in exchange for their support at the polls. Today, in cities throughout the LDCs, the poor use clientelistic relations to secure credit, government employment, and other economic goods. Dictators such as Zaire's Mobutu Sese Seko and Nicaragua's Anastasio Somoza maintained their regimes for years by dispensing patronage. Similarly, in democracies, such as India, Uruguay, and the Philippines, political bosses garner votes and volunteers similarly.

For most of the urban poor, however, collective rather than individual activity appears to be the most productive form of political participation. Many low-income neighborhoods have organized rather effectively to extract government benefits. Often, one of their first goals is to secure land titles for their homes along with basic services such as sanitation, sewage, tap water, schools, and paved streets.

Collective Goals: Housing and Urban Services

On the outskirts of Lima, Peru, several million people live in squatter communities. For the most part, these settlements were started through organized invasions of unoccupied land—be it government property, church property, or land whose ownership had been in dispute:

> Some invasions involve relatively small groups of families who cooperate on an informal basis shortly before the occupation of the land. Others involve hundreds of families and are planned with great care. The leaders of these invasions often organize well before the invasion occurs and meet many times to recruit members, choose a site, and plan the occupation itself.[37]

Although these land seizures were illegal, one study found that nearly half of the earliest ones were carried out with either the explicit or tacit approval of local government officials. While the authorities did not want invasions to get out of hand, they understood that permitting a controlled number of them onto low-value land (much of it public) enabled the poor to build their own homes with little cost to the state. There were political benefits to be gained as well. By protecting the invaders from police eviction, a political leader or party could secure electoral support from that community. In many cases, squatters paid off local authorities prior to their invasions.

When a leftist military regime seized power in Peru, it was anxious to mobilize the urban poor but, at the same time, it also wanted to preempt independent political activity. The generals issued an urban reform law legalizing most of the existing squatter communities. They tried to mobilize, yet control, the poor through SINAMOS, a state-run political organization for the rural and urban masses. Henry Dietz's study of six poor neighborhoods in Lima reveals that community leaders in several locations were adept at switching their tactics from Peru's earlier competitive electoral politics to the new rules of enlightened authoritarianism.[38] Mobilized neighborhoods used an impressive array of tactics to secure assistance from the military regime. These included: working through SINAMOS, enlisting the aid of a sympathetic Catholic bishop whom the church had assigned to the shantytowns, gaining the support of foreign NGOs, publishing letters in major newspapers, pressuring local government bureaucrats, and directly petitioning the president.

Although Lima's squatter settlements have been unusually well organized, the urban poor in many other developing countries have also established useful ties between their neighborhoods and the state. For example, in her study of low-income neighborhoods in Mexico City, Susan Eckstein described how neighborhood leaders became active in the long-ruling political party at the time (the PRI), thereby establishing themselves as the links between the government and their communities. Because these community organizations were controlled from the top down and tended to be short-lived, Eckstein was skeptical about how much the poor really gained through this clientelistic system. Still, she conceded that, over the years, poor neighborhoods had successfully petitioned the government for such benefits as running water, electricity, local food markets, schools, and better public transportation. Following the PRI's defeat in the 2000 presidential election (after seventy-one years in power) and Mexico's transition to democracy, many low-income neighborhoods have been forced to establish new clientelistic relationships.

The politics of low-income neighborhoods throughout the LDCs generally resemble the Peruvian and Mexican models in two important respects: the scope of their claims and their relationship to the national political system. Studies of politics in India, Pakistan, the Philippines, and other LDCs demonstrate that the poor usually have limited and pragmatic demands. For example, when their demands focus on housing, as they often do, they may simply demand protection against eviction from their illegal settlements. Beyond this, they may ask for basic services (water, electricity, etc.) and titles to their plots so that they can build their own homes. Established neighborhoods often request a medical clinic, a market, or a preschool lunch program. None of these objectives presents a challenge to the established political system or a call for major redistribution of economic resources.

In fact, the very nature of their political organizations limits the demands of low-income communities since these groups tend to atrophy after a number of years. Consequently, as Alan Gilbert and Peter Ward charge, "The [the government's] main aim [in supporting] community-action programs is less to improve conditions for the poor . . . than to legitimate the state . . . to help maintain existing power relations in society."[39] As an alternative to clientelism, critics favor a more independent, and perhaps more radical, form of mobilization that would raise the urban poor's political consciousness and lead to more sweeping redistributive policies benefiting far more people.

Other analysts, however, hold a more positive view of clientelism. While recognizing its shortcomings, they insist that the benefits that it brings are clearly better than nothing. Viewed in the broader context of society's tremendous inequalities, paved streets, clean drinking water, or a clinic may not seem like sufficient improvements to some outside observers. Nevertheless, the low-income neighborhoods that receive them appreciate their value. A radical regime might redistribute more to the poor, but this usually is not a viable option. Furthermore, the performance of radical regimes in helping the poor has been mixed. Marxist governments often redistribute significant resources to the urban poor soon after taking power. However, with the notable exception of China (after it transformed to an essentially capitalist economy) and Vietnam, they have usually had a poor record of generating economic growth.

The benefits of clientelism vary from country to country, depending on the nature of the political system and the health of the economy. In relatively open and democratic systems, the poor have broader opportunities to organize, demonstrate, petition, and vote. Consequently, their capacity to *demand* rewards from the state is normally greater than under authoritarian regimes. At the same time, the level of benefits clientelistic systems can allocate to low-income neighborhoods is also constrained by the state's economic resources. During their petroleum booms, the Mexican and Venezuelan governments could be more generous to the urban poor. Even in more difficult economic times, the Mexican government used revenues from the sale of state enterprises to finance public works projects in the urban slums. When Venezuela reaped the rewards of its petroleum wealth, President Hugo Chávez financed extensive antipoverty programs, which earned him strong support among the urban poor. On the other hand, the remaining dictatorships in Sub-Saharan Africa, such as Zimbabwe, have neither the economic resources nor the political will to aid impoverished urban neighborhoods.

Whatever the merits or limits of clientelism, its scope and range refute certain earlier assumptions about the politics of the urban poor. On the one hand, their often delicate and complex patron-client negotiations demonstrate that numerous low-income neighborhood leaders are more politically skilled than many outside analysts had given them credit for. While many of the urban poor suffer from fatalism and excessive individualism, others are capable of sophisticated political organization and tough bargaining with the state or political parties. On the other hand, the universality of clientelism indicates that the poor rarely engage in the radical politics, the violent upheavals, or the revolutionary activities that other political scientists had expected. During the recent global economic crisis and in regional economic meltdowns, various urban neighborhoods have erupted in violence. Nevertheless, the extent of rioting and social unrest has remained surprisingly limited. To be sure, unemployment and other economic difficulties helped motivate the slum dwellers of Tunis and Cairo to join in the mass protests that brought down the dictators of Egypt and Tunisia. But both these prodemocratic uprisings were started and led by young people from the middle class.

Radical Political Behavior

While most of the urban poor favor moderate and pragmatic forms of political expression, there have been important exceptions. In some countries, such as El Salvador since the mid-1990s, low-income neighborhoods have voted in substantial numbers for Marxist political candidates. And, in a few cases, residents of urban slums and shantytowns have been important players in revolutionary upheavals. In 1970, Salvador Allende, candidate of Chile's leftist Popular Unity (UP) coalition, became the developing world's first democratically elected Marxist president. Allende received considerable electoral support from the *campamentos* (squatter settlements) that ring the capital city of Santiago. In fact, a number of these neighborhoods were politically organized either by the UP or by the MIR (Revolutionary Left Movement), a more radical group than UP, which periodically engaged in armed action. The poor of Lima played a major role in electing a Marxist mayor, Alfonso Barrantes. These examples, as well as the Communist Party's electoral successes in several large Indian cities, indicate that the poor do support radical political parties under certain circumstances. However, they will favor those parties only if they have a realistic chance of winning at the local or national level so that they can be in a position to deliver tangible benefits to their supporters. Thus, even a slum dweller's decision to vote for a radical candidate is often based on very pragmatic calculations. Not long after supporting Barrantes for mayor, Lima's poor gave him few votes when he ran for the nation's presidency, believing that his Marxist policies might succeed in Lima but were not viable at the national level.

More often, the urban poor are attracted to charismatic populists (such as Venezuelan president Hugo Chávez) or to moderate leftists (such as Brazilian president Luiz Inácio Lula da Silva). Squatters or slum dwellers are much less likely to embrace urban guerrillas or other revolutionary movements. Teodoro Petkoff, a former leader of the Venezuelan communists' urban guerrilla wing, noted that residents of Caracas's poor barrios, even those who belonged to leftist unions, rejected the guerrillas. Blue-collar workers often elected communist union representatives in those days, Petkoff observed, because they felt that those union militants would deliver more at the bargaining table. On the other hand, in national elections, the urban poor were more likely to vote for the two mainstream parties (Social Democrats and Christian Democrats) or for the country's former right-wing dictator, all of whom were more capable of quickly delivering rewards to their supporters than the guerrillas were.[40]

In the 1980s and 1990s, Peru's *Sendero Luminoso* (Shining Path) guerrillas had some success in the shantytowns of Lima. However, as often as not, they only earned that "support" through intimidation. For example, when a popular, women's political organizer in the large shantytown Villa El Salvador failed to cooperate with it, the guerrilla group assassinated her in front of her family and neighbors.

This is not to suggest that the urban poor never support revolutions. During the second half of the twentieth century, the cities played a central role in four of the developing world's revolutions—in Bolivia, Cuba, Iran, and Nicaragua. However, in most cases, other social classes took the lead: miners, unionized blue-collar workers, artisans, the lower middle class, and the national police in Bolivia; students and university graduates in Cuba; and theology students and petroleum workers in Iran. In contrast, Douglas Butterworth's study of the former inhabitants of a Havana slum, *Las Yaguas*, conducted almost twenty years after the revolutionary victory, found that most respondents were barely aware of Fidel Castro's existence during his rise to power.[41]

In the past years, many of the urban poor in Muslim countries have been attracted to a different type of revolutionary vision, Islamism and Islamist extremism. In Tunisia and Egypt, Islamist organizations played a secondary role in the mass protests of the Arab Spring. However, Egypt's Muslim Brotherhood and Tunisia's Ennahdha (Renaissance) Party, both avowedly moderate Islamist parties, won the first democratic elections held in their country.

CONCLUSION: THE ROLE OF THE RURAL AND URBAN POOR IN DEMOCRATIC CHANGE

In future decades, the LDCs will continue to experience a shift in population from its rural areas to its urban centers. While the *rate* of urbanization has slowed in parts of the developing world, *absolute increases* in urban populations (the increases in raw numbers) will be greater than ever in the coming decades. Thus, governments will have to heed urban needs, including those of the poor. Still, even with the best-intentioned public policies, developing economies will be hard-pressed to provide sufficient jobs, housing, sanitation, and social services. Various economic crises over the past few decades have made the task all the more difficult. Urban crime, pollution, and AIDS will add tremendously to the burdens on the political and economic systems. In countries such as South Africa and Guatemala, the fall of authoritarian regimes has led to a surge in crime. To the extent that rural-urban migration can be slowed by agrarian reform, rural development programs, and improved rural education and health care, it will give both urban planners and the urban poor more time and opportunity to deal with these problems.

As the developing countries try to consolidate their new democracies, they will find the urban poor better equipped than their rural counterparts to become participatory citizens. But they are also more volatile and, should democratic governments disappoint them, they are more likely to turn to forms of antisystemic behavior. Both the rural and urban poor will need to refine and improve their strategies for securing state resources, while governments will have to become more responsive to both groups' needs. In many developing countries, however, urban crime and drug usage are more likely than radical politics to threaten stability in the proximate future. Faced with rising crime rates and economic deprivation, the poor may become disillusioned with democracy. If the military and the middle class also fear rising crime and disorder, democracies may fall to repressive governments.

Practice and Review Online
http://textbooks.rowman.com/handelman8e#ch6

KEY TERMS

agrarian reform
collectivization (collective farms)
culture of poverty
economies of scale
greenhouse effect
moral economy
patron-client relationships
    (clientelism)

peasant
shantytowns
smallholder
spontaneous housing
squatter settlements

DISCUSSION QUESTIONS

1. Peasants were the major foot soldiers in most twentieth-century revolutions (China, Cuba, Mexico, and Vietnam). Is this likely to be true of twenty-first-century revolutions in the developing world? Why or why not?
2. What kind of rural reform or development projects do you think would most benefit the rural poor? Why?
3. Although agrarian reform programs have fallen out of favor in contemporary government policies, there are those who still argue for their value. What are some arguments for restarting agrarian reform in LDCs?
4. Discuss the political orientations of the urban poor. What does survey research tell us about the way that the urban poor look at their present circumstances and about their views on the prospects of improving their lot?
5. Discuss the growth of urban crime in the LDCs, the major obstacles to reducing crime, and the possible political consequences of rising crime rates.

6. How might rapid urban growth contribute to the growth of demo-cratic governments in the LDCs? Under what circumstances might it *undermine* democracy?

NOTES

1. George Foster, "Introduction: What Is a Peasant?," in *Peasant Society*, eds. Jack Potter, George Foster, and May Diaz (Boston, MA: Little, Brown, 1967), 2–14.

2. Eric R. Wolf, *Peasants* (Upper Saddle River, NJ: Prentice Hall, 1966), 10.

3. Robert Redfield, *Peasant Society and Culture: An Anthropological Approach* (Chicago, IL: University of Chicago Press, 1965), 77.

4. Phyllis Arora, "Patterns of Political Response in Indian Peasant Society," *Western Political Quarterly* 20 (September 1967): 654.

5. James C. Scott, *Weapons of the Week: Everyday Forms of Peasant Resistance* (New Haven, CT: Yale University Press, 1986).

6. One of the most insightful books on the role of the peasantry in twentieth-century revolutions is Eric R. Wolf, *Peasant Wars of the Twentieth Century* (New York: Harper & Row, 1969).

7. James C. Scott, *The Moral Economy of the Peasant: Rebellion and Subsistence in Southeast Asia* (New Haven, CT: Yale University Press, 1976).

8. Wolf, *Peasant Wars*.

9. Samuel P. Huntington, *Political Order in Changing Societies* (New Haven, CT: Yale University Press, 1968), 375.

10. Binswanger-Mkhize, Hans et al., "Agricultural Land Redistribution: Toward Greater Consensus" (Paper delivered to the World Bank, 2010), 299.

11. T. S. Jane et al., "Smallholder Income and Land Distribution in Africa," *Food Policy* 28 (2003): 253–75, https://www.msu.edu/~chapotoa/Land%20 Paper.pdf.

12. Huntington, *Political Order*, 375.

13. Binswanger-Mkhize et al., "Agricultural Land Redistribution," 95.

14. James Grant, "Development: The End of Trickle Down," *Foreign Policy* 12 (Fall 1973): 43–65.

15. "FAO's Contribution to Good Policies and Practices in Agrarian Reform and Rural Development: A Brief Overview," 3.

16. Peter Baker and Rachel Donadio, "Obama Wins More Food Aid but Presses African Nations on Corruption," *New York Times*, July 11, 2009.

17. Manuel Castells and Alejandro Portes, "World Underneath: The Origins, Dynamics and Effects of the Informal Economy," in *The Informal Economy: Studies in Advanced and Developing Economies*, eds. Alejandro Portes, Manuel Castells, and Lauren A. Benton (Baltimore, MD: Johns Hopkins University Press, 1989), 12.

18. UN-Habitat (United Nations Human Settlements Programme), *Statistics*.

19. UN Habitat, *State of the World's Cities 2010/2011*.

20. Silvia Schmitt, "Housing Conditions and Policies," in Poverty and Democracy—Self-Help and Political Participation in Third World Cities, eds. Dirk Berg-Schlosser and Norbert Kersting (London and New York: Zed Books, 2003), 61.

21. Howard Handelman, "The Role of the State in Sheltering the Urban Poor," in *Spontaneous Shelter*, ed. Carl V. Patton (Philadelphia, PA: Temple University Press, 1988), 332–33.

22. Susan Eckstein, *The Poverty of Revolution: The State and the Urban Poor in Mexico*, 2nd ed. (Princeton, NJ: Princeton University Press, 1988), 41.

23. Alan Gilbert and Peter Ward, *Housing, the State, and the Poor* (New York: Cambridge University Press, 1985), 86–87.

24. For example, United Nations Office on Drugs and Crime, *Global Study on Homicide, 2015* (online).

25. All the crime and corruption data in this paragraph come from the UNDP, *Human Development Report 2000* (New York: Oxford University Press, 2000), 220–21.

26. *New York Times*, August 4, 2004.

27. "Trust in the National Police," based on a 2010 survey of 44,000 people by Americas Barometer, www.AmericasBarometer.org.

28. James Coleman, "Conclusion: The Political Systems of Developing Nations," in *The Politics of Developing Areas*, eds. Gabriel Almond and James Coleman (Princeton, NJ: Princeton University Press, 1960), 537.

29. Samuel Huntington, *Political Order in Changing Societies* (New Haven, CT: Yale University Press, 1968), 283.

30. Barbara Ward, "Creating Man's Future Goals for a World of Plenty," *Saturday Review* 9 (August 1964): 192.

31. Joan Nelson, *Migrants, Urban Poverty, and Instability in Developing Nations* (Cambridge, MA: AMS Press and the Harvard University Center for International Affairs, 1969).

32. Jorge Giusti, "Organizational Characteristics of the Latin American Urban Marginal Settler," *International Journal of Politics* 1, no. 1 (1971): 57.

33. Barbara Happe and Sylvia Schmit, "Political Culture," in *Poverty and Democracy*, 130.

34. Bryan R. Roberts, *Organizing Strangers: Poor Families in Guatemala City* (Austin, TX: University of Texas Press, 1973), 299.

35. Happe and Schmit, "Political Culture," 125. All of the survey results that follow come from that chapter (121–52) and from Norbert Kersting and Jaime Sperberg, "Political Participation," in *Poverty and Democracy*, 153–80.

36. Both quotes come from A. Bank, "Poverty, Politics and the Shaping of Urban Space: A Brazilian Example," *International Journal of Urban and Regional Research* 10, no. 4 (1986): 523.

37. David Collier, *Squatters and Oligarchs* (Baltimore, MD: Johns Hopkins University Press, 1976), 41, 44.

38. Henry Dietz, *Poverty and Problem Solving Under Military Rule* (Austin, TX: University of Texas Press, 1980).

39. Gilbert and Ward, *Housing, the State and the Poor*, 175.

40. Interviews with Petkoff in 1976 and 1978.

41. Douglas Butterworth, *The People of Buena Ventura* (Urbana, IL: University of Illinois Press, 1980), 19–20.

7
Revolutionary Change

Soldiers of the Islamic State (also known as ISIS) in Iraq. Since the end of the twentieth century (and the collapse of the Soviet Union), militant Islamic groups such as al-Qaeda and the Islamic State have replaced communists as the most powerful revolutionary force in many LDCs. *Handout/Alamy Stock Photo*

THE OPENING DECADES of the twentieth century ushered in the Mexican and Russian revolutions. The closing decades witnessed the collapse of Soviet Communism and the transformation of the Chinese and Vietnamese revolutions.* Just when it looked as this "age of revolution" was over, a new type of revolutionary movement has erupted in the Arab World—the rise of radical Islam. No era in world history had encompassed more revolutionary upheaval.

Karl Marx, the most influential prophet of revolution, expected insurrections to take place in industrialized European nations where the organized working class would rise up against the oppressive capitalist system. Instead, communist revolutions have taken place almost exclusively in the developing world, fought primarily by the peasantry. Islamist revolutionary movement, on the other hand, has drawn support from a wide variety of social classes and groups (see chapter 3).

In the LDCs, the appeal of revolutionary change has been its pledge of rapid and sweeping solutions to the problems of underdevelopment. Marxist revolutions promised to end colonial rule, terminate dependency, protect national sovereignty, reduce social and economic inequalities, accelerate economic development, mobilize the population, and transform the political culture. Islamist uprisings promise to drive out allegedly corrupt Western influence and values. Not surprisingly, many of the developing world's poor and oppressed along with numerous intellectuals and alienated members of the middle class have found revolutionary ideologies appealing.

Some revolutionary governments—in China, Cuba, and Mexico, for example—were able to deliver on a number of their promises. Under Mao Zedong's leadership, the Chinese Communist Party (CCP) redistributed land to the peasantry, industrialized the economy, and transformed the country into a world power. Fidel Castro's government implemented extensive land reform, an impressive adult literacy campaign, and significant public health programs. Mexico's revolutionary party reestablished national sovereignty over the country's most valuable natural resources (most notably, petroleum), initiated agrarian reform, and industrialized the nation.

Often, however, these gains have come at great cost, including considerable human suffering and loss of life during the revolutionary struggle and after its victory (Cambodia), political repression (China and Iran), and rampant corruption (Mexico, Laos). As a result of their revolution, the Chinese people now enjoy far better medical care, education,

---

*Leninist regimes remain in place in China and Vietnam (they still are officially communist), but their governments have abandoned communist economics and class-based politics. The Cuban government has also made more modest transformations of its economy.

and general living conditions than ever before. At the same time, however, perhaps thirty million people starved to death in the 1950s due to the mistaken experiments of Mao's Great Leap Forward.* Millions more suffered humiliation or imprisonment and perhaps 400,000 people died during the ultraradical period called the Cultural Revolution (1966–1976). Many other communist governments had their own *gulags* (networks of prisons or forced labor camps) for real and imagined political opponents. In Vietnam, the revolutionary government sent many suspected dissidents to "reeducation" camps, and in Cuba, a smaller, but still significant, number were imprisoned. Iran's Islamist revolution has produced military and some social gains, but has done so at the cost of internal repression and international isolation.

In the most unfortunate cases—Angola, Mozambique, and Cambodia—large portions of the population died as a result of the revolutionary conflicts and their aftermaths, with little or nothing positive to show for it.† In Cambodia, the fanatical *Khmer Rouge* government murdered or starved more than a million people, including much of the country's educated class, while failing to accomplish anything for its people. Over the years, even some of the more idealistic revolutionary regimes changed into corrupt bureaucracies, run by a new generation of opportunistic *apparatchiks* (party or government bureaucrats) who had never risked anything for the revolution's ideals. Currently, the IS has improved public services (water, sanitation, food distribution, and the like) in many areas that it controls, but at the cost of horrendous tyranny and mass slaughters especially of non-Muslims and Shi'ites.

After examining the meaning of the term *revolution* and classifying different types of twentieth- and twenty-first-century revolutions, this chapter will discuss the causes of revolutionary upheavals, their principal sources of leadership and support, and the policy objectives of their leaders once in power. Finally, it will discuss the decline of the revolutionary model at the end of the twentieth century and its possible resurrection in a new form in the twenty-first.

DEFINING REVOLUTION

Scholars have argued endlessly about what constitutes a revolution and whether particular upheavals such as the American Revolution or Iran's

---

*"The Great Leap Forward" (1958–1961) was Chinese leader, Mao Zedong's, tragic attempt to convert the economy to full communism rapidly. Government policies in agriculture, including the abolition of private farming, resulted in mass starvation.

†In Angola and Mozambique, most of the killings were carried out by counterrevolutionary forces. For the hundreds of thousands of butchered innocent civilians, however, it mattered little which side killed them.

Islamic revolution were, in fact, true social revolutions. Thus, Chalmers Johnson notes, "Half the battle will lie in answering the question, 'What is revolution?'"[1] In its broadest and least precise usage, the term is applied to any violent government overthrow. Peter Calvert offers the most open-ended definition when he maintains that revolution is "simply a form of governmental change through violence."[2] This kind of definition, however, seems too broad because it encompasses military coups and other upheavals that do little more than change the heads of government. Most scholars insist on a more rigorous definition, arguing that revolutions must bring fundamental political, economic, and social change. Samuel Huntington has suggested,

> A revolution is a rapid, fundamental, and violent domestic change in the dominant values and myths of society, in its political institutions, social structure, leadership and government activity and policies. Revolutions are thus to be distinguished from insurrections, revolts, coups and wars of independence.[3]

To be sure, it is frequently difficult to make the distinctions that Huntington proposes at the end of his definition. For example, some "wars of independence" (sometimes called "**wars of national liberation**"), such as Algeria's and Mozambique's, are generally considered authentic social revolutions because they ushered in fundamental societal change. On the other hand, Theda Skocpol accepts Huntington's starting definition but narrows it by claiming that "social revolutions are accompanied and in part effectuated through [massive] class upheavals."[4] She adds,

> Social revolutions are set apart from other sorts of conflicts by the combination of two coincidences: the coincidence of societal structural change with class upheaval; and the coincidence of the political with social transformation.[5]

Skocpol concedes that according to her more restrictive, class-based definition, only "a handful of successful social revolutions have ever occurred." The most clear-cut cases are the three she has studied in great detail: France (1789–1799), Russia (1917), and China (1911–1949). Other less restrictive definitions of revolution apply to Mexico, Cuba, Algeria, Ethiopia, South Africa, Vietnam, Cambodia, Turkey, and Iran. What is common to all of those is that insurgency brought sweeping changes to the country's political, economic, and social systems.

Because revolutions involve a fundamental transfer of political and economic powers, rather than a mere change in political leaders (as is the case of most military coups), they are almost always violent. Not surprisingly, the government officials and social classes that have long held (and often abused) power now face bleak futures and invariably fight to stay on top. If the revolutionaries triumph, they remove old elites from power and install new ones. And, at least in some respects, they broaden political, economic, and social participation to include those further down the social and economic ladder. This does not imply that revolutionary governments are democratic. They rarely are. But they are usually more broadly participatory and egalitarian than the regimes that they have toppled (this has not been the case in the areas controlled by the IS).

This chapter classifies as a revolution any insurgency that brings about these kinds of comprehensive political and socioeconomic changes. These insurrections may be rooted in class struggles (China and Vietnam), as Skocpol insists, or, contrary to Huntington, they may be wars of national liberation (Algeria and Angola), or even ethnic conflict (South Sudan) and religious revivalism (Iran and Syria), as long as they overturn critical political and economic institutions and change the country's underlying power structure and social values. In fact, the borderline between nationalist and class-based revolutions is often difficult to discern. The Vietnamese Revolution most clearly combined anticolonial and class struggles. Moreover, even primarily class-based revolutions, such as China's, Mexico's, Cuba's, and Nicaragua's, had important nationalist, anti-imperialist components to them.

Revolutions may be Marxist (China, Russia, Vietnam, Cambodia, and Cuba) or not (Mexico, Bolivia, Tunisia, and Iran). Marxism was particularly appealing to many revolutionaries because it promised the ideological rigor, social and economic "justice," and new political myths that they sought. But the revolutionary's vision of social justice need not be communist. It may also come from nationalism, Islam, democracy, or other ideologies and religions.

Revolutionaries generally come to power either through mass uprisings—featuring strikes, protest marches, and street riots (Russia, Bolivia, Egypt, and Iran)—and guerrilla warfare (China, Vietnam, and Cuba) or through a combination of both (Nicaragua and Libya). There have also been a few "elite revolutions" in which military officers or upper-level bureaucrats have overthrown governments and instituted far-reaching socioeconomic changes that far transcended the objectives of mere coups.[6] Primary examples include Mustafa Kemal Ataturk's military revolt in Turkey (1919), Gamal Abdel Nasser's officers' revolt in Egypt (1952), and Peru's "revolution from above" (1968)—all led by reformist military officers (see chapter 8).

The recent series of mass uprisings against authoritarian regimes in Tunisia, Egypt, Libya, Syria, Yemen, and Bahrain raises interesting challenges to these definitions of revolution. Do those mass uprisings against Arab dictators qualify as revolutions? Surely, the Tunisian transition to democracy and its apparent consolidation meets this test. However, in the other countries involved in the Arab Spring, their revolutions were aborted before they had gotten off the ground.

UNDERLYING CAUSES OF REVOLUTION

Just as experts have disagreed about the definition of revolution, they have also differed over the causes of revolutionary insurrection. Some theories focus on broad historical trends, including changes in the world order that make revolution possible or likely. Other explanations center on weaknesses in the *ancien régime* (the old political and socioeconomic systems), examining factors that caused the prerevolutionary state to fall. And yet others concentrate on the revolutions' major players, particularly the peasantry, seeking the factors that cause them to revolt.

Inexorable Historical Forces

Karl Marx viewed revolution as an unstoppable historical force growing out of class inequalities that are rooted in the ownership of the means of production. Those who command the economic system, he argued, control the state as well. Over time, however, subordinate classes will become alienated from the political-economic order and will attain sufficient political skills and vision (**class consciousness**) to overthrow the political system. Thus, Marx maintained that in the seventeenth and eighteenth centuries, an ascendant *bourgeoisie* (capitalists or, more broadly, the middle class) had toppled the old order dominated by the aristocracy and landed oligarchy. Examples of such bourgeois revolutions included the British Civil War (Revolution) of 1640 and the French Revolution (1789). Both of those were part of a broader European transition from agrarian feudalism to industrial capitalism. Although Marx believed that this new capitalist order represented a more advanced and more productive historical stage, he also argued that it depended on the exploitation of the working class (**proletariat**). In time, he predicted, as the exploitation of the proletariat became more apparent and as workers developed sufficient class consciousness, they would overthrow capitalism and install revolutionary socialism.

More than any other revolutionary theorist, Marx influenced the course of history, as most of the leaders of the twentieth century's major revolutions—including V. I. Lenin, Mao Zedong, Ho Chi Minh, Che Guevara, and Fidel Castro—fervently believed in his ideology. His writings evoked the centrality of class struggle in most revolutionary movements. But as even sympathetic analysts have noted, "He was, first and foremost a nineteenth-century man" whose ideology was closely linked to the era in which he lived.[7] "Marx's theoretical approach," writes

Irving Zeitlin, "enabled him to explain the past but failed him in his predictions."[8] Indeed, *no* country has ever had the succession of revolutions that he predicted, first capitalist, then socialist.* Instead, the primary locus of modern revolution has been the developing world—not advanced capitalist nations—and the foremost protagonists, at least in the twentieth century, were peasants rather than industrial workers. In this century, leadership in the Arab Spring has come principally from students and young professionals (joined by tribal leaders in Libya and Yemen).

Mao Zedong, the leader of the Chinese Revolution, accepted Marx's view of revolution as part of an unfolding historical process. Like other developing world Marxists, he viewed capitalist exploitation and its resulting class conflict as the root causes of communist upheavals. However, the CCP's military defeats in the 1920s convinced him that its orthodox commitment to **proletarian** revolution was not viable in a country in which the working class constituted only a small percentage of the population. Consequently, he reinterpreted Marxist theory to make it more applicable to China and other parts of the developing world. Mao established a model of peasant-based struggle and a military strategy designed to encircle and conquer China's cities following a period of protracted rural guerrilla conflict. The success of his strategy in the world's most populous country and its frequent use in other developing nations made Mao the most influential practitioner of revolutionary warfare in the twentieth century.

In Vietnam and Cuba, Ho Chi Minh and Che Guevara refined Mao's vision of "peoples' war" to make it more compatible with conditions in Southeast Asia and Latin America. While all of them demonstrated that communist revolutions could take place in countries that are not highly industrialized, those leaders still adhered to Marx's theory of history and his vision of class struggle.

Regime Decay

Even before the collapse of the Soviet bloc, it had become obvious that there was no *inevitable* march toward revolution and that, in fact, successful revolutions have been rather rare. Skocpol argues that neither the repression of the masses nor the skills of revolutionary leadership alone can bring about successful social revolutions. These factors may be necessary, but they are not sufficient. Rather, true revolutions succeed only when international pressures such as war, economic competition, or an

---

*In other words, no Marxist revolution took place in a country where capitalism was entrenched. And, by the end of the twentieth century, in a complete reversal of Marxist theory, communist regimes in the Soviet Union and Central Europe were changing to capitalism.

arms race undermine the state. The modernization of Britain and other European powers, she contends, created severe military and economic pressures on competing countries within and outside Europe. Some of those states, such as royalist France, Czarist Russia, and imperial China, were unable to adjust to these challenges and hence fell victim to revolutionary forces.[9]

In Russia, excessive military entanglements, foreign indebtedness, and a disastrous involvement in World War I undermined the Czarist state. Successive military defeats in two wars—first by the Japanese (1905) and then by the Germans (1917)—helped undermine the Czarist regime. Similarly, China's Manchu dynasty, having been fatally weakened by European and Japanese imperialism, was toppled by Nationalist forces in 1911, who, in turn, were overthrown by the communists nearly forty years later. Elsewhere, stronger regimes were able to withstand comparable challenges, but the Russian and Chinese states were too weak. Ultimately, disgruntled soldiers, workers, and peasants, led by "marginal elites" (university students and middle-class professionals alienated from the system), toppled the old orders.[10] Ironically, just as military competition undermined the Czarist government and set the stage for the Russian Revolution, some seventy years later, the Soviet-American arms race undercut the Soviet Union's financial health and contributed to the system's collapse.

Thus, Skocpol and others have argued that the most significant factor contributing to a successful revolutionary struggle is not the revolutionary leadership's strategy, tactics, or zeal, but rather the internal rot of the decaying old order. For example, Japan's invasion of China prior to World War II undercut the legitimacy of the Kuomintang government. The Japanese occupation demonstrated that the Nationalist regime was too corrupt and incompetent to resist a foreign threat, while the communist People's Liberation Army (PLA) was far more effective. When the Chinese revolutionary war resumed after World War II, many of the areas in which the communists won major military victories were the same ones in which they had organized mass resistance against the Japanese.

In fact, military defeats have frequently delegitimized the existing political order, setting the stage for subsequent revolutions. Thus, the destruction of the Ottoman Empire in World War I and the Japanese capture of British, French, and Dutch colonies in Asia during World War II (including Burma, Vietnam, and Indonesia) all undermined the imperial or colonial governments' legitimacy and led, respectively, to Ataturk's military revolt in Turkey, the communist revolution in Vietnam, and various independence movements in South and Southeast Asia. Similarly, Egypt's defeat by Israel (1948–1949) helped precipitate Colonel Nasser's revolution from above.

War has the additional effect of disrupting peasant life, forcing many to seek the new social structure and physical protection offered by the revolutionary forces. For example, in accounts of life in rural China during its civil war and the Japanese invasion, "one is struck by the number of peasants . . . who had their routines upset through the [war-related] death of their kin before they joined revolutionary organizations."[11]

Of course, there are other factors besides military defeats that may undermine governments. In Cuba and Nicaragua, prolonged dictatorships became obscenely corrupt. Fulgencio Batista rose from the rank of army sergeant in 1933 to become Cuba's dominant political actor over the next two decades. During that period, corruption infested all ranks of government. Batista's links to the American mafia helped turn Havana into a playground for affluent foreign tourists seeking gambling and prostitution. Elsewhere, members of the ruling Somoza dynasty commandeered a huge share of Nicaragua's economy for decades. The National Guard—virtually the Somozas' personal army—enriched themselves as well. For example, when an earthquake leveled the nation's capital (Managua) in 1972, the guard intercepted and sold U.S. relief supplies intended for the earthquake's victims.

A further element undermining the legitimacy of both the Cuban and the Nicaraguan dictatorships was their subservience to the United States, which offended their peoples' national pride. Because the U.S. military had occupied both countries for years early in the twentieth century, this was a particularly sensitive issue. The occupying American Marines had installed Anastasio Somoza Sr., the dynasty's founder, as the first commander of the country's hated National Guard (the country had no army), a position that he subsequently used to seize the presidency. Decades later, in the years preceding their revolution, Nicaraguans derisively referred to his son President Anastasio Somoza Jr., a graduate of West Point, as "the last [American] Marine." In both Cuba and Nicaragua, the combination of rampant corruption and injuries to nationalist self-respect united people across class lines against the government—from peasants to students to business owners. Lacking any real commitment to Batista's dictatorship, the undisciplined Cuban army offered surprisingly little resistance to Fidel Castro's small guerrilla force. In Nicaragua, the National Guardsmen, knowing that they faced popular retribution if they lost power, put up a stronger fight against the Sandinista revolutionaries, yet also fell relatively quickly.

Revolutionary opportunities may also arise when the economy deteriorates, standards of living decline, and the government is unable to meet long-standing economic responsibilities to its people. For example, runaway inflation undermined support for China's Kuomintang government. And declining living standards helped spark the Kenyan rebellion against British colonialism. Thus, maintains Charles Tilly, one cause of revolution is "the sudden failure of government to meet specific obligations which members of the subject population regarded as well established and crucial to their welfare."[12]

While Skocpol, Tilly, and others emphasize the decay of state authority at the *national* level, revolutions can also arise from the breakdown of authority at the local level. We observed earlier (chapter 6) that a web of patron-client relationships linking peasants to their landlords and other local power brokers helps maintain stability in the countryside. Peasants will tolerate considerable injustice if their landlords and the village political bosses compensate by providing them with needed benefits, such as secure access to land, credit, and protection from harassment by the police. However, if the expansion of market forces makes rural patrons unwilling or unable to continue providing benefits that peasants had come to expect, their authority will likely break down. At this point, the state may try to replace the traditional patrons by providing social services such as credit, technical assistance, schools, and clinics. If, however, government authorities fail to satisfy the peasants' needs as well, the rural poor may turn to revolutionary groups as their new patrons and protectors.

Challenges from Below

While revolutionary movements generally succeed only against discredited or weakened governments, they must also mount a well-organized and politically coherent challenge from below. Without this, the old regime, weak though it may be, will either cling to power or collapse into disorder or anarchy (as in Yemen and Somalia currently).

Tilly contends that three things must happen before a revolutionary movement can succeed: first, the revolutionaries must establish themselves as an "alternative sovereignty"; that is, the rebel leadership must convince its would-be supporters that it can function as a viable alternate government. Second, a sizable portion of the population must support that revolutionary option. Finally, the established government must be incapable of suppressing the revolutionary opposition.[13] There are a number of well-known cases in which revolutionaries successfully established alternative sovereignties. Following the collapse of Czarist rule in Russia, the Bolsheviks (Communist Party) established a network of workers' soviets (local leftist councils) to challenge the sovereignty of Alexander Kerensky's moderate provisional government. Asia's protracted guerrilla wars also illustrate the phenomenon. During the Chinese Revolution, the PLA (the Communist Party's military arm) controlled **"liberated zones"** in which the communists distributed land to the peasants, organized military and political support, and demonstrated their ability to govern.

The same was true of South Vietnam's National Liberation Front (Viet Cong).

But, even after understanding these broad preconditions for successful revolutionary activity, we still must ask what causes a revolution to break out in a particular country, at a particular time and not in others. Huntington maintains that the probability of a successful insurrection is determined by the balance of power between the capabilities of government political institutions, on the one hand, and the level of antigovernment political and social mobilization, on the other. Most revolutions, he notes, do not take place in either highly traditional or modern societies.* Rather, they are most likely to erupt in modernizing countries—those in transition from traditional culture to modernity. As greater urbanization, increased education and literacy, and expanded mass-media communication stimulate widespread political mobilization, civil society (the network of organized groups independent of government control) increases its demands on the political system. Unless the governing order can establish institutions capable of accommodating some of these demands in a timely manner, the system will become overloaded and hence more unstable.

Huntington then distinguishes two distinct revolutionary patterns: a *Western* model in which "the political institutions of the old regime collapse *followed* by the mobilization of new groups into politics and then by the creation of new [revolutionary] political institutions" (i.e., the regime's collapse *precedes* a well-organized challenge from below); and an *Eastern* (Asian) revolutionary model that "*begins* with the mobilization of new groups into politics and the creation of new [revolutionary] political institutions and ends with the violent overthrow of the political institutions of the old order."[14]

The French, Russian, and Mexican revolutions fit the Western model, while communist revolutions in China and Vietnam followed the Eastern model.† The recent prodemocracy movements in the Arab World do not seem to fit either model very well as there has been little in the way of coordinated, revolutionary political institutions either before or after the fall of the old regimes.

James C. Davies shifts our attention from the broad historical-social forces that make revolution possible to the question of why particular individuals choose to join a revolt or a revolution. He asserts

---

*However, in recent times, the spread of Facebook, the Web, and other IT media to very underdeveloped countries, such as Yemen, seems to allow revolutionaries to spread their message even in very traditional societies and for latecomers (such as Syria) to learn from earlier uprisings (Tunisia, Egypt).

†But, not all Asian revolutions followed the Eastern model, nor did all Latin American insurgencies conform to the Western model.

Figure 7.1 Davies's psychological model showing the gap between people's expectations and economic reality.

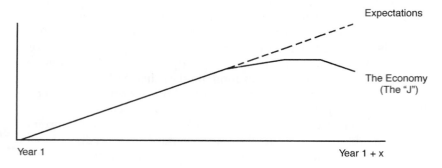

that, contrary to what we might expect, people rarely rebel when they are experiencing prolonged or permanent suffering. "Far from making people revolutionaries, enduring poverty makes for concern with one's solitary self or solitary family, at best, resignation or mute despair at worst."[15] To uncover the source of political upheavals, Davies combines economic and psychological explanations. Unlike Marx, Skocpol, or Tilly, his analysis lumps together mass revolutions with local uprisings and military "revolutions from above." Drawing upon historical data ranging from the Dorr Rebellion (an 1842 uprising in Rhode Island) to the Egyptian military revolution of 1952, he concludes that each upheaval took place after a period of sustained economic growth that was followed by a sharp downturn. A diagram of that growth and subsequent downturn (Figure 7.1) produces what Davies calls the "J-curve."* As a country's economy grows for a period of time, he suggests, people's expectations rise correspondingly (parallel to the long side of the "J"). However, these expectations continue to rise even after the economy experiences a downturn. What emerges is "an intolerable gap between what people want and what they get."[16] Davies argues that this economic J-curve also explains the American and French revolutions, the American Civil War, the rise of German Nazism, student unrest in the United States during the 1960s, and the African-American civil rights movement.

---

*More precisely, the economic pattern he described can be drawn as the letter "J" tipped over, with the long side representing the period of economic growth and the rounded part depicting the downturn.

Using only *twentieth-century* data from seventeen LDCs, Raymond Tanter and Manus Midlarsky confirmed Davies's thesis in Asia and the Middle East (long before the recent uprisings), but not in Latin America. Interestingly, their Asian and Middle Eastern cases also indicated that the higher the rate of economic growth prior to a downturn and the sharper the slide immediately preceding the outbreak of unrest, the longer and more violent the upheaval will be.[17]

Davies's theory is one of the most influential psychologically based explanations of revolutionary behavior. There is, however, an important limitation to his findings. He based his conclusions exclusively on data from countries that have experienced revolts or revolutions. This raises the question of whether there are countries that experienced a J-curve of growth and decline in their economies, yet did not have social upheavals. In fact, Davies admits that there are. For example, he notes the absence of mass unrest in the United States during the Great Depression, a devastating economic downturn. The same holds true for many Latin American countries that enjoyed strong economic growth in the 1960s and 1970s followed by a precipitous decline in the 1980s. Argentina had a comparable cycle from 1990 to 1998. Thus, as Davies concedes, his theory identifies common but not sufficient conditions for unrest. Although a J-curve often leads to revolution, it does not necessarily do so.

Ted Gurr has also developed a psychological model examining the gap between expectations and reality. Like Davies, he examines various types of civil violence, not just revolution. Gurr argues that "the necessary precondition for violent civil conflict is **relative deprivation** defined as [the] actors' perception of the discrepancy between their value expectations [i.e., what people believe they deserve] and value capabilities . . . conditions that determine people's perceived chances of getting . . . what they . . . expect to attain."[18] In other words, relative deprivation is the gap between what people want or expect from life and what they actually get.

Unlike Davies's theory, however, Gurr's notion of relative deprivation is not solely economic. Thus, he posits that there is also a high probability of civil unrest if many people are deprived of an important, noneconomic benefit that they have come to expect, or if they have suffered a blow to their status and their preferred social order. For example, although Westerners admired the Shah of Iran's attempts to modernize women's dress (prohibiting the veil) and improve their status, many of these changes violated the "preferred social order" of the nation's Shi'ite population. This, as we have seen, helped set the stage for the Islamist revolution. Furthermore, adds Gurr, the closer people are to attaining their goals, the greater will be their frustration if they fail to achieve them. Note, for example, the growing radicalization of Palestinians as the once-promising peace process between Israelis and the Palestine Liberation Organization stalled and the dreams of a Palestinian state have faded.

Finally, Gurr maintains that the type of civil violence that a country experiences will depend on which segments of society are experiencing relative deprivation. If the poor alone feel frustrated, there may be political "turmoil" (spontaneous, disorganized violence) but not a revolution. Only if important elements of the middle class and the elite—more educated and politically experienced individuals who can provide political leadership— also suffer relative deprivation can there be revolutionary upheaval. This was certainly true in the recent upheavals in the Arab World, especially in Egypt, where young professionals and students often took the lead.

Explaining Islamist Uprising

The sudden, explosive rise of the IS was not anticipated by experts on the Middle East and does not fit easily into previous theories of revolution. Nor are there revolutionary theorists or scholars within that movement who have developed sophisticated historical or socioeconomic explanations.[19] There were, of course, elements of regime decay as neither of the old dictatorships in Iraq (Saddam) and Syria (Assad) had been responsive to their populations' hunger for better living standards and cultural revitalization. The ancien régimes repression of Islamist movements had only added to their militancy and support. Iraq's Shi'a-dominated governments, which followed the American and allied overthrow of Saddam, disappointed many Iraqis when they also turned out to be extremely corrupt and turned Saddam's repression of the Shi'ites into Shi'a discrimination against Sunnis.

The revolutionary groups most analogous to the IS are the millenarian movements that periodically have erupted in other areas of the world. Often tied to devotedly religious faiths, they believe in the imminent destruction of their present social order followed by the creation of an ideal society in which everything will be changed. These movements often are peaceful (including many Evangelical groups) or, like the IS, may be violent (such as the Taiping Rebellion in nineteenth-century China or the 1990s Branch Davidians in Texas).

Like the class-based revolutions that we have discussed (in countries such as China, Vietnam, and Cuba), Islamist revolutionary leaders frequently came out of the more educated middle or even upper class. We have noted that the founders of al-Qaeda, bin Laden and al-Zawahiri, were respectively the son of a Saudi multimillionaire and an Egyptian surgeon. But, Abu Musab al-Zarqawi, the founder of "al-Qaeda in Iraq," which eventually evolved into the IS, was a high-school dropout, who then turned to drug and alcohol abuse and violent crime.

Causes of Revolution: A Summary

None of these theories of revolution offers a single "correct" explanation. For one thing, they often focus on different aspects of the question. For example, while Gurr and Davies ask why individuals join revolts or revolutionary movements, Skocpol focuses on the international economic and military factors that have weakened the state prior to successful revolutionary insurrections.

Clearly, revolutions are never inevitable and, in fact, successful revolutions are rare. While the causes of unrest may lie in relative deprivation or the regime's loss of legitimacy, the ultimate success or failure of revolutionary movements also depends on the relative military and political capabilities of the contending forces. Only by comparing the political-military strength of those who rebel with the state's capacity to defend itself can we understand why some revolutionary movements succeed, while others fail.

As we have seen, revolutions often occur after a country has been defeated or badly weakened in war (Russia, China, and Turkey) or after its government has been ousted temporarily (as several colonial powers were in World War II). They may also take place when a government is particularly corrupt (Cuba and Egypt) or subservient to foreign powers (Cuba, Mexico, and Iran). In all of these cases, the incumbent regime lost its legitimacy. Thus, Russia's Czarist regime and China's Kuomintang government both fell when they proved incapable of defending their people's sovereignty against foreign armies. Similarly, Cuba's president Fulgencio Batista lost his authority when he turned Havana into "the brothel of the Caribbean" in league with the American mafia. And, the Shah of Iran lost his legitimacy after his modernization program offended Iran's Muslim clerics. British, French, and Dutch colonial rule in Asia was secure as long as the indigenous populations believed that Europeans were too powerful to topple and perhaps better equipped to govern. When the Japanese ousted the colonial governments of Burma, Malaysia, Vietnam, and Indonesia, they demonstrated that Asian armed forces could defeat the European powers. Once the Europeans lost their aura of invincibility, they were unable to reestablish sustained colonial rule after World War II.

Finally, the very authoritarianism of many governments often ultimately undermines them. Cuba's Batista, the Shah of Iran, and Nicaragua's Anastasio Somoza Jr. illustrate this point. Because their governments had never been legitimized through free and honest elections, they could not convincingly claim to represent the people. Ignoring this problem during the Cold War, the United States supported authoritarian governments in countries such as El Salvador, Chile, Zaire (Congo), South Korea, Iran, and Pakistan. Responding to criticisms by human rights groups, Washington argued that, whatever their faults, these repressive governments were the last remaining firewalls against communist subversion and the rise of totalitarianism. In truth, however, a democratic government offers the best inoculation against revolution. Indeed, no consolidated democracy has ever been toppled by a revolution.*

LEVELS OF POPULAR SUPPORT

Che Guevara, the leading military strategist of the Cuban Revolution, once observed that those who undertake revolutions either win or die. Though perhaps overstating his point, Guevara's remark highlights the tremendous risk revolutionary fighters take, be they poor peasants or radicalized university students. Rebels almost always face superior firepower and a range of formidable state institutions (including the police and the military). Not surprisingly, most of the time the insurgents lose. One study counted twenty-eight guerrilla movements in Latin America from 1956 to 1990. Of this total, only two succeeded (Cuba's July 26 movement and Nicaragua's Sandinistas). Asia and Africa are also littered with the corpses of failed revolutionaries. Even victorious revolutions, such as Vietnam's and China's, leave behind vast numbers of fallen rebel fighters and supporters. Those who survive often return home to devastated villages and suffering families. Not surprisingly, then, peasants, workers, students, and professionals do not take lightly the decision to join a revolutionary force.

What portion of the population must support a revolution if it is to succeed? What types of people are most likely to join the movement? The answer to the first question is uncertain. There is no fixed or knowable percentage of the population that must support an insurrection in order for it to triumph. Following World War II, a majority of Ukrainians are believed to have supported a separatist movement fighting to end Russian control, yet this uprising was crushed by the powerful Soviet army. On the other hand, insurgencies elsewhere have succeeded with the active support of less than 20 percent of the civilian population.

Any evaluation of popular sentiment during a revolutionary upheaval needs to identify at least five different groups. First, there are those who strongly support the incumbent government and believe that their own fates are linked to the regime's survival. Government officials, military officers, landowners, and businesspeople with close links to the prerevolutionary state normally fall in this category. It may also include ethnic

---

*The only case of a communist regime replacing a democratic government is in postwar Czechoslovakia. But the new government took power through a Russian-supported coup, not through revolution.

groups tied to the regime (such as the Hmong people of Laos), people ideologically committed to the political system, and an assortment of others with a stake in preserving the status quo.

A second group in society also supports the government, but more conditionally. For example, during the 1960s, most Venezuelans supported the government's battle against Marxist guerrillas. Even though many of them shared the guerrillas' objections to the country's severe inequality and poverty, they were repulsed by the rebels' use of violence and their refusal to work within the country's new democratic framework. Because the government's public support was broad but thin (i.e., many Venezuelans were conditional supporters), it could easily have lost its advantage had it used the repressive antiguerrilla tactics so widely employed elsewhere in Latin America. By showing moderation, the government held its ground.

A third, often critical, segment of the population supports neither the revolutionaries nor the government. Its members are generally alienated and probably dislike both sides. In the 1980s and 1990s, many Peruvian Indian villages were victimized by the *Sendero Luminoso* (Shining Path) guerrillas, an extremely fanatical and brutal revolutionary movement. At the same time, these peasants were also often brutalized by the Peruvian army, which flagrantly violated their human rights. Not surprisingly, most peasants feared and hated both sides. Caught in the middle, for their own preservation they avoided taking sides, though some did join government-supported defense militias.

A fourth group—drawn primarily from the peasantry, workers, the urban poor, and alienated members of the middle class who sympathize with the revolutionary cause—occasionally lends support to the insurgents but does not actually join them. For example, sympathetic peasants in China, Cuba, and Vietnam offered intelligence information, food, and shelter to rebel guerrillas. In countries such as China and El Salvador, where the guerrillas controlled "liberated zones" for long periods of time, these support networks were very extensive. In other countries where the revolution was fought primarily through urban street protests rather than guerrilla war (Iran) and in revolutions with important urban and rural components (Mexico, Nicaragua), revolutionaries also depended on the sympathy and occasional support of the urban poor, workers, and parts of the middle class.

Finally, there is a relatively small portion of the population that fully involves itself in the revolutionary struggle. In Cuba and Mexico, for example, committed students, teachers, and professionals assumed leadership positions. In those countries, as well as in China, Vietnam, and El Salvador, many peasants became the revolution's foot soldiers. Given the enormous risks involved for the participants and their families, it is not surprising that only a small portion of the people took up arms. Some peasants joined out of desperation, because the armed forces had destroyed their farms or villages or because they feared being drafted into an army that they despised. Others were attracted to the revolutionaries' promises of a more just social order.

One can only guess the proportion of a country's population in each of these five groups at a particular point in time. Public opinion surveys in countries experiencing revolutionary upheavals are unlikely to elicit honest responses. But we do know that if they are to succeed, revolutionary movements must attract a core of firmly committed activists willing to risk their lives for the cause, as well as a larger circle of sympathizers. How large their numbers must be depends on the extent of government decay and loss of legitimacy. It also depends on how well armed and committed government troops are, how effectively those troops fight, and how much foreign support they have. Thus, for example, Fidel Castro's small rural force of only a few hundred troops (supported by a comparable number of urban guerrillas) defeated Batista's much larger but dispirited army. On the other hand, El Salvador's FMLN (the Farabundo Martí National Liberation Front)—a far larger and better-equipped guerrilla army than Castro's—could not unseat a government that was bolstered by extensive American economic and military aid. Yet even the United States' commitment of massive military assistance could not save the South Vietnamese government from the Viet Cong (communist) guerrillas and their North Vietnamese allies.

The people in the second category (mild government supporters) and the third (neutrals) are equally important targets for any revolutionary movement. In developing countries that have substantial urban populations, governments can maintain power in the face of considerable peasant unrest and rural guerrilla activity as long as they control the cities and retain the support of the urban middle class, particularly civil servants, businesspeople, and professionals. These middle-class groups are not normally radical, but they can become disenchanted with particularly corrupt, repressive, or ineffectual regimes. In Iran, the tide turned in favor of the revolutionary mullahs when Tehran's bazaar shopkeepers lost confidence in the Shah's government.

Nicaragua's revolution also illustrates this point. Because the Somoza family had expropriated such a large share of the national economy, its greed not only injured the poor but also hurt the business community. As the uprising spread and the National Guard became progressively more repressive, the country's private sector grew increasingly alienated from the government. Prominent business leaders—including the head of the country's Coca-Cola bottling plant, the nation's most prominent newspaper owner, and the directors of several important banks—demanded

Anastasio Somoza Jr.'s resignation and organized business shutdowns to express their opposition. While most of these businessmen were wary of the Sandinista movement (which made no secret of its leftist ideology), they shared its desire to oust the Somoza regime.

While flying from Panama to Miami during the height of the insurrection, I found myself seated next to the chief executive of an important Nicaraguan agrochemical plant. In the course of our conversation about events in his country, he declared, "Somoza has to go. He's too damned corrupt and he's wrecking the country." "But what if reformist business leaders such as you have to share power with the [Marxist-oriented] Sandinistas after he falls?" I asked. "I don't like those guys," he replied, "but if sharing power with them is what it takes to get rid of Somoza, then we'll have to do it." In the face of such broad ideological and cross-class opposition to the government, it was just a matter of time before the Somoza regime fell.*

In short, if a revolutionary movement is to gain power, there must be widespread alienation from the government, a disaffection that reaches beyond the ranks of the poor and the oppressed to the heart of the middle class and the business community. It is neither likely nor necessary for a large portion of those groups to actively support the insurrection. For the revolution to succeed, it is only essential that some of them, including a highly committed core, do so, while many others, like the Nicaraguan business executive on the plane, simply cease supporting the government.

PEASANTS AS REVOLUTIONARIES

Let us now turn our attention to the ranks of committed revolutionary supporters, particularly the last group, revolutionary activists. Most revolutions in LDCs have been fought primarily by peasants. The Chinese Red Army and the Viet Cong, for example, consisted overwhelmingly of the rural poor. Indeed, almost all African and Asian revolutionary movements have been overwhelmingly rural in character (the recent urban uprisings in the Arab World being obvious exceptions). And even in Latin America's revolutions, where the urban populations often played key roles, peasants were also very important actors. Consequently, it is important to ask, "What factors induce some peasants to risk joining a revolution, and what types of peasants join?"

Why Peasants Rebel
In our analysis of rural society (chapter 6), we noted that traditional peasant culture tends to be rather conservative. Because early economic

---

*After the rebels ousted the Somoza regime, the Sandinista-led revolutionary government did initially include progressive business leaders, but the two sides soon parted ways.

modernization frequently affects them negatively, they have good reason to cling to tradition. But the intrusion of market forces into their communities sometimes so unsettles their world that it radicalizes them as they struggle to protect what they have. For one thing, increasing numbers of subsistence farmers (peasants producing primarily for their family's consumption) in a modernizing economy are induced or pressured to enter the commercial market for the first time. Once involved in commercial agriculture, however, they must deal with fluctuations in the price of their crops, including volatile shifts that they are ill-equipped to handle.

At the same time, rural landlords, whose precapitalist exploitation of local peasants had been constrained by their neofeudal obligations, now viewed their tenants merely as factors of production in the new market economy. In Latin America, many landlords, who had previously funded their peons' *fiestas* or lent them money when they were in special need, concluded that such expenditures were no longer financially prudent in the more competitive market environment. Other landlords entering the commercial market decided to mechanize production and evict tenant farmers from their lands. For all of these reasons, rural society's transition from neofeudal to capitalist production precipitated many of the Third World's twentieth-century revolutions.[20] James Scott notes that the pain peasants suffered during that transformation was not merely economic or physical but also psychological.

To be sure, the precapitalist rural order had its share of grave injustices, but these inequities were somewhat mitigated by a web of reciprocal obligations between landlords and peasants and among peasants. It is the collapse of this "**moral economy**," Scott argues, that drives many peasants to revolution.[21] Similarly, as noted in chapter 6, Eric Wolf insists that in countries as disparate as Cuba, Mexico, Algeria, Vietnam, and China, most peasant participants in revolutionary movements were not trying to create a new socialist order. Rather, they were seeking to restore the security of their old way of life.

Which Peasants Rebel

Even in a single country or region, peasants are not a homogeneous mass. Some of them own comparatively large plots of land and employ other peasants to work on their farms with them. Others are landless or own extremely small plots. And still others work as wage laborers on large estates or rent parcels of land from the landlord, paying their rent in cash, labor, or sharecropping.* Each group has distinct political and economic needs.

---

*Sharecroppers are tenant farmers who pay their rent by giving the landlord a portion of their crop.

The peasants most threatened by the economic modernization of the countryside are the ones most likely to join local revolts or broader revolutionary movements. Analyzing data collected from seventy developing nations over a twenty-year period, Jeffrey M. Paige found that the peasant groups most liable to join insurgencies were wage laborers and sharecroppers who worked for landlords.[22] Not only are these peasants particularly vulnerable to changing economic conditions, but their landlords are also less likely to grant them financial concessions because they depend exclusively on their farmland for their incomes. Research on Latin American guerrilla movements reveals that squatters (poor farmers who illegally occupy land) and other peasants who face eviction from the land that they cultivate are also more prone to rebel.[23]

But even peasants with more secure access to the land may feel threatened by declining crop prices. For example, in Peru's Ayacucho province, the birthplace of the Shining Path guerrilla movement, peasants suffered from declining terms of trade for two decades; that is, the cost of the goods they consumed had been rising faster than the price of the crops that they sold. Caught in an ongoing financial squeeze, they felt increasingly insecure and hence became more receptive to the Shining Path's appeals.[24]

Peasants who are more prone to support revolutions, then, have one element in common—they are threatened by the prospect of losing their land and/or their livelihood. Conversely, the most conservative peasants are those with secure titles to their landholdings and relatively stable prices for their crops. It is for this reason that many analysts maintain that the best protection against rural revolution is an agrarian reform program that distributes land and offers the recipients secure titles and support services (see chapter 6).

Peasant insurrections are also more likely to arise in areas that have traditions of rebellion. For example, the revolutionary forces in China, Vietnam, Cuba, Mexico, and Nicaragua all received their greatest support in regions that had long records of peasant resistance, what one author calls a "rebellious culture."[25] Fidel Castro's home province of Oriente, known as "the cradle of the Cuban Revolution," had a history of unrest dating back to nineteenth-century slave revolts against their owners and against Spanish colonial rule. China's Hunan province (Mao Zedong's home) also had a rebellious tradition. Similarly, some revolutionary movements take root in areas with a long record of lawlessness and hostility toward the legal authorities. For example, Mexican revolutionary leader Pancho Villa operated in a region known for cattle rustling and other forms of social banditry. Villa himself was a bandit-turned-revolutionary. And Castro's guerrillas based themselves in the Sierra Maestra Mountains, a region with a history of smuggling, marijuana production, and banditry.

The IS is perhaps the only revolutionary movement in which not only the leadership but also a large portion of the rank-and-file rebels come from educated, middle-class backgrounds, particularly among the unusually high proportion of foreign troops in the revolutionary army.*

REVOLUTIONARY LEADERSHIP

Although peasants furnish the foot soldiers for revolutions, they rarely hold the highest leadership posts. They may stage spontaneous uprisings or even more extensive revolts on their own, but they usually lack the organizational and political skills needed to lead a national revolution. Consequently, the top revolutionary leaders and many at the middle level are typically people with more education and greater political experience. To be sure, there are exceptions. Mexico's Emiliano Zapata was a horse trainer from a peasant family who only became literate as an adult. Pancho Villa was also of humble origins. Today, peasants hold important leadership posts in the Colombian Revolutionary Armed Forces of Colombia (FARC) guerrillas. Ultimately, however, their political inexperience and lack of external contacts proved costly. Thus, Villa and Zapata jointly conquered Mexico City, the nation's capital, but then left it because neither man felt ready to run the country.

More typically, then, the top revolutionary leadership comes from middle-class or even upper-class origins. In Latin America, for example, "they are drawn disproportionately from the intelligentsia, not only highly educated, but also largely involved in the production of theories."[26] Trained as a librarian, China's Mao Zedong was the son of a grain merchant. In Vietnam, Ho Chi Minh, the son of a rural schoolteacher, practiced a number of professions, including photography, while living in Paris, where he became an activist in the French Communist Party. Fidel Castro received a law degree at the University of Havana, where he was a leader in student politics. His father, a Spanish immigrant, had started life in Cuba as a worker, but eventually became a well-to-do landowner. Castro's comrade, Che Guevara, was a doctor whose parents, though not rich, were of aristocratic origin. Similarly, most of the nine *comandantes* who directed the Sandinista Revolution came from solid middle- or upper-class families and were well educated. For example, President Daniel Ortega and his brother, Defense Minister Humberto Ortega, were the sons of an accountant-businessman. Luis Carrión, the son of a millionaire, had attended an American prep school. Only one *comandante*, Henry Ruiz, came from a poor urban family, and none were of peasant

---

*As we have previously noted, perhaps 30 percent of the IS's troops are foreign volunteers, many of them university educated.

origin.[27] Finally, a Vietnamese Communist Party study of nearly two thousand party activists (conducted after World War II, at the start of their long revolutionary struggle) revealed that 74 percent of them were either intellectuals or were from bourgeois (middle-class or capitalist) families, while only 7 percent were the children of workers, and 19 percent came from peasant families.[28] These are remarkable statistics for a party trying to speak for the country's peasantry and working class.

Not surprisingly, a larger number of lower-ranking revolutionary leaders are of peasant or working-class backgrounds. Compared to Latin America, more of the rural poor have held leadership positions in Asia's revolutionary governments (including China, Vietnam, and Cambodia), in countries where peasants accounted for most of the national population. During their two-decade revolutionary struggle and after taking power, the CCP and its Red Army offered peasant activists unprecedented opportunities for upward mobility. From its early days, the party gave peasants and children of peasants—heretofore at the bottom of the social ladder—preference for admission to its ranks. And as recently as 1985, decades after it took power, one-third of all CCP members were peasants (some 25 percent of whom were illiterate).* Similarly, many of the lower- and middle-level guerrilla leaders in El Salvador and Peru were of peasant origin, although they often were upwardly mobile children of peasants, who themselves had become teachers, health workers, and the like.

The educational and social gaps separating aspiring revolutionary leaders from the peasant rank and file can be considerable problems unless those leaders have a firm understanding of the local culture. Although Mao Zedong was an urban professional, his rural upbringing had given him an understanding of village life. Fidel Castro was no peasant, but his childhood on his father's farm had familiarized him with the region's rural poor. And in Venezuela, several of the FALN (the Armed Forces of National Liberation) commanders were sons of local landlords who built on their fathers' patron-client ties to the local peasants.

On the other hand, the rural poor often spurn aspiring guerrilla organizers who come to them with little understanding of their problems. Hence, they usually reject the overtures of radical university students from other regions of the country, other countries, or other ethnic backgrounds. Given their history of exploitation, peasants tend to be understandably wary of outsiders. The wider the language, cultural, or racial gaps between would-be revolutionary leaders and the local villagers, and

---

*Although the percentages of peasants and illiterates in the party were still well below their corresponding shares of the general population, they were higher than in most LDCs. Since the late 1980s, however, the educational level and professional training of mid-level party leaders have risen, meaning that they are more skilled but somewhat less representative of the population.

the greater the peasants' prior suspicion of outsiders, the harder it is for aspiring organizers to break through that wall of distrust. In Cuba, where racial and ethnic divisions were relatively less important, the peasants of the Sierra Maestra Mountains accepted Che Guevara, an urban middle-class Argentinean. So when he later ventured to Bolivia to spread the revolution, he was ill-prepared for the Indian peasants' deep mistrust of White outsiders such as himself. There, an antiguerrilla unit of the Bolivian armed forces captured and killed him, aided by local villagers who saw no reason to risk their safety for an outside agitator. Similarly, Hector Béjar, a failed Peruvian guerrilla leader, later wrote candidly in his memoirs about how he—a coastal, White journalist and poet—was unable to gain the trust of the highland Indians whom he had hoped to lead.[29]

REVOLUTIONARIES IN POWER

While many comparative studies have examined the causes of revolution, there is less cross-national research on the *policies* revolutionary regimes implement once in office. Perhaps guerrilla fighters in the hills have inspired more interest and romanticism (or fear) than have revolutionary bureaucrats in the corridors of power. The record suggests that revolutions in developing nations commonly have accomplished more than their detractors admit but less than their supporters claim.

A major goal of many revolutionary governments (especially Marxist ones) has been to achieve greater socioeconomic equality. This quest usually begins with the struggle for power itself, when revolutionary leaders use egalitarian appeals to garner support from downtrodden peasants and workers. Recognizing the critical importance of this support, Mao Zedong wrote that the peasantry is to the guerrilla army what water is to a fish. To win their loyalty, the Red Army treated peasants whom they encountered with greater respect than other Chinese military forces or governments had. Similarly, in Cuba, "the army's brutal treatment of the peasants" contrasted with "Castro's policy of paying for the food purchased from the peasants . . . and putting his [mostly urban] men to work in the . . . fields."[30]

Once in power, revolutionary governments have generally continued to emphasize economic and social equality. In addition to redistributing land and other economic resources, they also introduce egalitarian cultural reforms. We have noted, for example, that at meetings of Cuba's Committees for the Defense of the Revolution (CDRs), neighbors may pressure husbands to share household tasks with their spouses. Efforts at economic and social egalitarianism have been more limited in non-Marxist revolutions. Still, insurgencies such as Bolivia's and

Mexico's have improved the social status of the rural poor, including that of the indigenous (Native American) peoples.

As we have seen, revolutions open up new channels of upward social mobility for peasants and workers who previously had few such opportunities. To be sure, people of middle-class origins hold most of the government and party leadership positions. And ethnic minorities are also underrepresented at that level. For example, Cuba's Black and Mulatto populations and China's (non-Han) ethnic minorities have been severely underrepresented in their Communist Party politburos and government cabinets. But many revolutionary activists from humble backgrounds *do* hold political offices that they could never have attained under the old order. Consequently, revolutionary parties and mass organizations such as Cuba's CDRs often give peasants and workers a greater sense of participation in the political system.

Finally, revolutions usually reduce economic inequality, though the degree of change varies from country to country. Agrarian reform programs in China, Vietnam, Bolivia, Cuba, Mexico, and Nicaragua redistributed land from the rural oligarchy to the peasantry. Many Marxist regimes have offered guaranteed employment, subsidized food and housing, state-sponsored medical care, and other measures that particularly benefit the poor. In countries such as Cuba, government wage policies have reduced prior income inequalities. On the other hand, however, in more moderate revolutions, such as Mexico's, the prerevolutionary concentration of income has continued or even worsened.

To be sure, inequalities persist even in radical revolutionary societies. For example, while many of them have reduced disparities between rural and urban living standards, significant gaps persist. Since China has applied free-market reforms to its economy, income inequality—which had declined substantially in the 1980s—has increased sharply. In fact, currently economic inequality (as measured by the Gini index) is greater in China than in the United States, India, Mexico, or any country in Europe. On the other hand, other communist countries in Asia—such as Vietnam and Laos—as well as many former communist nations— Mongolia, Eastern European countries, and many of the former republics of the Soviet Union—have relatively low income inequality.[31]

At the same time, a new form of inequality invariably emerges in revolutionary societies as newly entrenched party and government officials begin to appropriate special perquisites for themselves and their families. Many years ago, Milovan Djilas, a disillusioned former leader of Yugoslavia's communist government, complained about the rise of a "new class" in revolutionary regimes, a new elite of party officials who enjoy special privileges and a better standard of living.[32] Today in China, the foremost Communist Party leaders are well known for their lavish lifestyles, while the children of party cadre are despised for their arrogance and corruption. While the effect of this "new class" is not sufficient to substantially affect their nations' Gini indexes, it often demoralizes the public. Widespread government corruption (even technically legal corruption) is disheartening in any setting, but even more so in a population that fought a revolution in the name of equality.*

Another major revolutionary objective has been mass political mobilization. As Huntington notes, "A full-scale revolution involves the rapid and violent destruction of existing political institutions, the mobilization of new groups into politics, and the creation of new political institutions."[33] Thus, in China, Vietnam, Cuba, and Nicaragua, the revolutionary governments created incentives and pressures that induced a large portion of the population to join revolutionary support groups. At one time, close to 90 percent of Cuban adults belonged to their neighborhood CDRs. In the 1980s, substantial portions of the Nicaraguan population joined Sandinista Defense Committees.

At its best, mass political mobilization has increased the government's capacity to build the economy by mobilizing volunteer labor and spreading labor discipline. At times, revolutionary support groups have also helped combat sexism, racism, and crime. At their worst, however, these groups have been used as vigilantes against alleged counterrevolutionaries and as agents of thought control. At Cuban CDR meetings, government spokespersons familiarize the members with current government political positions, while citizens are allegedly imbued with greater revolutionary consciousness and are encouraged to volunteer for projects such as planting neighborhood gardens or conducting mass inoculations. But in Mao Zedong's China, **mass mobilization** often involved brutal political campaigns that called upon citizens to root out and punish alleged enemies of the revolution. Hundreds of thousands, perhaps more, were persecuted, jailed, or killed during the government's Anti-Rightist Campaign (1957) and its Cultural Revolution (1966–1976).

Mass mobilization can be used either to activate citizens who support the revolution's goals or to isolate and persecute those who do not. Most revolutionary regimes are led by a dominant party, such as the CCP or the Mexican PRI (Institutionalized Party of the Revolution), which stands at the center of the mobilization process. Opposition parties are either prohibited or are only tolerated in a weakened condition. Among Marxist governments, only Nicaragua's Sandinistas allowed themselves to be voted out of office. Elsewhere, a number of non-Marxist revolutionary

---

*The British essayist George Orwell (himself an active radical) foresaw this danger in his famed novel *Animal Farm* (1945). It notes that "all animals [who had carried out a successful revolution against the humans] are equal, but some animals are more equal."

parties have lost favor over time. They may resort to fraud when faced with the prospect of losing control (as in Mexico until 2000), cancel elections that the opposition is expected to win (Algeria), or hand over the reins of power and become just another competing party (Bolivia and, most recently, Mexico).

In short, while revolutionary regimes often have broad popular support, as we have already noted, they are *not* democratic. Because they view themselves as the *only* legitimate voice of the people and the sole custodians of the general good, most radical regimes tend to regard opposition groups as enemies of the people who should be denied political space. The Sandinistas, a rare exception, allowed opposition parties and interest groups to function, though they were occasionally harassed. Although the major opposition newspaper, *La Prensa*, was periodically censored or briefly shut down, it continued to vigorously, and sometimes outrageously, attack the government right up to the time its publisher, Violeta Chamorro, was elected the nation's president. For the most part, however, even communist governments that have opened up their economies to free-market reforms (China and Vietnam) have maintained a repressive political structure that tightly limits opposition voices.

While members of the first generation of revolutionary leaders tend to be true believers in their movement's ideology, the next generation is frequently more corrupted by power. In China and Vietnam—where rapid economic growth and the expansion of the private sector have opened up new opportunities for corruption—bribing the right state official is often a necessity for doing business. Cubans, who generally had believed that their revolutionary leaders were more honest than their extremely corrupt predecessors, were shocked by the "Ochoa affair (1989)," which revealed that high-ranking military and security officers were involved in drug trafficking. Since the 1990s, more mundane government corruption has increased as a result of the frequent scarcities of consumer goods.[34] And, after the Sandinistas left office in 1990, disillusioned Nicaraguans learned that top party officials had kept for themselves some of the luxurious mansions that had been confiscated from the Somoza regime.* It is not that these revolutionary regimes are necessarily more corrupt than other governments in developing nations; often they are less so. Thus, Transparency International's rating of international corruption ranked Cuba and China better than average (i.e., less corrupt than over half the countries on the list), when compared to other developing countries.[35] It is just that their supporters, some of whom made considerable sacrifices for the revolutionary cause, had expected more.

---

*Yet, in spite of that, in 2006, Sandinista leader Daniel Ortega was once again elected president.

CONCLUSION: REVOLUTIONARY
CHANGE AND DEMOCRACY

Revolutionary change was an important force in many LDCs throughout the twentieth century. Its impact was probably greatest in Asia, where the Chinese Revolution transformed the lives of one-fifth of humanity and where revolutionary struggles in Vietnam, Laos, and Cambodia involved France and then the United States in major wars. Elsewhere in Asia, there were failed communist insurgencies in the Philippines and Malaysia and, most recently, a partially successful one in Nepal. Most of Africa's revolutions were wars of national liberation from European colonialism (Algeria, Angola, and Kenya, among others) or secessionist wars (including Biafra, Eritrea, and South Sudan). In some African nations, military rulers imposed revolutions from above—most notably in Ethiopia—usually with unfortunate results. Latin America experienced two Marxist revolutions (Cuba and Nicaragua), two non-Marxist insurrections (Bolivia and Mexico), and a number of unsuccessful revolutionary movements (including Colombia, El Salvador, Guatemala, and Peru). Both the revolutions and the failed insurgencies had spillover effects on neighboring countries. For example, the Cuban Revolution prompted a number of Latin American governments to initiate agrarian reform programs designed to avert "another Cuba." But it also intensified government repression in El Salvador and elsewhere.

However, in the past two decades, the appeal of classical revolutions, discussed earlier (those that fit the models of revolutionary theorists and analysts), particularly Marxist revolutions, seemed to have waned considerably. Indeed, today's world is a veritable graveyard of failed insurrections. The Soviet Union, once the fountainhead of Communism, collapsed. Communism is equally discredited throughout Eastern and Central Europe, where it held sway until recently. In Nicaragua, an American-backed counterrevolutionary war and the Sandinista regime's own errors undid many of the revolution's early social and economic gains and led to their defeat in the 1990 presidential election. Cuba's impressive achievements in education and health care were partially eroded in the 1990s after the collapse of the Soviet Union, previously a major source of economic assistance. Elsewhere in developing nations, other revolutionary governments performed far more poorly. Countries such as Angola, Cambodia, Ethiopia, and Mozambique suffered enormous losses of life and economic devastation, having achieved little or nothing in return.

Judging the accomplishment and failures of revolutionary change in countries such as China, Cuba, and Vietnam is not easy because evaluations are invariably influenced by the analysts' ideological orientations.

Furthermore, even the most objective social scientist finds it difficult to isolate the effects of revolutionary policy from a host of other overlapping factors. For example, critics of the Chinese Revolution argue that the socioeconomic gains attained under Mao were achieved in spite of his radical policies, not because of them. They further insist that the country's rapid economic growth since the 1980s demonstrates the advantages of free-market reforms. On the other hand, other analysts maintain that China could never have achieved its market-based economic boom without the revolution's earlier advances in education.

In the same way, the Cuban Revolution's detractors contend that the country's progress in health care and education could have been achieved under a democratic system, noting that Costa Rica (one of the strongest democracies in the region) has made comparable gains in social welfare. Furthermore, they maintain that Cuba's strong record in those areas was possible only because of massive Soviet aid over a period of thirty years. Nevertheless, more sympathetic observers note that Cuba achieved its impressive educational and health gains in spite of an American trade embargo.*

Neither side can definitively prove its position because there are so many independent variables that make it difficult or impossible to establish causal relationships. In any event, while there may yet be future revolutions in the developing world, it is likely that the era of leftist revolutions is drawing to an end. The demise of Soviet and Central European Communism exposed more clearly the deficiencies of Marxist-Leninist regimes. So too have China's and Vietnam's introduction of free-market (capitalist) components into their economic systems.

With Communism seemingly discredited, even among some of its once-fervent followers, it is unlikely to find many adherents willing to risk their lives fighting for its ideals. Marxist ideology, once chic among intellectuals and political activists, has become far less fashionable. At the end of the 1980s, facing defeat by its mujahideen opponents, Afghanistan's then-ruling People's Democratic Party (a communist party beholden to Moscow at the time) renounced its Marxist ideology in a failed effort to maintain power. One of its leaders dismissed the party's long-standing communist position by claiming that it had adopted that ideology at "a time when Marxism-Leninism was quite in fashion in underdeveloped countries." In Angola, where the governing party made a similar ideological conversion, the president explained that continuing to support the Marxist-Leninist model "would be rowing against the tide [of capitalist democracy]."[36] Similar transformations have occurred within Nicaragua's Sandinista party and El Salvador's FMLN, both former

---

*Prior to the revolution, the United States was Cuba's dominant trading partner.

revolutionary movements that subsequently transformed themselves into democratic socialist political parties. In his successful 2006 campaign to regain the presidency, Sandinista leader Daniel Ortega insisted that Jesus Christ, not Marx, was his first inspiration when he led the country's revolution nearly thirty years earlier. Modifying his earlier leftist views, he declared that "in this new context, to which we had to adjust, the market economy plays its role."

How many revolutionary upheavals will take place in the coming years is hard to predict, and the answer may be partly an issue of semantics (i.e., how we choose to define a revolution). However, now that colonialism has essentially come to an end in Africa and Asia, there are few possibilities for wars of national liberation. The collapse of the Soviet bloc, the abandonment of Marxist economics in China and Vietnam, and Cuba's economic problems after it lost Soviet aid have all substantially diminished the appeal of revolutionary Marxism. But, the rise of the IS indicates that other types of revolutions will very likely erupt in some LDCs.

Practice and Review Online
http://textbooks.rowman.com/handelman8e#ch7

KEY TERMS

ancien régime

class consciousness

liberated zones

mass mobilization

moral economy

proletariat

relative deprivation

wars of national liberation

DISCUSSION QUESTIONS

1. What conditions or developments have convinced people in LDCs to join revolutionary movements?
2. What is the likelihood of further revolutions in the twenty-first century? What kinds of revolutions are most likely to occur?
3. Discuss some of the major accomplishments and failures of revolutionary governments.
4. Does the recent Arab Spring indicate that the age of revolution is not yet over? Do the prodemocracy mass uprisings in Tunisia and Egypt qualify as revolutions?

NOTES

1. Chalmers Johnson, *Revolution and the Social System* (Stanford, CA: Hoover Institution, 1964), 2.

2. Peter Calvert, "Revolution: The Politics of Violence," *Political Studies* 15, no. 1 (1967): 2; and *Revolution and Counter Revolution* (Minneapolis, MN: University of Minnesota Press, 1990).

3. Samuel P. Huntington, *Political Order in Changing Societies* (New Haven, CT: Yale University Press, 1968), 264.

4. Theda Skocpol, "France, Russia, China: A Structural Analysis of Social Revolutions," *Comparative Studies in Society and History* 18, no. 2 (1976): 176.

5. Theda Skocpol, *States and Social Revolutions: A Comparative Analysis of France, Russia and China* (Cambridge, England: Cambridge University Press, 1979), 4.

6. Ellen Kay Trimberger, "A Theory of Elite Revolutions," *Studies in Comparative International Development* 7, no. 3 (1972): 191–207.

7. A. S. Cohan, *Theories of Revolution* (London: Thomas Nelson and Sons, 1975), 72.

8. Irving M. Zeitlin, *Marxism: A Re-examination* (Princeton, NJ: Princeton University Press, 1967), 142.

9. Skocpol, *States and Social Revolutions*.

10. Skocpol, "France, Russia, China."

11. Joel Migdal, *Peasants, Politics and Revolution* (Princeton, NJ: Princeton University Press, 1974), 252.

12. Charles Tilly, *From Mobilization to Revolution* (New York: Addison-Wesley, 1978), 204–05.

13. Charles Tilly, "Does Modernization Breed Revolution?" *Comparative Politics* 5, no. 3 (April 1974): 425–47.

14. Huntington, *Political Order in Changing Societies*, 265–66. Italics added.

15. James C. Davies, "Toward a Theory of Revolution," *American Sociological Review* 27, no. 1 (February 1962): 7.

16. Ibid. For other theories on the causes of revolution, see *When Men Revolt and Why*, ed. James C. Davies (New York: Free Press, 1971).

17. Raymond Tanter and Manus Midlarsky, "A Theory of Revolution," *Journal of Conflict Resolution* 11, no. 3 (1967): 264–80.

18. Ted Robert Gurr, "Psychological Factors in Civil Violence," *World Politics* 20, no. 2 (1967–1968): 252–53; see also Ted Robert Gurr, *Why Men Rebel* (Princeton, NJ: Princeton University Press, 1970).

19. Jason Brownlee, Tarek Masoud, and Andrew Raynolds, *The Arab Spring* (New York: Oxford University Press, 2015), 98–168.

20. Eric R. Wolf, *Peasant Wars of the Twentieth Century* (New York: Harper & Row, 1969).

21. James C. Scott, *The Moral Economy of the Peasant: Rebellion and Subsistence in Southeast Asia* (New Haven, CT: Yale University Press, 1976).

22. Jeffrey M. Paige, *Agrarian Revolution: Social Movements and Export Agriculture in the Underdeveloped World* (New York: Free Press, 1975), chaps. 1–2.

23. Timothy P. Wickham-Crowley, *Guerrillas and Revolution in Latin America* (Princeton, NJ: Princeton University Press, 1992), chap. 6.

24. Cynthia McClintock, "*Sendero Luminoso:* Peru's Maoist Guerrillas," *Problems of Communism* 32, no. 5 (September to October 1983): 19–34.

25. Wickham-Crowley, *Guerrillas and Revolution*, 246–50; Wolf, *Peasant Wars*.

26. Ibid., 213.

27. Dennis Gilbert, *Sandinistas: The Party and the Revolution* (New York: B. Blackwell, 1988).

28. Thomas H. Green, *Comparative Revolutionary Movements* (Upper Saddle River, NJ: Prentice Hall, 1974), 18.

29. Hector Béjar, *Peru 1965: Notes on a Guerrilla Experience* (New York: Monthly Review Press, 1970).

30. Sebastian Balfour, *Fidel Castro* (New York: Longman, 1990), 49.

31. The exact Gini indices are found in the United Nations Development Program, *Human Development Report*, "Inequality in income or expenditure."

32. Milovan Djilas, *The New Class* (New York: Praeger, 1957).

33. Huntington, *Political Order in Changing Societies*, 266.

34. Sergio Díaz-Briquets and Jorge Pérez López, *Corruption in Cuba: Castro and Beyond* (Austin, TX: University of Texas Press, 2006).

35. "The 2006 Transparency International Corruption Perception Index."

36. Both quotations come from Forrest Colburn, *The Vogue of Revolution in Poor Countries* (Princeton, NJ: Princeton University Press, 1994), 89.

8

Soldiers and Politics

Thai Prime Minister General Prayuth Chan-ocha reviews the troops. Military coups (takeovers of government) have become less prevalent in the LDCs in recent decades. But in some countries, such as Thailand—which has had twelve military governments since 1932, most recently in 2006 and 2014—the armed forces remain a potent political force. *AP/Bullit Marquez*

FOR MANY YEARS, military governments were ubiquitous in much of the developing world—most notably in Latin America, Africa, and the Middle East. More recently, as democracy has advanced among the LDCs, military government has become comparatively rare. While the number of military governments has declined enormously in recent years, there are still many countries where the armed forces are the final power behind the scenes (such as Burma and Pakistan).

Of course, men emerging from the military ranks occasionally head even the most advanced industrial democracies. American president Dwight Eisenhower, French president Charles de Gaulle, and Israeli prime minister Ehud Barak all used distinguished military careers as stepping stones to the leadership of their respective nations. But each of them entered politics as a private citizen, having first retired from the armed forces. Moreover, they achieved high office through democratic elections, not through military **coups**.*

Over the years, the political systems of developing countries have been distinguished by their high degree of military interference, either through direct rule or as a dominant interest group. Unlike their counterparts in industrialized democracies, soldiers in the LDCs often reject any dividing line between military and political activity. A pronouncement by the Indonesian armed forces prior to their assumption of power in the 1960s illustrates this perspective well:

> The army, which was born in the cauldron of the Revolution, has never been a dead instrument of the government, concerned exclusively with security matters. The army, as a fighter for freedom, cannot remain neutral toward the course of state policy, the quality of government, and the safety of the state.[1]

To be sure, there are countries such as India, Malaysia, Kenya, Mexico, and Costa Rica where the armed forces have not ventured deeply into politics for decades. But, until the 1980s, such restraint was the exception rather than the rule. Indeed, until recently, the military's political involvement in most of the LDCs was so pervasive that it was almost a defining characteristic of political underdevelopment.

One early study of military intervention revealed that the fifty-nine developing nations scrutinized had had a total of 274 attempted coups between 1946 and 1970.[2] At the start of the 1980s, most countries in South America—most notably Argentina, Brazil, Chile, and Peru—were

---

*A military coup is a sudden and illegal removal of the incumbent government and the seizure of political power by the armed forces or a faction of the military, using violence or the threat of violence. Usually, the coup makers install themselves in power, but sometimes they install a new civilian government or call new elections.

governed by the armed forces. During that decade the armed forces also dominated politics in much of Africa, including Algeria, Ghana, Nigeria, and Sudan. From 1958 to 1984, there were more than sixty-two successful and sixty failed coup attempts in Sub-Saharan Africa alone, affecting more than 80 percent of the nations in that region.[3] During an average year in the 1980s, military rulers governed 65 percent of Africa's population. Noting the scarcity of democratic elections in the region for most of that period, one observer argued that "coups had become the functional equivalent of elections, virtually the sole manner of ousting incumbent political leaders."[4] In all, Sub-Saharan Africa had eighty coups and one hundred and eight failed coup attempts from 1956 to 2001, affecting forty-one of the region's forty-eight countries. Three countries (including Nigeria, the continent's most populous nation) had six successful coups each.[5]

Military intervention was less prevalent in Asia, where India, Sri Lanka, and Malaysia, among others, were able to maintain elected civilian governments. Elsewhere in Asia, authoritarian civilian governments in Singapore, Vietnam, and China also kept the armed forces in check. Still, military takeovers in some countries have continued into the twenty-first century.

Although several Arab nations in North Africa have been controlled directly by the armed forces or by military strongmen (including Egypt today), indirect military dominance has been more common in the Middle East. Former Egyptian president Hosni Mubarak (1981–2011) and Syria's longtime strongman Hafez al-Assad (1970–2000) entered politics as military men and then assumed civilian roles. Elsewhere in the region, monarchs in Morocco, Jordan, Saudi Arabia, Kuwait, and the smaller Gulf States have successfully controlled their armed forces.

Recent decades, however, have seen a sharp decline in the number of successful coups. With rare exceptions, such as Algeria, Thailand, and Pakistan, the coups that have taken place have occurred only in small, very poor nations. That change has been most dramatic in Latin America, where democratically elected governments have become the norm. In a remarkable turnabout, successful military coups have virtually ended in the region (excepting Ecuador, Haiti, and Honduras) since the end of the Cold War. In Asia, military regimes have ended in countries such as Indonesia, Bangladesh, and South Korea. But, since 2000, military rulers have returned to power in Bangladesh, Pakistan, and Thailand after previously having stepped down in favor of civilian governments. Finally, the military government in Burma (in power since 1962) still endures as one of the oldest dictatorships in the world. Even there, however, the military set up a sham civilian government in 2011 and has reduced the level of repression.

In Africa, where military governments predominated into the 1990s, important transitions to civilian government have occurred in such nations as Nigeria and Ghana, leaving few military governments in power (though periodic coups and attempted coups continue). Since 2001, the rate of new military coups in Sub-Saharan Africa has declined to less than one per year. Still, while fewer African countries remain under formal military rule today, several armed-forces leaders have resigned their positions and subsequently become presidents through rigged elections. Moreover, there have been a number of unsuccessful coup attempts (multiple times in some nations), which have destabilized their political systems.

While the number of military governments throughout the developing world has declined substantially, the armed forces continue to wield considerable political influence over many civilian regimes. Often they are able to veto decisions by elected civilian officials regarding national security and foreign policy. In some countries, military leaders protect their own budgets, determine who serves as defense minister, or control military promotions. For example, while elected civilian presidents have governed Guatemala since 1985, they still hesitate to pursue policies that threaten the army's interests. In some countries, such as Algeria, Nigeria, and Pakistan, the armed forces remain a commanding force in politics. On the other hand, in a number of other nations once dominated by the military (such as Argentina, Brazil, and Turkey), the generals now accept civilian control.

In order to examine military participation in developing-world politics and the changing nature of civil-military relations, this chapter explores a series of interrelated questions: What accounts for so much military involvement in politics? How do the structures of military regimes differ from one country to another? What do the armed forces hope to accomplish when they seize power? How successfully have military governments achieved their political and economic goals? Is military rule generally beneficial or detrimental to economic and political development? What factors have induced military governments to step down in recent decades? What political roles do the armed forces continue to play after the establishment or reestablishment of civilian rule? How can civilian governments best control the military?

THE CAUSES OF MILITARY INTERVENTION

Political scientists have offered two alternative perspectives for explaining the frequency and nature of military intervention in developing countries. The first focuses on the *internal characteristics* of the armed forces themselves. The second stresses the broader *political environment* in which the military operates, most notably the weakness of civilian regimes.

The Nature of the Armed Forces

In early research on the less developed nations, many analysts maintained that the armed forces enjoyed greater organizational cohesion and clarity of purpose than civilian political institutions did, hence their penchant for intervention. As one leading analyst concluded, "The ability of officers to intervene in domestic politics and produce stable leadership is [directly] related to internal [military] social cohesion."[6] In their efforts to better understand the military's inner workings, scholars examined the class origins, educational levels, ideological orientations, and internal organization of the officer corps. These factors all seemed to affect the probability of military involvement in politics and to influence the officers' goals.

Obviously, the officers' education and training greatly influence their political values. A country wishing to keep the military out of politics must impart professional values to its officers. Ideally, as military training and tactics become more sophisticated, officers develop specialized and complex military skills, while distancing themselves from politics. However, such a division of function will develop only if military training focuses on external threats such as wars with other nations. Should the focus of military education shift toward **internal warfare**—controlling guerrilla unrest or other civil insurrections—professionalization will not suffice to keep the military out of politics.

Building on this theme, Alfred Stepan distinguished between "old" and "new" military professionalism. The former, typical of developed countries such as the United States, emphasizes skills relevant to "external security." As military officers train to repel foreign enemies we can expect them to remove themselves from domestic politics. In many developing nations, however, military training (the new professionalism) has primarily prepared officers for internal warfare against class-based or ethnically based insurgencies.

In his study of civilian relations with the military, Michael Desch found that the level of civilian control over the armed forces correlates with the level of external threat that the country faces from a foreign adversary and the extent of any domestic threat from internal upheaval. He argues that civilian control over the military is likely to be strongest when the country faces a high external threat and a low internal threat. Conversely, civilian control is generally weakest when the country faces a low external threat and a high internal threat, precisely the situation that has prevailed in many Latin American and African nations in the recent past.

The Nature of Civil Society

Though research into the internal structure and dynamics of the armed forces is very useful, it fails to tell the entire story. In other words, we cannot ascertain the probability of military intervention in politics and the objectives of this intervention merely by evaluating internal military factors such as the armed forces' cohesion, size, professionalism and ideological orientation. For example, there is surprisingly little correlation between the military's size and firepower, on the one hand, and its propensity to topple civilian governments, on the other. Indeed, Africa, home to some of the world's smallest militaries, has had one of the highest incidences of military rule. In Togo, an army of only 250 men and a small number of retirees from the former French colonial force carried out West Africa's first military coup. In Benin, one president was overthrown by only sixty paratroopers. Indeed, small and poorly armed military units executed a number of other takeovers in the region. In the closing years of the twentieth century, of nearly forty-five African countries, thirty-five had armed forces of fewer than thirty thousand, and twenty-three of these had fewer than ten thousand men. In contrast, China, India, Israel, Sweden, and the United States—with far larger militaries—have never suffered a coup.

Ultimately, then, the military's propensity to intervene in politics is less a function of its own capabilities than a consequence of the weaknesses of civilian political institutions. As Samuel Huntington insisted, "The most important causes of military intervention in politics are not military, but political and reflect, not the social and organizational characteristics of the military establishment, but the political and institutional structure of society."[7] Hence, the second group of explanatory theories focuses its attention on the nature of civil society.

If a civilian government enjoys substantial support from political and economic elites, influential political parties, and the general public, and if it provides political stability and a healthy economy, it is relatively immune from military coups. Conversely, "In times of uncertainty and the breakdown of [civilian political] institutions, soldiers come into their own; when there is no other effective organization of society, even a small, weak army may take command over a large, unorganized mass."[8] Samuel E. Finer maintained that the quality of a nation's political culture helps determine whether or not its civilian government can resist military intervention. Countries are relatively safe from coups if their citizens (including political and military elites) believe that only *civilian* political leaders and institutions are legitimate and that elections are the only legitimate means of changing governments. Civilian government is also more secure if a country has a strong civil society, that is, a network of independent groups such as labor unions and business organizations.[9] But, in many developing nations, civilian governments have low legitimacy and few members of civil society are willing to defend them. Consequently, disgruntled military leaders have more opportunities to overthrow them, while civilians and other troops are less likely to risk their lives defending them.

From an institutional perspective, civilian regimes are strongest when broadly based political parties support them. Where party systems are deeply entrenched in the fabric of society and elicit widespread support, the likelihood of military intervention is greatly diminished. In fact, a country's susceptibility to coups is more strongly influenced by the degree to which its party system penetrates and organizes society than by how democratic it is. Thus, once-authoritarian governments in Mexico and Taiwan (dominated by a single party) controlled the military effectively for years, just as the autocratic CCP does now. But when placed under great stress, not even a strong party system can fully immunize a political system from military interference. For example, strong party systems, which had kept Uruguay and Chile free of military coups for decades, collapsed under the strains of intense class conflict in the 1970s.

Civilian governments are most vulnerable during periods of economic decline or high inflation. They are also at risk when they are perceived as corrupt and when they are unable to maintain political stability. All these circumstances undermine their legitimacy and often increase popular expectations (or hopes) that military rule could improve the situation. In nations such as Nigeria, Thailand, and Pakistan, soon after taking power, military leaders declared their intention to root out widespread corruption. In such cases, military intervention has often drawn broad support initially from civil society. Following severe economic and political crises in Argentina, Brazil, Chile, and Uruguay, the new military dictatorships committed themselves to crush leftist movements, restore social order, and reinvigorate the economy.

As modernization theory would lead us to believe, countries that are more socioeconomically developed are less likely to suffer military takeovers.

> Countries with per-capita GNPs of $1,000 or more [in 1995 dollars] do not [normally] have *successful* coups; countries with per-capita GNPs of $3,000 or more do not have coup *attempts*. The area between $1,000 and $3,000 per-capita GNP is where unsuccessful coups occur, while successful coups . . . were [most common] in countries with per-capita GNPs under $500.[10]

While there have been a few exceptions to that claim, it has remained largely true.*

In summary, a nation's ability to limit military intervention reflects, in large part, the strength of its political institutions, the values of its

---

*These GNP levels are expressed in constant dollars to eliminate the effects of inflation.

political culture, and its level of economic development. Yet, these factors alone do not account for all the variations in civil-military relations. Elite values and behavior also play an important role. For example, India and Costa Rica, with political and socioeconomic circumstances comparable to those of their neighbors, have experienced little or no military intervention in politics. The explanation may lie in the values of their political and economic elites: elected officials, government bureaucrats, political party leaders, business leaders, and labor leaders, as well as military officers themselves.

India illustrates this point well. Located near several countries with long histories of military intervention (Pakistan, Bangladesh, Burma, and Thailand), it has been governed exclusively by civilians since independence. There is little to suggest that the Indian public, still heavily rural and one-third illiterate, has a political culture more modern or informed than that all of its neighbors have. Nor, until the 1990s, was its economy much more advanced than theirs. It appears, however, that political and economic elites in India have long endorsed civilian control more strongly than have their counterparts in neighboring countries.

Elite values, however, may change more quickly than entire political cultures do. In a process of "political learning," a nation's civilian leaders may understand from previous experience how better to avert military coups. The armed forces governed Venezuela for much of the first half of the twentieth century. From 1959 into the mid-1990s, nearly four decades of elected government transformed the country into one of Latin America's most stable democracies until government corruption and a declining economy undermined the political establishment's legitimacy. While a number of factors contributed to the prolonged period of civilian governance, one critical element was a change in the attitudes of political elites following the collapse of Venezuela's first experiment with democracy (1945–1948). Recognizing that political polarization had precipitated a 1948 military coup, leaders of the major political parties agreed to moderate their political conflict. In 1958, the foremost democratically oriented political parties signed the Pact of *Punto Fijo*, which increased interparty cooperation and set the basis for decades of civilian political dominance. Long viewed as a model for democratic reform in the region, Venezuela was one of the only Latin American countries that avoided military rule in the 1970s and 1980s. More recently, elite political pacts, often modeled after Punto Fijo, helped terminate civil wars and establish democratic governments in several Central American countries.

By the end of the 1980s, however, Venezuela's deep economic crisis and its pervasive government corruption had severely eroded civilian support for the political parties that had dominated government since the interparty pact. An unsuccessful coup attempt in 1992 received considerable popular approval and turned the coup's leader, Lieutenant Colonel Hugo Chávez, into a national hero, at least among the poor. Elected government has survived, but Chávez, who spent two years in jail for his coup activity, easily won the 1998 presidential elections. The two political parties that had dominated Venezuelan politics for the previous forty years were practically wiped off the electoral map. Since then, Chávez and his handpicked successor have subverted many of the country's democratic institutions and given the armed forces a much greater foothold in politics. Still, while not panaceas, political pacts such as Punto Fijo have often been valuable tools for establishing more stable civilian governments.

PROGRESSIVE SOLDIERS AND MILITARY CONSERVATIVES

Having examined the factors that either promote or inhibit military intervention, we will now consider the political behavior and policies of military regimes after they have established control. Given the disorder and conflict that characterize so many developing world nations, we must ask whether military rule produces greater political stability and socioeconomic development, at least in the short run. Also, once in office, are the generals and colonels likely to be a force for progressive change or defenders of the status quo?

Many of the early modernization theorists felt strongly that the armed forces could contribute to development. Marion Levy was impressed by the military's alleged rationality, disciplined organization, and commitment to modern values. Taking their critics to task, he maintained that the armed forces might be "the most efficient type of organization for combining maximum rates of modernization with maximum levels of stability and control."[11] Lucian Pye also saw the military as one of the best-organized national institutions in otherwise "disorganized transitional societies." It was, said Pye, at the forefront of technical training and a leader in imparting the values of citizenship to the public.[12] For Manfred Halpern, the Middle Eastern military was "the vanguard of nationalism and social change."[13]

Positive evaluations such as these predominated in the early modernization literature. Frequently they were based on an idealized vision of the professional soldier: trained in modern organizational skills, nationalistic, and above narrow tribal, class, and regional interests. At times, these writings reflected the authors' strong preference for order and stability, coupled with the assumption that the military could bring order out of political and economic chaos. Occasionally, they drew on a few military success stories and projected them onto a larger screen. One early model was the Turkish military revolt led by Ataturk (Mustafa Kemal) in 1919.

During the next two decades, Ataturk and his followers modernized the country before eventually turning it over to civilian rule. Another frequently cited military reformer was Egypt's Colonel Abdul Gamal Nasser, who rose to power in the 1950s seeking to reform his country's social and economic institutions while strengthening its military.

Over the years, very different kinds of officers (and sometimes enlisted men) have seized power, promising to modernize their countries through industrialization, greater labor discipline, expanded education, agrarian reform, or other fundamental reforms. In countries such as Upper Volta, Libya, and Peru, leftist militaries have promoted one or more of the following causes: economic redistribution, greater state intervention in the economy, mass mobilization, agrarian reform, or a struggle against imperialism. On the other hand, conservative generals in Brazil, Chile, Indonesia, and South Korea repressed mass political participation while encouraging investment by domestic firms and **multinational corporations (MNCs)**.

Why have some military governments championed the poor, while others have supported wealthy corporate and landowning interests? To find the answer, we must examine the class origins of the officers' corps, their nation's level of socioeconomic development, and the class alliances that had developed in their political system. Research in a range of LDCs has shown that officers tend to come from middle-class backgrounds, particularly in Asia and Latin America. Typically, their fathers were military officers, shopkeepers, merchants, midsized landowners, teachers, or civil servants. Not surprisingly, then, military regimes have commonly identified with the goals and aspirations of their country's civilian middle class.

But what are those goals, and what political ideologies and development policies have emerged from them? In the least developed countries, officers have often viewed economic elites, including large landowners and foreign corporations, as the source of their country's backwardness. Members of the middle class frequently resent those same elites for obstructing their own rise to political and economic prominence. In such a setting, both the armed forces and the civilian middle class may perceive the relatively unmobilized lower class as a potential ally in the battle against the oligarchy. For example, soon after taking power, Peruvian general Juan Velasco blamed the traditional landowning class and Peru's economic dependency for the nation's underdevelopment. In the following years, the military's ambitious land redistribution, shantytown reform, expropriations of property belonging to MNCs, expansion of the state economic sector, and mass mobilization greatly altered the country's political and economic landscape. Elsewhere, "General Omar Torrijos of Panama railed against oligarchic control and encouraged the lower class to participate in politics."[14] Muammar Qaddafi's government in Libya and a number of Marxist military governments in Africa used similar revolutionary rhetoric, but were quick to enrich themselves, their friends, and their relatives.

In the more modern and industrialized developing nations, however, where workers and the poor are more mobilized, the military confronts a different political landscape. Urbanization, the spread of secondary and university education, and economic development all have enlarged and strengthened the middle class, enabling it to wrest a share of political power from the economic elites. At the same time, industrialization has increased the size of the working class and enhanced the trade union movement. Urbanization also creates a growing and sometimes organized shantytown population. And the commercialization of agriculture often triggers unrest in the countryside. Not surprisingly, the middle class (having achieved a share of political influence) and its military partners see the more galvanized and politicized lower classes as a threat rather than a useful ally.

If left-wing political parties and trade unions have gained considerable mass support and if there has been growing political unrest, the military and the middle class are more likely to ally themselves with the economic elite and to repress mass mobilization. In Chile, the election of Salvador Allende's Marxist government and the accompanying mobilization of workers, peasants, and urban poor polarized the country along class lines. In nearby Uruguay, the Left's electoral appeal was not as strong, but labor-industrial conflict was intense, and the Tupamaros, a potent urban guerrilla group, were engaged in a campaign of political kidnappings and insurgency. In both countries, the perceived threat of guerrilla groups, mass mobilization, and an ascendant Left (including strong leftist political parties) prompted the military to topple longstanding democracies.

In short, then, the more underdeveloped a country is and the weaker its middle class, the greater the likelihood that the country will have a left-of-center military.* However, notes Eric Nordlinger, "the soldiers who have power in countries with an established middle class . . . act as more or less ardent defenders of the status quo."[15] Similarly, Huntington observes,

> In the world of the oligarchy, the soldier is a radical; in the middle class world, he is a participant and arbitrator; as mass society looms on the

---

*But the armed forces in the least developed nations are not *always* reform oriented. In Africa and other impoverished areas, the military often has seized power out of self-interest or for narrow ethnic goals. Similarly, while the military has often been progressive in the less developed nations of South America, Africa, and the Middle East, it has generally been reactionary in Central America and the Caribbean, where it has been co-opted by the upper class.

horizon he becomes the guardian of the existing order. . . . The more advanced a society becomes, the more conservative and reactionary becomes the role of the military.[16]

The conservative military officers' concerns are not limited to leftist mass movements. They generally oppose any mobilization of lower-class groups that threaten the nation's stability. For example, in recent times, the Algerian and Egyptian armed forces have stood in the way of mass mobilization by Islamic fundamentalists.

THE TYPES AND GOALS OF MILITARY REGIMES

Having observed the range of ideological orientations among military governments, we now examine the structures and goals of those regimes.

Personalistic Regimes

In the least developed countries—those with low levels of military professionalization, limited mass political participation, extensive political corruption, and little semblance of representative government—military officers frequently seize power for their own personal enrichment and aggrandizement, usually with little or no interest in economic or political reform. Their governments tend to be personalistic; that is, a single charismatic officer with a strong personal following leads them. In order to bolster his support, however, the leader allows part of the government plunder to pass on to the military and civilian cliques surrounding him. "Legitimacy is secured through patronage, clientelistic alliances, [and] systemic intimidation."[17]

In Latin America, personalistic dictatorships were most common in the less developed political and economic systems of Central America and the Caribbean. One of the most prominent examples was the Somoza dynasty in Nicaragua. As leader of the country's National Guard (its only military force), Anastasio Somoza Sr. overthrew the government in 1937, primarily seeking his own enrichment. Governing a small and impoverished nation, he amassed a fortune of several hundred million dollars using state resources to purchase construction firms, urban real estate, electrical power plants, air and shipping lines, cement factories, and much of the nation's best farmland. Following Somoza's assassination in 1956, his political and financial empire passed to his two sons, who ruled the country in succession until the 1979 Sandinista Revolution. Other personalistic regimes in the Americas included the Batista government in Cuba (eventually toppled by Fidel Castro's revolutionary army) and Alfredo Stroessner's long dictatorship in Paraguay (1954–1989). Batista had links to the American mafia's gambling and prostitution operations in Havana. Stroessner and his associates enriched themselves by collaborating with international smugglers and drug dealers.*

Personalistic military regimes have been especially common in Sub-Saharan Africa, sometimes led by upwardly mobile junior officers or even enlisted men such as Ghana's Flight Sergeant Jerry Rawlings and Liberia's Sergeant-Major Samuel Doe. While some were well intentioned, most have done little to develop their countries. The most infamous personalistic dictators in the continent have been Uganda's Idi Amin Dada, the Central African Republic's Jean-Bédel Bokassa, and Congo's Mobutu Sese Seko. Ironically, in light of his regime's subsequent enormous brutality, Amin initially justified his coup by citing the human rights violations of ousted President Milton Obote. Enamored of power as much as wealth, Amin played upon and exacerbated Uganda's ethnic divisions during his brutal eight-year reign (1971–1979). He not only expelled the country's sizable Asian population (mostly Indian) but also murdered an estimated 300,000–500,000 people, most notably members of the previously influential Langi and Acholi tribes. Seeing enemies at every turn, he even executed one of his wives. In an attempt to maintain absolute control over the armed forces, he purged or executed a large portion of the officers' corps, eventually creating an army composed largely of foreign troops (principally Sudanese and Zairian).

Equally megalomaniacal, the Central African Republic's Jean-Bedel Bokassa unleashed a reign of death and terror on his country following his takeover in a 1966 coup. Plundering the treasury of one of the world's more impoverished nations, he concluded that the presidency was not a sufficiently exalted position, so he lavished millions of dollars on his own coronation as the country's new emperor. In time, Amin and Bokassa so outraged the world community that they were ousted through external intervention. Amin fell to a Tanzanian invasion, while a French-supported coup toppled Bokassa.

Because most personalistic dictators lack a meaningful ideology or program to legitimize their regime, they typically must share some of the spoils with their military and civilian supporters in order to maintain themselves in office. For example, President Mobutu, Africa's most enduring military dictator (1965–1997), made himself a multibillionaire while opening up the floodgates of corruption to benefit his military and civil service. In this manner, he kept himself in office for decades while bankrupting the national government and destroying a once-dynamic economy. By the late 1990s, however, as the Zairian economy collapsed,

---

*To be sure, a few personalistic dictators, such as Argentina's Juan Perón and Venezuela's Hugo Chávez, introduced broad social and economic reform programs. But even benevolent personalistic military regimes are usually corrupt and concentrate excessive power in the hands of one person.

his regime unraveled, falling rapidly to a rebel force whose new government, unfortunately, turned out to be almost as corrupt and even more repressive. More recently, warlords (regionally based, military/political bosses who plunder the region they control) in Sierra Leone and Liberia overthrew the government with few goals other than looting the country. In Nicaragua, the Somoza dynasty maintained the National Guard's critical support by allowing its officers to enrich themselves.

Institutional Military Regimes

As developing countries' political and economic systems modernize, corresponding changes take place in military institutions and attitudes. Frequently, officers attend advanced military academies at home or abroad. Sometimes, they enroll in specialized seminars with civilian leaders, establishing links with politicians, businesspeople, and academics. These programs more intensely expose military officers to their country's political and economic challenges.

If these "new soldiers" seize power, they are likely to govern collectively rather than vest authority in the hands of a single leader. To be sure, many **institutional military regimes** have been dominated by a single figure, such as Libya's Qaddafi, Indonesia's Suharto, and Chile's Augusto Pinochet. Like purely personalistic dictators, some of these men are motivated by ambition, fear, and greed. Even in such cases, a substantial number of officers hold influential government positions (not just the paramount leader), and there is a degree of institutional decision making. In Indonesia, for example, active and retired military officers at one time held nearly half the positions in the national bureaucracy and some two-thirds of the provincial governorships. Furthermore, the goals of these institutional regimes are broader than any single leader's ambitions.

Institutional military governments have generally been headed by councils or juntas such as Niger's Supreme Military Council and Burma's Revolutionary Council. Comparable groups have governed Algeria, Argentina, Brazil, Ethiopia, Thailand, Uruguay, and a number of other countries. These are relatively small governing committees made up of officers from the various branches of the armed forces.* Typically, one active or retired officer serves as president and wields the most influence. Often, however, his term of office is limited. For example, in Argentina and Brazil, the military juntas limited the president to a single term. In contrast, Chile's General Augusto Pinochet was all-powerful and was not constrained by term limits. In some countries, including

---

*In some cases such councils have been mere façades, with one officer really in power. Thus, it is not always easy to distinguish between personalistic and institutional military regimes. Ultimately, the determining factor is where real power resides rather than what the formal structures are.

South Korea, Brazil, and Indonesia, the armed forces tried to legitimize its rule by creating a ruling political party that ran candidates in tightly controlled elections. Frequently, presidents and other leading government officials retire from active military duty before taking office. And in Egypt and Syria, military and civilian elites joined together to form a ruling party.

Institutional military regimes can be as repressive and brutal as personalistic dictatorships—sometimes even more so. Their day-to-day governing style, however, is generally more bureaucratic and sophisticated—commonly drawing on the talents of highly trained civilian technocrats. Moreover, unlike self-aggrandizing personalistic leaders, they are more likely to support the aspirations of the middle class, more prone to espouse a coherent political ideology, and more likely to champion nationalistic goals. Most institutional military governments pursue four broad objectives, or at least claim to do so.

First, they usually justify their seizure of power by denouncing the alleged corruption of the government that they have ousted. Thus, when Bangladesh's Lieutenant General Hussain Muhammad Ershad led a 1982 army coup, he charged that the outgoing administration had "failed totally because of [its] petty selfishness . . . and unbounded corruption."[18] Incoming military leaders in Uruguay, Pakistan, Thailand, and much of Africa have made similar proclamations. All of them promised to clean up the mess.

A *second* goal—one not normally publicly articulated or acknowledged—is the advancement of the military's own corporate interests. As Ruth First observed, while African coup leaders may claim to have acted for the good of the nation or for other noble political purposes, "when the army acts, it generally acts for army reasons."[19] When officers are unhappy with their salaries, the size of the defense budget, or the quantity and quality of their weapons, they often take action. They also react negatively to civilian "interference" in military affairs, such as the president deviating from normal promotion practices for officers.

Ever since the 1960s—a decade featuring coups in Togo, Ghana, Mali, Congo-Brazzaville, and Algeria—a number of African armies have taken power to protect themselves from competing military units (such as presidential guards), to increase their troop strength, to raise their salaries, or to augment their budgets. In South Asia, repeated coups in Bangladesh have been motivated by resentment over civilian interference in military promotions and by desires for greater military spending.

A *third* common goal is to maintain or restore order and stability. Institutional coups have often occurred during periods of civil unrest, guerrilla insurgencies, or civil war. For example, the army first involved itself deeply in South Korean politics when student demonstrations and labor protests challenged the civilian administrations of Syngman Rhee and Chang Myon. Thailand's many coups have usually followed strikes and street demonstrations in Bangkok.

Military officers are particularly troubled by radical challenges to the political and economic systems and by threats to the safety and integrity of the armed forces. During the early 1960s, Indonesia's civilian president, Sukarno, moved his regime leftward and became increasingly dependent on the country's large communist party, much to the discomfort of his conservative military commanders. Their fears intensified in 1965, when a small group of leftist officers assassinated Lieutenant General Ahmad Yani and five other officers, claiming that these men had been plotting a coup against Sukarno. The country's top military command responded with a massive attack against the communist party, eventually killing some half million alleged party supporters. At the same time, many Indonesian civilians used the chaos as an opportunity to loot and kill members of the country's prosperous Chinese minority. In time, army chief General Suharto ousted Sukarno and established a military dictatorship that lasted more than thirty years.*

Similarly, in Argentina, Brazil, Chile, and Uruguay, the generals' fear of leftist unions, guerrillas, and radical political parties prompted extended military dictatorships. In 1992, the Algerian armed forces halted the second round of parliamentary elections that seemed certain to result in victory for the Islamic Salvation Front, a party of militant Islamic fundamentalists.

A *final* goal of many institutional military regimes has been to revive and stimulate the economy. As we have noted, coups frequently follow periods of rampant inflation, labor conflict, or economic stagnation. A study of thirty-eight Sub-Saharan African governments over a two-decade period revealed that military takeovers were most likely to occur after an economic downturn. Asian and Latin American coups have frequently followed this pattern as well.

Developing-world militaries are frequently committed to industrialization. For one thing, industrial growth can provide them with arms and supplies that previously needed to be imported. In the least developed countries, such production may be limited to uniforms or rifles. On the other hand, in countries such as Brazil, Indonesia, and South Korea, highly advanced arms industries now produce planes, tanks, and other sophisticated weaponry for both domestic consumption and export. Even when it has no direct military payoff, industrialization contributes to national pride and international prestige. Small wonder, then, that

---

*Like many Indonesians, both Suharto and Sukarno had only one name and did not use a family name.

many Latin American and Asian countries have seen a political alliance between industrialists and the armed forces.

Having reviewed the goals of institutional military governments in general, we now focus on two distinct regime types that have received considerable attention in recent years: the bureaucratic-authoritarian regime and the revolutionary military government. While each type has represented only a minority of military governments, they have had a significant impact both within and outside their borders.

Bureaucratic-Authoritarian Regimes

Beginning with the Brazilian coup d'état of 1964, through the 1973 coups in Uruguay and Chile, to the Argentine military takeovers of 1966 and 1976, four of the most socioeconomically developed countries in South America succumbed to military rule. Chile and Uruguay had also been the strongest democracies in the region, free of military domination for decades. Thus, their coups contradicted the widely held assumption that both socioeconomic development and a strong political party system limit military intervention.

Once in power, these regimes lasted longer than typical military governments in the region, from twelve years (in Uruguay) to twenty-one (in Brazil). They suspended political party activity, crushed labor unions and other grassroots organizations, prohibited strikes, and jailed and tortured many suspected political dissidents. In Argentina and Chile, thousands of people were murdered or "disappeared" (covertly taken away, never to be seen again).

Argentine political scientist Guillermo O'Donnell referred to these military governments as **bureaucratic-authoritarian (BA) regimes**. Compared to previous military dictatorships, they had a more extensive bureaucratic structure that included like-minded civilian technocrats; they penetrated more deeply into civil society; established close links to MNCs; and were particularly repressive. O'Donnell focused on the closely related economic and political factors that explained the rise of these BA regimes in Latin America's most developed nations. First, he noted, economic growth in these countries had begun to stagnate by the 1960s. Many analysts argued that further growth would require investment in capital goods industries and new technologies, which only MNCs had the resources to provide. But international corporations (as well as domestic companies) had been reluctant to invest because of the rising labor strife, civil unrest, and leftist electoral strength, all caused by the countries' economic stagnation, high inflation, and declining living standards.

Growing radicalism among the poor and portions of the middle class and the resulting political polarization of society deeply alarmed the armed forces. In Argentina, Chile, and Uruguay, urban guerrillas added to the perceived threat. The goals of the new BA regimes, then, were to crush leftist political parties, unions, and guerrilla movements; limit workers' wages; create a "stable environment for investment"; and work closely with MNCs and domestic corporations to control inflation and reinvigorate the economy. Beyond repressing the Left, the generals wanted to depoliticize society and terminate most forms of political participation for an extended period. In addition, they wanted to extend the role of the private sector and roll back state economic activity, including welfare programs, minimum-wage guarantees, and public ownership of economic resources. While the analysis of BA regimes focused on Latin America, this type of military government later developed in South Korea and other East Asian countries.

Revolutionary Military Regimes

In a number of developing nations, the military has pursued goals diametrically different from those of the conservative BA regimes. Rather than excluding most of the population from the political system, they instead *extended* political and economic participation to formerly excluded groups. At the same time, however, their authoritarian political structure tightly controlled mass participation. In Africa, a number of Marxist, military governments proclaimed policies of cultural nationalism, anti-imperialism, peasant and working-class political mobilization, expansion of the state's economic role, and redistribution of economic resources to the poor.

Revolutionary coups have often been led by radicalized officers from the middle ranks (captains, majors, colonels), rather than generals. In a speech outlining the goals of Upper Volta's military government, Captain Thomas Sankara articulated the Marxist rhetoric typical of such regimes:

> The triumph of the Revolution [i.e., the military takeover] . . . is the crowning moment of the struggle of the Volta People against its internal enemies. It is a victory against international imperialism and its internal allies. . . . These enemies of the people . . . are: the bourgeoisie of Volta [and] . . . reactionary forces whose strength derives from the traditional feudal structures of our society. . . . The People in our revolution comprises: The working class . . . the petty bourgeoisie . . . the peasantry . . . [and] the lumpenproletariat [the poorest urban inhabitants].[20]

Military governments in Ethiopia, Sudan, Somalia, Congo-Brazzaville, Benin, and Madagascar made similarly radical declarations. Like most African military regimes, however, these governments have been led by men without significant political skills or advanced education. Consequently, their Marxist ideals were "self-taught, ideologically immature and crude, and riddled with inconsistencies."[21] For some of them, Marxism simply expressed their strong nationalism and distaste for the European nations that had colonized the continent. For others, revolutionary rhetoric came almost as an afterthought, a means of justifying their earlier seizure of power and authoritarian control. Thus, the government of Colonel Mengistu in Ethiopia, perhaps Africa's most prominent radical military government, did not embrace Marxism-Leninism until it had been in office for three years. In Benin (called Dahomey at that time), General Mathieu Kerekou declared his government to be Marxist and created "revolution committees" simply as a pretext for spying on the civil service.

In other world regions, leftist (though not Marxist) military regimes have governed countries as disparate as Libya, Panama, and Peru. Peru's military came to power seeking to curtail the influence of the rural oligarchy and incorporate the peasantry, working class, and urban poor into the political system. Finally, military governments in Panama and Ecuador introduced comparable, though far more modest, reform programs.

THE ACCOMPLISHMENTS AND FAILURES OF MILITARY REGIMES

How successfully have military governments achieved their goals and how well have they served their countries? Little needs to be said about personalistic military dictatorships. With a few notable exceptions, they are rarely seriously interested in benefiting their countries. Even those with broader goals have had blatantly self-serving objectives. Thus, it would be very hard to argue seriously that dictators such as Batista (Cuba), Somoza (Nicaragua), Stroessner (Paraguay), Amin (Uganda), and Bokassa (Central African Republic) contributed to the long-term political or economic growth of their respective nations. Consequently, the analysis in our next section focuses exclusively on the record of institutional military governments, which often have serious intentions, be it for left-wing or right-wing reform.

Combating Corruption

Let us first look at one of the most commonly professed objectives of institutional regimes—eliminating government corruption. Because government malfeasance is so pervasive, denouncing corruption is a convenient means of legitimizing the armed forces' unconstitutional seizure of power. Yet, most soldiers in office prove every bit as corrupt as their predecessors, or more so. To be sure, a few military governments have been quite honest, but they are the exceptions. As one leading scholar has observed,

> Every Nigerian and Ghanaian coup . . . has had as its prime goal the elimination of deeply ingrained corruption from society. Yet, not one military administration has made truly consistent efforts in that direction . . . or for that matter remained immune to it itself. . . . [Elsewhere in Africa] in two . . . military regimes—Guinea and Burkina Faso—nepotism and accumulation of wealth commenced the very day the officers' hierarchy took office.[22]

Ironically, the continent's continual military intervention has tended to increase corruption in the civilian governments that they oust. "The fear that [civilian] power may not last encourages the incoming politicians to grab what is grabbable."[23] In Asian nations such as Thailand and Indonesia, the military's record has been equally disappointing. In those few military governments that avoid *gross* corruption, the more modest lure of contraband automobiles and tax-supported vacation homes often proves irresistible. In short, even those military governments that seized power with noble intentions are generally soon corrupted.

Defending Military Interests

When it comes to pursuing their second major objective—advancing their own corporate interests—not surprisingly, military governments have been more successful, at least in the short term. More often than not, military rulers enhance the nation's defense budget. Unfortunately, however, these outlays draw government resources away from badly needed programs such as health care and education.

Typically, military governments increase spending on armaments, military salaries, military housing, and officers' clubs. In much of Asia, officers have benefited from preferential treatment in the distribution of governmental contracts. After leading a coup in Libya, Colonel Qaddafi insured his officers' loyalty by doubling their salaries, thereby making them the highest paid army in the LDCs. So, even in the face of a mass insurgency and the defection of many regular army troops, the military's elite units (those best-armed and trained) remained loyal to the colonel right to the end. In their first five years in office, Uruguay's generals raised the military and security share of the national budget from 26 percent to more than 40 percent. A parallel "bias in favor of army, police and civil-service salaries and benefits can be observed in practically every military regime in Africa."[24]

Throughout the LDCs, even when soldiers do not actually govern, the mere specter of intervention has often led civilian governments to bestow salary hikes and expensive weapon systems on the armed forces. For example, it would be very imprudent for elected leaders in the Philippines or Thailand to slash their country's defense budget. Even Malaysia and Singapore, with no history of coups d'état, pay their officers generously to keep them out of politics. Similarly, Colombia and Venezuela, with two of Latin America's most long-lived civilian governments (though military involvement in politics has risen sharply in both since the 1990s), have supported healthy defense budgets aimed at keeping the generals at bay.

But, while military rule may enlarge military budgets, it usually damages the armed forces in the long run by reducing their institutional cohesion. The longer the armed forces stay in power, the more generals, colonels, and admirals begin to squabble over resource allocation and other policy issues. New economic and political challenges inevitably arise, which drive a wedge between the officers in command. Furthermore, even military governments that took power with considerable popular support usually lose their legitimacy as they confront difficult economic and social problems. As a consequence, in some regions, most notably Sub-Saharan Africa, internal coups (one military faction ousting another) have produced a series of unstable military governments. Nearly half of Africa's twentieth-century coups and failed coup attempts sought to topple incumbent military regimes.[25] Hence, for the most part in recent decades, militaries have returned to the barracks to avoid further internal divisions, restoring the government to civilian hands.

Patterns in Military Spending

As we have seen, the major "accomplishment" of most military governments in the LDCs—budgetary gains for the armed forces—was frequently the nation's loss. Military spending is often higher than the country can afford, thereby reducing badly needed social and economic investment. Countries in South America that have not fought a foreign war in decades have spent fortunes on naval vessels and state-of-the-art combat jets. And, in Sub-Saharan Africa, home to many of the world's poorest countries, military budgets are frequently particularly disproportionate to economic capacities.

But, the demise of so many military governments during the 1980s and 1990s generally has *not* caused widespread cuts in defense spending that we might have expected. Table 8.1 indicates the amount of military spending in constant dollars over a twenty-two-year period in a number of regions of the developing world. The last column in the table indicates the percentage changes in military spending for each region between 1988 and 2010.*

At the start of that period, the Middle East and East Asia spent far more than any other world region. Both regions perceived serious

---

*Tables 8.1–8.3 present the latest data years available at the time this edition of the textbook was written.

Table 8.1   Trends in Military Expenditures, 1988–2010 (in billions of constant dollars)

Region	1988	1998	2010	Percentage Increase, 1988–2010
Sub-Saharan Africa	10.6	8.5	17.9	69
South America	23.9	31.7	54.8	129
East Asia	88.4	118.0	222.0	151
South Asia	18.3	24.0	42.6	132
Middle East	52.3	62.2	98.6	89

Source: Information from the Stockholm International Peace Research Institute (SIPRI): Military Expenditure Database (2011).

military threats—the Arab-Israeli conflict in the Middle East and the proximity of China, North Korea, and Vietnam in East Asia. And both regions included countries with substantial economic resources to spend on the armed forces (including Israel, the oil-exporting Arab States, China, South Korea, and Taiwan). Between 1988 and 1998 (data columns 1 and 2), military outlays actually fell in Sub-Saharan Africa and rose by one-third or less in the Middle East, South America, East Asia, and South Asia. But the pace of spending picked up considerably from 1998 to 2010, particularly in East Asia, South Asia, and South America.

Currently, defense consumes a disproportionate share of many LDC's GDP and thereby limits government spending on education, health care, rural development, and other social needs. Table 8.2 demonstrates that while some developing nations have tightly limited their military spending, others, particularly those facing external military threats or civil unrest, have enormous military budgets relative to their expenditures on basic socioeconomic needs. The table compares government spending in 2012 on two important "public welfare" needs with outlays for the military in four groups of countries: two highly industrialized democracies (the United States and Japan), three "upper-middle-income" developing nations (Mexico, Thailand, and Jordan), two "lower-middle-income" nations (Angola and India), and two "low income" LDCs (Ghana and Chad).*

The first data column indicates the combined percentage of each nation's GDP that was devoted to health and education. The next column

---

*These are categories used by the World Bank to classify economies throughout the entire world. Thus, even though countries such as India and Angola may seem extremely poor to Western observers, the World Bank still classifies them as "lower middle income" nations compared to all other countries in the world.

Table 8.2   Public Welfare (Health and Education) versus Military Expenditures as a Percentage of GDP

Country	Public Welfare (PW) Spending as a % of GDP	Military (M) Spending as a % of GDP	Ratio of Public Welfare Spending to Military Spending (PW:M)
United States	12.6	4.2	3:1
Japan	9.9	1.0	9.9:1
Mexico	7.5	0.6	12.5:1
Thailand	7.6	1.5	5.1:1
Jordan	10.3	4.0	2.5:1
India	4.3	2.5	1.7:1
Angola	4.6	3.6	1.3:1
Ghana	9.7	0.8	12.1:1
Chad	4.6	6.6	0.7:1

Source: UNDP, *Human Development Report*, 2014, Human Development Indicators; The World Bank: Data Bank by Countries—online. The table uses 2012 economic data (the latest data available at the time).

shows the percentage of each country's GDP spent on the military (M). Obviously, poorer and smaller countries, such as Ghana and Chad, cannot possibly spend nearly as much money on either public welfare or the military as the United States and Japan do. But, the table allows us to compare each country's expenditures relative to the size of its own economy (GDP). The last column in the table compares the two previous columns by showing each country's ratio of public welfare spending to its military outlays (PW:M).

All of the world's highly industrialized countries as well as most LDCs devote a greater portion of their GDPs to public welfare than to the military. This holds for all the countries in Table 8.2 except for the small African nation of Chad. But, their ratios vary greatly, from Mexico and Ghana (which expend over twelve times as much on public welfare) to Angola (which has a PW: M ratio of only 1.3:1). If we examine the four countries with the lowest ratios of welfare to military spending: Angola, India (1.7:1), Jordan (2.5:1), and Chad (0.7:1)—the only country in the table that spent more on the military than on public welfare—we find that each has faced hostile neighbors, domestic insurgencies, or both for many years. In countries such as India and Chad, each having per capita incomes lower than $1,500 annually, some of their substantial military expenditures could be going to badly needed educational and health care programs.

As elected civilian governments replaced military dictatorships, a number of countries *initially* cut the economic importance of military outlays sharply. From 1985 to 1993, military expenditures as a percentage

Table 8.3   Trends in Military Expenditures as a Percentage of GDP

Country	1990	2000	2013
Eritrea	21.3[a]	32.7	NA
Nigeria	0.9	0.8	0.9
Chile	3.4	2.8	1.0
Colombia	1.6	3.0	1.9
South Korea	4.0	2.6	2.8
India	3.2	3.1	2.5
Jordan	7.8	6.3	3.5
Saudi Arabia	14.0	10.6	9.3

Source: Information from the Stockholm International Peace Research Institute (SIPRI): Military Expenditure Database.

[a] The Eritrean figure is from 1993 because it became independent in that year.

of GDP fell from 2.9 to 1.7 percent in Argentina, from 6.8 to 2.1 percent in Chile, and from 4.4 to 1.6 percent in El Salvador. But, these cuts were usually short-lived and the percentage spent on the military rose again from the mid-1990s onward.

Table 8.3 presents data on military expenditures as a percentage of national GDP in eight developing nations (two from each of four world regions) during a twenty-three-year period (1990–2013). These figures show what percentage of each country's **Gross National Product** (GNP) was devoted to military spending over time. If a country allocates a large percentage of its annual production to the armed forces, it has less to spend on education, health, housing, and other types of human welfare.

As a point of comparison, we can compare the percentage of GNP allotted to the military in the table to the expenditures of two highly industrialized nations not in the table: France (3.4 percent in 1990 and 2.2 percent in 2013) and the United States (5.3 percent in 1990, during the Cold War, and 3.8 percent in 2013 after the collapse of the Soviet Union).

As the table indicates, LDCs allocated widely varying percentages, some spending a comparable percentage to that of the United States and France (Chile, South Korea, and India), others spending less (Colombia and, especially, Nigeria), and still others devoting far more (Jordan and, especially, Saudi Arabia and Eritrea).* LDCs with very high military spending percentages usually (but not always) face significant external threats from neighboring countries and/or internal threats from guerrilla or terrorist groups at home. Thus, Jordan and Saudi Arabia both view Israel

---

*The nations selected for the table are not meant to be representative of military spending in their regions, but were picked to indicate the wide range of such outlays among developing countries.

as a major external threat, while Saudi Arabia also fears Iran. Eritrea, a very poor African nation, won independence in 1993, after a protracted war of secession from Ethiopia. Since that time, it has had very hostile relations with Ethiopia, including a war (1998–2000) and in 2000 spent an incredible 32.7 percent of its GNP on the armed forces. In general, developing nations have reduced the percentage of GNP spent on the military during the past two decades. This does not mean that their actual military spending has gone down (almost always they have risen), but rather, that their GNPs have grown faster than spending. Development specialists applaud the decreased percentage of GDP spent on the military. But critics insist that most LDCs (especially the poorest) still spend too much on the military relative to human services and welfare expenditures.

Establishing Stability

Military officers almost always react negatively to popular unrest and political instability. For one thing, disorder violates their hierarchical view of society. Furthermore, it frequently threatens the interests of their middle-class and industrialist allies. Often, mass protests or other types of unrest pose an imminent danger to the armed forces themselves. The generals and colonels of Latin America, for example, have been keenly aware that Marxist revolutions in Cuba and Nicaragua destroyed their country's old military establishment. In Cuba, a number of Batista's officers faced the firing squad, while in Nicaragua, many National Guardsmen were imprisoned or had to flee the country. In Chile and Brazil, leftist political leaders threatened the officers' hierarchical control of the armed forces. Similarly, the generals in Algeria felt endangered by the growing strength of Islamic fundamentalists. Even "revolutionary soldiers" in Ethiopia, Libya, and Peru preferred to dictate change from the top, with tight government controls over mass mobilization.

In many respects, military governments are particularly well suited for controlling civil unrest. They can use force with impunity to combat guerrilla insurrections, disperse street demonstrations, and ban strikes. In some cases, their extensive intelligence agencies, such as South Korea's KCIA, enabled them to penetrate deeply into society to control dissent. The Argentine, Brazilian, Chilean, and Uruguayan armies used mass arrests, torture, and death squads to crush potent urban guerrilla movements. In Indonesia, the military destroyed one of the world's largest communist parties and later decimated various separatist movements.

But the generals restored order in these countries at a tremendous cost in human suffering. Some twenty to thirty thousand people died in the Argentine army's "dirty war" against the Left, while many more were imprisoned and tortured. Students and other young people were the primary victims, many of them incorrectly identified as part of the leftist opposition. In Chile, thousands of intellectuals and professionals fled the country, devastating one of the developing world's most advanced university systems and artistic communities. Some three thousand Chileans died; many others were the victims of torture. During Indonesia's "year of living dangerously," perhaps 500,000 communists and ethnic Chinese were massacred, while some 150,000 other people died subsequently (largely from starvation) in the army's struggle against East Timorian separatists. Another twelve thousand died in the separatist rebellion in Aceh. Of course, many military regimes are not repressive. However, it is precisely those that seize power to restore order in highly polarized societies that normally are the most brutal.

Moreover, *in the long term*, the military has not been particularly successful in providing political stability. To be sure, in several Asian and Latin American countries, state repression, coupled with technocratic development policies, either co-opted or decimated opposition groups. In South Korea, sharply improved living standards and a gradual political transition paved the way to a stable elected government. And in Argentina, Brazil, Chile, and Uruguay, the BA regimes' brutality against radical movements convinced political leaders on both sides of the ideological spectrum (but especially the Left) to moderate their positions so as not to provoke further military intervention. Ironically, all of these countries now have democratically elected leftist governments, not what the BA regimes hoped to achieve.

But these "successes" are the exception. Despite their brute strength, the armed forces' hold on power has generally been relatively brief. Eric Nordlinger's pioneering study of military governments found that, on average, they dissolved in five to seven years.[26] Karen Remmer's later work on twelve South American military governments between 1960 and 1990 showed four to be quite durable (twelve to thirty-five years); the remaining eight, however, averaged less than seven years.[27] Moreover, military rule, no matter what its accomplishments are, ultimately impedes the maturation of political parties and other civilian institutions necessary for long-term stability.

In Africa, more often than not, coups have only led to further coups, hampering political development as they turned politics into a fight for survival. The brutal regime of Sergeant Samuel Doe exposed Liberia to a devastating civil war and to a far more sinister ruler, Charles Taylor, who fomented unspeakably brutal internal warfare at home and in nearby Sierra Leone. Military rule in Ethiopia and the Sudan only worsened ethnically based civil wars. Elsewhere, extended suppression of dissident groups will likely lead to greater upheavals after those regimes eventually fall, as it did in Libya.

Improving the Economy

Earlier we noted that coups often are provoked by economic recessions or severe inflation. Consequently, many newly installed military governments promise to impose fiscal discipline and revitalize the economy. In South Korea, Indonesia, Brazil, and Chile, for example, conservative military governments curtailed union activity in order to suppress wage demands. By reducing strike activity and weakening unions, the generals expected to lower inflation and attract foreign investment.

Proponents of military dictatorships assert that they can more easily make economic decisions consistent with the national interest because they need not pander to special interest groups. Critics counter that soldiers lack the expertise to manage an economy. Even when well intentioned, they tend to allocate excessive funds to defense and to wasteful, chauvinistic projects. Examining the economic performance of specific military governments provides evidence to support both sides of the debate. South Korea demonstrated that a military government can oversee a very successful economic development program. Following General Park Chung Hee's seizure of power in 1961, the armed forces governed the country for more than twenty-five years. During this period, the Republic of Korea changed from an underdeveloped nation into one of the world's most dynamic industrial economies. Moreover, the country enjoyed sustained economic growth while still maintaining very equitable income distribution. Indeed, economists frequently cite South Korea as a model of well-executed economic modernization.

Elsewhere in Asia, Indonesia's military also presided over rapid economic growth from the mid-1960s to late 1990s. During the 1970s and early 1980s, the Suharto dictatorship plowed back a portion of the country's extensive petroleum revenues into labor-intensive export industries. At the same time, rural development programs and mass education improved income distribution and, coupled with economic growth, substantially reduced the number of Indonesians living in poverty. Nearby Thailand, governed by the military for much of the last seventy years, has also enjoyed an economic boom, though it was somewhat flawed by corruption and "**crony capitalism**" (plentiful government loans and contracts awarded to politically well-connected businesspeople).

Two of Latin America's major bureaucratic-authoritarian regimes—Brazil and, especially, Chile—also had relatively successful economic records. After several false starts, Chile's probusiness, export-oriented policies ushered in a period of strong economic expansion with low inflation. These achievements, however, followed a period of severe economic hardship, which forced the poor to bear a disproportionate share of the sacrifice. As with other BA regimes, income distribution deteriorated. After the restoration of democracy in 1990, the civilian governments of

Patricio Aylwin and Eduardo Frei maintained high growth rates while using targeted programs to reduce poverty. During that decade, that combination of high growth and remedial programs for those left behind halved the number of Chileans living in poverty.

Brazil's BA regime achieved dramatic economic growth during the late 1960s and 1970s, turning the country into an important industrial power. The benefits of this growth, however, were very poorly distributed, leaving many of the poor worse off than before. Moreover, Brazil's "economic miracle" was built on excessive foreign borrowing that turned the country into the LDCs' largest external debtor. In recent years, civilian president Luiz Inácio Lula da Silva's administration (2003–2010) was able to accelerate economic growth while sharply reducing the percentage of the population living in poverty.

Many other Latin American military governments, including the BA regimes in Argentina and Uruguay, performed poorly in the economic sphere. They spent far too much on defense, borrowed excessively, were corrupt, and frequently failed to understand development economics. In Africa, the armed forces' economic record, with few exceptions, has ranged from poor to disastrous. And, the Burmese military government wrecked the national economy.

Moving beyond examinations of individual cases such as these, some analysts have engaged in more systematic statistical comparison of regime types. Examining data on economic indicators such as growth rates and inflation, they have compared the economic performance of military and civilian governments in specific regions or throughout the LDCs. Unfortunately, these comparisons face a number of methodological problems. For one thing, the economies of individual LDCs are greatly influenced by world economic conditions, particularly the level of demand from highly industrialized countries for their major exports. Moreover, a military regime's economic policies may either negatively or positively influence the performance of civilian government that replaces it. Thus, for example, some military governments have stimulated short-term economic growth by borrowing excessively from foreign banks or institutions. But in doing so, they bequeathed high inflation and a debt crisis to their civilian successors. Few analytical comparisons have been able to control for all such factors. In general, though, cross-national statistical research has uncovered *little difference* between the economic growth rates of democratic and military governments, though in some regions (including Sub-Saharan Africa), civilian governments have outperformed military regimes.

MILITARY WITHDRAWAL FROM POLITICS

Once the armed forces have become entrenched in the political system, dislodging them is usually no easy task. Domestic protests (Indonesia) or external intervention (Uganda) sometimes induce the military to withdraw from power. More often, however, the armed forces voluntarily relinquish power for one or more of the following reasons: having accomplished their major objectives, they see no value in retaining power; deteriorating economic conditions make continued rule unappealing; extended rule has undermined internal military cohesion; or the regime has become so unpopular that staying in office would reduce the military's legitimacy as an institution.

Many military governments come into office as "caretakers" whose goal is to restore stability or solve a particular problem quickly and then return control to civilians. In Ecuador, for example, the armed forces frequently ousted elected leaders whom they considered too demagogic, too populist, or too incompetent. After ruling relatively briefly, they then voluntarily stepped down.

Because the perpetrators of institutional coups usually take power with expectations of augmenting military budgets and accelerating economic growth, their interest in governing, not surprisingly, wanes if the economy turns sour (as it does for at least some period of time in many LDCs). In countries such as Peru, Uruguay, and Thailand, economic downturns have convinced military governments to step down. These declines may also aggravate internal divisions within the armed forces.

In Sub-Saharan Africa, military rule may also aggravate ethnic tensions within the armed forces, particularly when officers from one tribe or religion dominate top government positions. For example, in Nigeria, the military's entry into the political arena unleashed four internal coups in a ten-year span, with ethnic divisions playing an important role. Two heads of government and a number of other senior officers were killed in the military's internal struggles. Elsewhere, other military governments, fearing similar deteriorations in military cohesiveness, have preferred to step down, leaving the nation's problems to civilian governments. In some countries, soldiers from one tribe or ethnic group may dominate the armed forces. For example, in Togo as of 2005, the Kabyé tribe made up only 15 percent of the country's population but constituted 70 percent of all soldiers and 90 percent of the officer corps. Ultimate power has been in the hands of a Kabyé military dictator who ruled the country for thirty-eight years (1967–2005) and his son who has reigned since 2005.

Just as military coups are most likely to take place when civilian governments lack legitimacy, the army is most likely to return to the barracks when its own legitimacy declines. This happens most dramatically when the country has been defeated in war. For example, following its humiliating defeat by the British in the Falklands (or Malvinas) war, the Argentine military regime was forced to step down. And Pakistan's military had to transfer power to its leading civilian critic after it lost East Pakistan (now Bangladesh) in a war with India.

In recent years, influential nations and international organizations in both developed countries and LDCs have taken a stronger stance against military takeovers. Thus, countries such as Madagascar and Ecuador, which have had coups during that period, found themselves isolated in the African Union (AU) or the Organization of American States (OAS) until they restored civilian government. Moreover, in 2009, the OAS unanimously ousted Honduras from that organization shortly after that country's armed forces removed an elected president, who was replaced with a more conservative civilian official. The coup was universally condemned by governments of all political stripes, whereas such a coup would have gone virtually unnoticed in decades past. Later in that year, both the European Union and the Economic Community of West African States imposed an arms embargo on Guinea when its military government's soldiers fired on opposition protesters, killing some 150 of them.

During the Cold War (1945–1991), the United States had worked closely with a number of military governments, occasionally even encouraging military coups against elected leftist governments (in Brazil and Chile, for example). Since the 1990s, however, it has opposed most military takeovers while members of the world community generally have toughened their position against military governments.

But these international pressures are usually ineffective unless the military has also lost its legitimacy at home. In Uruguay, economic decay and public revulsion against the regime's political repression so weakened the military government that it unexpectedly lost a national referendum that it had been confident it could tightly control. Eventually, popular discontent induced the generals to negotiate a return to civilian government. Similarly, in 1992, in Thailand, massive student-led prodemocracy demonstrations convinced the armed forces to withdraw. And in 2008, mass protests led by Pakistan's lawyers' association brought down the Pervez Musharraf dictatorship.

While some combination of these factors has accounted for the departure of most military regimes, it has not guaranteed that the armed forces would stay out of power. Indeed, until the 1980s, the soldiers were likely to return to power. Talukder Maniruzzaman examined seventy-one instances of military withdrawal from office from 1946 to 1984. He only considered cases in which military rulers were replaced by civilian government. In 65 percent of these cases examined, the armed forces were back in power within five years.[28] In 2006 the Thai military returned to power for several years and returned again in 2014. And the Pakistani military has been in and out of power a number of times.

This historical record notwithstanding, since the 1990s, those military governments that have stepped down have been more likely to stay out of office. In most of the developing world, there has been a dramatic decline in military rule. This trend has been weaker in Africa, where military governments or quasimilitary governments remain in such nations as Equatorial Guinea, Sudan, Algeria, Uganda, and Rwanda.* For example, as of 2015, the Latin American nations of Argentina, Ecuador, Brazil, Guatemala, and El Salvador, all with long histories of armed-forces intervention, had enjoyed anywhere from twenty-six to thirty-seven years without military government. In South Korea, decades of military dominance ended in 1993. Even in Sub-Saharan Africa, military regimes in several countries, including Nigeria, Benin, and Congo (Brazzaville), have given way to elected civilian governments in recent times.

In some cases, years of misrule undermined the military's institutional legitimacy. The brutality and incompetence of Argentine military dictatorship (1976–1983) so discredited it that succeeding civilian governments were able to reduce the armed forces to one-third their previous size. Elsewhere, as in Mozambique, El Salvador, and Nicaragua, peace treaties ending long civil wars also mandated sharp reductions in the size of the military.

Ultimately, if the armed forces are to relinquish political power and not return, they will need to find new responsibilities to justify their role in society and their share of the national budget. This is particularly true in countries that face no serious foreign threats. In Latin America and much of Africa, for example, wars between nation-states, as opposed to civil conflicts, have been quite rare. In assigning the military new roles, however, civilian governments must be careful not to involve it in tasks that may draw it back into politics—a danger some analysts see in the Latin American military's growing involvement in the "war on drugs." Furthermore, to *maintain* their restored political power and their control over the armed forces, civilian governments will have to establish more effective civil-military relationships.

NEW ROLES FOR THE ARMED FORCES

Many of the proposed "new roles" for the military are not really entirely new. They include combating drug trafficking (in parts of Latin America, the Caribbean, and Asia), antiterrorist activity, and emergency relief efforts following natural disasters. Unfortunately, in the past, some of these activities have brought as many new problems as solutions. In Mexico, Colombia, the Caribbean, and Central America, antidrug efforts have frequently corrupted the armed forces, as some officers have changed from enforcers to well-paid protectors of the drug cartels.

---

*Quasimilitary governments are nominally headed by civilians but depend on the backing of the military, which is the final authority.

In Mexico, for example, there have even been gun fights between military antidrug units and soldiers who were paid by the drug cartels to protect them. Furthermore, in countries such as Colombia and Sri Lanka, the armed forces have often used their mandates to combat terrorism and internal subversion as carte blanche for violating human rights and crushing peaceful and legitimate political opposition groups.

Another popular military activity is civic action—using troops in projects that are beneficial to the civilian population, such as building roads, medical clinics, sanitation projects, and schools. During the Cold War, U.S. military missions in the LDCs, particularly in Central America, encouraged and financed civic action designed to win local support for the government. Many governments have continued similar projects in countries such as Senegal, Thailand, and the Philippines. Unfortunately, these activities have been far too limited to make a significant dent in national poverty.

Finally, another role for militaries in the LDCs has emerged in recent times. Countries such as Argentina, India, Pakistan, and Uruguay have participated in UN peacekeeping forces in trouble spots such as Bosnia, Cambodia, and the Central African Republic. In addition to the UN missions, West African regional peacekeeping forces helped settle a bloody civil war in Liberia. Peacekeeping troops have sometimes been very effective. But, in cases such as Darfur, they have failed to adequately protect the civilian population. Sometimes—most notably in Burundi, Congo, the Central African Republic, Haiti and Liberia—"peacekeeping" troops have been guilty of raping and pillaging some of the people they were sent to protect.

The Military as the Deciding Factor in the Arab Spring

In the recent wave of prodemocracy uprisings across North Africa and the Middle East, the outside world has correctly focused its attention on the factors that led to the uprising and the character of the people who bravely put their lives on the line for a more open political system. But if we examine these rebellions closely, we find that the most important factor determining the success or failure of each uprising is probably the willingness or reluctance of the armed forces to defend the authoritarian regime.

In both Tunisia and Egypt, the armed forces were widely respected institutions. Early in both protest movements the military made a decision not to use force against the demonstrators despite the fact that Presidents Ben Ali and Mubarak had been high-ranking military officers before taking office. While it is impossible to know whether the two dictators would have been able to hold onto power had the armed forces defended them, at the very least overthrowing those regimes would have taken an enormous toll in human lives. But, the Egyptian case also shows the limits of a democratic transition facilitated by the military. Although the mass uprising coupled with military restraint led to the first democratically elected president in that country's history, the armed forces—long the most powerful force in Egyptian political life—remained as powerful as it always had. When the elected President, Mohamed Morsi, alienated the military, it overthrew him and reinstalled a military dictatorship more repressive than ever.

More so than many Arab nations, Syria is a country highly divided between various ethnic groups: Sunnis, Alawites, Kurds, Christians, and others. The Alawite minority is a sect that split from Shi'ite Islam centuries ago and suffered persecution over the years at the hands of the Sunni majority. Long one of the poorest and least powerful ethnic groups in the country, the Alawites were marginalized from Syrian society. Hence, unlike the Sunnis, they established a somewhat close relationship with the French colonial government that took power after World War I. The French, in turn, encouraged them to enter the colonial army, where they became entrenched in the officers' corps. In 1970, after independence, backed by his fellow Alawite officers, General Hafez al-Assad led a coup that put him in power until his death in 2000, when he was succeeded by his son, Bashar. While ethnically mixed, Syria's armed forces and security units are dominated by Alawite officers. Because the fall of the Assad dynasty would almost certainly strip them of their power and very likely subject them to discrimination, there is little chance that the country's elite troops will abandon the regime.

Improving Civil-Military Relationships

Although there are now far fewer military regimes, in many LDCs, particularly those with prior histories of military dominance, the armed forces continue to interfere frequently in politics. Consequently, civilian governments need to shore up their positions by modernizing and improving civil-military relationships. They must create or strengthen political institutions, attitudes, and behavior that reinforce civilian control.

One important area is the education of military officers. They are normally trained at military academies, often after graduating from military high schools. In the larger and more advanced LDCs, many senior officers continue their education through much of their careers, with the most promising ones attending advanced academies for specialized training. All of these schools are decisive in socializing military officers into the values of both the armed forces and the political system. If those officers are to stay out of national politics, their training must stress the importance of civilian control over the armed forces.

Second, the nation's constitution and legal system must bestow upon the chief executive (president or prime minister) final control over the armed forces. Unfortunately, in some countries, the constitution requires the civilian president to secure the approval of the military high command before appointing the defense minister or promoting the most senior generals and admirals. Other nations require the defense minister to be a military officer. To establish civilian control, governments need to eliminate such restrictions. Indeed, it is best if civilians serve as defense ministers.

Third, the country's political institutions must give the civilian president and defense minister clear and direct control over the armed forces. In the United States, for example, the president is legally the commander in chief and officers who criticize his policies publicly are often relieved of duty. In addition, it is important that the country's parliament or congress determines the defense budget and has some level of oversight (through committee hearings and the like) over the armed forces.

Fourth, an important, but rarely discussed, requirement for civilian dominance is that civilian officials control military intelligence activities. Primarily, these intelligence activities involve clandestine gathering of information at home and possibly abroad regarding national security. But often they also include covert operations. In countries such as Chile under General Pinochet and Pakistan today, military intelligence units have operated as an independent force in defense, foreign, and even domestic policy. For example, Pakistan's powerful Directorate for Inter-Service Intelligence has assisted the Afghan Taliban and probably al-Qaeda in the hopes of having an Afghan ally against India. It also is believed to maintain links to the Pakistani Taliban and to Muslim terrorist groups operating in India.

Finally, government leaders need to walk a fine line in their relationships with the armed forces. While insisting on civilian control, they also need to fund the military sufficiently to protect national security, and they must take seriously the opinions of military commanders in matters related to national defense. To do otherwise would be to invite a coup attempt.

CONCLUSION: DEMOCRACY AND THE MILITARY

By definition, the spread of democracy has reduced the number of military governments. This does not mean that the specter of military takeovers has disappeared. But, since the 1990s, attempted military coups have been largely limited to Sub-Saharan Africa and, to a lesser extent, Asia.

Even in democratically elected governments, the armed forces often exercise considerable political influence in certain policy areas.

Furthermore, in a number of countries, the military has remained outside civilian control. For example, in Chile, where General Pinochet's outgoing dictatorship was able to dictate the terms of the 1989 transition to democracy, the new constitution afforded the armed forces considerable influence. The military was granted amnesty for most of its human rights violations, including the murder of some two thousand to three thousand civilians. The elected president lacked authority to remove the military's chief of staff, and the armed forces appointed several members of the senate. General Pinochet himself, as a former president, served initially as senator for life. It took more than ten years until the Chilean Congress was able to end those special powers.

In order to consolidate democracy, LDCs must do more than merely restore elected governments. A stable and secure democracy requires a professionalized military that is committed to staying out of politics. In other words, there must be both "a high level of . . . professionalism and recognition by military officers of the limits of their professional competence" and "subordination of the military to the civilian political leaders who make the basic decisions on foreign and military policy" as well as domestic policy.[29] Officers must largely limit their professional role to defending their country from potential threats and must recognize that their involvement in national politics will only divide the armed forces and diminish their professional capacity. But just as the generals and colonels must keep out of national politics, civilian political leaders must respect the military's domain and not attempt to politicize the armed forces. All too often, aspiring political leaders or political parties who are unable to gain office through legitimate channels have approached the military for support. As David Mares has noted,

> If civilians are willing to accept democracy as a value, it is hard to see how a professional military would be drawn into politics. And if civilians, especially powerful corporate groups, do not accept the rules of the democratic game, it is difficult to see how democracy could be consolidated whether or not the military intervenes.[30]

Even the most successful military governments inhibit political development. They do so because their very rationale for taking office is "the politics of antipolitics." With their hierarchical perspective and their distaste for disorder, military commanders believe in a managed society. Most reject the give-and-take of political competition and the compromises inherent in politics. Consequently, they

> fail to see the functional aspects of the great game of politics: They severely restrict the free flow of the political process and force would-be politicians into a long period of hibernation. . . . The opportunity for

gaining political skills by a people once under a military regime is continually postponed by every new military regime.[31]

Practice and Review Online
http://textbooks.rowman.com/handelman8e#ch8

KEY TERMS

BA (bureaucratic authoritarian) regimes
coup (coup d'état)
crony capitalism
institutional military government (regime)

internal warfare
MNCs (multinational corporations)
personalistic military regimes

DISCUSSION QUESTIONS

1. Why do most political scientists today have a negative view of military rule in the LDCs? Under what circumstances, if any, might military government be a good thing for the country?
2. Discuss why you think the armed forces of developed countries such as the United States or Canada do not attempt military coups.
3. Where have military regimes successfully developed economies and where have they failed to do so? What seems to account for the difference?
4. What important role did the military play in determining the outcome of recent prodemocracy uprisings in the Arab World? Discuss how that role varied from country to country.

NOTES

1. Harold Crouch, *The Army and Politics in Indonesia* (Ithaca, NY: Cornell University Press, 1978), 345.
2. William Thompson, "Explanations of the Military Coup," PhD dissertation, University of Washington, Seattle, 1972, 11. Quoted in Amos Perlmutter, *The Military and Politics in Modern Times* (New Haven, CT: Yale University Press, 1977), 115.
3. Claude E. Welch, "Military Disengagements from Politics: Incentives and Obstacles in Political Change," in *Military Power and Politics in Black Africa*, ed. Simon Baynham (New York: St. Martin's Press, 1986), 89–90.
4. Samuel Decalo, *Coups and Army Rule in Africa* (New Haven, CT: Yale University Press, 1990), 2.
5. Patrick J. McGowan, "African Military Coups D'état, 1956–2001: Frequency, Trends and Distribution," *Journal of Modern African Studies* 41, no. 3 (September 2003): 339.

6. Morris Janowitz, *Military Institutions and Coercion in the Developing Nations: Expanded Edition of the Military in the Political Development of New Nations* (Chicago, IL: University of Chicago Press, 1977), 105.

7. Samuel P. Huntington, *Political Order in Changing Societies* (New Haven, CT: Yale University Press, 1968), 194.

8. Robert Wesson, "Preface," in *New Military Politics in Latin America*, ed. Robert Wesson (New York: Praeger, 1982), v.

9. Samuel E. Finer, *The Man on Horseback: The Role of the Military in Politics*, 2nd ed. (London: Penguin Books, 1976), 78–82.

10. Samuel P. Huntington, "Reforming Civil-Military Relations," in *Civil–Military Relations and Democracy*, eds. Larry Diamond and Marc F. Plattner (Baltimore, MD: Johns Hopkins University Press, 1996), 9. Italics added.

11. Marion J. Levy Jr., *Modernization and the Structure of Societies* (Princeton, NJ: Princeton University Press, 1966), vol. 2, 603.

12. Lucian W. Pye, "Armies in the Process of Political Modernization," in *The Role of the Military in Underdeveloped Countries*, ed. John J. Johnson (Princeton, NJ: Princeton University Press, 1962), 69–89.

13. Manfred Halpern, *The Politics of Social Change in the Middle East and North Africa* (Princeton, NJ: Princeton University Press, 1963), 75, 253.

14. Karen L. Remmer, *Military Rule in Latin America* (Boston, MA: Unwin Hyman, 1989), 3.

15. Eric A. Nordlinger, *Soldiers in Politics: Military Coups and Governments* (Englewood Cliffs, NJ: Prentice Hall, 1977), 173; also Huntington, *Political Order*, chap. 4.

16. Huntington, *Political Order*, 221.

17. Decalo, *Coups and Army Rule in Africa*, 133.

18. Jeffrey Lunstead, "The Armed Forces in Bangladesh Society," in *The Armed Forces in Contemporary Asian Society*, eds. Edward A Olsen et al. (Boulder, CO: Westview Press, 1986), 316.

19. Ruth First, *Power in Africa* (New York: Pantheon Books, 1970), 20.

20. "The Political Orientation Speech Delivered by Captain Thomas Sankara in Ouagadougou, Upper Volta, on October 2, 1983," in *Military Marxist Regimes in Africa*, eds. John Markakis and Michael Waller (London: Frank Cass, 1986), 145–53 (selected portions).

21. Samuel Decalo, "The Morphology of Radical Military Rule in Africa," in *Military Marxist Regimes in Africa*, 123.

22. Samuel Decalo, "Military Rule in Africa: Etiology and Morphology," in *Military Power and Politics in Black Africa*, 56, 58.

23. J. Bayo Adekanye, "The Post-Military State in Africa," in *The Political Dilemma of Military Regimes*, eds. Christopher Clapham and George Philip (London: Croom Helm, 1985), 87.

24. Decalo, *Coups and Army Rule in Africa*, 20.

25. McGowan, "African Military Coups D'état, 1956–2001," 347.

26. Nordlinger, *Soldiers in Politics*, 139.

27. Remmer, *Military Rule*, 40.

28. Talukder Maniruzzaman, *Military Withdrawal from Politics: A Comparative Study* (Cambridge, MA: Ballinger Publishing, 1987), 21, 24–25.

29. Huntington, "Reforming Civil-Military Relations," 3–4.

30. David R. Mares, "Civil-Military Relations, Democracy, and the Regional Neighbors," in *Civil-Military Relations*, ed. David R. Mares (Boulder, CO: Westview Press, 1998), 18, 59–75.

31. Brian Loveman and Thomas M. Davies Jr., eds., *The Politics of Antipolitics: The Military in Latin America*, 2nd ed. (Lincoln: University of Nebraska Press, 1989), 6.

9

The Political Economy of the Developing World

★ ★ ★

Factory workers in Tianjin, China. Since the 1960s a number of developing nations have become important industrial exporters, particularity in Asia—in countries such as Taiwan, South Korea, Singapore, India, and especially China—but also in Latin America—particularly Brazil, Argentina, Chile, and Mexico. *AP/Xiao Chu*

ALL GOVERNMENTS, except the most corrupt and incompetent, wish to promote economic development. Economic growth, coupled with reasonably equitable income distribution, offers the promise of improved living standards and, presumably, increased popular support for the ruling regime, at least in the long run.* It also provides added tax revenues, which enhance government capacity. And, economic development can augment a nation's military strength, diplomatic influence, and international prestige. But, the obvious benefits of growth should not obscure the many difficult questions that economic development policy entails. What government policies best promote economic growth and how can the conflicting goals of economic development be reconciled? How should countries share the inevitable sacrifices required for generating early economic development? How can a nation achieve economic development without doing irreparable harm to the environment?

During the 1980s, the optimism of early modernization theorists looked ill-founded in light of sharp economic declines in Africa and Latin America. Even today, despite some obvious progress, the war on poverty sometimes seems unwinnable in much of South Asia and Sub-Saharan Africa. At the same time, however, East Asia's spectacular growth since the 1960s and India's takeoff since the mid-1990s appear to belie dependency theory's pervasive pessimism about the limits of economic development in the periphery.

In recent decades, a substantial amount of the scholarship on LDCs has focused on its *political economy*. Martin Staniland defines this field as the study of "how politics determines aspects of the economy, and how economic institutions determine the political process," as well as "the dynamic interaction between the two forces."[1] This chapter focuses on several important issues: What should be the role of the state in stimulating and regulating economic growth and industrialization? What are the major strategies for development? How should countries deal with the deep economic inequalities that normally persist, or even increase, during the early modernization process?

THE ROLE OF THE STATE

The question of the state's proper economic role has been at the center of political and economic debates for hundreds of years, first in Western

---

*We have seen that in the short term, economic growth may be politically destabilizing. However, if growth is coupled with equitable income distribution, the chances of unrest diminish.

industrial economies, and more recently in the LDCs. During the sixteenth and seventeenth centuries, major European powers were guided by the philosophy of *mercantilism*, which looked at a nation's economic activity as a means of enhancing the political power of the state and its monarch. Consequently, mercantilists saw government as "both source and beneficiary of economic growth."[2] This perspective, however, drew the fire of the eighteenth-century Scottish economist Adam Smith, who favored a very limited state that gave market forces a free hand. The following century, Karl Marx, reacting to the exploitative nature of early capitalism, proposed giving the state a dominant economic role, at least initially, through ownership of the means of production and centralized planning. Finally, the twentieth-century economist Sir John Maynard Keynes, responding to the Great Depression, advocated a substantial degree of government economic intervention, but rejected Marxist prescriptions for state ownership and centralized planning.

In recent times, the collapse of the Soviet bloc's centrally controlled economy and the implementation of free-market (capitalist) reforms in communist countries, such as China and Vietnam, have discredited the advocates of state-controlled economies. At the same time, however, no government embraces full **laissez faire** (i.e., allowing market forces completely free reign, with no government intervention). All countries, for example, no matter how capitalistic, have laws regulating banking, domestic commerce, and international trade. Most have introduced some environmental regulations and work-safety rules. In the real world, then, governments must decide where to position themselves between the extreme poles of an unregulated economy and a command economy (an economy that is under centralized—state—control).

For a number of reasons, this choice is particularly contentious in the developing world. The fragile nature of less developed economies, their high level of poverty, their frequently poor distribution of wealth and income, their dependence on international market forces, and their relatively unchecked damage to the environment, all have encouraged many governments to assume an active economic role. Moreover, many developing nations lack a strong entrepreneurial class and sufficient private capital for investment. As a consequence, their governments have often built the steel mills, railroads, and sugar refineries that the private sector could not or would not provide. More recently, governments have been asked to protect the environment against the ravages of economic growth. Not surprisingly, then, state economic intervention traditionally has been more pronounced in the developing world than in the West. Since the 1980s, however, the spread of neoliberal economic policies— characterized by free trade, free markets, and relatively unrestrained capitalism—has sharply reduced government economic intervention in both the developing and the developed worlds.*

This chapter discusses a number of alternate models prescribing the role of the state in developing economies, ranging from command economies, such as North Korea's, to very limited state intervention, as in Hong Kong and Singapore. In considering these alternatives, the reader should keep in mind that these are ideal types. Few countries fit any of these models perfectly. Cuba's Marxist government, for example, permits private farming and some other small businesses. Also, many nations have introduced some mix of these approaches. While the options discussed below are not exhaustive, they cover the models most widely used in the LDCs today.

The Command Economy

Marxism began as a critique of capitalism in the Western world during the early stages of industrial development. Inherently, argued Karl Marx, capitalism produced an inequitable distribution of wealth and income with those who control the means of production (industrialists, landlords) exploiting those who worked for them (the working class, peasants). One of Marxism's appeals to its supporters was its promise of great equality and social justice. Because economic inequality often intensifies in the early stages of development, the ideology had special appeal for activists in the LDCs.

Marxist advocates further assert that only a revolutionary, political-economic system can free the LDCs from the yoke of dependency. That is to say, because dependency theorists believe that capitalist trade and investment in developing countries creates an exploitative relationship between core (industrial) nations and the periphery, they argued that radical change was needed.

Finally, another of Communism's appeals was its establishment of a centralized state control of the economy. A **command economy**, first established in the Soviet Union, has two central features. First, the state largely owns and manages the means of production. This includes factories, banks, major trade and commercial institutions, retail establishments, and, frequently, farms. While all communist nations have allowed some private economic activity, the private sector has been quite limited (aside from nations such as China and Vietnam, which have largely

---

*Originally, liberalism—first formulated as an ideology in the eighteenth century—advocated greater individual liberty (hence the name liberal) and less government intervention into people's lives, including their economic activities. Today, outside of the United States, the terms liberal, neoliberal policies, and **economic liberalization** normally refer to policies that *reduce* the role of government in the economy, contrary to the way the term liberal is used in the United States.

abandoned Marxist economics in recent years). Second, in a command economy, state planners, rather than market forces, shape basic decisions governing production.

Interestingly, Marxism saw market (capitalist) economies as anarchistic because they leave the most fundamental decisions about the allocation of resources and the determination of prices to the "whims" of supply and demand. Thus, Adam Przeworski has satirized the orthodox Marxists' attitude toward capitalism's "**invisible** [guiding] **hand**": people in capitalist countries such as Britain and Germany get up each morning and find their newspapers or milk bottles already sitting outside their doors without even knowing who delivered them. Yet, Przeworski notes wryly, orthodox Marxist theory insisted that the paper or milk bottle could not possibly have arrived without a central planner guaranteeing its delivery.[3] But, in reality, he observes, under a centrally planned economy, not only is home delivery unreliable, but there are also recurrent shortages of paper, milk containers, and milk. Ultimately, the collapse of Soviet and Eastern European Communism revealed the organizational failures of centralized command economies.

In fact, the command economy's flaws are so obvious today that most people are unaware of its earlier accomplishments. By dictating the movement of people and resources from one sector of the economy to another, communist countries such as the Soviet Union and China were able to jump-start their industrial development. During the 1920s and 1930s, "Entire industries were created [in the USSR], along with millions of jobs that drew peasants away from the countryside and into higher-paying jobs and higher living standards."[4] Western estimates of Soviet economic performance during its early industrialization phase indicate that between 1928 and 1955, GNP grew at a robust average annual rate of about 5 percent. After its revolution, China also moved quickly from a backward, agrarian economy to a far more industrialized society. According to a leading authority, between 1952 and 1975, that country's economy grew at an average annual rate of 8.2 percent, while industrial output surged ahead at 11.5 percent annually.[5] These rates far exceeded the norms in either capitalist developing nations or industrialized democracies. Other analysts believe that its growth rate could not have been that high because of the setbacks of the "**Great Leap Forward**" and the Cultural Revolution. Still, all agree that compared to Mexico, Pakistan, and most LDCs, China's growth during that period, like the Soviet Union's decades earlier, was very impressive. Small wonder that many LDCs were once attracted to the Soviet and Chinese communist development models.

Finally, command economies have frequently made great strides toward reducing income inequalities. Indeed, it is in this area that some communist LDCs clearly outperformed their capitalist counterparts.

In Cuba, for example, the revolution brought a substantial transfer of income from the richest 20 percent of the population to the poorest 40 percent. The poor also benefited from land reform, subsidized rents, and free health care, though some of those gains were undermined in the 1990s, following the loss of Soviet economic assistance. Greater educational opportunities for all and an extensive adult literacy program further advanced social equality. Nor was Cuba unique in this respect. Cross-national statistical comparisons indicate that communist countries as a whole had more equal income distribution than did capitalist nations at similar levels of development.

Eventually, however, the weaknesses of command economies overshadow their accomplishments.* Lacking measures of consumer demand, state planners have little basis for deciding what to produce and how much. Furthermore, centrally controlled economies typically reward producers for meeting their output quotas, with little concern for product quality. Even in the best of circumstances, to be at all efficient, a centralized command economy would need a highly skilled and honest bureaucracy equipped with sophisticated and accurate consumer surveys. Unfortunately, bureaucracies in the developing world rarely have these qualities. In addition, command economies handed inordinate power to state planners. And as Lord Acton once warned, "Power tends to corrupt, and absolute power tends to corrupt absolutely."

Thus, for example, Chinese private-business entrepreneurs know that the price of doing business is bribing government officials (cadres) or their adult children. Elsewhere as well, command economies have featured a large privileged class of state and party bureaucrats (*apparatchiks*), who enjoy perquisites unavailable to the rest of the population. Furthermore, while the Soviet Union and China enjoyed rapid growth in the early decades of their revolutions, both economies eventually lost momentum as they became more complex and therefore harder to control centrally. Finally, command economies are more adept at building heavy industries such as steel mills or public works projects—projects more common in the early stages of industrialization—than they are at developing sophisticated high-tech production techniques or at producing quality consumer goods. The Soviet Union, for example, turned out impressive military hardware and powerful space rockets, but was unable to produce a decent automobile or washing machine.

By the late 1970s in China and the 1980s in the Soviet Union, as both economies deteriorated, their leaders (Deng Xiaoping and Mikhail

---

*Of course, all command economies are also controlled by politically repressive governments. But this chapter analyzes only the economic record of command economies and not their politics.

Gorbachev, respectively) recognized the need for economic decentralization and reduced state economic control. China's subsequent transition to **market socialism** (a mix of free market and socialist economics) produced the world's second largest economy. However, in the Soviet Union and its major successor state, Russia, reforms resulted in an economic collapse that lasted for nearly a decade. The fall of Soviet bloc Communism and China's remarkable economic transformation have inspired market-oriented reforms in other command economies. Vietnam, for example, has transferred state farmland to the peasantry, attracted billions of dollars in foreign investment, and transferred a substantial portion of its industrial production from the state to the private sector. Elsewhere in Asia and Africa, governments such as Burma and Republic of the Congo (Brazzaville) have privatized much of the state sector (i.e., sold government-owned enterprises to private owners) and reduced government economic controls. The end of Soviet aid has undercut some of Cuba's gains in health care, nutrition, and education. Stripped of its primary benefactor, it too has been forced to accept limited free-market innovations.

In the former communist nations of Eastern and Central Europe, the demise of their command economies initially failed to improve living standards and usually lowered them sharply. Only in China and Vietnam did the transition toward free-market economics rapidly raise standards of living. In Eastern and Central Europe, especially Russia, it took a decade or more for living standards to equal or surpass their levels in the communist era.

Latin American Statism

Even in capitalist LDCs, the state has often played a major economic role, trying to be an engine of economic growth. In the period between the two World Wars, a number of Latin American nations first pursued state-led industrialization. This process accelerated during the Great Depression of the 1920s and 1930s, when countries in the region had difficulty finding markets for their food and raw material exports and, consequently had insufficient foreign exchange for industrial imports. Argentina, Brazil, and Mexico were among the early leaders in the push toward industrialization.

Unlike communist countries, Latin American nations left most economic activity in the hands of the private sector and did not centralize control of the economy. But their governments often owned strategically important enterprises and invested in industries that failed to attract sufficient private capital. Consequently, prior to the recent **privatization** of state enterprises, many of the region's railroads, airlines, petroleum companies, mines, steel mills, electric power plants, and telephone companies were state owned (though many of them originally had been built by foreign corporations that were subsequently nationalized).

In a number of ways, state ownership in the region contradicted common stereotypes. First, many government takeovers were supported by the business community. To begin with, the most important **nationalizations** (transfers of private firms to state ownership)—including the seizures of the petroleum industries in Mexico and Venezuela, mining operations in Chile and Peru, and railroads in Argentina—only affected companies that had been owned by foreign corporations rather than local capitalists. Second, after taking control of the petroleum industry, railroads, and utilities, the state often provided the country's private-sector industries with subsidized and inexpensive transportation, power, and other needed resources. In fact, until the 1980s, conservative governments in the region were as likely to expand government ownership as were left-leaning or **populist** regimes. For example, during the 1960s and 1970s, Brazil's right-wing, military regime substantially increased the size of the state sector. Such nationalizations typically were broadly popular and bolstered the government's legitimacy as a defender of national interests.

In addition to owning a number of essential enterprises, the state also played a pivotal role in fomenting private-sector industrial growth. In Latin America's largest economies, the government initiated **import-substituting industrialization (ISI)** programs in the early to mid-twentieth century. ISI (discussed more extensively later in this chapter) sought to replace imported consumer goods with domestically manufactured products. Import-substituting firms were normally privately owned, but depended heavily on government support. This included protective tariffs and quotas on competing imports, favorable exchange rates, subsidized energy and transport costs, and low-interest loans.

In countries such as Argentina, Brazil, Chile, and Mexico, these government-supported development policies were initially quite successful. From 1945 to 1970, rates of investment in Latin America were higher than in the Western industrial nations, and from 1960 to 1980, the region's manufacturing output grew faster as well.[6] Virtually every Latin American country began manufacturing basic consumer goods such as textiles, clothing, packaged food, and furniture. Larger nations such as Argentina, Brazil, and Mexico established automotive plants, steel mills, and other heavy industries. In time, industrialization altered the region's demographic and class structures. Massive rural migration to the cities transformed Latin America into the developing world's most urbanized region (see chapter 6). For decades, ISI also created blue-collar jobs and expanded the size of the middle class.

But hidden beneath these accomplishments, this strategy also promoted economic inefficiencies and income inequality. While it may have been necessary for the government to nurture industrialization in the early stages of economic development, Latin American countries maintained protectionist measures and subsidies too broadly and too long. Rather than serving as a finely calibrated tool for getting industrialization off the ground, ISI became a politically motivated juggernaut. With industrialists, the middle class, and organized labor all united behind these policies, elected officials were unwilling to wean established industries from government support and protection long after they should have become self-sufficient. Inefficient domestic industries received excessive protection; trade and fiscal policies designed to promote industrialization often harmed agricultural exports; and the income gaps widened between the urban and rural populations, between the urban middle and lower classes, and between skilled and unskilled urban workers.

Mexico illustrates both the initial accomplishments and the subsequent weaknesses of statism in the region. From the mid-1930s to 1970, the national government supplied 35–40 percent of the country's total capital investment. At the same time, the state petroleum, electric power, and railroad companies provided private industry with subsidized energy and transportation by selling those items at a loss. Government trade and labor policies protected Mexican companies from foreign competition and held down domestic wages as a means of stimulating domestic investment. As a consequence, between 1935 and 1970, industrial output grew at an average yearly rate of nearly 10 percent and GNP rose 6 percent annually, making Mexico one of the world's fastest-growing economies at that time. During the 1970s and early 1980s, however, the state's role in the economy spiraled out of control. By 1985, the government operated nearly 1,200 state enterprises (**parastatals**), involved in everything from petroleum extraction to food sales. At the same time, however, even during this era of strong economic growth, Mexico's "economic miracle" left the rural population and the urban poor behind, creating a highly unequal distribution of income and leaving substantial pockets of poverty.

Overall, Latin America's development model introduced two important areas of inefficiency, both of which typify state-led industrial growth elsewhere in the developing world. First, a large number of state-owned enterprises were overstaffed and poorly run. Contrary to the common stereotype, state enterprises are not inherently inefficient. In advanced economies such as France and Norway, governments have operated some enterprises quite productively. But few governments in the less developed world have the skilled and disciplined personnel needed to perform at that level. Furthermore, given the high rate of unemployment in almost all the LDCs, their governments are under great political pressure to hire more employees, whether the state enterprises need them or not. Consequently, parastatals are typically substantially overstaffed, with many employees who do little or nothing.

At the same time, labor unions and middle-class groups also have lobbied state enterprises to sell consumer goods and services at highly discounted prices. For example, in the past, Argentineans rode the state railroads for a nominal fee and received highly subsidized electricity in their homes. Elsewhere in the region, governments have subsidized or controlled prices for items such as gasoline, urban bus fares, and food. Ultimately, the combination of money-losing parastatals, consumer subsidies, and subsidies to private-sector producers helped bankrupt many Latin American governments. By 1982, virtually every government in the region was deeply in debt and suffering from severe fiscal problems.

A second important weakness of Latin America's development model was the inefficiency ISI policies encourage in the private sector. To be sure, governments throughout the world have effectively used protectionist measures to help infant industries get started during the early stages of development. Typically, in the ISI model, the state creates a wall of high import tariffs and quotas to protect emerging local manufacturers from foreign competition. But over time, the government needs to scale back the level of protection or else domestic firms will have little incentive to become more efficient and internationally competitive. But Latin American protectionism, rather than serving as a temporary stimulus, became embedded in the economy.

From the early 1980s to the mid-1990s, the region's severe debt crisis and economic depression compelled almost all Latin American nations to reverse their statist economic policies. For example, the Mexican government closed or privatized more than 80 percent of the country's 1,155 state enterprises, including the national airline, telephone companies, and banks. In Chile, the transition to a slimmed-down state began during the dictatorship of General Augusto Pinochet (1973–1990). But when democracy was restored, the new governing coalition (including the once-radical Socialist party) continued many of Pinochet's economic policies that they had once denounced.

While these reductions in public-sector activity were necessary, they also carried a great human cost. Throughout Latin America in the 1980s and early 1990s, millions of public- and private-sector workers lost their jobs, as the new owners of privatized parastatals fired excess workers as the region endured its most serious economic recession since the 1930s. Many other state-owned, money-losing plants simply shut down. In Mexico the government's economic restructuring program eliminated an estimated 400,000 jobs. For example, more than half the workers formerly employed in state steel mills were laid off when their companies were privatized. Argentina, Chile, Peru, and Venezuela had similar experiences. At the same time, reduced protectionism in much of the region opened the door to a surge of imported consumer goods, further slashing sales and jobs in local firms that were unable to compete. Finally, the reduction or elimination of government consumer subsidies sharply increased the cost of basic necessities including bread, milk, and rice.

In Mexico and Argentina, just as in Chile, populist and left-wing parties that had once been the leading advocates of government economic intervention reluctantly conceded that the state sector had grown too unwieldy and needed to be cut back. Excessive government spending, coupled with the middle and upper classes' failure to pay their fair share of taxes, had resulted in massive fiscal deficits and runaway inflation. Only by substantially cutting budgetary deficits since the 1980s have Latin America's governments been able to control inflation, which had reached rates over 1,000 percent annually in Argentina, Brazil, Nicaragua, and Peru. The debt crisis and the related economic recession contributed to a sharp decline in Latin American living standards from the early 1980s to the early 1990s (the lost decade). In Peru and Venezuela, for example, real incomes (wages that are adjusted for inflation and purchasing power) fell by nearly 40 percent.[7]

Since the 1990s, inflation has been brought under control. At the same time, the region's economy has grown at a healthier rate—more rapidly than North America's or Europe's, but not as fast as Africa's or Asia's. However, while most analysts agree that Latin America's level of state economic interventionism and protectionism had been excessive, reforms designed to scale down government often have not improved living standards, at least initially.

East Asia's Developmental State

In contrast to Latin America's economies, many Asian nations have grown at a phenomenal rate since the 1970s. South Korea, Taiwan, Hong Kong, Singapore, and China once received the most attention. But recently, India has made tremendous strides. Their impact on world trade has been enormous. China is now the world's leading exporter of manufactured goods. But several Southeast Asian economies—such as Thailand, Malaysia, and Indonesia—have also grown dramatically. From the mid-1960s until the region's financial crisis in 1997–1998, Taiwan, South Korea, Singapore, Hong Kong, Thailand, Malaysia, Indonesia, and China all grew at annual rates ranging from 4 to 10 percent, and China and South Korea sometimes exceeded those rates.[8] In fact, from 1960 to the late 1990s, these economies grew almost three times as fast as Latin America's and five times as fast as Sub-Saharan Africa's. While a number of East and Southeast Asian economies had serious setbacks during the late 1990s crisis, they quickly resumed rapid development. Moreover, the benefits of East and Southeast Asia's rapid growth have been distributed relatively equitably, with a far narrower gap between the rich and poor than in Latin America or Africa.

With the exception of Communist China and Vietnam (which have mixed socialist and free-market economies and thus lie outside the "East Asian model"), most East and Southeast Asian countries have tied their growth to the free market. More than in other regions, the private sector has controlled most of the economy, with a relatively small state sector. Predictably, this has led conservative economists to hail the East Asian economic miracle as a triumph of unfettered capitalism, a testimony to keeping government out of the economy.

But many East Asian specialists insist that, on the contrary, governments in that region were key players in stimulating economic growth.[9] Examining the causes of Japan's spectacular postwar economic resurgence, Chalmers Johnson first formulated the notion of the **developmental state**.[10] We can best understand the meaning of this term by comparing the role of government in East Asia's high-growth capitalist nations to its function in Western nations during their initial industrial expansions some 150 years earlier. At that time, Western nations created *regulatory states* in which "government refrained from interfering in the marketplace, except to insure certain limited goals" (e.g., banking regulation). In contrast, the East Asian developmental states "intervene actively in the economy in order to guide or promote particular substantive goals" (e.g., full employment, export competitiveness, or energy self-sufficiency).[11]

Japan's powerful Ministry of International Trade and Industry (MITI), Johnson noted, directed the country's postwar industrial resurgence. Subsequently, South Korea, Taiwan, Singapore, Indonesia, and other industrializing nations in East and Southeast Asia adopted many features of Japan's state-guided, capitalist development model. Typically, each country had a powerful government ministry or agency "charged with the task of planning, guiding, and coordinating industrial policies."[12] They included South Korea's Economic Planning Board, Taiwan's Council for Economic Planning and Development, and Singapore's Economic Development Board, all modeled after MITI. Under the developmental state, their government economic intervention was far more extensive and direct than in the West, targeting entire economic sectors (such as agriculture or industry), whole industries (such as computers, software, and automobiles), and particular companies (such as South Korea's Hyundai).

All of the developmental states did not pursue identical policies. For example, the bonds between government and big business have been tighter in South Korea than in Taiwan, while state enterprises have been more important in Taiwan. In Singapore, government control over labor has been more comprehensive than in the other two countries. But in all of them, the state played an important role, guiding the private sector toward targeted economic activities and stimulating growth in areas that the government wished to expand. Sometimes, government planners even pressured particular industries or companies to specialize in certain products and abandon others.

For example, when the South Korean and Taiwanese governments wished to develop the electronics and computer industries, they intervened aggressively, rather than leaving it to the marketplace. They established relevant research institutes; granted firms in the targeted industries' preferential access to credit; temporarily required companies that had been importing those targeted products to switch to domestic manufacturers; and offered trade protection to new industries for limited periods of time. South Korea temporarily banned all imports of computers when it promoted that industry, and Taiwan did the same for textiles.[13]

While the East Asian development model's tremendous success has earned it widespread admiration, some observers have remained skeptical about its applicability elsewhere. One concern is the model's apparent political requirements. Most developmental states have been authoritarian—or what Johnson calls "soft authoritarian"—during their major industrialization push. Authoritarian rule allowed government to repress or control labor unions and to direct management. Taiwan, South Korea, and Indonesia all industrialized under authoritarian governments, though they have subsequently democratized. The governments of Malaysia and Singapore continue to repress democratic expression in varying degrees. Hence, there is some doubt about how the developmental state would perform under the democratic pressures now spreading across the developing world. Still, India's very impressive economic growth since 1991 addresses some of those doubts. It has adopted some elements of the East Asian development model while maintaining its democratic government.

Another important question is the transferability of East Asian political and economic institutions and policies to other parts of the developing world. The developmental state seems to require qualities that are in short supply in other developing areas: a highly skilled government bureaucracy and close cooperation between business, labor, and agriculture. In Indonesia, for example, a team of government economists known as "the Berkeley Boys" (most of them holding doctoral degrees in economics from the University of California at Berkeley) oversaw the country's economic development. India's government bureaucracy is not as highly regarded, but macroeconomic planning in that country has been in the hands of some of the world's best economists (many of them having doctoral degrees from Oxford University).

South Korea's highly trained state technocrats worked closely with the country's all-powerful business conglomerates (*chaebols*), such as Hyundai and Samsung. Similar cooperation between sophisticated government planners and big business, together with a relatively docile working class, contributed to economic surges elsewhere in East and Southeast Asia. Outside of Asia, however, only Chile's "Chicago Boys" (economists trained at the University of Chicago) brought a comparable set of skills and enjoyed similar support from government and the business community.

While it is very possible that the model will eventually spread, few African, Latin American, or Middle Eastern nations currently offer promising conditions for its use. Furthermore, current free-trade regulations and neoliberal prescriptions (described immediately below) from the World Trade Organization (WTO) mean that future industrial development will probably involve less state intervention than in the initial East Asian model.

The Neoliberal Model

Quite unlike the preceding models, **neoliberal economics** assigns government a very limited economic role. The state, it argues, should provide certain fundamental "public goods" such as national defense, police protection, a judicial system, and an educational system. It may also supply a physical infrastructure, including sewers and harbors, when it is not feasible for private capital to do so. And, perhaps it should allocate some resources to meet the most basic needs of the very poor. But neoliberal economists believe that most of the governments in the developing world have injured their economies by moving far beyond that limited role. These critics attribute Africa's and Latin America's earlier economic development problems to excessive state intervention, while they credit East and Southeast Asia's success to their governments' allegedly limited role.

Neoliberals insist that free-market forces should determine production decisions and set prices without government interference. Consequently, they condemn state policies designed to stimulate industrial growth: protective tariffs and import quotas that restrict free trade and thereby drive up prices to the consumer; artificial **currency exchange rates** that distort the prices of exports and imports; state subsidies to producers and consumers; and government controls on prices and interest rates. All of these policies, they argue, distort the choices made by producers, consumers, and governments. Only when these artificial constraints are removed, they maintain, will the economy "get prices right" (by letting free-market forces determine them).

For several decades, the neoliberals have generally won the debate against advocates of extensive state intervention.*

As we have observed, in the past few decades, many developing countries (such as India and Mexico) liberalized their economies, deregulating the private sector, privatizing state enterprises, removing trade barriers, and freeing prices. They have also reduced subsidies for industry and for consumers, often out of budgetary necessity. In part, these changes resulted from pressures on the LDCs coming from international lending agencies—such as the World Bank and the IMF—and by the United States. Although only Hong Kong and Singapore come close to the pure neoliberal model, a large number of LDCs have moved in that direction.

While analysts continue to disagree on the broader economic effects of neoliberalism, the evidence seems to indicate that reducing government intervention has often stimulated economic growth, particularly in economies that had earlier imposed extensive state intervention. For example, when India and Chile substantially reduced government's economic role, both embarked on a period of rapid growth. At the same time, however, unfettered capitalist growth often has benefited only a portion of the population, leaving the poor behind. India illustrates this point well. The changeover to a predominantly free-market economy turned that nation into one of the world's fastest-growing major economies.

Yet, so far, less than one-third of the population has benefited from that growth—essentially city dwellers employed in the modern economy, especially the expanding middle class. To be sure, those beneficiaries comprise some 350 million people, certainly no small accomplishment. But, nearly two-thirds of India's population—primarily the barely educated rural poor—have gained little from the boom. Many of the country's most rapidly expanding industries are in the high-tech or tech-support sectors, which primarily hire people with more advanced educations. Furthermore, many of the other new industries (such as auto manufacturing) are **capital-intensive** and generate comparatively few jobs. Thus, despite India's rapid economic growth, almost one half of all children under five suffer from stunting, a form of malnutrition in which children are shorter than normal for their age.[†] Indeed, the childhood malnutrition rate has remained fairly unchanged since the 1990s and is about the

---

*Since the turn of the century, leftist governments have been elected in much of Latin America (including Bolivia, Brazil, Chile, and Venezuela). But, while they have introduced many antipoverty programs, many have moderated their previous positions and have accepted many of their predecessors' neoliberal reforms.

†Even though, on average, Indian children eat more food than most of their Sub-Saharan counterparts, they are still more malnourished. Recent research suggests that this is explained by India's very poor sanitary conditions. Half the population lacks access to toilets and, therefore, defecates outside. This spreads diarrheal disease, which causes malnutrition even among adequately fed children.

same as impoverished Bangladesh and Burkina Faso and over five times as high as in China. Currently, over one million Indian children die of malnutrition every year.[14]

Elsewhere, as in India, the benefits of economic growth have not reached a significant portion of the population and in many countries wealth and income have become more concentrated. For example, Argentina had once enjoyed one of the more equitable income distributions in Latin America, but this has changed drastically. In the mid-1970s, the most prosperous 10 percent of the population had average incomes that were 12 times higher than the poorest 10 percent. But by the mid-1990s, following neoliberal restructuring, this ratio had risen to 18 to 1, and by 2002, the richest 10 percent of the population earned 43 times as much as the poorest 10 percent.[15]

In addition to its tendency to widen income inequality, neoliberal economics has been strongly criticized by environmentalists. From their perspective, even a modified policy of laissez faire that acknowledges some state responsibility for the environment, is inadequate. As Richard Albin noted,

> The idea that private interest, operating within unfettered markets, will tend to produce a close approximation of the socially optimal allocation of resources, was close to the truth when output (population, too) was so much smaller.[16]

But, he argues, as the world's population and associated pollution have reached dangerous levels, society can no longer afford to let free-market mechanisms allocate penalties for pollution. Such remedies would come far too late. Further discussion of economic growth and its impact on the environment follows later in this chapter.

Finding a Proper Role for the State

Political scientists and economists will continue to debate the state's proper role in less developed economies. As time goes on, new models will undoubtedly arise. Still, some areas of agreement have emerged in recent decades. On the one hand, the level of government intervention in both command economies and Latin American statism now seems excessive. On the other hand, the extremely limited government role advocated by the neoliberals appears to be unrealistic and inadequate in most LDCs. East Asia's developmental state model has been the most successful. But, it is unclear whether it can be replicated elsewhere. Indeed, a model that succeeds in one country or region will not necessarily work in another. Countries vary greatly in size, human capital, and natural resources. Thus, cookbook formulas for growth will likely fall short in many countries. As we have noted, the strong hand of the stereotypical developmentalist state—in Japan, South Korea, Singapore, and Taiwan— would have to be modified to meet current trade regulations under the WTO. Finally, new crises—such as the Latin American and African debt crises in the 1980s, the 1997–1998 Asian financial crisis, and the world's deep recession during 2008–2010—have forced planners to alter and adapt their development models.

INDUSTRIALIZATION STRATEGIES

Since the time of Britain's industrial revolution, governments have equated economic development and industrialization with national sovereignty and military strength. Starting in Latin America during the 1930s, industrial growth has been the centerpiece of economic development for many developing nations.

Neoliberal economists criticize industrialization programs in many LDCs, arguing that every country should specialize in economic activities for which it has a "**comparative advantage.**" That is, it should produce and export those goods it can provide most efficiently and cheaply relative to other nations. On the basis of this argument, neoliberals maintained that most less developed nations should abandon plans for industrialization and concentrate, instead, on the production and export of raw materials or agricultural products. Rather than manufacture goods such as cars, washing machines, or fertilizers, they insisted, countries such as Sri Lanka and Kenya would be better off increasing tea or coffee exports—products for which they have a comparative advantage—so they could use those earnings to import manufactured products.

Similarly, they contended that it made little sense for Nigeria to build steel mills or for Uruguay to produce refrigerators. Still, many LDCs have been reluctant to depend fully on revenues from the export of primary goods (agricultural products and raw materials such as coal, iron, and petroleum), because their prices are so volatile. One possible solution (easier said than done) is to pursue balanced growth, including some industrial development (presumably manufacturing products which draw on local natural resources and can be exported), while still stressing production of primary goods for export. For example, Brazil has supplemented its traditional agricultural and mineral exports with extensive manufactured exports, including products such as autos and aircraft.

Until now, industrializing nations have generally pursued one of two alternate strategies: import-substituting industrialization (ISI) and **export-oriented industrialization (EOI).** In the first case, as we have seen, LDCs try to reduce their dependency on manufactured imports by producing more goods, especially consumer goods, at home. Like Latin

America, Asian nations began their industrial development by producing for their own consumption. But, unlike Latin American ISI, which focused on consumer goods for the home market for an extended period of time, East Asian nations soon turned to EOI, linking their industrial development to manufactured exports. Although EOI has been most closely associated with East and Southeast Asia, it is a strategy now widely embraced in Latin America and other parts of the less developed world as well. Having started that strategy later, Latin America and other developing areas have yet to catch up with Asia's export capabilities. Consequently, shirts, blouses, electronics, and running shoes sold in Western department stores are still more likely to be manufactured in China, Singapore, Sri Lanka, Indonesia, or Thailand than in Brazil, Colombia, or Honduras.

Import-Substituting Industrialization

National economic policies are partly the product of deliberate choice and partly the result of political and socioeconomic opportunities and constraints. As we have seen, ISI emerged as a development strategy in Latin America during the 1930s as the worldwide depression sharply reduced international trade. Because North America and Europe reduced their purchases of primary goods (Uruguayan wool, Argentine beef, and Brazilian coffee, for example), Latin American nations no longer were able to earn enough foreign exchange to import the manufactured products that they needed. So, the region's early industrialization was designed, in part, to produce consumer goods that Latin American countries could no longer afford to import.

But although ISI began as a response to an international economic crisis, economic planners subsequently transformed it into a long-term strategy for industrial development. With substantial unemployment at home and an urban population pressing for economic growth and additional jobs, government leaders faced a political imperative to industrialize. Nationalist presidents such as Argentina's Juan Perón and Brazil's Getúlio Vargas forged populist political coalitions of industrialists, blue-collar workers, and the urban middle class, all committed to industrialization.

As previously noted, Latin American governments imposed quotas and tariffs on imported *consumer* goods in order to protect emerging national industries from international competition. But, planners also wanted to facilitate other types of imports, namely capital equipment (primarily machinery) and raw materials that domestic manufacturers needed. To reduce the cost of those imports, governments often overvalued their own currencies. Eventually, most Latin American countries established multiple currency exchange rates, with differing rates for transactions tied to imports, exports, and other financial activities. To further encourage industrial development, governments also offered domestic industries tax incentives, low-interest loans, and direct subsidies.

Because of ISI's impressive record in Latin America from the 1940s into the 1970s, the strategy was emulated in many parts of Africa and Asia as well, sometimes with comparable success. Turkey, for example, enjoyed strong ISI growth before shifting to EOI during the 1980s. Even East Asia began its industrial development using ISI. By the 1970s, however, the ISI strategy was undermining Latin America's economies. As John Sheahan notes, "It fostered production methods adverse for employment, hurt the poor, blocked the possible growth of industrial exports, [and] encouraged high-cost consumer goods industries."[17]

To understand how poorly Latin America's newly industrialized countries (NICs) fared in international trade compared to their East Asian competitors, it is useful to compare Mexico (one of Latin America's major industrial powers) with East Asia's four **Asian tigers** (South Korea, Taiwan, Hong Kong, and Singapore). Mexico has a substantially larger population than the combined total of the four Asian countries. It also has a considerable geographic advantage over them in the export market, being located closer to Western Europe and thousands of miles closer to the United States, the world's largest importer. Yet, as of the mid-1980s (prior to the North American Free Trade Agreement, NAFTA), the combined value of *manufactured* exports of the four Asian tigers was twenty times higher than Mexico's (since then, the gap has narrowed).[18]

In many Latin American countries, export taxes and overvalued currencies put traditional primary goods exporters at a competitive disadvantage, thereby depriving the country of badly needed foreign exchange. At the same time, because local consumer-goods industries could import their needed capital goods (machinery and other manufactured products used to manufacture other products) cheaply, the region never developed its own capital-goods industry and, instead, imported manufacturing technologies that were often inappropriate to local needs. Subsidized imports of machinery and heavy equipment also encouraged capital-intensive production (i.e., using more advanced technologies and machinery while employing fewer workers) rather than the labor-intensive production that predominated in Asia. The ISI model of industrialization benefited a small, relatively well-paid "labor elite" (i.e., skilled, unionized workers employed in more capital-intensive factories). But it failed to provide enough jobs for the region's workforce, leaving too many Latin Americans unemployed and underemployed.

Ironically, although ISI was originally designed to make Latin America more economically independent, in the end, it merely replaced dependence on consumer-goods imports with dependence on imported capital goods, foreign technologies, and credit. Traditional primary exports often languished, while deficits contributed to Latin America's spiraling foreign debt, leading eventually to a major debt crisis and a recession in the 1980s. This crisis, in stark contrast to East Asia's rapid growth at that time, induced Latin American governments to abandon their inwardly oriented economic policies as they tried to emulate East Asia's export-driven model. The NAFTA treaty between Mexico, Canada, and the United States is the most dramatic manifestation of that region's move toward EOI. Since that time, Latin American nations have established several regional trade associations, including Mercosur (a trade agreement involving two economic powers—Brazil and Argentina—and two smaller countries in the southern part of South America) and the Latin American Integration Association.

Export-Oriented Industrialization

East Asia's **NICs** began their industrialization drive through import substitution, just as their Latin American counterparts had done years earlier. Soon, however, they diversified into manufacturing for export. As governments phased out their early protectionist measures, they forced local companies to become more competitive in the world market. State planners shaped the market, pressuring industries and offering them incentives to export. By 1980, manufactured goods constituted more than 90 percent of all South Korean and Taiwanese exports but represented only 15 percent of Mexico's and 39 percent of Brazil's.[19] Fueled by their dynamic industrial export sectors, East Asia's booming economies became the envy of the developing world. More recently, India has enjoyed very impressive growth tied to the export of services.

There are a number of reasons why East Asia decided to stress manufactured exports early in its industrialization drive, while Latin America failed to do so for decades. For one thing, East Asian industrialization began in a period of unprecedented expansion in world trade, inspired by the West's enormous postwar economic boom (from the mid-1940s through early 1970s) and the broad assault on trade barriers in the years following the General Agreement on Trade and Tariffs (GATT) in 1947.* The opportunities offered by outward-oriented growth were obvious to Asian policy makers by the 1950s. Conversely, the expansion of Latin American industrialization started during the Great Depression of the 1930s, a period of greatly restricted world trade. Indeed, it was their very inability to export traditional products at that time that inspired Latin American nations to turn initially to ISI. In retrospect, Latin America should have moved to EOI after World War II, but ISI seemed to be

---

*In 1995, the WTO replaced the GATT.

working so well until the 1980s that there was little incentive to change. Ironically, another reason why East and Southeast Asian countries chose EOI was that their economic opportunities seemed more limited than Latin America's. Because of their smaller populations, Hong Kong, Singapore, and Taiwan (though not South Korea) did not believe that ISI, which relied upon the domestic market, was a feasible strategy for them as it had been for larger countries such as Mexico, Argentina, Brazil, and Colombia. Furthermore, with fewer agricultural goods or raw materials to export, East Asians turned their weakness into strength by emphasizing manufactured exports.

GROWTH WITH EQUITY

Until this point, our discussion has focused on the size of the national economy. Indeed, production is the primary measure of economic development used in popular and scholarly analysis. Typically, a country is thought to be performing well when its GDP (or its GNP) grows rapidly. Analysts focus less frequently on how equitably this growth is distributed. It is to this important dimension that we now turn.

Early debate on development often pitted mainstream social scientists against left-of-center analysts, with the first group primarily interested in the prerequisites of growth and the second focusing on the fairness of economic distribution. For example, while many mainstream economists were impressed with Brazil's rapid economic expansion in the late 1960s and early 1970s, critics pointed out that the country's extremely unequal income distribution meant that few benefits of that growth reached the poorest half of the population. On the other hand, although Cuba's income redistribution policies and social welfare programs have favorably impressed some observers, conservative critics criticize its generally weak record of economic growth since the late 1960s.

Many market-oriented economists insist that increased inequality is unavoidable, indeed desirable, in the early stages of economic development in order to concentrate capital in the hands of entrepreneurs, who can then invest more in the economy, expand their enterprises, and create jobs. Their critics counter that development of that sort did little to help the majority of the people. In many developing nations, they maintained, the bottom half of the population would benefit more from meaningful redistribution of wealth and income, even with less growth, than from strong economic growth without redistribution.

In time, however, analysts of varying ideological persuasions have concluded that there is no intrinsic contradiction between these two goals. In fact, a proper development strategy entails "growth with equity." One study indicates that since the 1960s, countries with higher income equality have developed faster than those with highly concentrated patterns. East Asia's economic takeoff since the 1970s and 1980s demonstrates that point. For example, Taiwan and South Korea have coupled spectacular economic growth rates with relatively equitable income distributions. Indeed, widely based purchasing power in both those countries has helped stimulate their economic growth. In South Korea, almost all peasant families own television sets, a feat hardly conceivable in Africa or Latin America. During the Korean television industry's takeoff, these domestic purchases supplemented exports in stimulating that industry's growth.

What accounts for the higher level of economic equality in East Asia compared to Africa or Latin America? One important factor is the pattern of land distribution in the countryside. For a number of reasons, farmland has historically been more equitably distributed in Asia (especially East Asia) than in Latin America. While the size of Latin America's largest land-holdings has declined in recent decades, estates of several thousand acres still exist and were common in the recent past. Today, large landowners still dominate the countryside in nations such as Brazil and Colombia. While the largest farms in Africa are not nearly as big, landownership is still very concentrated in countries such as South Africa, Kenya, and Ethiopia. On the other hand, the largest holdings in Asia, where there is much heavier population pressure, are rarely more than one or two hundred acres and they are far smaller in countries such as South Korea.

Landholding patterns reflect both historical legacies and contemporary government policies. Spanish colonialism established an agrarian structure in Latin America and the Philippines dominated by *latifundia* (large estates). In Africa, landholding is most concentrated in countries that had substantial numbers of White settlers(who carved out large agricultural estates) during their colonial period. These include Kenya, Mozambique, and Namibia. On the other hand, Japanese colonial authorities in Korea and Taiwan encouraged smallholder farming. Although European colonial regimes established large export-oriented plantations in Southeast Asia, landownership there was still never as concentrated as in Latin America. It is surely not coincidental that the Philippines, the only country in East Asia to share Latin America's Spanish colonial heritage, also has the region's most concentrated land and income distribution. In the twentieth century, South Korean and Taiwanese agrarian reform programs led to even more egalitarian land distribution in those countries, just as the American-imposed reform had done in Japan after World War II. By reducing rural poverty, land reform contributed to greater income equality (see chapter 6).

Another major component of national income distribution is the relationship between rural and urban living standards. Although city dwellers enjoy higher incomes and greater social services throughout the

LDCs, the urban-rural gap is particularly marked in Africa and Latin America. Residents of Mexico City, for example, have incomes averaging four to five times higher than those in the countryside, while in China the ratio of urban to rural population nationally is over 3:1. There are many reasons for such discrepancies, but government policy often plays an important role. In chapter 6, we noted that, until recently, governments in both regions often kept the prices of basic food crops below their market value in order to provide their urban political constituencies with cheap food. By contrast, East Asian farmers generally have received the free-market price for their crops or even obtained subsidized prices above market value.

Industrial policy also affects income distribution. Latin America's ISI strategy encouraged the importation of capital equipment for domestic industries. Such capital-intensive development created many relatively skilled and well-paid industrial jobs, but left behind a far larger number of poorly paid, "unskilled" urban workers and rural peasants. Conversely, East and Southeast Asia's EOI strategy benefited from the region's large labor force, thereby producing a great number of low-wage jobs in emerging industries.

By initially using labor-intensive methods that utilized their pools of cheap labor, Hong Kong, Taiwan, and South Korea successfully exported cheap low-tech goods such as textiles, toys, and footwear. Over time, as these industries needed increasing numbers of workers, two changes took place. First, greater demand for labor in low-end export industries caused factory wages to rise; second, rural-to-urban migrants seeking factory jobs reduced the supply of rural labor, thereby driving up wages for farm workers in the countryside. What had begun as a policy exploiting cheap labor eventually sponsored strong economic growth, higher wages, and greater income equality.

As factory wages rose substantially in the region's tigers, those countries shifted from low-tech manufactured products to more sophisticated exports such as electronics, commercial services (most notably in Singapore), computer software, computers, and automobiles (South Korea). Production of apparel and other low-wage items passed to lower-income Asian nations such as Malaysia, Thailand, Indonesia, Bangladesh, and Sri Lanka. China, which first became an industrial giant by manufacturing low-priced consumer goods and parts for foreign brands, is now also producing higher-end products, including some under Chinese brand names.

ECONOMIC DEVELOPMENT AND THE ENVIRONMENT

Throughout the world, economic development has inevitably caused environmental degradation. For example, prior to European settlement, the East Coast of the United States was covered with thick forest. Since then, increased human population, urban sprawl, and farming have destroyed almost all of that growth. Today, industrial and auto pollution in the United States and Europe contaminate the surrounding air and water, sometimes affecting areas thousands of miles away. In the LDCs, rapid population growth, natural-resource extraction, and industrialization have also damaged the environment. In Indonesia, for example, foreign-owned mines have dumped health-threatening waste into nearby water systems, while logging firms harvested vast tracks of jungle timber, bringing birth defects in mining areas and flooding in timber regions in their wake. Massive dams in China have flooded archeological treasures, farmland, and vacated villages. Since the 1970s, environmental groups in advanced industrialized nations have questioned the trade-offs between economic growth and the conservation of natural resources. Most ominously, the consequences of global warming may soon threaten living standards and lives throughout the planet. Some of the more radical environmentalists in the United States and Europe have proposed zero-growth strategies for highly developed nations. This could require limiting population growth (already on the decline in those countries) and creating a less consumer-oriented society.

But the option of zero growth, or even of reduced economic growth, which has never attracted significant support in the developed world, is totally unacceptable in the developing world. In countries such as Bangladesh, Brazil, Egypt, Indonesia, and Nigeria, where a substantial portion of the population lives in abject poverty, it would be politically suicidal and ethically questionable for government leaders to propose limiting economic growth. Unless and until the environmental consequences of economic growth can be mitigated, the trade-off between growth and environmental decay presents a horrible ethical dilemma. It would be unconscionable to tell poor Pakistanis or Ethiopians that they should not hope for a higher standard of living. But barring major technological and political breakthroughs, achieving an acceptable standard of living for all people could easily overtax the planet's natural resources.

Environmental regulations and controls are also far weaker in the LDCs, because of their urgent desire for economic growth and because their "green" (ecology) movements developed much later than in the West and lack the political influence of their American and European counterparts. Moreover, LDCs often lack the government infrastructure to enforce environmental controls. Finally, polluting industries (both foreign and domestic) often bribe public officials responsible for enforcing environmental laws.

The Costs of Growth

The world's industrialized nations continue to be the major consumers of natural resources, the leading polluters of air and water, and the greatest contributors to global warming, depletion of the ozone layer, and other looming environmental disasters. Yet, ironically, it is those same developed countries that now insist that the LDCs become better environmental citizens. In response, LDCs often point out that the United States, with less than 5 percent of the world's population, annually consumes roughly 20 percent of the planet's energy.[20] Hence, many of them bristle at the suggestion that developing nations make special efforts to protect the environment. Even so, because of their more fragile economic and ecological conditions, a number of developing nations face daunting environmental challenges. In African countries such as Sudan, Nigeria, and Burkina Faso, wood fires produce 75 percent or more of all energy, forcing peasants hungry for firewood to deplete the forests. Each year, rich cattle ranchers and poor peasants in Brazil burn vast areas of the Amazonian jungle to clear the land for ranching, agriculture, or logging. "During the past 40 years, close to 20 percent of the Amazon rain forest has been cut down—more than in all the previous 450 years since European colonization began."[21] In Malaysia and Indonesia, Japanese-owned logging firms cut down large tracts of rain forest. In places such as Central America and Sub-Saharan Africa, rains and waterways wash off topsoil, rainfall patterns shift, and both droughts and floods occur more frequently. In many parts of the developing world, the arable land area is declining and deserts are growing.

Cities such as Shanghai, Cairo, New Delhi, Nairobi, and São Paulo have grown tremendously in recent decades (chapter 6), producing enormous quantities of raw sewage, auto emissions, and industrial waste. As cars and buses (most without proper emission controls) choke the streets, air quality rapidly deteriorates. Elsewhere, mines, oil fields, chemical plants, and factories, operating with few environmental safeguards, pollute their surroundings. The consequences for local populations are often tragic—including infections, respiratory illnesses, birth defects, and loss of farmland. Other environmental costs—such as destruction of rain forests, which contributes to global warming—have consequences that extend far beyond the LDCs.

Environmental Decay as a Developing World Problem

The difficult trade-off between economic growth and environmental conservation is probably most starkly illustrated in China, home to almost one-fifth of the earth's population. From the time that its government introduced free-market economic reforms in the 1980s, that country has enjoyed one of the world's highest rates of economic growth, averaging about 8 percent annually. Living standards have tripled, and millions of Chinese citizens have moved out of poverty. The number of people spared from hunger, disease, and early death is staggering. Balanced against those gains, however, are enormous increases in air and water pollution and extensive destruction of the country's farmland, raising the danger of future famine just when China has finally managed to feed its population adequately. Moreover, as the country has built an average of two new coal-burning, electric power plants annually, added over 6.5 million motor vehicles every year, and vastly expanded its industrial production, it has surpassed the United States as the world's largest producer of **greenhouse gases** (emissions that trap the earth's heat in the atmosphere and contribute to global warming, principally carbon dioxide and, to a lesser extent, methane).

Seeking a better life, over one hundred million Chinese peasants have migrated to the cities, often abandoning farms in productive agricultural regions. In addition, substantial quantities of farmland have been paved over for highways, factories, and urban sprawl. Since the late 1950s, the country's total arable land has decreased by somewhere between 15 and 55 percent (depending on what estimate one accepts), while the nation's population has grown by some 80 percent. Though China's rate of population growth is currently relatively low (1 percent annually), loss of farmland caused by economic development continues to accelerate at an alarming rate. So far, the country has averted hunger by farming the remaining land more intensively, and some recent grain harvests have reached record or near-record levels. But this intensive use of fertilizers and pesticides eventually depletes the soil, and a food crunch probably looms in the coming decades. As this enormous country needs to import increasing amounts of food, it will likely drive up prices of grains and other foods in the world market, with serious consequences for the poor throughout the LDCs.

Environmental Decay and Global Warming

Not only does environmental decay pose dangers to the LDCs themselves, but it threatens developed countries as well. And, of course, the developed world's environmental sins similarly endanger developing countries. Of all the environmental threats currently facing the world, the most menacing is surely global warming. Although there are still some scientists who feel that the future risks of global warming have been exaggerated, there is now a general consensus within the scientific community and among most of the world's political leaders that the earth has been warming over the long term, that the causes are in large part man-made, and that the consequences will be horrendous if nothing is done to stop it. As Michael Klare has warned,

In general, adverse effects from global warming will produce suffering on an unprecedented scale. Many will starve; many more will perish from disease, flooding, or fire. Others, however, will attempt to survive in the same manner as their predecessors: by fighting among themselves for whatever food and water remain; by invading more favorable locales; or by migrating to distant lands, even in the face of violent resistance.[22]

Specific environmental consequences of warming, if current trends continue, may include more droughts in some regions, more frequent floods in others, declining food production, widespread hunger and starvation, intensified hurricane and typhoon activity, and flooding of coastal cities and low-lying rural areas.[23] Many countries in Africa would be among the hardest hit because they already are subject to frequent drought and severe food shortages and have the fewest economic resources to address the problem. But many other regions would also suffer because of their limited resources and the likelihood that global warming will affect countries closest to the equator most severely. Moreover, developed nations, experiencing their own diminished agricultural production, will not be as well-positioned to send famine relief to Africa and Asia as they have done so often before.

While these outcomes are already widely discussed, Klare points to a number of less well-known consequences that also threaten to create conflict and violence. Some severely affected nations would probably invade bordering countries that have more water or arable land, especially if they are stronger militarily than their neighbors. Somalia, Ethiopia, and Sudan have already fought wars linked to water and land rights. Similarly, within nations, regions or ethnic groups that are more adversely affected may attack their neighbors. In many of the most poverty-stricken countries, economic disasters and internal violence may cause states to fail, opening up the way for militias and roving bands, as has already happened in Somalia. Finally, the combination of hunger, warfare, and internal violence would almost certainly intensify population movement from stricken areas to more affluent ones, including intensified emigration from Africa to Western Europe and from Latin America to the United States and Canada.

In 2015, Pope Francis issued a strongly worded encyclical on the environment calling for action on climate change. His warnings may influence the governments of many Catholic countries and of many Catholics worldwide.

Moreover, there is an additional problem combating global warming. All countries, LDCs, and advanced industrial nations alike, would benefit from a significant reduction in the emission of carbon dioxide and other greenhouse gases. But for each individual country (say, Indonesia), the cost of reducing emissions is substantial, while their own country would only reap limited advantages because the benefits are spread around the entire world (since air flows freely across borders). Therefore, Indonesia (or any country) has incentives to "free-ride," that is, to let other countries (such as China and Germany) pay the costs of reducing their own emissions while every country, including Indonesia, would reap the benefits.

For the most part, then, First World (developed) countries are the primary sources of global warming, while developing nations—particularly in Africa and Asia—are potentially its greatest victims. At the same time, rapid industrialization in Asia and Latin America has sharply increased the LDCs' share of greenhouse gas emissions in recent years. As noted previously, China has surged past the United States as the world's largest source of these gases, while India now ranks third. Those two nations correctly respond that, since each of them is home to more than one billion people, they each pollute far less than the Western industrial giants on a per capita basis.* Still, the additional gases produced by these two new industrial powers alone are cause for great concern. In the fifteen-year span between 1992 and 2007, emissions rose by nearly 40 percent worldwide. While emissions actually *declined* during that period by almost 2 percent among the fifteen members of the European Union and grew by only 11 percent in Japan, emissions grew by 20 percent in the United States and jumped 103 percent in India and 150 percent in China.

THE SEARCH FOR SUSTAINABLE DEVELOPMENT

Discussion of the environmental consequences of economic growth often focuses on the objective of **sustainable development**, defined as economic development that "consumes resources to meet [this generation's] needs and aspirations in a way that does not compromise the ability of future generations to meet their needs."[24] Whenever feasible, it involves the use of *renewable resources* (such as wind and water power for generating electricity) in place of resources that cannot be replaced (e.g., coal and petroleum) or that are being consumed at a faster rate than they can be replaced (such as tropical rain forests and ocean fishing grounds). It also embraces consumption of resources in ways that least pollute the environment: limiting auto and industrial emissions, finding sustainable substitutes for pesticides and other agricultural chemicals that pollute the soil and the water system, and reducing the use of products that destroy the world's ozone layer.

---

*In recent years, the United States has emitted over ten times as much greenhouse gas per capita as India has and twice China's emissions per person.

In theory, these are goals to which all nations—rich and poor alike—can aspire. Even so, developed and developing nations have long debated which of them should take the lead and which should bear the greatest economic costs. At the groundbreaking international conferences and UN summits since the 1990s, tensions between the developed and less developed countries were obvious. As one analyst observed,

> The conflicts between the rich and poor [have become] evident. The Northern [industrialized] countries, which [feel] vulnerable to global environment problems such as climate change and biodiversity loss, [have] attempted to extract commitments on environmental conservation from the South [the LDCs]. However, the South, which [feels] more vulnerable to perceived underdevelopment, has been concerned with extracting [economic] transfers from the North.[25]

The difficult trade-off between growth and environmental protection was vividly brought home to this author at a meeting in Jamaica with local social scientists. After one U.S. scholar stressed the importance of preserving the island's ecology, a Jamaican economist sarcastically replied, "You Americans raped your environment in order to develop your country and raise your standard of living. Now we Jamaicans reserve the right to do the same." While such feelings are counterproductive, they are understandable. Many LDCs note that industrialized nations ask NICs such as China and Mexico to reduce smokestack emissions and beseech Thailand and Brazil to sustain their rain forests. But it is the developed countries that have wreaked the greatest havoc on the environment and have offered the LDCs little help to defray the costs of environmental controls.

U.S. policies created further problems. Although the United States was passed by China several years ago as the world's greatest source of greenhouse gases, it still produces close to 20 percent of the world's total emissions. During the eight years of the George Bush administration (2001–2009), the U.S. government questioned whether there was actually a danger of global warming and rejected mandatory caps on greenhouse gas emissions. In 1997, worldwide negotiations had produced the Kyoto Protocol, which envisioned a global contract binding industrialized nations to reduce their emissions of six greenhouse gases by 2012 to 5.2 percent below their 1990 level. This would be 29 percent below what they had been expected to reach without an accord. President Bill Clinton never submitted the Kyoto agreement to the U.S. Senate, which had made it clear that it would not ratify it unless it imposed mandatory targets on developing nations as well. In 2001, 178 nations agreed in Bonn, Germany, to meet objections from Japan and other nations by modifying the Kyoto agreement so as to lower the targeted 5 percent reduction to only 2 percent. In spite of these modifications, the United States upset its allies in the European Union and much of the world community by announcing that it would not ratify the Kyoto treaty or the Bonn modifications. The Bush White House—supported by a large segment of the business community and Congressional Republicans—had two major objections to the treaty: first, the Protocol called for no reduction in greenhouse gas emissions in the developing nations (including high-growth countries in Asia); second, it believed that Kyoto's mandatory environmental targets would undermine American economic growth.

By insisting that it would only accept voluntary targets, the United States reinforced the LDCs' belief that it was being held to a double standard when it came to making economic sacrifices for the environment. Most of the international community has committed itself, at least in theory, to Kyoto's goals. However, because the United States accounted for 25 percent of all greenhouse emissions at that time, its decision to pull out made it harder to reduce overall levels. In early 2005, following Russian ratification, the Kyoto accord went into effect without U.S. participation. The Protocol was due to expire in 2012 and environmentalists hoped that a new treaty could be successfully negotiated at the 2009 United Nations Climate Change Conference in Copenhagen. But, conflicting national interests—pitting China against the West and developing countries against the developed ones—limited progress and blocked agreement on a new treaty until 2015. At that time nearly 200 nations (including all the major generators of greenhouse gases) agreed to an ambitious plan for limiting global warming in the future. Although the agreement was nonbinding, many environmental groups and activists believed that it was a major step forward.

Some Signs of Progress

Despite these obstacles, there are some hopeful signs of progress. Today, there are few powerful voices in the United States or elsewhere denying the existence and threat of global warming (though some candidates for the 2016 presidential race continue to deny its dangers). At the very least, the governments of developing countries and international development agencies have become more conscious of the growth-environmental trade-off. Together many of them have begun searching for ways to achieve development that reduces damage to the environment. Many LDCs that previously saw the green movement as a Western conspiracy to keep them underdeveloped have come to realize that sustainable development is in their own interest. Conversely, the world's most developed nations have generally acknowledged that, to date, they have contributed the most to global warming and other environmental dangers and that they will have to help poorer nations pay the costs of future environmental protection.

Recently, the European Union and Japan have both taken new, more vigorous initiatives to reduce greenhouse gas emissions. In the United States, Barack Obama took office having made a strong commitment during his campaign to reduce greenhouse gas emissions, as well as by offering government support for several initiatives, including the development of more fuel-efficient, cleaner-burning automobiles; and greater use of alternate sources of energy, such as wind and solar power. The Obama administration has ruled out joining the Kyoto Protocol, arguing that the treaty would expire in only three years and it is far too late for the United States to reach its targets. Its goal is to cut American greenhouse gas emissions 17 percent by 2020, bringing it back to the 1990 level and to reduce emissions 80 percent by 2050. There have been some signs of progress (independent of government action). From 2006 to 2009, total greenhouse gas emissions in the United States declined in three of the four years, including a sharp 6.1 percent decrease in 2009. This brought emissions down to their lowest point since 1995. But, while conservation efforts accounted for a part of that drop, the largest decrease (in 2009) was largely caused by the global economic recession. So far, Congress has failed to pass the administration's environmental proposals. But, in 2011, President Obama announced that the automobile industry had agreed to slash emissions from new cars and light trucks on an average of 30 percent by 2016.

It is unlikely, however, that these efforts will substantially change the LDCs' skepticism toward environmental regulation (although the Chinese have announced a major initiative to cut energy consumption and greenhouse gas emissions). And the United States has trailed well behind the European Union in reducing carbon emissions. The new Republican majority in the House of Representatives made it clear that President Obama's proposed cap-and-trade legislation limiting emissions would not pass and the White House abandoned its efforts. There is considerable Congressional opposition to tough environmental legislation, much of it coming from Congressional representatives (including some Democrats) who represent districts fearful of being hurt by it. But, as he approaches his last years in office, he has introduced tough new standards for carbon emissions.*

Ultimately, even if LDCs applied strict environmental measures, these still would not fully reconcile the tension between economic growth and environmental protection. Furthermore, environmental controls are generally expensive and often reduce productivity. If the world's industrial

---

*As of the publishing of this book, Republican Congressional leaders have vowed to override some of these standards especially as they applied to coal-burning, electric power stations.

powers want the LDCs to make such sacrifices, they will probably have to underwrite much of the cost. This might involve debt forgiveness, subsidized technology transfers, and direct grants.

Which of the economic models discussed earlier in this chapter is best equipped to handle the environmental challenge? The answer is not clear. It seems certain that preserving the environment requires significant state intervention. For example, since it is unrealistic to expect industrialists to monitor and control their own pollution or to hope that all drivers will voluntarily purchase fuel-efficient cars, most analysts feel that some government regulation is needed. Consequently, the neoliberal model, which severely limits government economic intervention and depends heavily on free-market mechanisms, seems ill-suited to protect the environment (though market mechanisms, such as a cap-and-trade legislation, can be very helpful).

In theory, command economies seem particularly well suited to defend the environment because the state controls the means of production and can self-regulate. In fact, however, communist governments from the Soviet Union and Poland to China and North Korea have had very poor environmental records. For one thing, directives to managers of state enterprises usually demand that they maximize production, with little thought given to environmental consequences. At the same time, absent a free society and a free mass media, citizens are unable to organize environmental pressure groups or even to know the extent of ecological destruction.* Thus, it appears that if developing nations are to have any chance at sustainable development, they must combine an honest, effective, and responsible state with a free democratic society where green activists can mobilize popular support.

FINDING THE RIGHT MIX

It has often been easier to recognize what has not worked in developing countries than to identify what has. The dependency theorists' assumption that economic development was only possible if LDCs reduced their ties to the capitalist core has been shattered by the success of East Asia's export-oriented growth and the failures of protectionism in Latin America. Similarly, command economies, while often able to reduce economic inequalities, generally have had poor records of economic growth and modernization beyond the early stages of development. North Korea's dismal communist economy, in stark contrast to South Korea's

---

*The Chinese government has become more sensitive to environmental issues and sometimes responds to grassroots protest demonstrations in that area. But, it still has a long way to go.

prosperity, demonstrates that model's failures. And, China was able to stage its breathtaking economic expansion only after it had moved away from a command economy. On the other hand, the neoliberal minimal state can hardly address the deep inequities, societal cleavages, and looming ecological nightmares plaguing so many LDCs. The challenge for developing economies is to establish a strong and effective, but not overbearing, state—one that can promote growth, equitable income distribution, and a healthy environment, while avoiding **crony capitalism**, political repression, and unwarranted interference in the market.

Many developing countries have now embraced East Asia's export-oriented industrial model. Beyond the previously mentioned problem of transferability, however, there are at least two other fundamental concerns about universalizing the East Asian experience. The first concerns the extent to which the world economy can continue to absorb mounting industrial exports. East Asia launched its EOI strategy during a period of unparalleled economic expansion in the First World. International trade was expanding rapidly, and developed countries could absorb a rising tide of industrial exports. Since the 1970s, however, First World economic growth has slowed down due, in part, to factors such as periodic spikes in energy costs and the transfer of industrial jobs to the NICs. Even should the Japanese and Western European economies recover their former dynamism, some analysts question whether the international market can absorb an ever-enlarging flow of industrial exports, most notably from China, the world's emerging industrial giant, or whether a protectionist backlash from the First World might place a cap on imports.[26]

Supporters of EOI counter that there is no sign of a looming ceiling on industrial imports, particularly since the larger NICs have become major importers themselves. The evidence so far suggests that LDCs hoping to industrialize need to develop some type of export sector and to participate actively in the global economy. But they would be wise to also diversify their economy and to build protections against the negative aspects of globalization. At the start of the recent global economic crisis, many LDCs that are highly dependent on the developed world for trade and investment suffered sharp economic declines as demand for their exports waned. And to the surprise of many economists and unlike previous global recessions, less developed economies bounced back impressively in 2010 (growing by nearly 8 percent).

THE EFFECTS OF GLOBALIZATION ON DEVELOPING NATIONS

Perhaps the most important and hotly debated economic development affecting LDCs in recent years is **globalization**. The mass media and social scientists both define globalization in related, but somewhat distinct, ways. In its most fundamental sense, the term refers to the increasing interdependence of national economies throughout the world. It is characterized by rising world trade in goods and services, increasing flows of cross-national finance (including banking, stock market transactions, and corporate acquisitions), greater legal and illegal cross-national labor migration, accelerated international transfers of advanced technologies, expansion of MNCs, and mounting influence of global economic institutions such as the IMF, the World Bank, and the WTO. All of these changes enhance the interdependence of national economies. In short, globalization involves the free flow of information, goods, services, and capital across national borders. Beyond this, the term is often also understood to include the spread of culture, consumer tastes, and technology from the West (particularly the United States) to the rest of the world.

Scholarly debate over globalization has centered on several questions: Is this really a new phenomenon or merely a continuation of economic trends that have existed for centuries? If it is new, when did it begin? And, most importantly for our purposes, has globalization improved or harmed less developed economies? Some scholars who claim that globalization is not a particularly new or dramatic development actually trace the first wave of economic globalization back to the Roman Empire. Some date it to the rise and spread of Western European capitalism in the sixteenth century, while others trace it to the last decades of the nineteenth century.[27] Others question whether there is anything uniquely global about the present era, arguing that the present level of economic interdependence was matched or exceeded in earlier times. Thus, for example, the level of trade as a percentage of the world economy is no higher today than it was in the early years of the twentieth century.

Still, the speed and breadth of today's IT revolution have greatly accelerated the interconnectedness of national economies. The effects of debt default in Russia very quickly spill over to Argentina and Brazil. A sharp drop in China's rate of economic growth or its stock market or a liquidity crisis in a major French bank has quickly brought down prices on the New York Stock Exchange. And most recently, world financial markets responded quickly and dramatically when U.S. Treasury bonds ratings were downgraded and when Greece, Ireland, Italy, and other European nations were in danger of defaulting on their external debt. To be sure, skeptics point out that the volume of world trade grew only modestly from 1980 to 2000. However, as we have seen, certain regions of the developing world—Asia and, to a lesser extent, Latin America—increased their manufactured exports substantially. Furthermore, *financial* globalization escalated dramatically during that period. For example, in the last two decades of the twentieth century, direct foreign investment rose by 250 percent worldwide and by 400 percent in the LDCs.[28] The daily turnover of international currency exchanges increased more than tenfold during that same twenty-year period. Moreover, other indicators of globalization—such as the volume of foreign travel, international phone calls, and cross-border use of the Internet—have exploded. As one analyst has put it, recent globalization is fundamentally different from earlier forms of international trade and commerce because "national markets are *fused* transnationally rather than [merely] linked across borders."[29]

If we accept that globalization is an important and, in some respects, recent development, particularly as it affects LDCs, when did this process begin? Some analysts trace it to the resurgence of world trade after World War II. In the 1960s, the term "globalization" acquired its present meaning. But, it was in the 1970s and 1980s, aided by the IT revolution, that the process took off and it is since then that the phenomenon has become the focus of intense scrutiny by scholars, journalists, and political leaders.

One of the most contentious debates regarding globalization focuses on its economic consequences for the LDCs. Neoliberals and other supporters of free trade often see globalization as a panacea, able to stimulate the economies of developed and developing nations alike. They point to the benefits that export-led growth has brought to East Asia, Chile, and India. By allowing for the most rational allocations of investments, labor, and natural resources across national borders, they argue, globalization creates the most efficient and productive economic outcome. The IT revolution, for example, has permitted India's educated and technologically proficient middle class to provide tech support to the world. In books such as journalist Thomas Friedman's best-seller *The World Is Flat*, the optimists see globalization as a win-win situation for the developed and the developing worlds.[30]

Critics of globalization see its impact very differently. They view it as a force that has imposed greater Western economic control and cultural dominance over LDCs. Moreover, they insist, it has widened income gaps between industrialized and less developed countries—as well as *within* the LDCs—has caused environmental decay, and has extended poverty. One of the most influential analyses of that kind is Joseph Stiglitz's *Globalization and Its Discontents*.[31] Unlike many critics, Stiglitz—a Nobel-Prize–winning economist, former chair of President Bill Clinton's Council of Economic Advisers, and former chief economist for the World Bank—is the most respectable of establishment figures. Yet, his writings severely criticize the U.S. government, the World Bank, and, especially, the IMF for pressuring less developed nations to adopt free-trade and privatization policies that have inflicted substantial pain on their populations and made their economies more vulnerable to shifts in the global economy.

While we cannot explore all aspects of this debate, we will focus on what may be the most important question: Has recent globalization deepened or alleviated poverty in the less developed world? Much of this discussion, in turn, has centered on the issue of economic equality and inequality: Has globalization intensified or reduced the economic gaps within individual LDCs and those between LDCs and the world's wealthier nations? There seems to be general agreement that between 1945 (when the latest wave of economic integration began) and 1980, the gap between rich and poor nations widened. Evidence since the 1980s, when globalization accelerated, suggests that this economic gap may have begun to narrow.

Supporters of globalization argue that rapid industrialization in countries such as China, India, South Korea, and Brazil, and expansion of the international service industry by countries such as India have allowed the LDCs, or at least some of them, to begin catching up with the developed world. Further examination, however, suggests a more complex picture. Since the 1970s, the income gap between the developed and developing countries has narrowed. But this was entirely the consequence of East and Southeast Asia's economic surge. Advocates of globalization point out that the countries in which living standards have most improved and where poverty has most sharply declined in the past two to three decades—including China, Chile, Indonesia, India, and South Korea—are precisely the nations that are most intensely integrated into the global economy. At the same time, the poorest nations in the world and those that, until recently, were falling furthest behind are the countries of Sub-Saharan Africa, which have had the least globalized economies. Moreover, as a number of that region's countries have opened up their economies to world trade since 2000, Sub-Saharan Africa, though still poor, has had some of the world's fastest-growing economies.

If we turn to the issue of inequality *within* developing nations, the evidence is somewhat ambiguous. As countries such as Chile and China have entered the global economy more intensely, the gap between their poor and the middle and upper classes has widened. Looking more systematically at data from sixty-five countries from 1995 to 2001, economist Almas Heshmati found that income inequality was somewhat greater in more globalized economies. But, he also observed that globalization was but *one* of many factors contributing to inequality, explaining only about 10 percent of the difference between nations.[32] Furthermore, depending on how they analyze the data, some economists have argued that income inequality has intensified as a result of globalization in recent decades, while others contend that it has diminished. But, even if there were a consensus that inequality has increased, would that mean that standards of living for the poor are declining on an absolute basis (i.e., that the poor are actually getting poorer)? It might, but it could also mean that *all* income groups have benefited from globalization but that the upper and middle classes have gained the most.

The most serious charge leveled against globalization is that it has intensified poverty in LDCs. Case studies describe Nike factories that pay their workers shockingly low wages (at least by Western standards) and peasants who were pushed off their land by foreign-owned plantations and logging operations. But, while case studies often provide useful insights, we cannot know how representative they are of the general population. That is, while a careful case study may demonstrate how MNCs reduced economic opportunities in Nuevo Laredo, Mexico, or how free trade impoverished sugar plantation workers in Malaysia, we do not know whether these situations are typical of Mexico or Malaysia, much less of the developing world as a whole.

If, however, we examine more systematic statistics from the United Nations and the World Bank, we find that, contrary to globalization's critics, poverty in the developing world has actually *declined* significantly since globalization accelerated in the early 1980s. For example, according to World Bank statistics, the percentage of the LDCs' population living in "absolute poverty"—defined as those living on less than $1 a day (PPP) or, since 2008, $1.25 a day—fell from 40 percent in 1980 to 19 percent in 2002 (controlling for inflation). Since the start of the twenty-first century, when many countries in Sub-Saharan Africa inserted themselves more vigorously in the global economy, not only has that region enjoyed substantial economic growth, but life expectancy grew from under fifty years (in 2000) to fifty-seven years (in 2013).

A host of factors helped reduce absolute poverty and increase life expectancy (such as reducing the death rate from HIV/AIDS), and it would be an oversimplification to attribute all of this improvement to globalization. But, at the very least, the progress in recent decades does challenge allegations that rapid globalization has further impoverished the LDCs. Furthermore, the most dramatic declines in absolute poverty have occurred in China, other parts of East Asia, and India, the regions most intensely linked to the global economy. As its economies have become more globalized, poverty rates in Sub-Saharan Africa have declined somewhat more modestly.

At the same time, while *absolute* poverty fell sharply during this period, *total* poverty (which includes both those living in absolute poverty—below $1.25 daily—and those living on $1.25–2.50 per day) declined more gradually, from 67 to 50 percent, with most of this decline taking place in China, India, and East Asia. In fact, it appears that many of those who escaped absolute poverty have only advanced to a milder form of poverty (i.e., many of those who had been living on less than

$1.25 per day now earned $1.26–2.50 per day). Furthermore, even if the effect of globalization has generally been benign, it has also produced its share of losers. Even in a wealthy nation such as the United States, many textile mill employees and other workers in the manufacturing sector have seen their jobs disappear when their employer moved operations to Asia or Mexico. In developing countries, where workers and peasants are not protected by Western-style unemployment compensation or other safety nets, the consequences of economic dislocations are far more severe. During the Asian financial crisis in the late 1990s, an unintended consequence of globalization, millions lost their jobs, at least for a period of time. Elsewhere, reduced trade barriers in Latin America have allowed an influx of cheap foreign imports that destroys many local industries and put their employees out of work. This has led analysts such as Stiglitz to argue that since continued globalization seems inevitable, governments must take steps to mitigate its negative consequences on the biggest losers.[33]

Opponents of globalization maintain that the recent world economic recession showed ways in which it may be perilous for developing nations to link their economies to the world's advanced industrial nations. As the economy of developed nations declined in 2008–2011, remittances by the LDCs' workers employed abroad (money sent home to families or friends) fell as fewer people were able to find work overseas.[34] The World Bank estimated that total remittances to developing countries, though rarely discussed in the West, exceeded $300 billion at the start of the worldwide recession, substantially higher than the value of all foreign aid by developed countries.* In countries such as Haiti, Lebanon, and Honduras, these remittances accounted for more than 20 percent of the GDP at that time.

But, while globalization has in some respects worsened the effects of the recent financial crisis on the LDCs, its effects in the long run seem more benign. For example, it is true that this crisis has reduced overseas remittances. But the vast cross-national movement of workers thus far in the century (a product of globalization) had caused those remittances to multiply from $116 billion in 2002 to $440 billion in 2015. More importantly, the fact that the developing countries rebounded so quickly and impressively from the initial shock of the most recent global recession, puts into question some of the doomsday predictions from critics of globalization.

---

*This figure only includes formal remittances made through banks. Some experts estimate that an equal amount of funds or more are transferred informally through friends and relatives who bring the money home personally to avoid bank fees.

CONCLUSION: DEMOCRACY AND ECONOMIC DEVELOPMENT

Earlier in this chapter, we observed that in the second half of the twentieth century, the most dynamic developing economies were often governed by authoritarian regimes, at least at the start of their economic booms. Almost all of Asia's most impressive early economic performances—in Taiwan, South Korea, Thailand, Malaysia, Indonesia, China, and Vietnam—emerged from authoritarian or semiauthoritarian, developmental states or modified command economies. Chile initiated Latin America's most successful transition from ISI to export-led growth under General Pinochet's military dictatorship. On the basis of such evidence, some have argued that authoritarian governments are better equipped to start economic development because they can control workers' wage demands and can impose long-term development plans on business.

On the other hand, for every authoritarian success story, there have been several economic disasters. Corrupt dictatorships throughout Africa, the Middle East, and Latin America have plundered their country's limited wealth, created inefficient private or state monopolies, and used the economy to reward themselves and their political allies. That is, for every South Korea, Chile, or Singapore, there has been a Congo, Tajikistan, and Iran, all of them authoritarian regimes that experienced *negative* average annual growth rates from 1975 to 2004 (i.e., their economies lost ground). While Chile's bureaucratic authoritarian regime performed well economically, its counterparts in Argentina and Uruguay were much less successful. Overall, statistical analyses of the LDCs' economic growth rate in recent decades reveal that authoritarian governments do not perform any better than democratic ones do. And one recent study indicated that dictatorships perform less well. Bruce Bueno de Mesquita et al. ranked hundreds of specific governments worldwide for the second half of the twentieth century and compared the 179 most autocratic governments with the 176 most democratic ones (over that fifty-year span, every country had multiple governments; each of those governments was counted as a different case). During that period, democratic administrations achieved an average real annual growth rate (adjusted for inflation) of 3.04 percent, while autocratic governments had only 1.78 percent, a substantial gap. Moreover, the authors argue convincingly that the difference in performance has a logical explanation. Governments that need to appeal to a broad coalition of voters (democracies) are more inclined to pursue policies that promote broadly based economic gains. On the other hand, governments that owe their incumbency to a small coalition of strategic allies (dictatorships) are far more likely to be corrupt and to pursue policies designed to keep themselves in power, no matter what the cost is to the national economy.[35] In recent years, India, the world's most populous democracy, has also created one of the world's fastest-growing economies. Of course, the list of democratic governments includes both strong economic performers and weak ones, as does the list of authoritarian governments. But these findings, along with many others, offer hope that democratic governments and the worldwide movement toward democracy eventually may produce faster economic growth as well as greater political justice.

Practice and Review Online
http://textbooks.rowman.com/handelman8e#ch9

KEY TERMS

Asian Tigers
capital-intensive
command economy
comparative advantage
crony capitalism
currency exchange rates
developmental state
(economic) liberalization
EOI (export-oriented
    industrialization)
globalization
great leap forward
greenhouse gases

invisible hand
ISI (import-substituting
    industrialization)
laissez faire
market socialism
nationalizations
neoliberal economics
NICs
parastatals
populist
privatization
sustainable development

DISCUSSION QUESTIONS

1. What do you consider the major advantages and disadvantages of globalization? What measures might be implemented to alleviate those disadvantages?

2. Under what circumstances has substantial state intervention into the economy been helpful and in what cases has it had negative effects?

3. Any nation must resolve trade-offs between economic growth and environmental losses. If you were the leader of a developing nation, what criteria might you use to determine whether or not the economic benefits of a particular development project or private-sector investment were worth the environmental costs?

NOTES

1. Martin Staniland, *What Is Political Economy?* (New Haven, CT: Yale University Press, 1985), 6.

2. Ibid., 12.

3. Adapted from Adam Przeworski, *Democracy and the Market* (New York: Cambridge University Press, 1991), 105, fn. 10.

4. A. Hewett, ed., *Reforming the Soviet Economy: Equality versus Efficiency* (Washington, DC: Brookings Institution, 1988), 38.

5. Harry Harding, *China's Second Revolution* (Washington, DC: Brookings Institution, 1987), 30–31.

6. John Sheahan, *Patterns of Development in Latin America* (Princeton, NJ: Princeton University Press, 1987), 85.

7. Howard Handelman and Werner Baer, eds., *Paying the Costs of Austerity in Latin America* (Boulder, CO: Westview Press, 1989); Stephan Haggard and Robert R. Kaufman, eds., *The Politics of Economic Adjustment* (Princeton, NJ: Princeton University Press, 1992).

8. Extrapolated from Sinichi Ichimura and James W. Morley, "The Varieties of Asia-Pacific Experience," in *Driven by Growth*, ed. James W. Morley (Armonk, NY: M. E. Sharpe, 1992), 6; Steven Chan, *East Asian Dynamism* (Boulder, CO: Westview Press, 1990), 8; UNDP, Human Development Report, 1997 (New York: Oxford University Press, 1997), 21–22.

9. Robert Wade, *Governing the Market: Economic Theory and the Role of Government in East Asian Industrialization* (Princeton, NJ: Princeton University Press, 1990); Stephan Haggard, *Pathways from the Periphery* (Ithaca, NY: Cornell University Press, 1990).

10. Chalmers Johnson, *MITI and the Japanese Miracle* (Stanford, CA: Stanford University Press, 1982).

11. Steven Chan, *East Asian Dynamism* (Boulder, CO: Westview Press, 1990), 47–48.

12. Ibid., 49.

13. Robert Wade, "Industrial Policy in Asia: Does It Lead or Follow the Market?" in *Manufacturing Miracles*, 231–66; Wade, *Governing the Market*.

14. "A New Approach to Fighting Child Malnutrition in India," *Knowledge@ Wharton* (University of Pennsylvania), July 25, 2014.

15. *New York Times*, "A Widening Gap Erodes Argentina's Egalitarian Image," December 25, 2006.

16. Richard Albin, "Saving the Environment: The Shrinking Realm of Laissez-Faire," in *International Political Economy*, 2nd ed., ed. Jeffrey A. Frieden and David A. Lake (New York: St. Martin's, 1991), 454.

17. Sheahan, *Patterns of Development*, 86–87.

18. Wade, Governing the Market, 34, 36.

19. Gary Gereffi, "Paths of Industrialization: An Overview," in *Manufacturing Miracles*, ed. Gary Gereffi and Donald L. Wyman (Princeton, NJ: Princeton University Press, 1990), 15. But, Brazil's proportion grew steadily from 8 percent in 1965 to 45 percent in 1987.

20. U.S. Energy Information Administration (EIA), International Petroleum Monthly, October 6, 2009, http://www.eia.doe.gov/ipm.

21. Scott Wallace, "Farming the Amazon," National Geographic, http://environment.nationalgeographic.com.

22. Michael Klare, "Global Warming Battlefields: How Climate Change Threatens Security," *Current History* 106 (November 2007): 357. This section of the chapter draws heavily on that article.

23. Andrew Guzman, *Overheated: The Human Costs of Climate Change* (New York: Oxford University Press, 2013), 54–131.

24. Bhaskar Nath and Ilkden Talay, "Man, Science, Technology and Sustainable Development," in *Sustainable Development*, eds. Bhaskar Nath, Luc Hens, and Dimitri Devuyst (Brussels, Belgium: VUB University Press, 1996), 36.

25. Andrew Blowers and Pieter Leroy, "Environment and Society: Shaping the Future," in *Environmental Policy in an International Context: Prospects*, eds. Andrew Blowers and Pieter Glasbergen (New York: John Wiley & Sons, 1996), 262.

26. Robin Broad and John Cavanaugh, "No More NICs," *Foreign Policy* 72 (Fall 1988): 81–103.

27. Malcolm Waters, *Globalization* (New York: Routledge, 1995).

28. Mauro F. Guillén, "Is Globalization Civilizing, Destructive or Feeble?," *Annual Review of Sociology* 27 (August 2001): 235–60.

29. S. J. Kobrin, "The Architecture of Globalization," in *Governments, Globalization, and International Business*, ed. J. H. Dunning (New York: Oxford University Press, 1997), 148. Cited in Guillén, "Is Globalization Civilizing. . . ?"

30. Thomas Friedman, *The Earth Is Flat*, updated ed. (New York: Farrar, Straus, and Giroux, 2006).

31. Joseph E. Stiglitz, *Globalization and Its Discontents* (New York: W. W. Norton, 2002).

32. Almas Heshmati, *The Relationship Between Income Inequality and Globalization* (Helsinki, Finland: The United Nations University, 2003).

33. Joseph E. Stiglitz, *Making Globalization Work* (New York: W. W. Norton, 2006).

34. *The Global Financial Crisis and Developing Countries* (London: Overseas Development Institute, June 2009).

35. Bruce Buena de Mesquita et al., "Political Competition and Economic Growth," *Journal of Democracy* 12, no. 1 (2001): 58–72. See also, chapter 2 of this textbook for additional research by Halperin, Siegle, and Weinstein and by Rodrik supporting these findings.

Glossary

African Union (AU) An organization representing fifty-four African states and seeking to promote cooperation between them. It was founded in 2002 to succeed the Organization of African Unity.

agrarian reform Distribution of farmland to needy peasants along with government-support programs such as roads, technical assistance, and lines of credit needed to make beneficiaries economically viable.

ancien régime The old political order. The term is often used to describe a decaying regime threatened or ousted by a revolutionary movement.

Arab Spring The term used to describe the rise of prodemocracy movements in the Arab World, starting with Tunisia and Egypt in early 2011 and soon spreading to other Arab countries, including Libya, Syria, Yemen, and Bahrain. Now, only Tunisia remains democratic.

Arab States (Arab World) Countries in North Africa and the Middle East that speak Arabic and are mostly Muslim.

Asian tigers The so-called four Asian tigers are South Korea, Taiwan, Singapore, and Hong Kong—the first Asian nations, after Japan, to develop rapidly growing, export-oriented economies.

associated-dependent development A type of Third World industrialization based on an alliance of the local, political, economic, and military elites with multinational corporations and Western governments.

authoritarian government (regime, system) A political system that limits or prohibits opposition groups and otherwise restricts political activity and expression.

BA (bureaucratic-authoritarian) regimes Military dictatorships, found most often in Latin America's more developed countries, that were based on an alliance between the military, government bureaucrats, local business elites, and multinational corporations.

capital-intensive   Industrial or agricultural production that relies more heavily on machinery and technology than on human labor.

caste system   A rigid social hierarchy in which each person is born with a status that he or she retains regardless of his or her education or achievement.

CEBs (Christian or Ecclesial Base Communities)   Small Catholic neighborhood groups in Latin America that discuss religious questions and community problems. Commonly located in poor neighborhoods, many CEBs were politicized or radicalized in the 1960s and 1970s.

class consciousness   A measure of how much a social class (workers, peasants, or the middle class) views itself as having common goals that are distinct from, and often opposed to, the interests of other classes.

clientelism (clientelistic)   The dispensing of public resources by political power holders or seekers who offer them as favors in exchange for votes or other forms of public support. See also **patron-client relations**

collectivization (collective farm)   The act of merging individual farms into a collective (joint) unit. Collectivization may be undertaken voluntarily (as in the Israeli Kibbutz) or may be forced by the state against the will of the affected peasant smallholders. Forced collectivization led to considerable bloodshed in countries such as the Soviet Union.

colored(s)   A South African term coined during the period of White rule to describe people of mixed racial background.

command economy   An economy in which most of the means of production are owned and managed by the state and in which prices and production decisions are determined by state planners.

comparative advantage   A country's capacity to engage in a particular economic activity efficiently and cheaply relative to other nations.

conflict theory   A branch of modernization theory that believed that the various goals of political and socioeconomic modernization sometimes conflicted with each other.

constant dollars   When comparisons are made between, say, a country's military spending in five different years, all of the actual amounts for every year are converted to their value in a single year so as to factor out the effect of inflation.

core nations   The richer, highly industrialized nations of the world.

coup d'état (coup)   A seizure of political power by the military.

crony capitalism   A corrupt form of capitalism in which powerful, well-connected businessmen use their government ties to accumulate wealth.

cultural pluralism   A diversity of ethnic groups.

culture of poverty   A sense of powerlessness and fatalism allegedly found commonly among the urban poor.

currency exchange rates   The value of a nation's currency relative to major currencies such as the dollar and euro.

curse of oil   Economists have observed that countries with an abundance of oil often find that, paradoxically, rather than enriching them in the long term, oil wealth causes nations to skew their economic decisions in the wrong direction, to neglect other parts of their economy, and to fall victim to extensive corruption. More broadly, some scholars have observed that this often happens with other valuable natural resources (gold, diamonds, etc.) as well.

democratic consolidation   The process through which democratic norms (democratic "rules of the game") become accepted by all powerful groups in society, including labor unions, business, rural landlords, the church, and the military.

democratic transition   The process of moving from an authoritarian regime to a democratic one.

dependency theory   A theory that attributes LDC ("periphery") underdevelopment to its economic and political dependence on the advanced industrial nations ("the core").

developmental state   A government system that intervenes actively in the capitalist economy in order to guide or promote the state's economic development goals.

economies of scale   Economic efficiencies achieved through large-scale operations.

electoral democracy   A country is considered an electoral democracy if it has free and fair elections but does not honor its citizens' rights in some areas, such as freedom of expression.

EOI (export-oriented industrialization)   An industrialization model heavily tied to exporting manufactured goods. This strategy has been the linchpin of East Asia's economic boom.

ethnicity (ethnic group)   A group that feels it has common culture, traditions, beliefs, values, and history that unite it and distinguish it from other cultures.

export-oriented industrialization see **EOI**

fundamentalism   A theological doctrine that seeks to preserve a religion's traditional worldview and to resist any efforts by religious liberals to reform it. It also frequently seeks to revive the role of religion in private and public life, including dress, lifestyle, and politics. Used interchangeably with "revivalism."

GDI (gender-related development index)   An index measuring a country's key social indicators (literacy, income, life expectancy) for women as compared to men.

GDP (gross domestic product)   A measure of a nation's total production similar to the gross national product (GNP), but it excludes certain financial transfers that are included in GNP.

gender gap A systematic difference in social status or achievement between men and women (e.g., a difference in income levels).

gender inequality index see **GII**

gender-related development index see **GDI**

gender quotas A percentage of seats in an elected legislature or of candidates that are reserved for women.

GII (gender inequality index) The GII is a composite index comparing men and women on three dimensions—empowerment, labor force participation, and health.

gender parity index see **GPI**

gender-related development index see **GDI**

globalization The tendency of today's national economies to become increasingly intertwined and interdependent, usually coupled with increased interdependence of cultures.

GNP (gross national product) A measure of a country's total production. GNP per capita is often used as a measure of average income in an individual country.

GPI (gender parity index) An index comparing the female literacy rate to the male rate.

Great Leap Forward China's effort (1968–1960) to rapidly industrialize and increase agricultural production by forcing the peasantry into large communes (a type of collective farm) and by having the country's huge urban and rural workforce put forth tremendous effort. That experiment had disastrous effects on the economy and led to the starvation and death of millions of Chinese.

greenhouse effect (greenhouse gases) Carbon gases produced by burning fossil fuels that threaten to warm the world's climate dangerously by limiting the dispersion of heat from the atmosphere.

gross national product see **GNP**

HDI (Human Development Index) A composite measure of educational level, life expectancy, and per capita GDP.

honor killings Murders of women who have allegedly "dishonored" their families by engaging in sexual activity or some related "lesser offense" (sometimes as innocent as being seen in public with an unacceptable man). Honor killings are commonly committed by close male relatives of the victim.

human development index see **HDI**

import-substituting industrialization see **ISI**

informal sector (economy) The part of the economy that is unregulated by the government while similar activities are regulated and taxed. Also defined as "all unregistered (unincorporated) enterprises below a certain size."

infrastructure The underlying structures (including transportation, communication, and agricultural irrigation) that are needed for effective production.

institutional military regime (government) A government in which many of the armed forces' commanding officers take part. That is, the armed forces as an institution takes command of government, rather than a charismatic officer with a personal following.

internal warfare Military action aimed at controlling guerrilla unrest or other domestic civil insurrections.

invisible (guiding) hand The capitalist notion that the good of society is advanced most effectively when individual actors (businesspeople, workers) seek to maximize their own economic advantage.

ISI (import-substituting industrialization) A policy of industrial development based on manufacturing goods domestically that were previously imported. Pioneered in Latin America.

Islamism (Islamist) Islamic fundamentalism or revivalism. A movement designed to bring the Islamic faith to its fundamental, strictly interpreted beliefs and traditions. An Islamist is a believer in Islamism.

jihad An Islamic holy war.

Koran Divinely revealed law according to the Muslim religion.

labor-intensive industry Industries that make more extensive use of human labor, as opposed to machinery and technology.

laissez faire A policy of minimal state intervention in the economy.

LDCs (less developed countries) The term is used synonymously with the terms *Third World* and *developing countries.*

legitimacy The population's acceptance of the government's or its leaders' right to rule.

liberal democracy A democracy that not only has free and fair elections, but also respects civil liberties and upholds basic freedoms.

liberalization (of the economic system) Reducing the degree of state intervention in the economy (referring to the eighteenth-century classical liberalism of Adam Smith).

liberalization (of the political system) A process whereby dictatorial governments begin to reduce repression and loosen restraints on freedom, often in response to organized protest.

liberated zones Areas (most notably in the countryside) controlled by the revolutionary army. The term was used by the communists in China and Vietnam.

liberation theology See the **Theology of Liberation**

majoritarian democracy A type of democracy in which the party or group that wins an elections makes decisions without affording constitutional or other institutional protections to minority groups, who are not given any special representation.

market socialism A hybrid of Marxist economics and free enterprise that has been adopted by countries such as China.

mass mobilization The process whereby large segments of the population are activated politically. Governments or revolutionary movements may choose to mobilize the population.

MNCs (multinational corporations) Corporations with holdings and operations in a number of countries. Primarily based in the developed world, many of them exercise considerable economic power in the Third World.

modernization theory (Theorists) A popular theory (especially in the United States and the West) that argues that in order to attain modern economies and political systems, LDCs would need to adopt Western values and practices.

moral economy The web of economic and moral obligations that binds a social unit together. Often used in reference to peasant-landlord relations in the countryside.

mujahideen Islamic "freedom fighters" or guerrillas in a holy war.

mullah An educated Muslim trained in religious law and doctrine.

multinational corporations see **MNCs**

nationality A population with its own language, cultural traditions, and historical aspirations, who frequently claim sovereignty over a particular territory.

nationalization The transfer of private firms to state ownership.

neocolonialism Economic or cultural dominance of one sovereign nation over another.

neoliberal economics (reforms) Economic policies, now widely in favor, based on an adaptation of Adam Smith's "classical liberalism." These reforms reduce the role of the state in the economy, enhance the role of the private sector, and allow free-market forces to operate without government interference. Specific reforms have included balancing the budget, letting the market (not government regulations) determine the value of the national currency, removing barriers to free trade, and privatizing state enterprises.

NGO (nongovernmental organization) An organization at the local, national, or international level that is privately funded and has no connection with the government. Most NGOs stress grassroots organization. Commonly, they support goals such as democratization, human rights, women's rights, environmental protection, housing, health care, and education.

NIC (newly industrialized country) Countries in East Asia and Latin America (such as Taiwan and Mexico) that have developed a substantial industrial base in recent decades.

nongovernmental organization see **NGO**

new social movements (NSMs) Grassroots reformist movements that are free of traditional political party ties or class-based ideologies

nurturing role (professions) Occupations such as teaching and nursing that are commonly filled by women and that involve roles commonly associated with motherhood.

parastatals Semiautonomous, state-run business enterprises, such as government-owned power plants, petroleum firms, and food processing plants.

patron-client relations Relations between more powerful figures (patrons) and less powerful ones (clients), involving a series of reciprocal obligations that benefit both sides but are more advantageous to the patron. See also **clientelism**

peasant A person in a traditional rural society, who earns his living from agriculture either as the owner or renter of a small plot of land, who often produces (wholly or in part) for his/her own family's consumption. Peasants, by definition, have a culture and lifestyle that is distinct from urban society, and he or she is dependent for his or her survival on relationships with more powerful outsiders, such as landlords (who own larger farms), merchants, and moneylenders.

periphery Third World countries, commonly seen by dependency theorists as occupying a lesser rank in the international economy.

personalistic military regime A form of military dictatorship in which a single officer dominates. Often that regime's legitimacy is based on his charisma or his web of contacts with powerful groups.

pluralism (pluralist democracy) A form of government that allows a wide variety of groups and viewpoints to flourish and to engage in political activity independent of government control.

political culture The set of political beliefs and values that underlie a society's political system.

populist (reforms, leaders, parties) A multiclass, reformist political movement that promises increased welfare programs for the poor and middle class but rejects a basic restructuring of the economic order. Third World populist movements are often led by a charismatic (and sometimes demagogic) political leader.

private sector The sector of the economy that is owned by individuals or private companies.

privatization   The process of transferring to the private sector portions of the economy formerly owned by the state.

procedural democracy   Standards of democracy based on political procedures (such as free elections) rather than outcomes (such as social justice).

progressive church   The reformist and radical wings of the Catholic Church (primarily in Latin America).

proletariat   Marxist term for the working class (blue-collar workers).

proportional representation (PR)   A method of electing legislatures in which voters select from party lists in multimember districts; seats are then allocated in proportion to the percentage of votes each party receives.

reconciliation approach   A contemporary perspective in modernization theory that holds that it is possible for LDCs to simultaneously attain some development goals that were previously considered contradictory, at least in the short run (such as early economic growth and equitable income distribution).

relative deprivation   The gap between an individual's or group's expectations and desires and their actual achievement.

reserved seats   Seats in a government body, such as the national parliament, that are specifically set aside for women or other underrepresented groups.

revivalism   An attempt to revive traditional religious practices and, sometimes, to revive the role of religion in politics. See also **fundamentalism**

secularization   The separation of church and state and, more generally, the removal of religion from politics.

shantytown   A community of poor homes or shacks built by the inhabitants. Unlike slums, they are commonly in outlying urban areas rather than the central city.

single-member districts   see **SMDs**

sites-and-services (programs)   Housing arrangements in which the state sells or gives each inhabitant legal title to a plot with basic services such as electricity and water, leaving the recipient to build his or her own home.

smallholders   Peasants owning small plots of land.

SMDs (single-member districts)   An electoral system in which the country is divided into a relatively large number of districts with comparable populations, with only one representative (member) elected to the legislature in each district. SMD is largely confined to English-speaking countries such as Britain, Canada, and the United States. Other democracies are more likely to use proportional representation.

spontaneous housing   Urban housing built independently by the occupants without government permission.

squatter settlements   Communities built by the poor who illegally or semilegally occupy unused land.

Sub-Saharan Africa   Countries in Africa below the northern tier of Arab nations. Also called Black Africa.

substantive democracy   Standards of democracy that measure government policy outcomes, such as literacy and health levels or socioeconomic equality, not just democratic procedures (as distinguished from procedural democracy).

sustainable development   Economic development that "consumes resources to meet [this generation's] needs and aspirations in a way that does not compromise the ability of future generations to meet their needs."

technocrat   A government bureaucrat or adviser with technical expertise, who often has advanced training in fields such as engineering, economics and the hard sciences.

theocracy (theocratic state)   a country, state, or city that is subject to the rule of God as interpreted and enforced by religious leaders.

Theology of Liberation (liberation theology)   A reformist interpretation of Catholic doctrine that stresses the emancipation of the poor. It was born and spread in Latin America from the 1960s to the 1990s and still has many adherents today.

Third Wave   The widespread transition from authoritarian to democratic government that has taken place in the Third World and Eastern Europe since the mid-1970s (some say it ended around the year 2000, though some democratic transitions continue).

traditional culture (values, society)   A culture or society that adheres to very long-standing values and customs that have not been extensively transformed by modernization.

tribe (tribal)   Subnational groups who share a collective identity and language and believe themselves to hold a common lineage.

UNDP   The United Nations Development Programme, which publishes much of the data used in this text.

wars of national liberation   Wars of independence fought against colonial powers.

zipper-style quotas   A type of quota system for electoral lists of candidates for parliament or other government bodies, in which the candidates are ranked and the group that is assigned a quota of candidates (such as women) must be given rankings comparable to the majority group on the candidate list (in this case, men).

Index

About the Author

HOWARD HANDELMAN is professor emeritus at the University of
Wisconsin–Milwaukee. He has been director of the Center for Latin
America and Caribbean Studies, chair of the Department of Political
Science, and chair of the Department of Spanish and Portuguese.

His books include *Struggle in the Andes: Peasant Political Mobilization in Peru; Mexican Politics: The Dynamics of Change; Democracy
and Its Limits: Lessons from Asia, Latin America, and the Middle East;
Politics in a Changing World;* and *Paying the Costs of Austerity in Latin
America.*